SEAN BAIRD, MCSE, MCSD, MCT
DAVID BESCH, MCSD, MCT
DENIS DARVEAU, MCSE, MCT
WAYNE SMITH
DEANNA TOWNSEND, MCSD

MCSE
TRAINING GUIDE

SQL SERVER 6.5
DESIGN AND
IMPLEMENTATION

New Riders

MCSE Training Guide: SQL Server 6.5 Design and Implementation

By Sean Baird, David Besch, Denis Darveau, Wayne Smith, and Deanna Townsend

Published by:
New Riders Publishing
201 West 103rd Street
Indianapolis, IN 46290 USA

© 1997 by New Riders Publishing

Printed in the United States of America 1 2 3 4 5 6 7 8 9 0

Library of Congress Cataloging-in-Publication Data

CIP data available upon request

ISBN: 1-56205-830-4

Warning and Disclaimer

This book is designed to provide information about SQL Server 6.5 implementation and Microsoft's Implementing a Database Design on SQL Server 6.5 exam. Every effort has been made to make this book as complete and as accurate as possible, but no warranty or fitness is implied.

The information is provided on an "as is" basis. The authors and New Riders Publishing shall have neither liability nor responsibility to any person or entity with respect to any loss or damages arising from the information contained in this book or from the use of the discs or programs that may accompany it.

New Riders is an independent entity from Microsoft Corporation, and not affiliated with Microsoft Corporaation in any manner. This publication may be used in assisting students to prepare for a Microsoft Certified Professional Exam. Neither Microsoft Corporation nor New Riders warrants that use of this publication will ensure passing the relevant Exam.

Publisher	*David Dwyer*
Executive Editor	*Mary Foote*
Marketing Manager	*Kourtnaye Sturgeon*
Managing Editor	*Sarah Kearns*

Acquisitions Editor
Stephanie Layton

Development Editor
Chris Zahn

Project Editor
Christopher Morris

Copy Editor
Howard Jones

Technical Editor
Christoph Wille, MCSE, MCSD

Coordinator of Editorial Resources
Suzanne Snyder

Software Product Developer
Steve Flatt

Software Acquisitions and Development
Dustin Sullivan

Assistant Marketing Manager
Gretchen Schlesinger

Team Coordinators
Amy Lewis
Stacey Beheler

Manufacturing Coordinator
Brook Farling

Book Designer
Glenn Larsen

Cover Designer
Dan Armstrong

Cover Production
Casey Price

Director of Production
Larry Klein

Production Team Supervisor
Laurie Casey

Graphics Image Specialists
Kevin Cliburn, Wil Cruz

Production Analysts
Dan Harris
Erich J. Richter

Production Team
Aleata Howard, Cindy Fields,
Mary Hunt, Linda Knose,
Kristy Nash

Indexer
Joe Long

About the Authors

Sean Baird works in the Applications Development group at Empower Trainers & Consultants. As one of Empower's senior consultants, Sean spends his time leading projects and performing analysis and design on client-server and Internet systems. He has worked on a wide variety of business solutions for Empower's clients, and has technical experience with most of the Microsoft product line. Sean has worked with SQL Server for several years and is one of Empower's SQL Server experts. He obtained a bachelor's degree in Computer Science from the University of Missouri-Rolla, and holds MCSE, MCSD, and MCT certifications. Sean currently lives in Kansas City, where he enjoys hot-air ballooning in his spare time.

David Besch is currently a Senior Computer Consultant with Empower Trainers and Consultants, Inc., in Overland Park, Kansas. He received a BS in Computer Science from the University of Missouri-Rolla in 1993. After graduating, David went to work for the Flesh Company as a Senior Developer, programming in Pascal and C languages. He is certified as both an MCP and MCSD. He also holds certifications in Implementing and Administrating SQL Server 6.0, Visual Basic 3.0, Windows NT Workstation 3.51, WOSA I, WOSA II, and Networking Essentials. David lives in Lenexa, Kansas, with his wife, Cheryl, and their cat, Blaise.

Empower Trainers & Consultants, Inc. is a full-service technology firm headquartered in the Kansas City Metro area. Empower offers a variety of consulting services on Internet and traditional client-server applications development, as well as network systems integration. In addition, they offer training on Microsoft Office and BackOffice applications. Empower is aligned with Microsoft at the highest level as a Microsoft Solution Provider/Partner and an ATEC II (Authorized Technical Education Center—Status II Partner). To be a Microsoft Partner, an organization must demonstrate its competence and abilities as a Solution Provider. Organizations must also pass certification requirements and reviews by Microsoft. There are currently 140 companies recognized at Microsoft's Partner level, including industry giants IBM, Digital and Intel. For more information, visit Empower's web site at www.empower.com.

Denis Darveau is a Senior Network Operating Systems Consultant with Zen Systems, Inc., based in Sausalito, California. Denis has been involved with computer science since the early 1980s in his Air Force days as a Programmer/Analyst/Designer for the North American Air Defense Command (NORAD). After four years of teaching various operating systems, such as UNIX (programming, networking, and system administration) and Oracle DBA, in 1994, Denis became a Windows NT Microsoft Certified Professional (MCP) and became a Microsoft Certified System Engineer (MCSE) at the beginning of 1996. His specialty is SQL Server 6.x and TCP/IP. Denis is also a Microsoft Certified Trainer (MCT), having taught over 100 Microsoft Curriculum courses to over 1,000 students all over the United States and Canada.

Wayne Smith hails from Chesapeake, Virginia, and is currently in the employ of the ADESA Corporation in Indianapolis, Indiana, where he serves as a client/server developer with Microsoft SQL Server and Visual Basic.

Deanna Townsend is a consultant specializing in PowerBuilder development. Her database experience includes SQL Server, Sybase, and Informix. She has received her MCSD and CPD certifications. Previous to this book, she has co-authored three PowerBuilder textbooks for Que Education and Training and contributed to *JavaBeans Developers Reference* for New Riders.

Trademark Acknowledgments

All terms mentioned in this book that are known to be trademarks or service marks have been appropriately capitalized. New Riders Publishing cannot attest to the accuracy of this information. Use of a term in this book should not be regarded as affecting the validity of any trademark or service mark.

Dedication

Sean Baird would like to dedicate this book to his family.

Contents at a Glance

Table of Contents

2 System Databases and Tables 63

3   Data Definition   117

4   Retrieving Data   179

7   Indexes   313

Introduction

MCSE Training Guide: SQL Server 6.5 Design and Implementation is designed for advanced end-users, service technicians, and network administrators who are considering certification as a Microsoft Certified Systems Engineer (MCSE), Microsoft Certified Product (MCP) Specialist or as a Microsoft Certified Solution Developer (MCSD). The SQL Server 6.5 Design and Implementation exam ("Exam 70-27: Implementing a Database Design on Microsoft SQL Server 6.5") tests your ability to implement, administer, and troubleshoot information systems that incorporate SQL Server 6.5 as well as your ability to provide technical support to users of Microsoft SQL Server version 6.5.

Who Should Read This Book

This book is designed to help advanced users, service technicians, and network administrators who are working for MCSE or MCSD certification prepare for the MCSE/MCSD "Implementing a Database Design on Microsoft SQL Server 6.5" exam (#70-27).

This book is your one-stop-shop. Everything you need to know to pass the exam is here, and Microsoft has certified it as study material. You do not *need* to take a class in addition to buying this book to pass the exam. However, depending on your personal study habits or learning style, you may benefit from taking a class in addition to studying the book or buying this book in addition to a class.

This book also can help advanced users and administrators who are not studying for the MCSE/MCSD exam but are looking for a single-volume reference on SQL Server Design and Implementation.

How This Book Helps You

This book takes you on a self-guided tour of all the areas covered by the MCSE/MCSD SQL Server 6.5 Design and Implementation exam and teaches you the specific skills you need to achieve your MCSE certification. You'll also find helpful hints, tips, real-world examples, exercises, and references to additional study materials. Specifically, this book is set up to help you in the following ways:

✓ Objectives

▶ **Organization.** This book is organized by major exam topics (12 in all) and exam objectives. Every objective you need to know for the "Implementing a Database Design on Microsoft SQL Server 6.5" exam is covered in this book; we've include a margin icon, like the one in the margin here, to help you quickly locate these objectives. There are pointers at different elements to direct you to the appropriate place in the book if you find you need to review certain sections.

🔑 Key Concepts

▶ **Emphasis.** Another marginal icon you will see is one referring you to key concepts. Understanding these key concepts is crucial to your success on the exam. These concepts are also ones that serve as the basic foundation for further learning. You must master them in order to understand material that follows. In order to be able to build on your knowledge, you must make sure that you first understand these key concepts.

▶ **Deciding how to spend your time wisely.** Pre-chapter quizzes are at the beginning of each chapter to test your knowledge of the objectives contained within that chapter. If you already know the answers to those questions, you can make a time-management decision accordingly.

▶ **Extensive practice test options.** Plenty of questions are at the end of each chapter to test your comprehension of material covered within that chapter. An answer list follows the questions so you can check yourself. These practice test options will help you decide what you already understand and what requires extra review on your part. The CD-ROM also contains a sample test engine that will give you an accurate idea of what the test is really like.

**Note**

For a complete description of the test engine, please see Appendix D, "All About TestPrep."

For a complete description of what you can find on the CD-ROM, see Appendix C, "What's on the CD-ROM."

For more information about the exam or the certification process, contact Microsoft at:

Microsoft Education: Call (800) 636-7544

Internet: `ftp://ftp.microsoft.com/Services/MSEdCert`

World Wide Web: `http://www.microsoft.com/train_cert/default.htm`

CompuServe Forum: `GO MSEDCERT`

Understanding What the Implementing a Database Design on Microsoft SQL Server 6.5 Exam (#70-27) Covers

The "Implementing a Database Design on Microsoft SQL Server 6.5" exam (#70-27) covers 12 main topic areas, arranged in accordance with test objectives. The exam objectives, listed by topic area, are covered in the following sections.

Data Modeling

▶ Define entity, relationship, and attribute

▶ Identify and apply the different types of relationships used in designing a database

▶ Identify the relationship between a primary key and a foreign key

▶ Identify how key data-modeling components, such as no nulls, no duplicates, and no changes are implemented

System Databases and Tables

▶ Identify the role of the *master* database

▶ Identify the role of the *tempdb* database

▶ Identify the role of system tables

▶ Estimate space requirements

Data Definition

▶ Increase transaction log size

▶ Create and modify tables

▶ Apply an identity property to a table definition

▶ Identify the appropriate uses for the different types of constraints

▶ Apply REFERENCE constraints to enforce referential integrity

Retrieving Data

▶ Write SELECT statements

▶ Select specific rows based on specific operators

▶ Manipulate character, numeric, and date data by using TSQL functions

▶ Use wildcards to retrieve rows

▶ Write a SELECT statement using system functions

▶ Format and sort query results

Retrieving Data (Advanced Topics)

▶ Generate summary data by using aggregate functions

▶ Generate summary data by using the COMPUTE clause and COMPUTE BY clause

- ► Generate summary data by using the GROUP BY clause

- ► Generate summary data by using the HAVING clause

- ► Correlate data by using outer joins

- ► Correlate data by using self-joins

- ► Recognize and apply subqueries that use nested SELECT statements

Modifying Data

- ► Manipulate data by using INSERT statements

- ► Manipulate data by using UPDATE statements

- ► Manipulate data by using DELETE statements

- ► Import and export data

Indexes

- ► Identify appropriate uses of indexing

- ► Differentiate between clustered and non-clustered indexes

- ► Create unique and composite indexes

- ► Identify performance considerations when using indexes

- ► Use index management options

Using Views, Defaults, and Rules

- ► Create views

- ► Recognize the benefits of using views

- ► Create, bind, unbind, and drop defaults

- ► Create, bind, unbind, and drop rules

Programmability

▶ Identify control-of-flow statements

▶ Implement cursors

▶ Recognize the benefits of using stored procedures

▶ Identify capabilities of SQL Server and MAPI

▶ Implement string and variable extensions for the EXECUTE statement

▶ Manage user-defined error messages

Triggers

▶ Create triggers

▶ Enforce referential integrity

▶ Enforce data integrity

▶ Apply the inserted and deleted tables

Replication

▶ Apply replication appropriately

▶ Apply the appropriate replication model

▶ Recognize the roles of the publishing server

▶ Recognize the role of the distribution server

▶ Recognize the role of the subscription server

▶ Trace the replication process

Application Development and Open Data Services (ODS)

▶ Recognize and apply open architecture

▶ Recognize and apply Open Database Connectivity (ODBC)

▶ Identify the benefits of integrating OLE architecture with SQL Server

▶ Recognize how SQL Server takes advantages of the OLE architecture

Hardware and Software Needed

As a self-paced study guide, much of the book expects you to use SQL Server and follow along through the exercises while you learn. Microsoft designed SQL Server to operate in a wide range of actual situations, and the exercises in this book encompass that range. However, the exercises require only a single stand-alone computer running SQL Server. The computer should meet the following criteria:

▶ Computer on the Microsoft Hardware Compatibility List

▶ 486DX2 66-Mhz (or better) processor for Windows NT Server

▶ 16 MB of RAM (minimum) for Windows NT Server

▶ 340-MB (or larger) hard disk for Windows NT Server

▶ 3.5-inch 1.44-MB floppy drive

▶ VGA (or Super VGA) video adapter

▶ VGA (or Super VGA) monitor

▶ Mouse or equivalent pointing device

▶ Two-speed (or faster) CD-ROM drive (optional)

▶ Network Interface Card (NIC)

▶ Presence on an existing network, or use of a 2-port (or more) mini-port hub to create a test network

▶ MS-DOS 5.0 or 6.*x* and Microsoft Windows for Workgroups 3.*x* pre-installed

▶ Microsoft Windows 95 (floppy version)

▶ Microsoft Windows NT Server (CD-ROM version)

It is somewhat easier to get access to the necessary computer hardware and software in a corporate business environment. It is harder to allocate enough time within the busy workday to complete a self-study program. Most of your study time may occur after normal working hours, away from the everyday interruptions and pressures of your regular job.

Tips for the Exam

Remember the following tips as you prepare for the MCSE/MCSD certification exams:

▶ **Read all the material.** Microsoft has been known to include material not specified in the objectives. This course has included additional information not required by the objectives in an effort to give you the best possible preparation for the examination, and for the real-world network experiences to come.

▶ **Complete the exercises in each chapter.** They will help you gain experience using the Microsoft product. All Micro-soft exams are experienced-based and require you to have used the Microsoft product in a real networking environment. Exercises for each objective are placed at the end of each chapter.

▶ **Take each pre-chapter quiz to evaluate how well you know the topic of the chapter.** Each chapter opens with one essay question per exam objective covered in the chapter. Following the quiz are the answers and pointers to where in the chapter that objective is covered.

▶ **Complete all the questions in the "Review Questions" sections.** Complete the questions at the end of each chapter—they will help you remember key points. The questions are fairly simple, but be warned, some questions may have more than one answer.

Note

Although this book is designed to prepare you to take and pass the Implementing a Database Design on Microsoft SQL Server 6.5" certification exam, there are no guarantees. Read this book, work through the exercises, and take the practice assessment exams.

When taking the real certification exam, make sure you answer all the questions before your time limit expires. Do not spend too much time on any one question. If you are unsure about an answer, answer the question as best you can and mark it for later review when you have finished all the questions. It has been said, whether correctly or not, that any questions left unanswered will automatically cause you to fail.

Remember, the object is not to pass the exam, it is to understand the material. Once you understand the material, passing is simple. Knowledge is a pyramid; to build upward, you need a solid foundation. The Microsoft Certified System Engineer and Solution Developer programs are designed to ensure that you have that solid foundation.

Good luck!

New Riders Publishing

The staff of New Riders Publishing is committed to bringing you the very best in computer reference material. Each New Riders book is the result of months of work by authors and staff who research and refine the information contained within its covers.

As part of this commitment to you, the NRP reader, New Riders invites your input. Please let us know if you enjoy this book, if you have trouble with the information and examples presented, or if you have a suggestion for the next edition.

Please note, though: New Riders staff cannot serve as a technical resource during your preparation for the Microsoft MCSE/MCSD certification exams or for questions about software- or hardware-related problems. Please refer to the documentation that accompanies SQL Server or to the applications' Help systems.

If you have a question or comment about any New Riders book, there are several ways to contact New Riders Publishing. We will respond to as many readers as we can. Your name, address, or phone number will never become part of a mailing list or be used for any purpose other than to help us continue to bring you the best books possible. You can write us at the following address:

New Riders Publishing
Attn: Publisher
201 W. 103rd Street
Indianapolis, IN 46290

If you prefer, you can fax New Riders Publishing at (317) 817-7448.

You also can send e-mail to New Riders at the following Internet address:

`certification@.mcp.com`

If you have technical problems with the CD-ROM, contact Macmillan Computer Puglishing at the following Internet address:

`support@mcp.com.`

NRP is an imprint of Macmillan Computer Publishing. To obtain a catalog or information, or to purchase any Macmillan Computer Publishing book, call (800) 428-5331.

Thank you for selecting *MCSE Training Guide: SQL Server 6.5 Design and Implementation*!

C h a p t e r

Data Modeling

1

This chapter helps you prepare for the exam by covering the following objectives:

> ▶ Define entity, relationship, and attribute
>
> ▶ Identify and apply the different types of relationships used in designing a database
>
> ▶ Identify the relationship between a primary key and a foreign key
>
> ▶ Identify how key data modeling components, such as no nulls, no duplicates, and no changes are implemented

Test Yourself! Before reading this chapter, test yourself to determine how much study time you will need to devote to this section.

1. What is an entity?

2. What is an attribute?

3. What is a relationship?

4. What are the three main types of relationships used in a database model?

5. How are primary keys and foreign keys used to create a relationship?

6. How is a no nulls constraint implemented for an attribute?

7. How is a no changes constraint implemented for an attribute?

8. How is a no duplicates constraint implemented for an attribute?

Answers are located at the end of the chapter...

Creating a simple database in SQL Server is relatively easy, but one of the most important tasks you will perform as a database developer has little to do with the SQL Server product itself. Before creating a database, spend some time thinking about how you will represent the real-world information of your application in a relational database. Understanding the concepts presented in this chapter is vital to a successful database implementation.

This chapter covers the fundamentals of designing a database using relational database design methods. In addition, you learn how these modeling concepts are implemented in SQL Server. Because the process of data modeling deals with several abstract concepts, a case study is presented at the beginning of the chapter and is used to make the concepts and principles more accessible. This case study is referred throughout each chapter, and is used in the exercises.

Keep in mind that an in-depth discussion of relational database design is outside the scope of this book. Numerous reference materials are available on this topic, such as the following:

▶ Graeme Simsion, *Data Modeling Essentials* (Van Nostrand Reinhold, 1994).

▶ David C. Hay, *Data Model Patterns, Conventions of Thought* (Dorset House Publishing, 1996).

▶ E. F. Codd, *The Relational Model for Database Management* (Addison-Wesley Publishing Company, 1990).

The following topics are covered in this chapter:

▶ A case study of a college enrollment database

▶ An introduction to data modeling concepts: Entities, attributes, and relationships

▶ Implementing entities and attributes

▶ Implementing relationships

▶ Normalizing your database design

Case Study: A College Enrollment Database

A small Midwestern engineering college has contracted you to design and develop a database to automate their student enrollments and class scheduling. You begin by interviewing the Registrar to determine what types of information will be stored in the database. The Registrar tells you the following information:

"We have ten departments on campus that offer about 400 different courses—everything from Astronomy 101 to Zoology 410. Of course, we don't have enough professors to teach every course every semester, but we do manage to offer about 150 different courses each semester.

"One of the problems we'd like this database to solve is the difficulty we have scheduling all of the courses we offer in a semester. Typically, a course is offered at several different times during the week. For instance, Physics 150 may be offered on Monday, Wednesday, and Friday from 1:30 to 2:30 PM, and it may also be offered on Tuesdays and Thursdays from 7:30 to 9:00 AM. Right now, we have to worry about the different time slots and rooms assigned to each class. We stick bits of paper up on the wall to show what's been used and what hasn't. It's difficult and time-consuming to do it this way, especially if someone leaves a window open and the papers get scattered! Just to keep everything straight, we refer to these different scheduled courses as 'classes.' Since professors are in short supply, only one professor teaches a particular class.

"Sometimes we don't even have a tenured professor available to teach a class and we need to have a Teaching Assistant do the job. There isn't any difference as far as the class is concerned—we just assign the T/A as the teacher—but we do keep fairly different types of information on the two different categories of teachers. For instance, our T/As are paid by the hour, while the professors are salaried.

"Oh, another interesting point about our teachers. We're very proud of the new mentoring program we've just put in place. Our more experienced professors have the option to mentor some of our newer professors. This program ensures that our newer professors have someone to talk to in case they need advice. We're not forcing this on anyone, so not everyone will have a mentor, but we would like to document in the database who has a mentor and who doesn't.

"Now, we have about 4,000 students that can enroll themselves in any of these classes. Right now we use paper enrollment forms— you can imagine the paperwork we have to go through in order to process everyone's enrollments! Eventually, we'd like the students to be able to enroll over the Internet, but before we can have someone write that application, we need this database to keep track of everything. Not only that, but several professors want to start tracking attendance more closely so they can correlate attendance with students' grades. They want to do this for each time the class meets."

The Registrar concludes by telling you that her descriptions of the campus's operations are not at all complete, and that you should interview the department heads for more information. However, you decide to begin modeling the database on what you've learned so far.

Introduction to Data Modeling Concepts: Entities, Attributes, and Relationships

 Objective

The relational design process provides a structured approach to modeling an information system's data and the business rules for that data. Once you learn the fundamentals of this process, you will be able to take the information learned from the requirements gathered for the system (such as the information presented in the case study) and easily design a database.

The three key components used in relational database design are outlined in the following table; this section describes each in more detail.

Table 1.1

The Three Key Components Used in Relational Database Design		
Design Component	Implemented in SQL Server	Examples
Entities	Tables	Student, Course
Attributes	Columns in a Table	Student's Name, Course number
Relationships	Primary/Foreign Key Columns or Tables	Teacher to Class

The next section of this chapter briefly discusses how these components are implemented in SQL Server, but don't worry about the details for now. Implementing tables, columns, and relationships is covered in more detail in Chapter 4, "Retrieving Data."

Entities

 Key Concepts

Entities are the basic building blocks of relational database design.

 Note

An *entity* defines any person, place, thing, or concept for which data will be collected.

Some examples of entities include:

▶ Person: student, teacher

▶ Place: classroom, building

▶ Thing: computer, lab equipment

▶ Concept: course, student's attendance

When you are trying to discover possible entities in your data model, it is often helpful to look (or listen) for noun phrases during the requirements analysis. Because nouns describe people, places, things, or concepts, this trick usually leads you to an entity.

The challenge is to distinguish between the relevant and the irrelevant concepts. Consider the following excerpt from the case study:

"We have ten *departments* on campus that offer about 400 different *courses*—everything from Astronomy 101 to Zoology 410. Of course, we don't have enough *professors* to teach every course every *semester*, but we do manage to offer about 150 different courses each semester."

The highlighted words or phrases are likely candidates for modeling as an entity. The *professor*, or *teacher*, concept is an obvious choice, as are the ideas of a *course* and a *department*. The database will have to keep track of many different teachers and courses. In addition, the database will be used over many semesters, so if detailed information needs to be kept about each semester, the concept of a semester should be modeled as an entity. Notice that the idea of a campus, while important to a college, is not a candidate for an entity in this example. This is because a small college with only one campus will probably build any campus-specific information directly into its data model. If the college planned to expand to multiple campuses in the future, then creating a campus entity would be important because it would allow you to collect information about each distinct campus.

A good practice is to list all of the entities in your database with a one-sentence description of what that entity represents. For example, a Teacher may be defined as "A person employed by the college who is responsible for instructing students in a class." Usually, a good entity can be described in one sentence, unless it is a very abstract concept.

 **Tip**

Defining each entity in your database in this way may seem unnecessary, but it is especially helpful when you're dealing with concepts that are more abstract than a teacher. Also, creating these definitions can draw attention to any relationships between entities.

Review the case study and see if you can identify some entities that will be used in the data model. Then, review the following list of entities:

Teacher: A person employed by the college who is responsible for instructing a class of students.

Student: A person who is enrolled in classes at the college and attends class sessions.

Course: A course defines the subject material taught in a class.

Class: A scheduled instance of a course that is taught by one teacher and that meets in a particular room during specific times of the week.

Class Session: An instance of a class that occurs at a particular date and time.

When we talk about an entity in the data model, we usually are talking about an *instance* of that entity. An *instance* is a particular occurrence of an entity that is distinguishable from all other occurrences of that entity. For example, the college has multiple professors, such as Professor Noel, Professor Press, and Professor Smith. Each is an instance of a teacher. The concept of an instance is important to understanding relationships.

In a data model diagram (often referred to as an *Entity-Relationship (ER) diagram*, or the database *schema*), entities are most often drawn as boxes, occasionally with their definition inside. See figure 1.1 for an example of the case study's data model up to this point.

 Tip

Several good database modeling tools are available on the market. These tools help you create professional ER diagrams and fully define all aspects of your data model. In addition, many of these tools automatically create the final database in SQL Server.

Figure 1.1

Example ER diagram (entities and definitions) for the college enrollment database.

Teacher

> A TEACHER is a person employed by the college who is responsible for instructing a CLASS of STUDENTS.

Course

> A COURSE defines the subject material taught in a CLASS.

Student

> A STUDENT is a person who is enrolled in CLASSES at the college and attends CLASS SESSIONS.

Class Session

> A CLASS SESSION is an instance of a CLASS that occurs at a particular date and time.

Class

> A CLASS is a scheduled instance of a COURSE that is taught by one TEACHER and that meets in a particular room during specific times of the week.

Now that you are familiar with the concept of an entity, you are ready to describe your entities in greater detail.

Attributes

Key Concepts

The second major data-modeling concept that you must understand is that of attributes.

Note

Attributes are additional characteristics or information defined for an entity.

An entity's attributes don't define an entity, but they provide additional information about an entity that may be useful elsewhere. For example, the concept of a *teacher* can be defined without knowing the teacher's name, salary, or educational level. However, knowing nothing about its teachers doesn't do the college any good.

Review the case study and the entities described in the previous session. Try to list some attributes for each entity, then review the following list of possible attributes for each entity:

Teacher: Name, gender, social security number, address, salary, years tenured

Student: Name, gender, social security number, billing address, college address, class level, grade point average

Course: Course number, course name, prerequisites

Class: Course number, scheduled meeting time, scheduled room, assigned teacher, maximum enrollment, students enrolled

Class Session: Course number, date and time of session, students attending

There is a set method or trick for discovering attributes of a particular entity. Usually, brainstorming on the different characteristics of an entity is sufficient. If you find that you are having difficulty, you may want to check the definition of the entity to see if it is specific enough.

In an ER diagram, attributes are listed by name inside their entity's box, as shown in figure 1.2.

Figure 1.2

Example ER diagram (entities and attributes) for the college enrollment database.

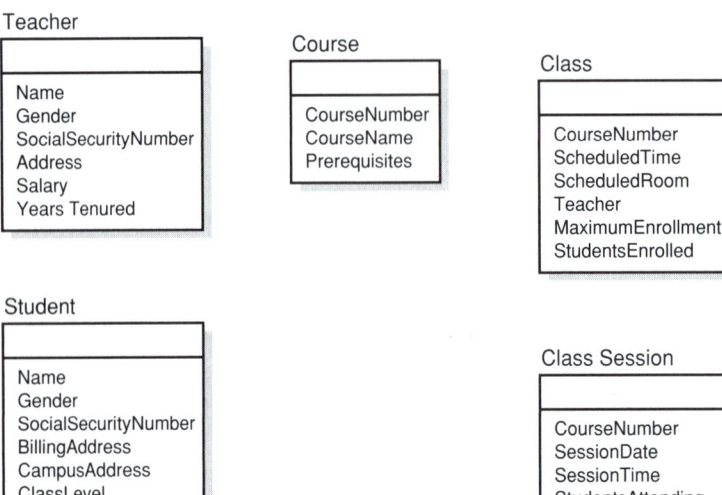

Teacher

Name
Gender
SocialSecurityNumber
Address
Salary
Years Tenured

Course

CourseNumber
CourseName
Prerequisites

Class

CourseNumber
ScheduledTime
ScheduledRoom
Teacher
MaximumEnrollment
StudentsEnrolled

Student

Name
Gender
SocialSecurityNumber
BillingAddress
CampusAddress
ClassLevel
GradePointAverage

Class Session

CourseNumber
SessionDate
SessionTime
StudentsAttending

Relationships

Entities and attributes enable you to explicitly define what information is being stored in the database. Relationships are the other powerful feature of relational modeling, and give the modeling technique its name.

> A *relationship* is a logical linkage between two entities that describes how the entities are associated with each other.

For instance, our definition of a teacher reads: "A person employed by the college who is responsible for instructing students in a class." Clearly, the teacher entity and the class entity are somehow associated with each other. Creating a relationship explicitly defines an association between entities in the data model.

Identifying Relationships in a Data Model

If entities can be thought of as the nouns in data modeling, then relationships are best described as the verbs. In fact, relationships often have a verb phrase associated with them in the data model, much like entities have an associated definition. One trick to discovering relationships between entities is to look closely at the entity definitions. Consider the following entity definitions from earlier in the chapter:

Teacher: A person employed by the college who is responsible for *instructing* a CLASS of STUDENTS.

Student: A person who is *enrolled* in CLASSES at the college and *attends* CLASS SESSIONS.

Course: A COURSE *defines* the subject material taught in a CLASS.

Class: A scheduled instance of a COURSE that is *taught* by one TEACHER and that meets in particular room during specific times of the week.

Class Session: An instance of a CLASS that *occurs* at a particular date and time.

Notice that the definitions now are written to show other entities in all caps, and significant verbs or verb phrases appear in italics. Formatting your entity definitions in this way makes it easy to identify possible relationships between entities. These definitions can be distilled into several simple statements that highlight the relationships between the entities in this case study:

A TEACHER instructs CLASSES.

A COURSE defines subject material for CLASSES.

STUDENTS are enrolled in CLASSES.

STUDENTS attend CLASS SESSIONS.

A CLASS occurs as CLASS SESSIONS.

In an ER diagram, relationships are represented as lines drawn between entities. Often, the verb phrase appears near the line to describe the relationship further. See figure 1.3 for the case study's data model with relationships.

Types of Relationships

√ Objective

You may notice that some of the relationship lines in figure 1.3 have dots on one or both of their ends. This is because there are several different ways to classify a relationship.

The most important (and most commonly referred to) classification of a relationship is called its *cardinality*. The cardinality of a relationship allows the database modeler to specify how instances of each entity relate to each other. There are three major types of cardinality:

▶ **One-to-One**: A single instance of one entity is associated with a single instance of another entity. This type of relationship is relatively uncommon; it is typically used when an entity can be classified into several sub-types. See exercise 1.4 for an example of where a one-to-one relationship might be used.

Figure 1.3

Example ER diagram (entities and relationships) for the college enrollment database.

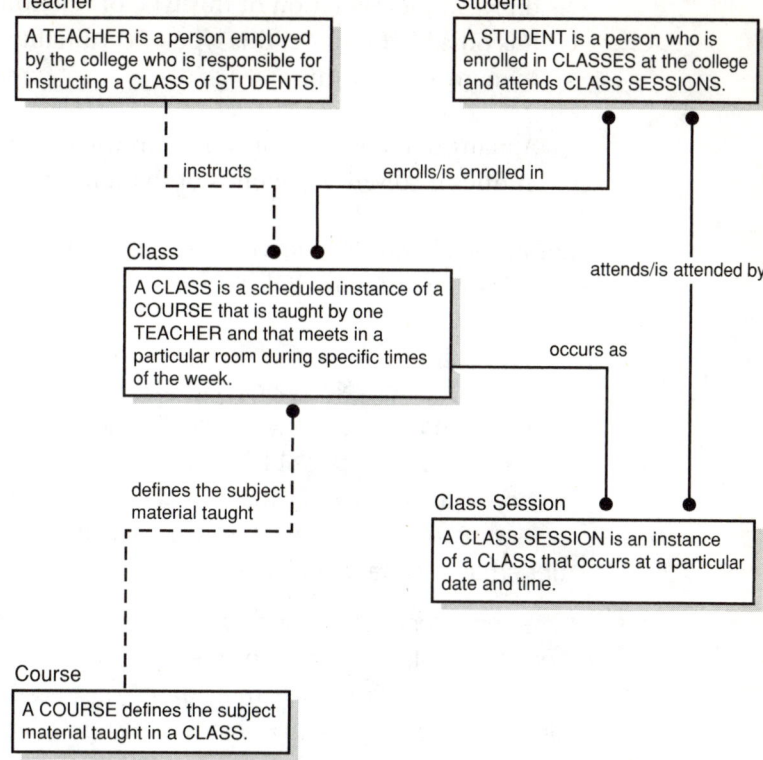

Teacher

A TEACHER is a person employed by the college who is responsible for instructing a CLASS of STUDENTS.

Student

A STUDENT is a person who is enrolled in CLASSES at the college and attends CLASS SESSIONS.

instructs

enrolls/is enrolled in

Class

A CLASS is a scheduled instance of a COURSE that is taught by one TEACHER and that meets in a particular room during specific times of the week.

attends/is attended by

occurs as

defines the subject material taught

Class Session

A CLASS SESSION is an instance of a CLASS that occurs at a particular date and time.

Course

A COURSE defines the subject material taught in a CLASS.

▶ **One-to-Many**: An instance of an entity (called the *parent*) is associated with zero or several instances of another entity (called the *child*). An example of this type of relationship can be found by examining the teacher and class entities. A teacher may instruct zero or more classes during the course of a semester.

A one-to-many relationship is drawn as a line between the entities involved. The child end of the relationship typically has a dot.

▶ **Many-to-Many**: Many instances of an entity are associated with many instances of another entity. Consider the enrollment relationship between a student and a class. A single student may be enrolled in many classes, and a single class may enroll many students. SQL Server does not support a direct implementation of this type of relationship; however, it is possible to model this type of cardinality using two one-to-many relationships.

A many-to-many relationship is drawn as a line between the entities involved. Both ends of the line have a dot.

Later in the chapter you learn how each of these types of relationships is implemented in SQL Server.

 Note

The one-to-many relationship actually has a sub-classification. Typically, the one-to-many cardinality means "one to zero, one, or more." It is possible to specify that at least one instance of the child entity must exist, in other words, "one to one or more." In most notation systems, this is denoted by an uppercase P near the child end of the relationship line.

The one-to-one relationship is actually a special case of a "one to exactly *n*" type of relationship, in which exactly *n* instances of the child entity must exist. Most notation systems denote this type of relationship by putting the number of instances required near the child end of the relationship line.

Finally, another special type of cardinality is the "one to zero or one." This specifies that either zero or one instances of the child entity exist for each instance of the parent. Most notation systems denote this condition with an uppercase Z near the child end of the relationship.

Implementing Entities and Attributes

Now that you've become familiar with the three main concepts used in relational modeling, it's time to see how these concepts are used in SQL Server. Entities and attributes are implemented in SQL Server as tables and columns. The following section deals with how relationships are defined between tables in a database.

Chapter 3, "Data Definition" covers the actual commands used to define tables and relationships in a database.

Characteristics of Tables

Recall that the earlier discussion of entities introduced the concept of an *instance* of an entity. In SQL Server, tables are used to store information about each instance of an entity. A sample table for the Teacher entity is presented in figure 1.4.

Figure 1.4

The teacher entity as a table.

First Name	Last Name	Gender	Social Security Number	Salary	Years Tenured
Warren	Press	M	001-03-1869	$45,000	12
Marie	Noel	F	079-91-2060	$52,500	15
Michael	Barry	M	114-78-1342	$59,000	16
Christopher	Smith	M	001-23-1903	$60,100	18

Note that a table stores each instance of an entity as a row in the table, with each attribute stored in a column. So, in figure 1.4, the table has four teachers, and each column describes information about each teacher. Rows and columns are sometimes referred to as *records* and *fields*, respectively. The order of the rows and columns in a table is not important, although columns that store related information should be grouped together. Note that in the example table, the FirstName and LastName columns are grouped in this way.

The following list summarizes this terminology:

▶ *Entities* are modeled as *tables*.

▶ In a *table*, each instance of an entity is called a *row*.

▶ *Attributes* are modeled as *columns* in a table.

▶ Programmers often refer to *rows* and *columns* as *records* and *fields*.

Although you may choose any names you want for tables and columns, following a couple of guidelines makes your data model consistent and easier to read. These guidelines include:

▶ Table and column names are usually singular; this is a relational modeling convention. Tables are almost always named after the entity they represent.

▶ Also, mixed case is preferable to using underscores to separate words.

▶ Ensure that columns that store the same type of information in different tables have the same name. For instance, if the teacher table and the student table both store address information, make sure that the column storing the ZIP code is named the same in both tables.

These guidelines may seem basic, but developers writing applications that use your database will appreciate the consistency.

SQL Server does place some restrictions on table and column names. The restrictions include:

▶ Table and column names cannot be longer than thirty characters.

▶ Table names must be unique within the database.

▶ Column names must be unique within a table.

 Tip

Most object names within SQL Server are limited to thirty characters.

SQL Server enforces the uniqueness of table and column names for you, but for a relational model to work properly, each row must also be unique. This concept is known as *entity integrity* or *row integrity*. In other words, each instance of an entity must be distinguishable from all other instances. Otherwise, it would be very difficult to change a particular instance of an entity. Imagine trying to change some information about one teacher without knowing how to distinguish that teacher from the others! Because SQL Server does not automatically enforce it, the person designing the database must build this row uniqueness into the data model. Row uniqueness is enforced by using a special column in the table called the *primary key*.

Choosing and Defining the Primary Key

As mentioned in the preceding section, the *primary key* is a special column or group of columns in the table that can be used to identify any one row. The important thing to remember is that the value in the primary key column (or combination of values in the group of columns) *must be unique in the table in which it resides.* Fortunately, SQL Server provides several ways to enforce the uniqueness of the primary key:

▶ Using a primary key constraint when the table is defined. See Chapter 3 for more information about constraints.

▶ Using the sp_primarykey stored procedure to define the primary key for an existing table.

▶ Creating a unique index on the primary key column(s). See Chapter 7, "Indexes," for more information about indexes.

A primary key may be chosen out of the existing columns in a table, or a new column may be created expressly for this purpose.

The easiest way to create a primary key is to create a special column called an *identity* column, also known as an *auto-number* or a *sequence* column. An identity column contains numbers assigned automatically by SQL Server. SQL Server just adds one to the prior value in the column to get a new, unique number to use as a key value. In data modeling terms, this type of primary key is known as a *surrogate key,* because the key values themselves have no inherent meaning.

To choose a primary key, look at the existing attributes of an entity to see if there's an attribute of group of attributes that could serve to identify instances of that entity. The important question to ask yourself when you're considering these possible keys is "are the values of this column or group of columns guaranteed to be unique?" If the answer is yes, then you have found a *candidate key.* You will ultimately define a primary key by choosing one of these candidate keys. This type of primary key is known as an *intelligent key,* because the key value has some business meaning associated with it as well.

Note

There are advantages and disadvantages to using surrogate and intelligent keys. Consult one of the data modeling texts listed at the beginning of the chapter for more information.

Consider the teacher table shown in figure 1.4. We could choose to identify a teacher by name, using a combination of the FirstName and LastName columns. Of course, we know that many people have the same name, so this is a poor choice for a primary key. Now, consider the teacher's social security number. Social security numbers are supposed to be unique, which would make this column a good choice for a primary key. Unfortunately, social security numbers can be duplicated by accident, which not only causes a lot of confusion for the people involved, but causes our choice of a primary key to fail. So, for the teacher table, we will just assign a surrogate key called TeacherID, as shown in figure 1.5.

Figure 1.5

The teacher table with a primary key defined.

Teacher ID (PK)	First Name	Last Name	Gender	Social Security Number	Salary	Years Tenured
1	Warren	Press	M	001-03-1869	$45,000	12
2	Marie	Noel	F	079-91-2060	$52,500	15
3	Michael	Barry	M	114-78-1342	$59,000	16
4	Christopher	Smith	M	001-23-1903	$60,100	18

Surrogate primary key names usually end with *Code*, *Number*, or *ID*. Primary keys are denoted in the data model with the letters *PK*, or separated from the other attributes by a line in the ER diagram. Typically, the primary key column(s) are the first in the table.

Note

SQL Server only allows one primary key to be defined per table, even though there may be several valid candidate keys. In situations like this, the data modeler usually defines the other candidate keys as *alternate keys* by creating a uniqueness constraint on the candidate key column(s). SQL Server then enforces uniqueness on the alternate key(s) as well as the primary key.

Alternate keys are usually denoted in a data model by the letters *AK*.

In addition to defining a column as a primary key, the database designer may define additional constraints on columns. These are discussed in the next section.

Column Constraints

You may specify additional constraints on columns when designing your database. These constraints enable you to build basic business requirements into your data model. There are three fundamental types of column constraints used in a database design: *not null (NN)*, *no duplicates (ND)*, and *no changes (NC)*. These constraints may be combined, as in the case of a primary key, which is usually marked as NN and ND.

The not null concept allows the database designer to require the entry of a value in a particular column. For example, if a teacher's name, gender, and social security number are required for tax purposes, these columns can be marked as not null. The not null concept is also used for columns involved in a primary key. SQL Server implements the not null concept by keeping information about the *null option* of each column. This option must be set when a table is created, and is set by using the NULL or NOT NULL keywords. See Chapter 3 for more information about creating tables.

Note

Null is a special value used in relational databases that means "no value has been entered" or "the value is unknown." It is not the same as an empty string ("") or a zero value.

Null has two special properties of which you should be aware. First, it propagates through any arithmetic expression, so "2 + null" results in null. Next, comparing null to any value, including itself, results in a null.

The no duplicates concept specifies that the values in a column must be unique. This concept is used in primary keys and alternate keys. For example, disallowing duplicates on the TeacherID column in the teacher table allows that column to be used to uniquely identify any row in that table. SQL Server implements this concept in a number of ways, including a primary key constraint, a unique constraint, or a unique index.

The no changes concept allows the database designer to prohibit changes to the values in a column. This concept is used mainly for columns participating in a primary key. Preventing changes to a primary key is recommended because primary key values are used to create relationships between tables, and changes to a primary key could result in a referential integrity violation. (For more information on the role of primary keys in relationships, see the following section on implementing relationships.) SQL Server implements this concept using reference constraints or triggers.

 Note

You also may assign security permissions to columns so that only certain users of the database may make changes to values in those columns. For instance, you may want only the department chairs at the college to have the ability to change teachers' salaries.

SQL Server also enables you to build custom constraints on columns to enforce more complex rules, like "the number of years tenured for a teacher cannot be less than zero." Custom constraints are discussed in Chapter 3.

Figure 1.6 shows the sample teacher table with constraints defined. Note that the primary key column, TeacherID, has several constraints defined.

Non-Decomposable Columns

One important consideration when implementing attributes in a table involves decomposing an attribute into several columns. Typically, attributes should be broken down into columns that contain information that cannot be decomposed any further. Consider the Teacher entity shown in figure 1.2. Two attributes in this entity—name and address—should be broken into multiple columns. The name attribute should be decomposed into columns for FirstName, LastName, and MiddleInitial. The address attribute should be decomposed into columns for Address1,

Address2, City, State, and ZipCode (and possibly Country). Storing values in columns that cannot be decomposed further has several advantages:

▶ Columns are easier to update. For instance, decomposing the address attribute into multiple columns allows a developer to easily change any part of the address without having to worry about the other parts.

▶ Columns are easier to query. For instance, finding all teachers that live in a certain city can be accomplished by querying the city portion of the address. If this attribute were not decomposed, finding where the city was in the address would be difficult.

▶ Data integrity is more specific. Each column may have its own data type, null option, or other constraints as needed. For instance, not every person has a middle initial, so this column could allow nulls, whereas the FirstName and LastName columns would require a value.

Figure 1.6

The teacher table with column constraints.

Teacher ID (NN,NC,ND)	First Name (NN)	Last Name (NN)	Gender (NN)	Social Security Number (NN)	Salary	Years Tenured
1	Warren	Press	M	001-03-1869	$45,000	12
2	Marie	Noel	F	079-91-2060	$52,500	15
3	Michael	Barry	M	114-78-1342	$59,000	16
4	Christopher	Smith	M	001-23-1903	$60,100	18

There are no specific rules about when to decompose a column or how far to decompose a column. Phone numbers are a good example of columns that could be decomposed further. It would be possible to decompose a phone number into its area code and number, or area code, prefix, and number. Another example is a ZIP code field, which could be decomposed into a ZIP code and a ZIP+4 code. Both of the aforementioned examples are rarely decomposed into separate columns. As a database designer, you need to evaluate the need to decompose these types of columns, based on how the information is updated or queried, or based on special data integrity rules.

Considering all of the implementation issues presented in this section leads us to the data model presented in figure 1.7. This diagram shows what would be a typical implementation of the entities and attributes for the enrollment database.

Figure 1.7

The enrollment database ER diagram (Completed Entities and Attributes) with primary keys and column characteristics shown.

Course

CourseID: NOT NULL
Description: NOT NULL

Student

StudentID: NOT NULL
FirstName: NOT NULL
LastName: NOT NULL
MiddleInitial: NULL
Gender: NOT NULL
SocialSecurityNumber: NOTNULL
BillingAddress1: NOT NULL
Billing Address2: NULL
BillingCity: NOT NULL
BillingState: NOT NULL
BillingZipCode: NOT NULL
CampusAddress1: NOT NULL
CampusAddress2: NULL
CampusCity: NOT NULL
CampusState: NOT NULL
CampusZipCode: NOT NULL
ClassLevel: NULL
GradePointAverage: NULL

Teacher

TeacherID: NOT NULL
FirstName: NOT NULL
LastName: NOT NULL
MiddleInitial: NULL
Gender: NOT NULL
SocialSecurityNumber: NOTNULL
Address1: NOT NULL
Address2: NULL
City: NOT NULL
State: NOT NULL
ZipCode: NOT NULL
Salary: NULL
Years Tenured: NULL

Class

ClassID: NOT NULL
Course: NOT NULL
ScheduledTime: NOT NULL
ScheduledRoom: NOT NULL
Teacher: NOT NULL
MaximumEnrollment: NOT NULL
Students Enrolled: NOT NULL

Class_Session

ClassID: NOT NULL
SessionDate: NOT NULL
SessionTime: NOT NULL

Implementing Relationships

Entities and attributes are physically represented in a SQL Server database by tables and columns. Relationships between tables differ in that they are not represented by any particular object in the database. Instead, relationships are created by logically linking the primary key column(s) of the parent table with a *foreign key* column (or columns) in the child table.

Primary Keys and Foreign Keys

Understanding how primary keys and foreign keys relate to each other is vital to understanding relationships in SQL Server. When a relationship is created between two tables (say, teacher and class), the parent table in the relationship contributes its primary key to the child table, where it is known as a foreign key, as shown in figure 1.8.

Figure 1.8

Implementation of the relationships between the teacher, class, and course tables.

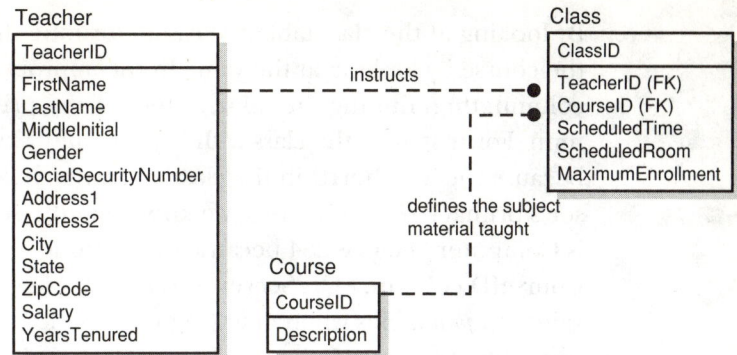

Note how a new TeacherID column is present in the class table, and that it carries the *FK* designation. Note also how the CourseID column (the primary key of the course table) is contributed to the class table as a foreign key. The foreign key columns in the class table are said to have a *reference* to the associated primary key columns in the parent tables.

The link between entities in the tables is created by storing the value of the primary key for the parent row in the foreign key column of the child row. Refer to figure 1.9, which shows some sample data for these three tables to illustrate this concept.

Figure 1.9

The teacher, course, and class tables, showing the related data in the primary key and foreign key columns.

Teacher ID (PK)	First Name	Last Name	Gender	Social Security Number
1	Warren	Press	M	001-03-1869
2	Marie	Noel	F	079-91-2060
3	Michael	Barry	M	114-78-1342
4	Christopher	Smith	M	001-23-1903

Course ID (PK)	Description
1	Physics 109
2	Electrical Engineering 213
3	Computer Science 284

Class ID (PK)	Teacher ID (FK)	Course ID (FK)	Scheduled Time		Scheduled Room	Maximum Enrollment
1	2	1	MWF	7:30 AM	Phys 104	30
2	4	1	TR	11:30 AM	Phys 114	35
3	1	3	M	6:00 PM	CSC 215	40
4	3	2	TR	2:30 PM	EE 119	20
5	1	3	MWF	4:30 PM	CSC 210	25

By looking at the class table, we can determine the teacher and the course by looking at the value in the appropriate foreign key column, then finding the value in the related primary key column. For instance, the class with ID 3 is taught by Professor Press, because the TeacherID in the class table matches with that professor's primary key value. Also, we know that the subject of this class is Computer Science 284 because of the value stored in the CourseID column. SQL Server uses primary key and foreign key values to *join* tables when querying information from more than one table. For more information, see Chapter 5, "Retrieving Data (Advanced Topics)."

Now that you have seen how primary keys and foreign keys are used in relationships, let's look at some specifics of implementing relationships of different cardinalities.

One-to-One and One-to-Many Relationships

One-to-one and one-to-many relationships are implemented as described in the previous section. The primary key of the parent table is contributed to the child table as a foreign key. In the case of a one-to-one relationship, one primary key value corresponds to one foreign key value. In the case of a one-to-many relationship, one primary key value corresponds to multiple foreign key values.

If the primary key column is contributed to the child table's primary key (in other words, the foreign key is one of the columns in the child table's primary key), then this relationship is known as an *identifying* relationship. In this case, the child entity is known as a *dependent* entity because its identification depends on the parent entity. Foreign keys in identifying relationships cannot contain null values.

The relationships in figure 1.8 could be implemented as identifying relationships, because a class can be identified uniquely by the combination of its teacher, course, scheduled time and scheduled room attributes.

The other type of relationship (in which the foreign key is not part of the child's primary key) is known as a *non-identifying* relationship, because the child entity can be identified without knowing about the parent. In this case, the child entity is said to be *independent* of its parent. Foreign keys in non-identifying relationships may be marked as not null (NN), in which case they are known as a *mandatory non-identifying* relationship.

Figure 1.8 shows two non-identifying relationships between the Class table and the Teacher and Course tables. A Class is identified by its class ID, and the relationships provide additional information about the class. The relationships are mandatory because that information about a class must be known.

Many-to-Many Relationships

Many-to-many relationships are implemented a bit differently than a one-to-one or one-to-many relationship. A simple primary key to foreign key link does not suffice. Consider the relationship between the student entity and the class entity. This relationship defines which classes students are enrolled in, or which students are enrolled in which classes. Simply taking the primary key from one table and using it as a foreign key in another will not work, because only half of the relationship is defined; furthermore, this would result in the duplication of data in one or the other tables.

One possible way to implement this type of relationship would be to use a column in each table that lists all of the classes for each student, or all the students in each class. This type of implementation is shown in figure 1.10.

Unfortunately, while a person can look at the two tables and determine which students are enrolled in which class, SQL Server has no way to efficiently use this information. SQL Server has no built-in way to match key values stored in this manner. In addition, implementing the relationship in this way violates the idea of using non-decomposable columns (as discussed earlier in the chapter).

Figure 1.10

A many-to-many relationship between the student table and the class table, using multiple primary key values in a column.

Student ID	Name	Class Enrollment
1	C. Brunswick	1,3,4
2	D. Hughes	2,4
3	B. Smith	1,4,5
4	K. Davies	2,5

Class ID	Teacher ID	Course ID	Scheduled Time	Students Enrolled
1	2	1	MWF 7:30 AM	1,3
2	4	1	TR 11:30 AM	2,4
3	1	3	M 6:00 PM	1
4	3	2	TR 2:30 PM	1,2,3
5	1	3	MWF 4:30 PM	3,4

Because the enrollment columns shown in figure 1.10 can be decomposed, let's see how effective that implementation option is. Consider figure 1.11. In this case, the enrollment column in the student and class tables has been decomposed into a list of columns.

Figure 1.11

Many-to-many relationship between the student table and the class table, using multiple primary key values in multiple columns.

Student ID	Name	Enrollment 1	Enrollment 2	Enrollment 3	Enrollment 4	Enrollment 5
1	C. Brunswick	1	3	4	Null	Null
2	D. Hughes	2	4	Null	Null	Null
3	B. Smith	1	4	5	Null	Null
4	K. Davies	2	5	Null	Null	Null

Class ID	Teacher ID	Course ID	Scheduled Time	Enrollment 1	Enrollment 2	Enrollment 3	Enrollment 4	Enrollment 5
1	2	1	MWF 7:30 AM	1	3	Null	Null	Null
2	4	1	TR 11:30 AM	2	4	Null	Null	Null
3	1	3	M 6:00 PM	1	Null	Null	Null	Null
4	3	2	TR 2:30 PM	1	2	3	Null	Null
5	1	3	MWF 4:30 PM	3	4	Null	Null	Null

This may seem like a viable solution at first, because now SQL Server has distinct columns that it can use to join the tables. However, this implementation has two problems. First, SQL Server cannot join multiple columns in this manner any easier than it can join columns with lists of values. Secondly, this implementation restricts students to enrolling in only five classes, and restricts classes to a maximum of five students. True, it would be possible to increase the number of enrollment columns in each table to handle all possible situations, but this would waste storage space when a student was enrolled in only a few classes, or a class only had a few students enrolled.

 **Note**

> The second implementation option presented is also a violation of *first normal form.* For more information on normal forms, see the next section.

So how is a many-to-many relationship implemented? The trick is to use another table. In data modeling lingo, the entity used in building a many-to-many relationship is called an *associative entity,* but many database designers simply refer to it as a *join table.* To implement a many-to-many relationship, define the associative entity in the data model and create a one-to-many relationship from each of the original entities to the associative entity, as shown in figure 1.12. Note that the primary keys of the original tables migrate as foreign keys to the primary key of the join table. In most many-to-many implementations, the join table is a dependent entity.

Figure 1.12

An ER diagram of a many-to-many relationship between the student table and the class table, using an associative entity.

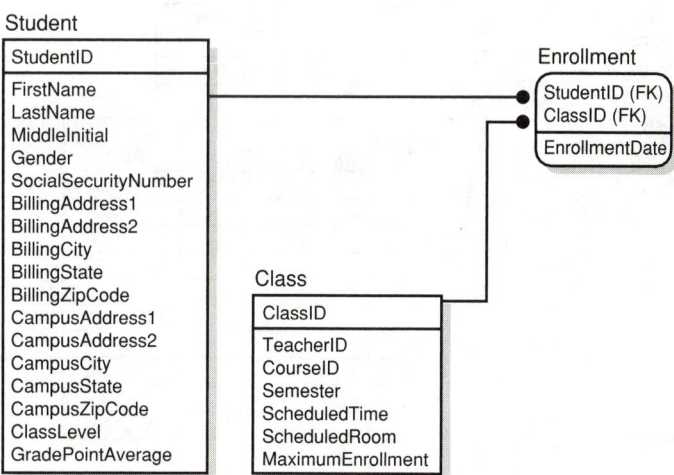

You also may need to define additional columns for the primary key to ensure that it will be unique. Refer again to figure 1.12. In this case, no additional fields are required, because the combination of a student ID and class ID is guaranteed to be unique. If a student has the misfortune to fail a course and has to repeat it in a later semester, he or she will be enrolled in a new instance of a class, because a course has new classes defined for each semester. See exercise 1.3 for an example of when additional primary key attributes are required.

Creating a new entity for a many-to-many relationship also opens an opportunity for defining new attributes for this entity. Doing this enables you to store additional information about the relationship. Figure 1.12 illustrates this by adding an enrollment date column to the enrollment table. Now we know not only that a student *is* enrolled in a class, we know *when* that student enrolled.

Implementing a many-to-many relationship in this way eliminates the problems discussed at the beginning of this section. All columns are non-decomposable, and first normal form isn't violated. See figure 1.13 for an example of a correct many-to-many implementation.

Figure 1.13

Example of a many-to-many relationship between the student table and the class table, using the enrollment table as a join table.

Student ID (PK)	Name
1	C. Brunswick
2	D. Hughes
3	B. Smith
4	K. Davies

Student ID (PK)	Class ID (PK)	Enrollment Date
1	1	5/20/1997
1	3	5/20/1997
1	4	5/20/1997
2	2	5/22/1997
2	4	5/22/1997
3	1	5/22/1997
3	4	5/23/1997
3	5	5/22/1997
4	2	5/19/1997
4	5	5/20/1997

Class ID (PK)	Teacher ID	Course ID	Scheduled Time	
1	2	1	MWF	7:30 AM
2	4	1	TR	11:30 AM
3	1	3	M	6:00 PM
4	3	2	TR	2:30 PM
5	1	3	MWF	4:30 PM

Recursive Relationships

Recursive relationships aren't covered on the exam, yet they are used in some special cases. Consider the following excerpt from the case study:

"Oh, another interesting point about our teachers. We're very proud of the new mentoring program we've just put in place. Our more experienced professors have the option to mentor some of our newer professors. This program ensures that our newer professors have someone to talk to in case they need advice. We're not forcing this on anyone, so not everyone will have a mentor, but we would like to document in the database who has a mentor and who doesn't."

In this case, the teacher entity needs to have a relationship to itself, because a more experienced teacher acts as a mentor to a less experienced teacher. A recursive relationship is implemented just like a normal one-to-one or one-to-many relationship, except that the same table acts as both the parent and the child in the relationship. Figure 1.14 shows how the relationship described in the case study would be modeled.

Figure 1.14

ER diagram of a recursive relationship on the teacher entity.

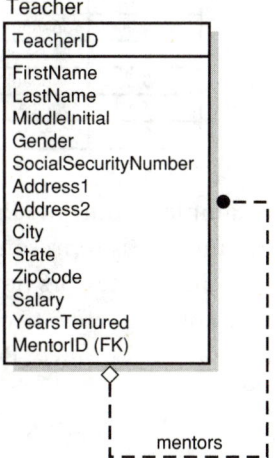

Note how the primary key of the teacher table is contributed back to the teacher table as a foreign key. Also, note that the foreign key is renamed from TeacherID to MentorID—this is known as *rolenaming*, and clarifies the foreign key's role in describing the entity.

 **Note**

Rolenaming can be used in any type of relationship, but is required for a recursive relationship. Otherwise, the foreign key would have the same name as the primary key!

A recursive relationship is always non-identifying, and may be either mandatory or non-mandatory. In the example presented in figure 1.14, the relationship is non-mandatory, because not every teacher has a mentor. If every teacher was required to have a mentor, then the relationship would be made mandatory by indicating that the MentorID column could not contain nulls. Figure 1.15 shows a sample teacher table.

Figure 1.15

Example teacher table, showing the relationship between the TeacherID column and the MentorID column.

Teacher ID (PK)	First Name	Last Name	Mentor ID (FK)
1	Warren	Press	Null
2	J.C.	Brunswick	8
3	Marie	Noel	Null
4	Joshua	Smith	3
5	Elizabeth	Green	6
6	Michael	Barry	3
7	Janice	Saint	1
8	Christopher	Smith	Null

In the example, professors Press, Noel, and Smith do not have mentors, and this is represented by a null in the MentorID column. All other professors do have a mentor, and the value in the MentorID column refers back to the primary key of that professor's mentor. For instance, Professor Noel mentors Professor Joshua Smith.

Referential Integrity

One final concept important to implementing relationships deals with *referential integrity*. Referential integrity is a way of ensuring that the primary key and foreign key values used to create a relationship never get out of sync. Otherwise, it would be possible to have child entities that had no corresponding parent entity. If this happens, the child entity is said to be *orphaned*. Figure 1.16 and the next few paragraphs describe how this can happen.

Figure 1.16

Course and Class tables, with example data.

Course ID (PK)	Description
1	Physics 109
2	Electrical Engineering 213
3	Computer Science 284

Class ID (PK)	Teacher ID (FK)	Course ID (FK)	Scheduled Time		Scheduled Room	Maximum Enrollment
1	2	1	MWF	7:30 AM	Phys 104	30
2	4	1	TR	11:30 AM	Phys 114	35
3	1	3	M	6:00 PM	CSC 215	40
4	3	2	TR	2:30 PM	EE 119	20
5	1	3	MWF	4:30 PM	CSC 210	25

Referential integrity violations are a concern any time data is inserted into a table, removed from a table, or updated in the table:

▶ **The insert problem**: If a row is inserted into a child table that has a foreign key value that does not match any primary key in the parent table, then the child row will be an orphan. For instance, inserting a class that has a CourseID of 4 results in a class that has no corresponding course. The two options for preserving referential integrity are to restrict the insert—to not allow it to happen—or to set the CourseID column to null. Typically, the insert is restricted.

▶ **The delete problem**: If a row is deleted from the parent table, then any rows in the child table that refer to the parent row are orphaned. For example, deleting the Physics 109 course leaves the associated classes without a valid CourseID. When a parent row is deleted, there are three options. The delete may cascade to the child rows, in which case they are also deleted. For example, deleting the Physics 109 course would also delete the classes with IDs of 1 and 2. Instead of cascading, the delete may be restricted, or the child rows' foreign key values may be set to null. Typically, the delete cascades or is restricted.

 **Warning**

Use cascading deletes with caution; if a lot of child tables reference a single parent table and cascading deletes are in place, it is possible to destroy a large amount of data very quickly!

▶ **The update problem**: If the primary key value of the parent table is changed, then any rows in the child table that refer to the parent row are orphaned. Also, if the foreign key value in a child row is updated to refer to a nonexistent parent row, then the child row is orphaned. For updates to the parent table, the update may be cascaded to the child table, the update may be restricted, or the child's foreign key may be set to null. For updates to the child table, the update may be restricted, or the foreign key may be set to null. It is standard practice to disallow updates to a primary key column, and to restrict updates to foreign key columns so that only valid values may be entered.

Referential integrity is maintained by using triggers or declarative referential integrity (DRI) constraints. DRI constraints can only restrict inserts, deletes, or updates to preserve referential integrity. Triggers are more flexible and can implement a restriction, a cascade, or a set null operation to preserve referential integrity. Triggers are discussed more in Chapter 10, "Triggers," and constraints are covered in Chapter 3.

Normalizing Your Database Design

In 1970, E.F. Codd formalized three rules for relational database design known as *normal forms*. In later years, additional normal forms have been defined (there are now six), but the first three are the most widely used. Although normalization is not covered extensively on the exam, it is a very important step in developing a good database design. Normalizing your database ensures the following things:

> ▶ Dependencies between data are identified

> ▶ Redundant data (and all of the problems associated with it) is minimized

> ▶ The data model is flexible and easier to maintain

Codd's normal forms were derived from set-based calculus, but you don't need to be a mathematician to use them. The next three sections discuss the three normal forms and how to identify and correct violations of each. Before normalizing an entity, it is helpful to first identify or create a primary key. In addition, columns should be decomposed before normalization.

Normalization, if carried too far, can adversely affect performance by increasing the number of tables joined in a query. In some cases, *denormalizing* the data model is appropriate. However, it is usually best to take the data model to third normal form before considering what data to denormalize.

First Normal Form

The purpose of first normal form (1NF) is to eliminate repeating groups of attributes in an entity. For example, let's say that the college wants to track students' degrees, whether they have already been earned (as in the case of a graduate student that already has a BS degree), or if they are still in progress (such as a freshman who has just started working towards his or her BS). The initial ER diagram for the student entity may look something like the one presented in figure 1.17.

To discover a violation of first normal form, look at each attribute for an entity and ask "does this attribute occur repeatedly for any particular instance of this entity?" If the answer is yes, as in the case of the DegreeID, DegreeName, DegreeWhenEarned, and DegreeInProgress attributes in figure 1.17, then you must correct the 1NF violation.

Figure 1.17

First normal form violation in the student entity.

Student

StudentID
FirstName
LastName
MiddleInitial
BillingAddress1
BillingAddress2
BillingCity
BillingState
BillingZipCode
CampusAddress1
CampusAddress2
CampusCity
CampusState
CampusZipCode
DegreeID1
DegreeName1
DegreeWhenEarned1
DegreeInProgress1
DegreeID2
DegreeName2
DegreeWhenEarned2
DegreeInProgress2

Note

The address fields in the student table also are a violation of 1NF. In this case, we will leave these fields in the student table because the college only requires these two addresses to be kept for a student. We are normalizing the degree fields because a student may hold any number of degrees, and normalizing makes the data model more flexible.

If the college was interested in storing a variety of different addresses for each student, or past addresses for each student, those attributes would be a good candidate for normalization.

To correct a violation of first normal form, create and name a new entity that describes the repeating groups. For this example, create a new entity called *Student Degree*. Eliminate the repeating groups of attributes and move them to the new entity. Finally, decide on a primary key for the new entity (in this example, we'll use the DegreeID) and create an identifying one-to-many relationship between the original entity and the new entity. The results will be similar to those shown in figure 1.18.

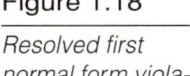

Figure 1.18

Resolved first normal form violation in the student entity.

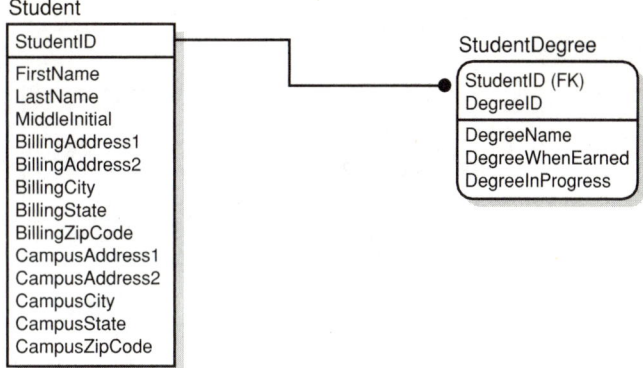

In general, 1NF violations cause the data model to be less flexible and less efficient in storing data. Resolving this particular violation has made the data model more flexible because we are no longer limited to storing two degrees per student. In addition, we save storage space when a student has only one degree.

Second Normal Form

The purpose of second normal form (2NF) is to eliminate partial key dependencies. In other words, each attribute in an entity must depend on the whole key, not just a part of it.

 **Tip**

Second normal form violations can only occur in entities that have primary keys composed of more than one attribute.

Consider figure 1.19. This ER diagram shows the data model from the last section, with an additional attribute (DegreeCreditsRequired) stored about each degree in the StudentDegree entity.

To identify a 2NF violation, look at each attribute not involved in the primary key and ask "does this attribute only depend on part of the primary key?" In figure 1.19, the answer is "yes" for the DegreeName and DegreeCreditsRequired attributes, which only depend on the DegreeID. In other words, we don't need to know about a student to know a degree's name or the credit hours required to obtain it. We do need to know about the particular student for the DegreeWhenEarned and DegreeInProgress attributes.

Figure 1.19

Second normal form violation in the StudentDegree entity.

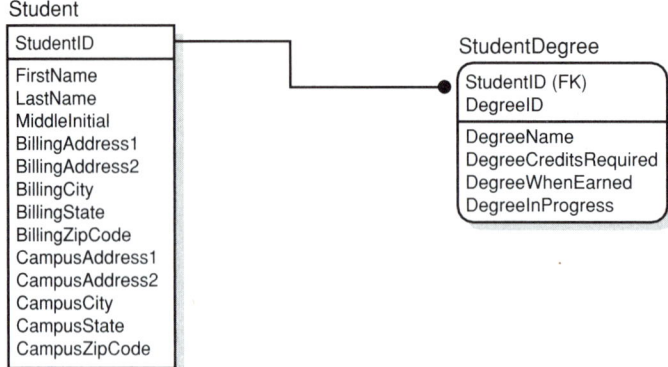

To correct a violation of second normal form, create a new entity for the attributes that depends on only part of the primary key. In this example, we will create a new *Degree* entity that describes each degree program and the credit hours required to obtain it. Then, move the partially dependent attributes to the new entity and create an identifying relationship between the new entity and the entity that had the violation, as shown in figure 1.20.

Figure 1.20

Resolved second normal form violation in the StudentDegree entity.

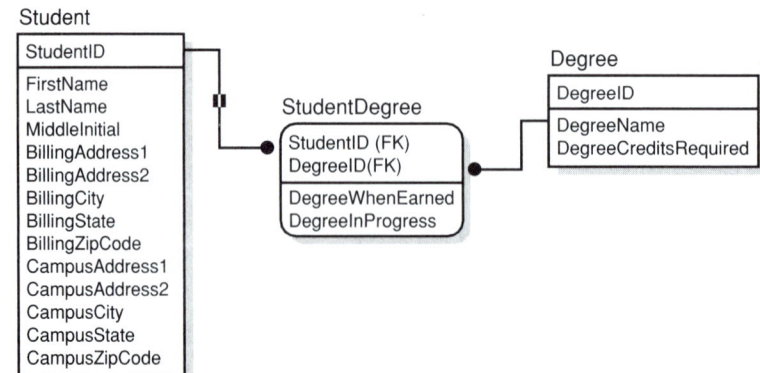

2NF violations typically cause data to be duplicated. In the example in this section, the degree name and credit hours required were duplicated for each student that had a particular type of degree (BA, BS, MS, and so on.) Moving the attributes for a degree to the new entity eliminates this redundancy.

Third Normal Form

Third normal form (3NF) also helps eliminate redundant information by eliminating interdependencies between non-key attributes. To identify a violation of this kind, look at each attribute not participating in the primary key and ask if the attribute depends on some other non-key attribute. See figure 1.21 for an example of a violation of third normal form in the Class entity.

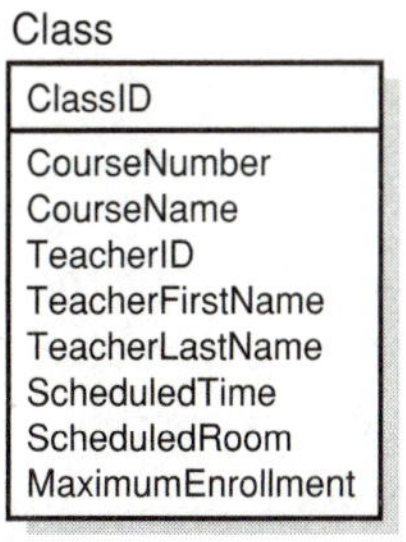

Figure 1.21

Third normal form violation in the Class entity.

Class

ClassID
CourseNumber
CourseName
TeacherID
TeacherFirstName
TeacherLastName
ScheduledTime
ScheduledRoom
MaximumEnrollment

In this diagram, there are actually two violations of the third normal form. The first occurs because of the dependency between the CourseNumber and CourseName attributes, and the second occurs because of the dependency between the TeacherID, TeacherFirstName, and TeacherLastName attributes.

To resolve a 3NF violation, create a new entity that contains all of the non-key attributes that depend on each other. In this example, we've created two new entities, one for the interdependent course attributes, and one for the interdependent teacher attributes. For the new entity, choose or create a primary key, then create a non-identifying relationship back to the original entity. The resolution of the normal form violations shown in figure 1.21 is shown in figure 1.22.

The third normal form is very similar to the second normal form, except that it deals entirely with dependencies that don't involve the key. In both cases, however, redundant data is eliminated, which makes the database more reliable and easier to update.

Figure 1.22

Resolution of the third normal form violations in the Class entity.

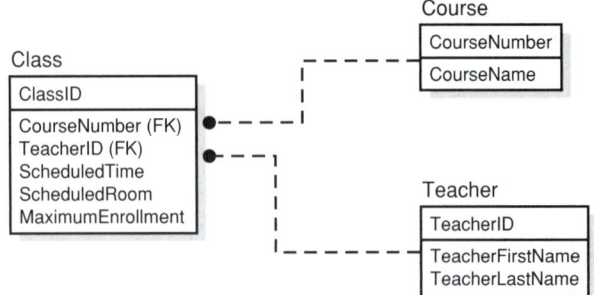

Summary

This chapter covered the fundamentals of designing a database using relational database design methods. You learned the data modeling concepts that must be understood before the database can be implemented. You also learned how these modeling concepts are executed in SQL Server. While it is important to learn the SQL Server commands and code, you must first understand the basic concepts of entities, attributes, and relationships before you can successfully design a database.

Exercises

Exercise 1.1:   Modeling a New Entity

Recall that the case study made mention of the fact that several academic departments existed at the college. This exercise walks you through the steps required to create the department entity, define its attributes, and identify a primary key.

1. Identify the person, place, thing, or concept that will be represented in the data model by the new entity. This exercise uses the concept of an academic department at the college.

2. Develop a sentence that defines the entity. For the academic department, we use "A department is a unit of administration that offers at least one type of degree and employs one or more teachers."

3. Identify any attributes of the entity. For this example, we want to store information about the department's name and chairperson, as well as the office location and phone number for the department.

4. Place restrictions on any attributes as required. For the department entity, the department name and chairperson are required information, so we place a no nulls restriction on those attributes.

5. Identify or create a primary key attribute. For the department entity, we could use the department name as the primary key, because two departments on campus are unlikely to have the same name. However, remember that a primary key usually has a no changes restriction. This would make it difficult to change a department's name if required. Therefore, we will create a surrogate key called DepartmentID.

6. The new entity will look similar to the one presented in figure 1.23. You may now implement the new entity in SQL Server. For more information on how to do this, see Chapter 3.

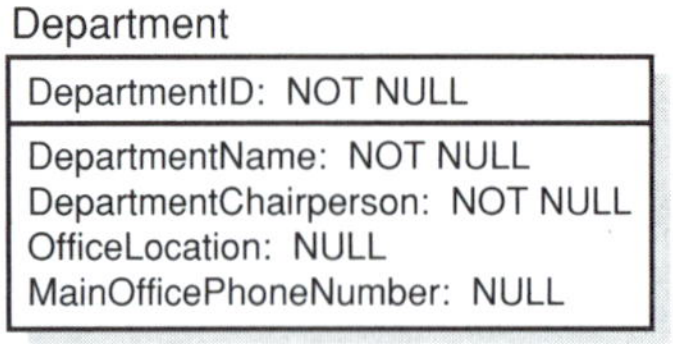

Figure 1.23

The Department entity.

Department

DepartmentID: NOT NULL
DepartmentName: NOT NULL DepartmentChairperson: NOT NULL OfficeLocation: NULL MainOfficePhoneNumber: NULL

Exercise 1.2: Creating a One-to-Many Relationship

Exercise 1.1 walked you through the process of creating the department entity. You may have noticed that the definition of a department includes the phrase "employs one or more teachers." This phrase indicates that a relationship exists between the department entity and the teacher entity. This exercise walks you through the steps required to create this relationship.

1. If you have not already done so, define each entity that participates in the relationship and define the primary key for each. The department and teacher entities participate in the relationship in this example.

2. Create the foreign key attribute in the child table for the relationship and denote it with the *FK* indicator. If the parent entity helps define the child entity, then include the foreign key in the child entity's primary key. Otherwise, just include the foreign key with the other attributes of the child entity.

   In the department-teacher example, a department does not help define a teacher, so the foreign key from the department entity is not included in the primary key of the teacher entity.

3. Draw a line between the two entities and indicate the cardinality of the relationship. In this case, the relationship requires that a department employ at least one teacher. The *P* designation indicates that the cardinality is "one-to-one or more."

4. If desired, write the verb phrase that describes the relationship on or near the relationship line. The resulting data model will look similar to the one presented in figure 1.24.

Figure 1.24

The one-to-many relationship between the department entity and the teacher entity.

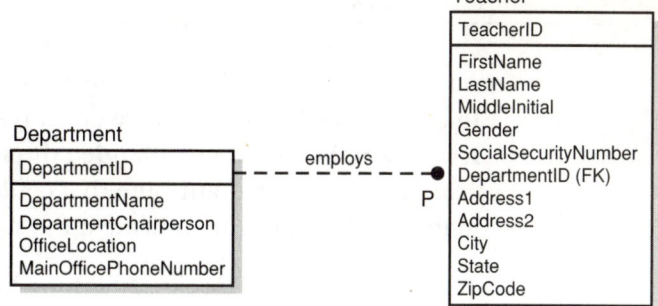

Exercise 1.3:   Creating a Many-to-Many Relationship

Recall that a many-to-many relationship exists between the student entity and the class session entity. This relationship defines which students attended a particular class session. This exercise walks you through the steps required to create the many-to-many relationship.

1. If you have not already done so, define each entity that participates in the relationship and define the primary key for each. The student and class session entities participate in the relationship in this example.

2. Define and name the associative entity used in the many-to-many relationship. In this example, name the entity *ClassSessionAttendance.*

3. Create an identifying one-to-many relationship from each of the original entities to the associative entity. In other words, create foreign keys in the associative entity's primary key. These foreign keys reference the primary keys of the original entities in the relationship.

   The class session attendance example entity will have a primary key composed of the StudentID and SessionID foreign key attributes.

4. Verify that the primary key of the new table will be unique, and add any attributes to the primary key if required. For this example, the combination of the student and session information is sufficient.

continues

Exercise 1.3:   Continued

5. Add any non-key attributes to the associative entity if needed. In this example, the associative entity is simply used to record whether a student attended the session or not. One example of a non-key attribute that could have been added to this entity is a flag to indicate if the student was tardy.

The final data model looks something like the one presented in figure 1.25.

Figure 1.25

The many-to-many relationship between the class session entity and the student entity.

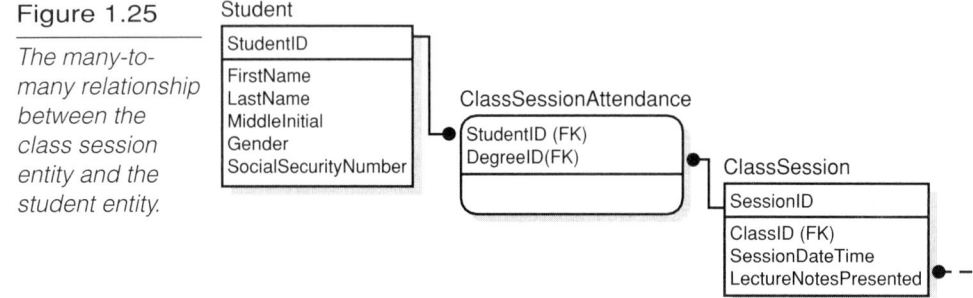

Exercise 1.4:   Creating a One-to-One Relationship

Exercise 1.4 explains one scenario in which a one-to-one relationship is useful and shows you how to create a one-to-one relationship in a data model. Consider the following excerpt from the case study:

"Sometimes we don't even have a tenured professor available to teach a class and we need to have a Teaching Assistant do the job. There isn't any difference as far as the class is concerned—we just assign the T/A as the teacher—but we do keep fairly different types of information on the two different categories of teachers. For instance, our T/As are paid by the hour, while the professors are salaried."

The previous paragraph explains that there are two different categories of teachers about which data is maintained. It would be possible to store all of this information in a single teacher table, but if the two categories of teacher don't share much common information, many columns in the teacher table would contain null values. A better solution is to categorize the entity, as follows:

1. Determine which attributes are common to all categories of the entity. For this example, every teacher has a name and address. These attributes stay in the main entity.

2. Determine how many categories exist for the entity, and create that number of new entities. In this example, the teacher entity can be categorized into a T/A type or a tenured professor type, so two new entities should be created.

3. Move the attributes specific for each category to the new entities. In this example, the TeacherTADetail receives the hourly rate attribute and a foreign key that links a T/A's information to a student's information. The TeacherTenuredDetail receives the attributes specific only to tenured professors, such as salary and benefits information.

4. Create the primary keys for the new entities by creating a foreign key that references the original entity. In this example, both the TeacherTADetail and TeacherTenuredDetail entities have a TeacherID foreign key as their primary keys.

Because the primary key of each child entity is composed of only the foreign key from the parent table, there can be at most one row in the child table for each row in the parent table. The resulting data model will look something like the one presented in figure 1.26.

Figure 1.26

Teacher entity after being categorized into T/A detail and tenured professor detail. Note the one-to-one cardinality in the relationships.

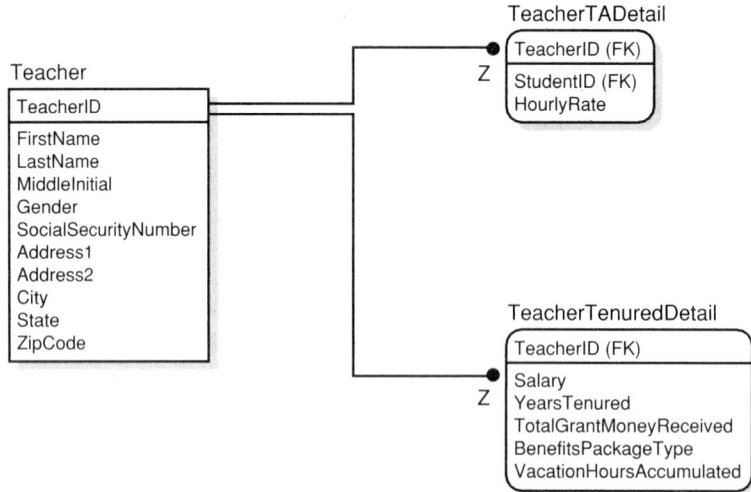

Review Questions

1. Before it is implemented in SQL Server, a data model is most often represented in what kind of diagram?

    A. Object-Relational diagram

    B. Codd diagram

    C. Entity-Relationship diagram

    D. Table structure diagram

2. An instance of an entity is implemented in SQL Server by a:

    A. view

    B. table

    C. column

    D. row

3. In a database model, each entity may have multiple:

    A. attributes

    B. primary keys

    C. names

    D. relationships to other entities

4. In a data model, any person, place, thing, or concept about which data is collected is:

    A. a relationship

    B. an attribute

    C. an instance

    D. an entity

5. In a data model, an attribute is used to:

    A. store additional information about an entity

    B. define an entity

    C. create an instance of an entity

    D. enforce entity integrity

6. Choose all of the statements that are true about relationships:

    A. Relationships are stored in the database as relationship objects.

    B. Relationships explicitly define an association between two entities.

    C. Relationships are most easily identified during requirements analysis by looking or listening for noun phrases.

    D. Relationships are a logical link between tables implemented with primary keys and foreign keys.

    E. Relationships are most often characterized by their cardinality.

7. An attribute is also known as a:

    A. column

    B. field

    C. row

    D. tuple

8. What are the three general types of constraints used for attributes in a data model?

    A. no updates

    B. no duplicates

    C. no nulls

    D. no deletes

    E. no changes

9. Using _____ columns makes them easier to update and query.

    A. decomposable

    B. unique

    C. not null

    D. non-decomposable

10. Which of the following are true about table and column names?

    A. Table and column names are limited to 40 characters.

    B. Table names must be unique within the database.

    C. Column names must be unique within the database.

    D. Table and column names must be in all uppercase.

    E. Column names must be unique within a table.

11. How is a no nulls restriction implemented for a column?

    A. By using a not null constraint when the table is created

    B. By using an index that does not allow nulls

    C. By specifying the null option on the column when the table is created

    D. By using a reference constraint

12. How is a no changes restriction implemented for a column?

    A. By using a foreign key/reference constraint

    B. By using a primary key constraint

    C. By using a trigger

    D. By using column permissions

13. How is a no duplicates restriction implemented for a column?

    A. By using a reference constraint

    B. By using a unique index on the column

    C. By using a unique constraint

    D. By using column permissions

    E. By using a trigger

    F. By using a primary key constraint

14. The primary key of a table enforces:

    A. referential integrity

    B. entity or row integrity

    C. column integrity

    D. identity constraints

15. What is the relationship between a primary key and a foreign key?

    A. A foreign key value is contributed to a primary key value in a column to create a link between two instances of an entity or two instances of two different entities.

    B. A primary key value is contributed to a foreign key value in a column to create a link between two instances of an entity or two instances of two different entities.

    C. There is no relationship; primary keys and foreign keys are two different ways to ensure entity integrity.

16. In a one-to-many relationship,

    A. The foreign key value of a single instance of the parent entity is contributed to many primary key values in multiple instances of the child entity.

B. The primary key value of a single instance of the parent entity is contributed to many foreign key values in multiple instances of the child entity.

C. A parent entity may be identified by its child entity.

D. A child entity may be identified by its parent entity.

17. A one-to-one relationship:

   A. is typically the result of normalizing an entity

   B. is characterized by one primary key value corresponding to zero or one foreign key values

   C. is characterized by one primary key value corresponding to zero or more foreign key values

   D. is typically the result of an entity being categorized into two or more different types

18. A one-to-many relationship:

   A. is typically the result of normalizing an entity

   B. is characterized by one primary key value corresponding to zero or one foreign key values

   C. is characterized by one primary key value corresponding to zero or more foreign key values

   D. is typically the result of an entity being categorized into two or more different types

19. What is the most commonly used cardinality in a relationship?

   A. One-to-many

   B. One-to-one

   C. Many-to-one

   D. Many-to-many

20. A many-to-many relationship is implemented with:

    A. two one-to-many relationships

    B. multiple columns in each participating entity that contain the primary key values of the referenced entity

    C. a column in each participating entity that lists the primary keys referenced in the other entity

    D. an associative entity

21. In a recursive relationship,

    A. the parent instance of one entity is associated with one or more child instances of another entity

    B. the parent instance of one entity is associated with one or more child instances of the same entity

    C. an instance of an entity always has an association with itself

    D. multiple parent instances of one entity are associated with one child instance of another entity

22. Referential integrity refers to what?

    A. The enforced uniqueness of a row in a table

    B. The enforced uniqueness of a column in a table

    C. Ensuring that a foreign key attribute cannot be null

    D. The enforced synchronization of primary key and foreign key values

23. An identity column is used to:

    A. identify an attribute

    B. provide unique, sequenced primary key values

    C. enforce the no changes restriction on a column

    D. define a foreign key

24. What are the benefits of a normalized data model?

    A. Redundant data is minimized

    B. Storage space is used more efficiently

    C. The data model is more flexible

    D. Performance is improved

25. Denormalizing a data model is best done:

    A. only after fully normalizing the database

    B. when the entities are being designed

    C. if performance is slow due to many tables being joined together

    D. to reduce redundant data

Answers to Review Questions

1. C

2. D

3. A,D

4. D

5. A

6. B,D,E

7. A,B

8. B,C,E

9. D

10. B,E

11. C

12. A,C,D

13. B,C,E,F

14. B

15. B

16. B,D

17. B,D

18. A,C

19. A

20. A,D

21. B

22. D

23. B

24. A,B,C

25. A,C

Answers to Test Yourself Questions at Beginning of Chapter

1. An *entity* defines any person, place, thing, or concept for which data will be collected. See "Entities."

2. An *attribute* is any additional characteristic or information defined for an entity. See "Attributes."

3. A *relationship* is a logical linkage between two entities that describes how the entities are associated with each other. See "Relationships."

4. One-to-one, one-to-many, and many-to-many. See "Types of Relationships."

5. The primary key value for an instance of an entity is used in the foreign key attribute of the instance(s) of the associated entity. See "Primary Keys and Foreign Keys."

6. Use the SQL Server null option for a column when creating a table to define whether or not the column may contain nulls. See "Column Constraints."

7. Use an identity property on the column (when creating a table), or use a trigger to prevent changes to a column. Security permissions also may be assigned to a particular column to prevent certain users from modifying its contents. See "Column Constraints."

8. Use a primary key or unique constraint on a column to ensure its uniqueness. The stored procedure sp_primarykey also may be used to define a primary key, and a unique index on a column prevents duplicate values. See "Column Constraints."

Chapter 2

System Databases and Tables

Test Objectives

This chapter helps you prepare for the exam by covering the following objectives:

 Objectives

▶ Identify the role of the *master* database

▶ Identify the role of *tempdb* database

▶ Identify the roles of the system tables

▶ Estimate space requirements

Test Yourself! Before reading this chapter, test yourself to determine how much study time you will need to devote to this section.

1. What is the purpose of the *master* database?

2. What is the purpose of the *model* database?

3. What is the purpose of the *msdb* database?

4. What is the purpose of the *tempdb* database?

5. Describe the use of the system catalog and a database catalog.

6. Define these terms: *page, extent, allocation unit.*

7. What is a *device?*

8. What are the Transact-SQL commands used to create, delete, and expand a device?

9. Explain the relationship between databases and devices.

Answers are located at the end of the chapter...

Chapter 1 discussed the process of creating a model, or schema, for a database. Before a database can be created, some physical storage, such as files on a hard drive, must be created for the database. This chapter covers the information you need to know in order to create the physical storage for a database.

This chapter also introduces you to some special databases on a SQL Server known as the *system* databases. Without the information stored in these databases, SQL Server would not function properly. Understanding these databases helps you understand how the schema of a database is stored in the server and how the operating system files used to store a database are tracked by SQL Server.

Finally, this chapter covers the many useful stored procedures provided by Microsoft with SQL Server. These stored procedures help you gather information about the server, perform common implementation tasks, and configure the server.

Thus the following topics are covered in this chapter:

- ▶ Defining physical database storage

- ▶ System databases

- ▶ System tables

- ▶ Using system stored procedures

- ▶ Server configuration

Much of the information in this chapter is especially relevant if you plan to also study SQL Server database administration. Because the system databases and tables contain critical information about the server and its databases, understanding them can help with troubleshooting and maintenance.

Defining Physical Database Storage

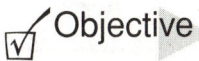 The first step in physically implementing a database after the creation of the data model is the allocation of physical storage for the database. Creating a *device* in SQL Server also creates a physical

file on the disk. Thoroughly understanding how SQL Server stores its data will help you better estimate the space required for a particular database. This will help you avoid running out of storage space for a database, or over-allocating storage and wasting disk space.

 **Tip**

> In this section, pay special attention to the units of storage used by SQL Server; the exam will most likely have several questions to test your knowledge in this area. In addition, make sure you are familiar with how to manage devices in both Enterprise Manager and Transact-SQL.

Units of Storage in SQL Server

SQL Server stores data in five basic units of storage. The different storage structures are used in such a way that performance is maximized. In order of increasing size, these units of storage are:

▶ **Page**: The page is the basic unit of storage in SQL Server. It is 2 KB (2048 bytes) in size. One or more rows of table data or index information is stored on a page.

 **Note**

> The page also is the basic unit of locking in SQL Server, except if *insert row-level locking* (IRL) is turned on for a table. This means that if a user process has a row locked for any reason, updates to that row and *any other row on the same page* are prohibited. While this slightly decreases concurrency, it improves the performance of SQL Server. Plans for future versions include the introduction of optional row-level locking.

▶ **Extent**: Eight contiguous pages make an extent, which is 16 KB in size. Tables and indexes are always created on their own extent. When the data in a table or index grows beyond the capacity of the original extent, another one is allocated. For instance, if a table contained 7 KB of data, and another 5 KB were added, SQL Server would allocate another extent to store the additional information.

- ▶ **Allocation Unit**: Thirty-two contiguous extents make an allocation unit, which is 1/2 MB (524,288 bytes) in size. A database's storage is incrementally allocated by using two or more allocation units.

Typically, a database's minimum size is 1 MB (2 allocation units). However, increasing the size of the *model* database (see the *"Model"* section in this chapter) may change the minimum size of a database.

- ▶ **Device**: A device is an operating system file that contains two or more allocation units (devices can be up to 32,768 MB in size).

- ▶ **Database**: Databases are stored on one or more devices, and may be from 1 MB to 1 terabyte (TB) in size. Databases may reside on devices spread across multiple hard disks, which makes very large databases possible.

For more information about creating databases, see the next chapter.

The end of this section describes how you can use this information to estimate the size of a database.

Managing Database Devices

As mentioned previously, database devices are mapped to physical files on disk. A device is known by two names. Its physical name is the fully qualified filename of the operating system file on disk. Its logical name (which can be up to thirty characters in length) is how the device is referred to in SQL Server. When you are creating a database, you always refer to its device(s) by logical name.

Remember that a database may be stored on multiple devices, which may exist on different physical disks. In addition, a device may hold fragments of one or more databases.

The next few sections introduce you to the commands you will use to manage database devices.

 Tip

Although it is not required, backing up the *master* database after managing system devices (or databases) is strongly recommended. Refer to the *"Master"* section in this chapter for more information.

Creating a Device

To create a database device in SQL Enterprise Manager, perform the following steps:

1. From the Server Manager window, select a server, and expand the tree view by clicking the plus sign to the left of the stoplight icon (which represents the server). Select the Database Devices folder, right-click so the context menu appears, and select the New Device option. The New Database Device dialog box appears, as shown in figure 2.1.

Figure 2.1

The New Database Device dialog box.

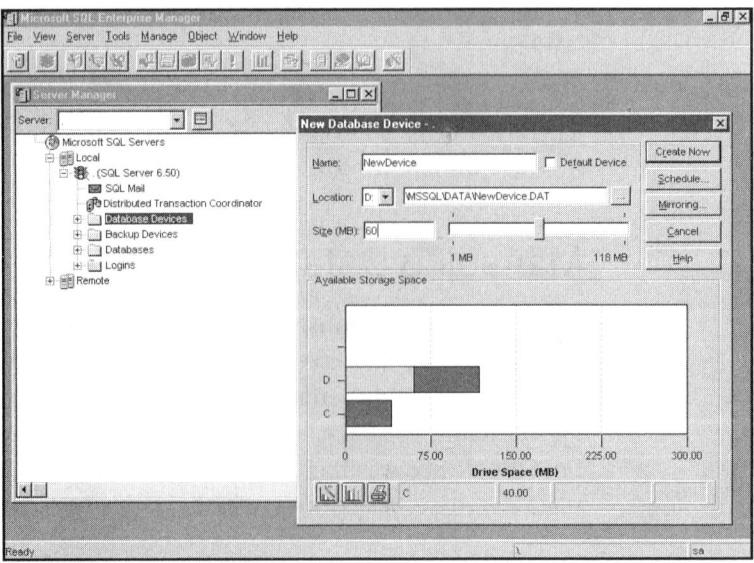

You also may get to a Manage Database Devices dialog box by selecting Manage, Database Devices from the Enterprise Manager menu. This dialog box has commands that enable you to add, expand, and delete devices on the server.

2. Enter the logical name of the device in the Name box. This may be up to thirty characters in length.

3. Select a drive letter and enter a path and filename for the device in the Location box. SQL Server provides a default filename that is the same as the logical name. You also may click the browse button (marked by an ellipsis, (…)) to select a location for the file.

4. In the Size box, enter the size, in megabytes, for the new device, or use the slider bar to select a device size. The available free space on each physical disk is represented in a graph at the bottom of the screen.

5. You have now entered all of the information required to create a device. Clicking the Create Now button creates the device and returns you to the Server Manager window. Clicking the Schedule button enables you to schedule the device's creation for a later time. The SQL Executive must be running to schedule the device creation.

If you are creating a very large device, or creating a device on a FAT partition, schedule the device creation, even if you want it executed immediately. Schedule the command for immediate execution, and Enterprise Manager will start the task in the background and return control to you immediately. If you don't schedule the device creation, Enterprise Manager will be totally unresponsive while the device is being built.

You also may create a device by using the Transact-SQL command:

1. Open the ISQL_W application, or open the query window from SQL Enterprise Manager by selecting the server, and selecting Tools, Query Tool from the menu.

2. You must be in the master database to execute this command. Select master from the DB combo box in the query window.

3. Type the following command:

```
DISK INIT
    NAME =      'logical_name',
    PHYSNAME = 'physical_name',
    VDEVNO =    virtual_device_number,
    SIZE =      number_of_2KB_pages
```

Name is the logical name for the device.

Physname is the fully-qualified filename (path and file name) for the device.

Vdevno is the virtual device number used by SQL Server to identify the device. Valid device numbers range from 0 to 255; 0 is reserved for the *master* database device, and 51 and 52 are reserved for the *msdb* database devices.

Size is size of the device *in 2-KB pages.* The easiest way to calculate this is by taking the desired size of the device in megabytes and multiplying this number by 512. (There are 512 2-KB pages in a megabyte.)

4. This example creates a device with a logical name of 'MyDevice' in the file D:\MSSQL\Data\MyDevice.DAT. The device has a virtual device number of 42, and is 15 MB in size:

```
DISK INIT
    NAME =      'MyDevice',
    PHYSNAME = ' D:\MSSQL\Data\MyDevice.DAT',
    VDEVNO =    42,
    SIZE =      7680
```

5. Execute the query by typing Alt-X or clicking the Execute Query button. The new database device will be created.

Note Any time a device is created or dropped by using the Transact-SQL commands, you need to manually refresh the device list in the Server Manager window to see the changes. You may do this by right-clicking the Database Devices folder and selecting the Refresh option from the context menu.

Windows NT initializes the new device file by setting all of its bytes to zero. This may take some time on a FAT partition, because NT must manually clear the file. Once a device is created, an entry is made in the master database in the *sysdevices* table. See the section titled "System Tables" for more information about this table.

Removing a Device

You can remove a device from the server using SQL Enterprise Manager. Perform the following steps:

1. From the Server Manager window, select a server, and expand the tree view by clicking the plus sign to the left of the stoplight icon (which represents the server). Select the Database Devices folder, and expand it by clicking the plus sign. Select a device, right-click so the context menu appears, and select the Delete option, as shown in figure 2.2.

Figure 2.2

Deleting a device from Enterprise Manager.

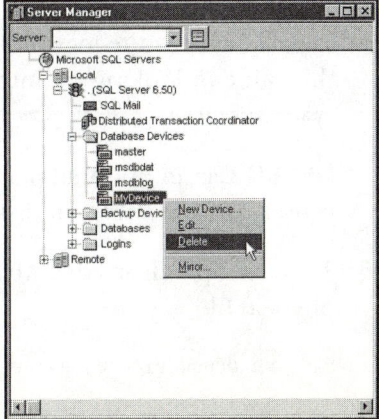

2. A dialog box appears, confirming the deletion of the device. To delete the device, click Yes, and the device will be removed from SQL Server. If one or more databases exist on the device, a different dialog will appear and alert you to the fact that these databases will also be dropped. To drop the device, click the Delete Device button.

Note   Dropping the device from Enterprise Manager will not delete the physical file. To free disk space, manually delete the file from the disk.

To drop a device using Transact-SQL, do the following:

1. Open the ISQL_W application, or open the query window from SQL Enterprise Manager by selecting the server, and selecting Tools, Query Tool… from the menu.

2. You must be in the master database to execute this command. Select master from the DB combo box in the query window.

3. Drop any databases that exist on the device by using the DROP DATABASE statement. This statement is covered in Chapter 3, "Data Definition."

4. Type the following command:

```
EXEC sp_dropdevice logical_name [, DELFILE]
```

logical_name is the logical name for the device. You can find this value by looking in Enterprise Manager or querying the *sysdevices* table.

DELFILE is an optional parameter. Adding this parameter causes the device file on disk to be deleted.

5. This example drops the 'MyDevice' device and deletes the physical file:

```
EXEC sp_dropdevice MyDevice, DELFILE
```

6. Execute the query by typing Alt-X or clicking the Execute Query button. The device is removed from the system. The query fails if the device still contains any databases.

Expanding a Device

Any database device may be expanded if needed without affecting any of the databases on the device. This feature is especially useful if a database has grown to capacity. Adequate disk space must exist for the expanded device. Also, keep in mind that a device can never be shrunk—plan your expansions carefully!

To increase the size of a database device in SQL Enterprise Manager, perform the following steps:

1. From the Server Manager window, select a server, and expand the tree view by clicking the plus sign to the left of the stoplight icon (which represents the server). Select the Database Devices folder, and expand it by clicking the plus sign. Select a device, right-click so the context menu appears, and select the Edit option. The Edit Database Device dialog box appears, as shown in figure 2.3.

Figure 2.3

Editing a device in Enterprise Manager using the Edit Database Device dialog box.

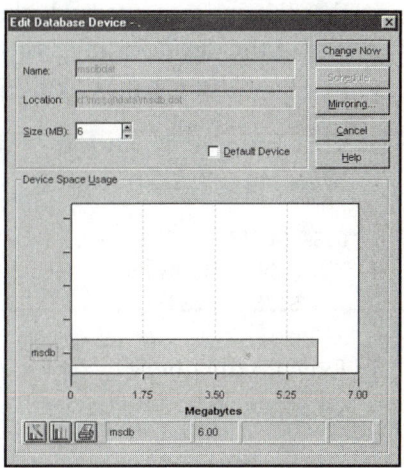

2. In the Size box, type the new size for the device, or use the spinner button to increase the size.

3. Click the Change Now button to expand the device. Alternately, you may schedule the device expansion by clicking the Schedule button.

You also may create a device using the Transact-SQL command:

1. Open the ISQL_W application, or open the query window from SQL Enterprise Manager by selecting the server, and selecting Tools, Query Tool... from the menu.

2. You must be in the *master* database to execute this command. Select master from the DB combo box in the query window.

3. Type the following command:

```
DISK RESIZE
    NAME = logical_device_name,
    SIZE = final_size_in_2K_pages
```

NAME is the logical name for the device. You can find this value by looking in Enterprise Manager or querying the *sysdevices* table.

SIZE is the *new* size of the device *in 2-KB pages*. Remember that the easiest way to calculate this is by taking the desired size of the device in megabytes and multiplying this number by 512. (There are 512 2-KB pages in a megabyte.)

4. This example expands the 'MyDevice' device to 30 megabytes (15,360 2-KB pages):

```
DISK RESIZE
    NAME = MyDevice,
    SIZE = 15360
```

5. Execute the query by typing Alt-X or clicking the Execute Query button. The device is expanded to its new size.

Using Default Devices

Typically, only the system administrator (SA) can create databases on a SQL Server. It is possible for the SA to grant this permission to certain users so that they may create databases of their own.

However, the ability to manage devices always resides with the system administrator and cannot be transferred.

Instead of constantly administering devices for the users, the system administrator can set up a pool of *default* devices that users may create databases on. Any device can be a default device. If a device is not specified when a database is created, the database is created in available space in the pool of default devices. The default devices in the pool are used in alphabetical order.

 **Tip**

> The *master* database device is set up as a default device when SQL Server is installed. If you plan to set up a pool of default devices, remove the master device from the pool so user databases do not compete for space with the *master* database.

A device can be added or removed from the default pool by using Enterprise Manager or a Transact-SQL command. In Enterprise Manager, the New Database Device and Edit Database Device dialog boxes (see figures 2.1 and 2.3) each have a check box that determines if a device is a member of the default pool. If the box is checked, then the device is used as a default device.

To change the default status of a device using Transact-SQL, do the following:

1. Open the ISQL_W application, or open the query window from SQL Enterprise Manager by selecting the server, and selecting Tools, Query Tool from the menu.

2. Type the following command:

   ```
   sp_diskdefault database_device, {defaulton ,  defaultoff}
   ```

   Database_device is the logical name of the database device for which you are changing the default option

   Specifying **defaulton** or **defaultoff** for the next parameter adds or removes the specified device from the default pool.

3. This example removes the master device from the default pool:

```
sp_diskdefault master, defaultoff
```

4. Execute the query by typing Alt-X or clicking the Execute Query button. The device's default status is changed.

Considerations for Space Planning

Before creating a database, it is a good idea to estimate its size and growth potential. This will ensure that you allocate adequate storage to the database without wasting space. This section walks you through the steps required to estimate the size of a table's data and the size of its indexes. Keep in mind that you need to estimate the size of each table in your database, as well as the size of each index on a table.

 Tip

The formulas in this section will help you determine the number of 2-KB pages required for a table and its indexes. You may convert from these numbers into megabytes by multiplying by 2,048 (the number of bytes in a 2-KB page), then dividing by 1,048,576 (the number of bytes in a megabyte).

To increase the accuracy of your estimates, you should have a good idea of the data types you plan to use in each table, as well as the type and number of indexes on a table. More information about tables and data types can be found in Chapter 3, and more information about indexes may be found in Chapter 7, "Indexes." In addition, Appendix B in the Administrator's Guide in the SQL Server Books Online is devoted entirely to this topic.

Be sure to plan for future growth when estimating the size of your database. Although it is possible to expand or shrink a database, doing so can make a database difficult to recover. See the next chapter for more detail about altering the size of a database.

Exercise 2.1 gives an example of estimating the size of a table.

Estimating the Number of Data Pages

The first step to estimating the size of a table is to estimate the number of pages that contain the table's data. (If the table has no indexes, this is also the last step.) To estimate the number of data pages for the table, first estimate the number of bytes in a row of data, then divide that number into the number of bytes available on a page.

To determine the number of bytes in a data row:

1. Start with 2 bytes as overhead.

2. To this, add the sum of the bytes in all of the fixed-length columns in the table. Character, binary, and any numeric data types are considered fixed-length. However, if a column allows NULLs, it does not count as fixed-length. The size of each data type may be found by looking in the books online or by using the sp_help stored procedure.

3. If the table has nothing but fixed-length columns, then you are done calculating the data row size. Continue with the rest of the calculation.

4. To the total in #2, add the sum of the bytes in all of the variable-length columns in the table.

5. Compute the overhead for the variable-length columns by using this formula: Overhead = ((Total from #4 / 256) + 1) + (number of variable-length columns)+ 3. Round this number down to the nearest whole number.

6. The data row size is the number of bytes from #4 plus the number of bytes of overhead from #5.

Now that you know the number of bytes in a data row, you can determine how many data rows will fit on a page. Because SQL Server uses 32 bytes per page as overhead, this formula gives you the number of data rows per page: 2,016 / Data Row Size.

Finally, divide the estimated number of rows in the table by the number of data rows per page (Number of Rows / Data Rows per Page). This gives you the approximate number of data pages required to store the table's data.

 **Tip**

For the best accuracy, round down on any calculations that determine the number of data rows per page. Also, round up on any calculations that determine a number of pages.

Estimating the Number of Clustered Index Pages

In a clustered index, the data pages themselves are actually the leaf pages of the index. This reduces the amount of storage required for the index. There are two steps to calculating the size of a clustered index: calculating the row size of the clustered index, and calculating the number of pages in the clustered index.

Calculating the Clustered Index Row Size

The calculation to determine the index row size is very similar to the calculation to determine the data row size. If all of the columns in the clustered index are fixed-length, then the row size can be determined by this formula (SQL Server uses 5 bytes of overhead for a clustered index row):

Row Size = 5 + (Sum of bytes in the key columns)

If one or more of the columns are variable-length, use these formulas:

Key Size = 5 + (Sum of bytes in the fixed-length key columns) + (Sum of bytes in variable-length key columns)

Overhead = ((Key Size / 256) + 1) + (Number of variable-length key columns + 3)

Row Size = Key Size + Overhead Size

Calculating the Number of Clustered Index Pages

Now that you have the Row Size for the clustered index, calculate the number of pages in the index as follows:

1. Determine the number of index rows per page:

   (2,016 / Row Size) − 2

2. Determine the number of pages at level 0 of the index:

(Number of data pages) / (Index rows per page)

3. If the result from step #2 is greater than one, determine the number of index pages at each level by dividing the number of index pages at the previous level by the number of index rows per page:

(Number of index pages on previous level) / (Index rows per page)

4. Continue with step #3 until you get a result of less than or equal to one. This is the root page of the index.

To determine the total size of the clustered index, add up the number of pages from each level of the index.

Estimating the Number of Non-Clustered Index Pages

In a non-clustered index, the leaf pages point to the data pages in a table. There are two steps to calculating the size of a non-clustered index: calculating the number of leaf pages, and calculating the number of nonleaf pages. Adding these two values together yields the total size of the index.

Calculating the Number of Leaf Pages

To determine the number of leaf pages, first determine the row size of a leaf row. Use these formulas:

If the key columns are all fixed-length, then the row size is simply:

Row Size = 7 + (Sum of bytes in key columns)

If one or more of the key columns is variable-length, then use these formulas to determine the row size:

Key Size = 9 + (Sum of bytes in fixed-length key columns) + (Sum of bytes in variable-length key columns) + (Number of variable-length key columns) + 1

Overhead Size = (Key Size / 256) + 1

Row Size = Key Size + Overhead Size

Now that you know the leaf row size, calculate the number of leaf row pages:

Number of leaf pages =

(Number of rows in table) / (2,016 / (Size of leaf index row))

Note that dividing the size of the leaf index row into 2016 gives us the number of leaf rows per page. We then divide that number into the number of data rows because each leaf row corresponds to one data row.

Calculating the Number of Nonleaf Pages

To determine the number of nonleaf pages, first determine the row size of a nonleaf row. Use this formula:

Nonleaf Row Size = (Size of leaf index row) + 4

Then, determine the number of nonleaf index rows per page:

Nonleaf Rows per Page = (2,016 / Nonleaf Row Size – 2

Finally, calculate the number of nonleaf pages:

1. Determine the number of pages at level 1 of the index:

   (Number of leaf pages) / (Nonleaf Rows per Page)

2. If the result from step #1 is greater than one, determine the number of index pages at the next index level by dividing the number of index pages at the previous level by the number of index rows per page:

   (Number of index pages on previous level) / (Nonleaf Rows per Page)

3. Continue with step #2 until you get a result of less than or equal to one. This is the root page of the index.

To determine the total size of the non-clustered index, add up the number of pages from each level of the index (the preceding ones you computed), then add in the number of leaf pages.

System Databases

When SQL Server is first installed, four databases are created on the server by the setup program. These databases are known as the system databases because they contain information required by SQL Server to operate. They cannot be deleted. The four system databases covered in this section are named *master, model, msdb,* and *tempdb,* they are shown in figure 2.4.

Figure 2.4

The system databases in Enterprise Manager.

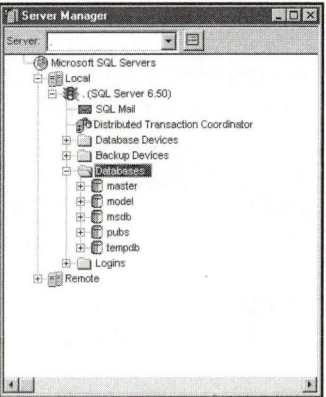

Note

SQL Server uses another system database, known as the distribution database, for data replication. It is only created if you set up replication on a server. More information about replication and this database may be found in the SQL Server Administration study guide.

You may note that figure 2.4 also shows another database, called Pubs. This sample database is created when SQL Server is installed. It falls into the category of a *user* database. The database administrator has full control over the user databases on a SQL Server.

Master

Objective

The *master* database is by far the most important of the system databases. The *master* database controls not only the operation of all of the user databases but also contains server-wide configuration information. Some of the information contained in the *master* database includes:

▶ Database devices stored on the server. Database devices correspond to the physical files that contain a database. Database devices were covered in more detail earlier in the chapter.

▶ Databases stored on the server, their size, and which devices they reside on.

▶ Backup devices on the server. Backup devices correspond to either a file or a tape drive and are used to back up and recover databases.

▶ Login accounts for the server. Server logins define which network users are allowed to access the SQL Server.

▶ Configuration options for the server. There are about 50 different settings that may be changed for a server.

▶ Error messages defined for the server. There are about 2,200 error messages predefined when SQL Server is installed; you may add your own if you wish.

▶ Information about current processes and locked objects.

▶ System stored procedures and extended stored procedures used to administer databases and the server. These are covered in more detail later in the chapter.

All of this information is stored in 13 special tables known as the *system catalog*. The system catalog is discussed in more detail later on.

As mentioned previously, the *master* database cannot be deleted. In addition, the information stored in its tables cannot be modified directly. However, by using Enterprise Manager or the system stored procedures you can indirectly update this information.

Because the *master* database is so important to SQL Server, be sure to perform a backup when critical information is changed. Backing up the *master* database is especially important after:

▶ changing the server configuration

▶ adding or modifying one or more devices

▶ adding or modifying one or more databases

The *master* database is created on the master database device, which has a default size of 25 MB. If you anticipate that the server will contain a large number of databases or devices, you may want to specify a larger size during installation of the product. It is also possible to expand the size of the device and the database later on.

Model

The *model* database is used as a template for new user databases. When the database administrator creates a new user database, SQL Server copies the contents of the *model* database into the new database. *Model* is similar to a cookie cutter; SQL Server stamps out identical databases in its image.

By default, the *model* database only contains the 18 tables that make up the *database catalog*, which is described in more detail later in the chapter. However, it is possible to modify the *model* database. Making changes to the *model* database is particularly useful when you plan on creating many similar databases or want all new databases to have special settings. The following list describes some typical changes made to the *model* database:

▶ Database options, which are covered in detail in Chapter 3, may be set in *model* and will be in place for all subsequently created databases.

▶ Users who have access to all databases on a server can be added and default permissions defined.

▶ Commonly used database objects, such as stored procedures, defaults, ruled, user-defined types, and even tables with data may be added.

The *model* database defaults to 1 MB in size, though this may be expanded if needed. A new database must be at least as big as the model database because all of *model*'s information is copied to the new database. *Model* resides on the master database device.

Msdb

The *msdb* database supports the SQL Server Executive, which was introduced in version 6.0. The Executive provides for proactive server management by allowing a database administrator to schedule routine backups and maintenance. This service also keeps history information about backups for each database and can maintain the history of a scheduled task. Finally, the Executive can store information about the server's operators, and even automatically notify them if a problem occurs.

Note   The SQL Executive is covered in more detail in the SQL Server Administration study guide.

The *msdb* database contains ten tables (in addition to its database catalog) that store information used by the SQL Executive. These tables are:

▶ *sysalerts:* An alert is triggered in response to an event, and can write an event to the event log, e-mail an operator, or page an operator. This table contains a row for each alert defined in the Executive.

▶ *sysbackuphistory, sysbackupdetail:* These two tables maintain the history information of every database or table backup operation performed on the server.

▶ *syshistory:* This table functions as a sort of event log for the Executive. It contains historical information (such as success/failure codes and time to complete) for every time an alert or task is executed.

▶ *sysnotifications:* This table associates an operator with an alert by describing how an operator will be notified when an alert is fired.

▶ *sysoperators:* This table has a row for every operator defined on the server. Operators are people responsible for administering the server.

▶ *sysrestoredetail, sysrestorehistory:* These two tables maintain the history information of every database or table restore operation performed on the server.

▶ *sysservermessages:* This table contains error and warning messages used by the server as a whole.

▶ *systasks:* The systasks table contains a row for every user-defined scheduled task on the server. Tasks may occur on a schedule (such as a backup) or in response to an alert.

During setup, *msdb* is created on two different devices. The data device, MSDBDATA, defaults to 2 MB in size. The log device, MSDBLOG, defaults to 1 MB in size. Both reside on the same disk and directory as the master device.

Tempdb

As its name implies, *tempdb* stores any temporary information generated by the SQL Server. This temporary information is usually the intermediate results of a query that included a join, sort, or grouping. Data stored in server-side cursors is also stored in *tempdb*. In addition, users of the SQL Server may create temporary tables in the tempdb database. These tables are deleted when the user closes his or her connection to the server, or when the server is shut down.

When SQL Server is installed, *tempdb* is placed on the master device with a default size of 2 MB. Typically, *tempdb* needs to be expanded to a larger size. The size depends on the size of the largest user database on the server, and the number of queries that use grouping, sorting, or joins.

System Tables

 Objective

As mentioned previously, every SQL Server database contains system tables known as the *database catalog*. The *master* database contains some additional tables known as the *system catalog*. The basic ER diagram for these tables can be found at:

`http://premium.microsoft.com/msdn/library/sdkdoc/admn_c_3ucz.htm`

This section provides an overview of the purpose of each table. For the detailed ER diagram, and more information about each of the system tables, see the SQL Server Books Online.

While it is not necessary to fully understand the system tables in order to use SQL Server, knowing about the information in these tables is often useful. As an example, consider the case of a programmer writing a front-end for a SQL Server database. The programmer may want any column default values in a table to show up on a data entry form when the user begins to add a record. The programmer could query the database catalog to obtain this information.

Database Catalog

The eighteen tables that compose the database catalog are used to define the structure of a database. The four most important elements of a database are stored in five tables. These four elements are:

- ▶ **Basic Objects:** These objects are the main building blocks of a database. Information about each of these objects (including the system tables themselves) is stored in the *sysobjects* table. The six most important objects stored in *sysobjects* are as follows:

  - ▶ **Table**: A table stores data in columns and rows. Table creation is discussed in the next chapter.

  - ▶ **View**: A view is a predefined query that provides an alternate way to look at data in one or more tables.

Views are discussed more in Chapter 8, "Using Views, Defaults, and Rules."

▶ **Stored Procedure**: A stored procedure is a set of pre-compiled Transact-SQL statements that are stored on the server. Later in this chapter, you will learn about some of the system stored procedures that come with SQL Server. Refer to Chapter 9, "Programmability."

▶ **Trigger**: A trigger is also a set of pre-compiled SQL statements, but triggers execute when the data in a table is modified. They are most often used to enforce referential integrity or complex business rules. Refer to Chapter 10, "Triggers," for more information.

▶ **Default**: A default is an initial value for a column that SQL Server inserts if the user does not provide a value when inserting data. Defaults are covered in Chapter 8.

▶ **Rule**: Rules provide a way to perform column-level data validation in a table. Rules are covered in Chapter 8.

▶ **Index**: An index provides a quicker way to access data in a table by maintaining a hierarchical tree of ordered pointers to the data rows. Chapter 7 discusses indexes in more detail. Information about the indexes in a database is stored in the *sysindexes* table.

▶ **Constraint**: Constraints are used for a variety of purposes. DEFAULT and CHECK constraints provide the same functionality as defaults and rules, and other constraints are used to enforce referential integrity. Refer to the next chapter for information about constraints. Information about the constraints in a database is stored in the *sysconstraints* and *sysreferences* tables.

▶ **Data Type**: A data type indicates what kind of information is stored in a column. Examples would include integers, characters, and floating point numbers. Data types are stored in the *systypes* table. This table includes information on user-defined data types in addition to the system data types.

The remaining tables in the database catalog are used as follows:

▶ Detailed information about system objects is stored in these tables:

  ▶ *sysprocedures*: Contains information about stored procedures, triggers, views, defaults, and rules.

  ▶ *syscolumns*: Has a row for every column in every table and view in the database and has rows for each parameter passed to a stored procedure.

  ▶ *syscomments*: This table contains the SQL statements for all of the database's stored procedures, triggers, views, defaults, and rules.

  ▶ *sysdepends*: Defines interdependencies between database objects. For instance, a trigger has a dependency to a table. When the table is dropped, so is the trigger.

  ▶ *syskeys*: Contains a row for every primary key or foreign key in the database.

▶ Three tables store information related to database security:

  ▶ *sysusers*: Defines valid users of the database.

  ▶ *sysalternates*: Defines server logins that are aliased to a database user.

  ▶ *sysprotects*: Defines user's permissions for each object in the database.

▶ Three tables are used for replication. (For more information on replication, see Chapter 11, "Replication.")

  ▶ *sysarticles*: Defines each article (the information being replicated from a table) published for replication.

  ▶ *syssubscriptions*: Defines which remote servers are subscribing to articles from the database.

  ▶ *syspublications*: Defines each publication (group of articles) available from a database.

▶ The database's transaction log is stored in the *syslogs* table. The transaction log records all changes to the database to ensure recoverability.

▶ The *syssegments* table stores information about each database segment. Segments are an advanced way to partition a database among different devices, and are not covered in this book. For more information, see the SQL Server Books Online.

System Catalog

The system catalog consists of thirteen tables found only in the master database. These tables contain information relevant to the server as a whole. Briefly, these tables are:

▶ *syscharsets*: Stores character set and sort order information.

▶ *sysconfigures, syscurconfigs*: Stores server configuration options. These are discussed in more detail later in the chapter.

▶ *sysdatabases*: Maintains a list of all databases on the system.

▶ *sysdevices, sysusages*: *Sysdevices* keeps a list of all devices on the server, and *sysusages* maps databases to devices.

▶ *syslanguages*: Maintains a list of all foreign languages used on the server. English is always available for use by SQL Server, and is not represented in this table.

▶ *sysprocesses, syslocks*: These tables maintain information about the current processes executing on the server and which resources those processes have locked for use.

▶ *syslogins, sysremotelogins*: These tables maintain information about user accounts that are permitted to log into SQL Server. The *sysremotelogins* table contains users from other SQL Servers that are allowed to access the server.

▶ *sysmessages*: This table contains the message text for every informational, warning, or error message produced by the server.

▶ *sysservers*: Maintains a list of remote SQL Servers accessible from this server. This information is used primarily for replication.

Using System Stored Procedures

The master database contains about 300 stored procedures that are known as system stored procedures. Recall that a stored procedure is a collection of Transact-SQL commands that is precompiled and stored on the server. These stored procedures come as part of the master database when SQL Server is installed, and are used mainly by administrators to manage the server. Except in a few cases, they may be invoked from any database. All of the stored procedures provided by Microsoft begin with the sp_ prefix, unless they are extended stored procedures, in which case they begin with xp_.

There are five broad categories that these stored procedures fall into:

▶ **Catalog**: Catalog stored procedures provide a well-defined interface between SQL Server and Microsoft's Open Database Connectivity (ODBC) API. They provide information about the SQL Server and the structure of a database to ODBC or other database gateways. For example, the sp_server_info stored procedure returns information about the SQL Server, such as the version number of the software and the maximum length for an object name.

▶ **Extended**: Extended stored procedures provide functionality not normally supported in SQL Server. Running an extended stored procedure actually invokes a function in a DLL. These procedures are primarily used for integration with Windows NT security, support for SQL Mail, and replication. It is possible for developers to create and add new extended stored procedures to the server.

▶ **Replication**: These stored procedures are used to manage the replication of data between servers. They provide the interface to manage articles, publications, and subscriptions.

▶ **SQL Executive**: These stored procedures provide the interface to the SQL Executive service and provide a way to manage alerts, tasks, and operators.

▶ **System**: System stored procedures are the most numerous of those listed so far. They fall into two broad categories:

  ▶ **Informational** stored procedures return information about the server or a database to a user. They take information from the raw system or database catalog tables and present it in a more user-friendly form. The sp_help group of stored procedures are the most commonly used from this group, and are discussed in more detail later in this section.

  ▶ **Administrative** stored procedures are used by an administrator to manage the server or a database. They typically make changes to the system tables in master, msdb, or a user database. Calling the stored procedure isolates the administrator from the complexity of the system tables and ensures that all updates to the system or database catalog are consistent. We have already seen an example of this class of stored procedure with the sp_dropdevice and sp_diskdefault stored procedures.

Note

SQL Enterprise Manager makes extensive use of these stored procedures by executing them behind the scenes to perform a particular task.

sp_help Stored Procedures

Thirty of the system stored procedures are used to provide helpful information about nearly every aspect of SQL Server. They may be run from any database by any user on the system. The most commonly used sp_help procedures are listed here. More details may be found in the SQL Server Books Online.

▶ **sp_help**: The most commonly used of all the help procedures, sp_help returns information on any of the SQL Server base objects (tables, views, stored procedures, triggers, rules, and defaults) as well as data types. The syntax is:

```
sp_help [objectname]
```

Running sp_help without an object name returns a list of all objects in the current database.

 Tip

If you are writing a SQL script using the SQL Query tool and need help with an object, highlight the object name and type Alt-F1. This will run sp_help on the selected object.

▶ **sp_helpconstraint**: This stored procedure returns a detailed list of the constraints on a particular table. The syntax is as follows:

```
sp_helpconstraint tablename
```

The table name is required. Note that information about a table's constraints is returned when sp_help is called for a table.

▶ **sp_helpdb**: This procedure returns the name of the database, its total size (including its transaction log) and the options that are set for the database. Detailed information about the database's host devices is also shown. The syntax is:

```
sp_helpdb [dbname]
```

If no database name is given, then a summary of all databases on the server is returned.

▶ **sp_helpdevice**: Returns information about one or all devices on the server, including devices used for backup operations. The syntax is:

```
sp_helpdevice [devicename]
```

▶ **sp_helpindex**: Returns information about all of the indexes on a table. The syntax is:

```
sp_helpindex tablename
```

The table name is required.

▶ **sp_helpsql**: This stored procedure is useful for retrieving the syntax for any Transact-SQL command or system stored procedure. The syntax is:

```
sp_helpsql ['topic']
```

You may use wildcards (% and _) in the topic text; all matching topics will be returned.

▶ **sp_helptext**: This stored procedure returns the SQL statements used to create a view, trigger, stored procedure, default, or rule. The syntax is:

```
sp_helptext objectname
```

The object name is required.

▶ **sp_helpuser**: Returns information about all of the users in the database, or a specific user. The syntax is:

```
sp_helpuser [username]
```

Using Stored Procedures

Stored procedures are invoked from the query tool in Enterprise Manager or from the ISQL application. The generic steps to follow when executing a stored procedure are as follows:

1. Start the ISQL application, or open the query tool in Enterprise Manager by selecting Tools, SQL Query Tool from the menu. In either case, the query window that appears (see figure 2.5) is exactly the same.

Figure 2.5

The SQL Query Tool dialog box in Enterprise Manager.

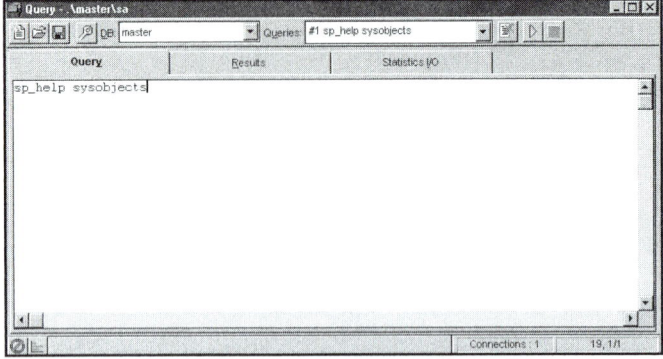

2. Select the database that you want the stored procedure to operate on. This can be done by executing a query or by selecting the database from the DB combo box on the toolbar. To switch to another database using SQL statements, use the following command:

```
USE <dbname>
```

For example, to switch to the Pubs sample database, you would execute the following query:

```
USE pubs
```

3. Enter the name of the stored procedure and any parameters it takes. If you will be executing more than one stored procedure, you need to type EXEC (or EXECUTE) before each stored procedure name. In the example in figure 2.5, the sp_help stored procedure is about to be run.

 **Tip**

To quickly look up the syntax of a SQL statement, highlight the SQL keywords or stored procedure name and type Shift-F1. This causes the Transact-SQL help file to be displayed with the appropriate help topic.

4. Execute the query by typing Alt-X or clicking the Execute button on the top right of the toolbar. Any results will be returned on the results tab.

**Note**

Do not be alarmed if you see the message "This command did not return data, and it did not return any rows." This simply indicates that the query or stored procedure ran successfully. Most of the system stored procedures do not explicitly report success, so you will generally see this message.

Server Configuration

Before discussing server configuration, a word of caution is in order.

**Warning**

Changing the server configuration is a potentially dangerous activity. Improperly changing a configuration value can disable your SQL Server. Be sure that you understand the implications of the changes you make.

SQL Server Books Online and Microsoft TechNet are two good references for understanding each configuration setting.

Recall from the earlier discussion on the master database that the system catalog stores configuration information for the server as a whole. There are about fifty different configuration settings for a server. Examples of such settings are as follows:

▶ Maximum number of user connections

▶ Memory used by SQL Server

▶ Default user options

▶ Number of locks available on the server and locking thresholds

▶ Other performance tuning settings

There are two different types of configuration settings: dynamic and static. Dynamic settings take effect immediately after they are changed, while static settings require the server to be stopped and restarted (or *bounced*) to take effect.

 Tip

If you find that a configuration change has disabled the server, you may start the server in a minimal configuration from the command prompt. Open a command prompt window and type *sqlservr –f*. This starts the server in single-user mode with a default configuration so you can correct the problem.

The server's configuration can only be changed by a system administrator. This is done by using a system stored procedure (sp_configure) or Enterprise Manager.

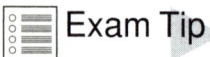 **Exam Tip**

Be sure that you understand both methods for the exam.

Changing Configuration Options

To change a configuration option from SQL Enterprise manager, follow these steps:

1. From Enterprise Manager Server Manager window, right-click the server name, and select Configure from the context menu. You also can choose Server, SQL Server, Configure from the main menu.

2. The Server Configuration/Options dialog appears. Select the Configuration tab, as shown in figure 2.6. The grid shows each configurable option, the minimum and maximum values, the value in use by the server, and the current setting.

3. Scroll through the list to find the option you would like to change. Selecting an option brings up a description of that option and when the change takes effect (dynamic or static). Change the option to the desired value.

4. Click the OK button or the Apply Now button to save the change. If the option is dynamic, then the change takes effect immediately. Otherwise, you will need to stop and restart the SQL Server service.

Figure 2.6

The Server Configuration dialog box in Enterprise Manager.

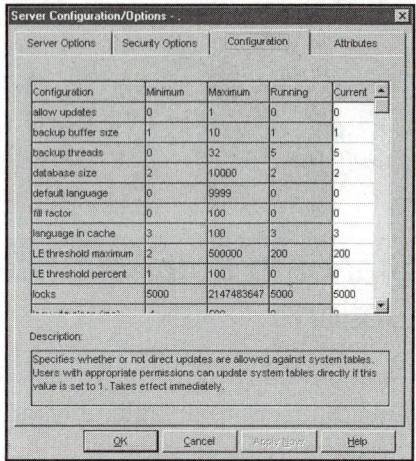

You also can change configuration options using sp_configure by doing the following:

1. Open the ISQL_W application, or open the query window from SQL Enterprise Manager by selecting the server, and selecting Tools, Query Tool from the menu.

2. Type the following command:

```
sp_configure ['option name', new value]
```

A list of available options (and their current settings) are printed if you run sp_configure without any parameters.

3. For example, to change the maximum number of client connections from the default of 15 to 50, run the following:

```
sp_configure 'user connections', 50
```

4. Run the RECONFIGURE command from the query window after changing a dynamic option. This causes the server to start using the new setting immediately. If you change a static

option (the number of user connections used in the example is a static option), you need to stop and restart the SQL Server for the change to take effect.

 Tip

To shut down the server from the query window, you may run the SHUTDOWN command. This immediately initiates a shutdown of the SQL Server. You may restart the server by using the SQL Service Manager, Enterprise Manager, or the Service Control Manager in the Control Panel.

Standard and Advanced Configuration Options

Configuration options are grouped into two categories: standard and advanced. By default, only the standard options are shown by sp_configure or the Server Configuration/Options dialog box. You do not typically need to change any of the advanced settings, as they are used mainly for fine-tuning the performance of the server under special circumstances.

To set the server so that you may see and change the advanced options, change the Show advanced options option to have a value of 1. This configuration setting is dynamic, so the change occurs immediately.

Summary

This chapter covered the information you need to know in order to create the physical storage for a database. It also introduced you to some special SQL Server databases known as the *system* databases. You learned that these databases contain the underlying schema of a database. You also learned how the operating system files used to store a database are tracked by SQL Server.

Finally, this chapter covered the stored procedures provided by Microsoft with SQL Server. These stored procedures help you gather information about the server, perform common implementation tasks, and configure the server.

Exercises

Exercise 2.1: Estimating the Size of a Table

This exercise shows you how to estimate the size of a table. The table has the following columns:

EmployeeID: int data type, not NULL, non-clustered index

FirstName: varchar(30), not NULL, first column in clustered index

LastName: varchar(30), not NULL, second column in clustered index

BirthDate: datetime, NULL

There are initially 5,000 employees in the table.

The first step is to calculate the number of data pages. Do the following:

1. This table has three variable-length columns (FirstName and LastName because they are varchars, and BirthDate because it is NULLable).

2. The number of bytes of fixed overhead and column data is:

   2 + (Size of fixed-length columns) + (Size of variable-length columns)

   The int column is 4 bytes, the two varchar columns are 30 bytes each, and the datetime column is 8 bytes. This gives you a total data size of 74 bytes.

3. The number of bytes of overhead for the variable-length columns is:

   (Data Size / 256) + 1 + (Number of variable-length columns)+ 3

   So you have (75 / 256) + 1 = 1 (rounding down) + 6 = 7 bytes

continues

Exercise 2.1: Continued

4. The total size of a data row is 74 + 7 bytes = 81 bytes.

5. The number of data rows per page is 2,016 / 81 = 24 (rounding down).

6. The number of data pages is 5,000 rows / 24 rows per page = 209 2-K pages (rounding up).

Next, calculate the size of the non-clustered index:

1. Because the index has a single, fixed-length column, the size of a leaf page row is:

   7 + (Sum of fixed-length key columns) = 7 + 4 = 11 bytes

2. The number of leaf rows per page is:

   2,016 / (Size of leaf page row) = 2,016 / 11 = 183 leaf rows per page

3. The number of leaf pages is:

   (Number of data rows) / (Number of leaf rows per page) = 5,000 / 183 = 28 leaf pages (rounding up)

4. The size of a nonleaf row is:

   (Size of leaf row) + 4 = 11 + 4 = 15 bytes

5. The number of nonleaf index rows per page = 2,016 / (Size of nonleaf row) = 2,016 / 15 = 134 nonleaf rows per page

6. The number of nonleaf pages in level 1 of the index is:

   (Number of leaf pages) / (Number of nonleaf rows per page) = 28 / 134 = 1 (rounded up—this is the root page of the index)

7. The total size of the index is:

   (Number of leaf pages) + (Number of nonleaf pages) = 28 + 1 = 29 pages.

And finally, the size of the clustered index:

1. The clustered index is composed of two variable-length columns. The size for the key columns is:

   5 + (Sum of fixed-length key columns) + (Sum of variable-length key columns) = 5 + 0 + 60

   The size for the overhead of the variable-length columns is:

   ((Key Size) / 256)+ 1 + (Number of variable-length key columns) + 3 = (60 / 256) + 6 = 6 (rounding down)

   So, the total size of the clustered index row is 66 bytes.

2. The number of clustered index rows per page is:

   (2,016 / Clustered index row size) − 2 = (2,016/66) − 2 = 28 (rounding down)

3. The number of level 0 pages is:

   (Number of data pages) / (Clustered index rows per page) = 209 / 28 = 8 pages (rounding up)

4. The number of level 1 index pages is:

   (Number of index pages in previous level) / (Clustered index rows per page) = 8 / 28 = 1 (rounding up, this is the root page of the index)

5. The total size of the clustered index is the sum of the pages in each index level, or 9 pages.

Adding the number of data pages (209), non-clustered index pages (29), and clustered index pages (9) gives a total of 247 pages, or approximately a half-megabyte.

Exercise 2.2:   Creating a Database Device Using Enterprise Manager

This exercise walks you through the steps of creating a database device using the Enterprise Manager Application. You must create one or more devices before creating a database.

continues

Exercise 2.2: Continued

1. Start the SQL Enterprise Manager application.

2. From the Server Manager window, select a server, and expand the tree view by clicking the plus sign to the left of the stoplight icon (which represents the server). A list of the server's folders appears.

3. Select the Database Devices folder, right-click so the context menu appears, and select the New Device... option. The New Database Device dialog appears.

4. Enter the logical name of the device in the Name box. This may be up to thirty characters in length. Use the name MyDevice1.

5. Select a drive letter and enter a path and filename for the device in the Location box. SQL Server provides a default filename that is the same as the logical name. You also may click the browse button (marked by an ellipsis, (...)) to select a location for the file.

   The path that appears depends on where you installed SQL Server. If SQL Server is installed on your C drive, the path will likely be C:\MSSQL\DATA\MyDevice1.Dat.

6. In the Size box, enter the size, in megabytes, for the new device, or use the slider bar to select a device size. Create a 1 megabyte device.

7. Click the Create Now button. A 1 megabyte device named MyDevice1 is created on the disk. Use File Manager or Explorer to find the file.

Exercise 2.3: Creating a Database Device Using Transact-SQL

Exercise 2.3 shows you how to create a database device using the DISK INIT Transact-SQL command.

1. Start the SQL Enterprise Manager application.

2. Select your server in the Server Manager window, and select Tools, Query Tool... from the application menu. The Query Tool window appears.

3. If it is not already selected, select the *master* database in the DB combo box on the query window's toolbar.

4. Type the following command, making modifications if needed for your system.

```
DISK INIT
    NAME =      'MyDevice2',
    PHYSNAME = ' C:\MSSQL\Data\MyDevice2.DAT',
    VDEVNO =    42,
    SIZE =      512
```

5. Execute the query by typing Alt-X or clicking the Execute Query button. A 1 megabyte device named MyDevice2 is created on the disk. Use File Manager or Explorer to verify that the device was created.

Exercise 2.4: Expanding a Database Device Using Enterprise Manager

This exercise shows you how to expand the database device you created in Exercise 2.2. You expand MyDevice1 from 1 MB to 2 MB in size.

1. Start the SQL Enterprise Manager application.

2. From the Server Manager window, select a server, and expand the tree view by clicking the plus sign to the left of the stoplight icon (which represents the server). A list of the server's folders appears.

3. Select the Database Devices folder, and expand the tree view by clicking the plus sign to the left of the folder icon.

4. Select MyDevice1 from the list of devices. Right-click so the context menu appears, and select the Edit... option. The Edit Database Device dialog appears.

5. Type in the new size of the device, or use the spinner button next to the Size box to increase the size to 2 MB.

continues

Exercise 2.4: Continued

6. Click the Change Now button. The device is increased in size from 1 MB to 2 MB. Use File Manager or Explorer to verify the new size of the file.

Exercise 2.5: Expanding a Database Device Using Transact-SQL

This exercise shows you how to expand the database device you created in Exercise 2.3. You expand MyDevice2 from 1 MB to 2 MB in size.

1. Start the SQL Enterprise Manager application.

2. Select your server in the Server Manager window, and select Tools, Query Tool from the application menu. The Query Tool window appears.

3. If it is not already selected, select the *master* database in the DB combo box on the query window's toolbar.

4. Type the following command:

```
DISK RESIZE
    NAME =     MyDevice2,
    SIZE =     1024
```

5. Execute the query by typing Alt-X or clicking the Execute Query button. MyDevice2 is expanded from 1 MB to 2 MB. Use File Manager or Explorer to verify the new size of the device.

Exercise 2.6: Adding a Device to the Default Pool Using Transact-SQL

Exercise 2.6 shows you how to add the device you created in Exercise 2.3 to the default pool of devices by using the system stored procedure sp_diskdefault.

1. Start the SQL Enterprise Manager application.

2. Select your server in the Server Manager window, and select Tools, Query Tool... from the application menu. The Query Tool window appears.

3. Type the following command:

```
sp_diskdefault MyDevice2, defaulton
```

4. Execute the query by typing Alt-X or clicking the Execute Query button. MyDevice2 is added to the default pool of devices.

Exercise 2.7:   Dropping a Database Device Using Enterprise Manager

This exercise shows you how to use Enterprise Manager to delete the database device you created in Exercise 2.2.

1. Start the SQL Enterprise Manager application.

2. From the Server Manager window, select a server, and expand the tree view by clicking the plus sign to the left of the stoplight icon (which represents the server). A list of the server's folders appears.

3. Select the Database Devices folder, and expand the tree view by clicking the plus sign to the left of the folder icon.

4. Select MyDevice1 from the list of devices. Right-click so the context menu appears, and select the Delete option. The device is dropped from the server.

5. Use File Manager or Explorer to verify that the physical file is still present on the disk. Delete the file manually.

Exercise 2.8:   Dropping a Database Device Using Transact-SQL

This exercise shows you how to use the sp_dropdevice stored procedure to delete the database device you created in Exercise 2.3.

1. Start the SQL Enterprise Manager application.

2. Select your server in the Server Manager window, and select Tools, Query Tool... from the application menu. The Query Tool window appears.

continues

Exercise 2.8: Continued

3. Type the following command:

```
sp_dropdevice MyDevice2, DELFILE
```

4. Execute the query by typing Alt-X or clicking the Execute Query button. MyDevice2 is dropped from the server. Use File Manager or Explorer to verify that the physical file has also been deleted.

Review Questions

1. How large is an extent?

    A. 16 KB

    B. 2 KB

    C. 8 pages

    D. 16 pages

2. When a database is created, its space is allocated in 1/2 MB increments called:

    A. Extents

    B. Allocation units

    C. Devices

    D. Segments

3. Which database objects are placed on their own extents and expanded one extent at a time?

    A. Tables

    B. Views

    C. Stored procedures

    D. Triggers

    E. Indexes

4. When creating a device with the DISK INIT command, the size of the device is expressed in:

    A. Megabytes

    B. Number of extents

    C. Number of pages

    D. Kilobytes

5. Which of the following are true about databases and devices?

   A. Databases may contain more than one device.

   B. Different devices can reside on separate physical disks.

   C. Devices may contain more than one database.

   D. Databases may reside on more than one device.

   E. Databases may not reside on devices that are on different physical disks.

6. Which of the following are NOT true about pages?

   A. A page is 2-KB in size.

   B. A page is the basic unit of storage in SQL Server.

   C. Only 2,032 bytes are available per page for data storage; the other 16 are overhead.

   D. 16 pages make an extent.

   E. A page is the basic unit of locking in SQL Server.

7. A device is administered in SQL Server by using its:

   A. Physical name

   B. Segment name

   C. Virtual device number

   D. Logical name

8. When using the DISK RESIZE statement, the size parameter is used to:

   A. Define the new size of the device in 2-KB pages.

   B. Define the new size of the device in megabytes.

   C. Define the number of 2-KB pages by which to expand the device.

   D. Define the number of megabytes by which to expand the device.

9. When expanding a device in SQL Enterprise Manager, the size parameter is used to:

    A. Define the new size of the device in 2-KB pages.

    B. Define the new size of the device in megabytes.

    C. Define the number of 2-KB pages by which to expand the device.

    D. Define the number of megabytes by which to expand the device.

10. When are default devices used?

    A. When users besides the system administrator create databases.

    B. When space runs out on existing devices.

    C. When no device name is specified when a database is created.

    D. When the DBA wants to reduce his/her time spent creating devices for user databases.

11. When planning the size of a database, it is helpful to know:

    A. The data type and NULL option for the columns in each table.

    B. The number but not the type of indexes on each table.

    C. The predicted number of rows in each table.

    D. The potential growth of each table.

12. How does placing a non-clustered index on a table compare to placing a clustered index on a table in terms of space used?

    A. There is virtually no difference in the amount of space used.

    B. A non-clustered index consumes less space than a clustered index.

C. A non-clustered index consumes less space than a clustered index, but only if all of its key columns are of fixed-length.

D. A non-clustered index consumes more space than a clustered index.

13. Which of the following statements about space estimating are true?

A. A char(30) column that is marked as NULLable is considered to be a fixed-length column for estimating purposes.

B. Variable-length columns add more overhead per row.

C. Variable-length columns do not affect the amount of overhead in a row.

D. Estimates are more accurate if you always round down the result of a division.

14. The database responsible for storing intermediate results from a query, or storing cursor information is:

A. *msdb*

B. *tempdb*

C. *master*

D. *model*

15. How many tables are there in the system catalog?

A. 13

B. 10

C. 18

D. 12

16. What happens if changes are made to the *model* database?

    A. Changes are not permitted to the *model* database because it is a system database.

    B. All databases have their database catalogs updated.

    C. Changing the *model* database does not affect the behavior of SQL Server.

    D. New databases reflect the changes made to the *model* database.

17. The *msdb* database is responsible for:

    A. Supporting the SQL Executive service

    B. Storing the filename of each backup device

    C. Storing the server's configuration

    D. Storing detailed information about backup and restore operations that have occurred in the past

18. Which of the following are NOT true about the *master* database?

    A. The *master* database should be backed up regularly.

    B. The *master* database contains both the system catalog and the database catalog.

    C. Direct updates are commonly made to the *master* database tables.

    D. Tables in the *master* database are used to store server configuration information.

    E. The *master* database device defaults to 5 megabytes.

19. Which system tables store information about devices on the server?

    A. The database catalog

    B. The system catalog

    C. *syssegments*

    D. *sysdevices*

    E. *sysusages*

20. It is a good idea to back up the *master* database after:

    A. Dropping a database

    B. Creating a device

    C. Making changes to the server configuration

    D. Resizing a database

    E. Creating a database

21. Which of the following tables in the database catalog are responsible for storing the bulk of the schema information?

    A. *sysobjects*

    B. *sysprocedures*

    C. *sysindexes*

    D. *syslogs*

    E. *sysconstraints*

22. How can the information in system tables be modified?

    A. Directly, after setting a special configuration option or starting the server in single-user mode

    B. By users modifying the design of a database

    C. By the administrator using system stored procedures

    D. By making changes to data in a database

23. Which objects are stored in the *sysobjects* table?

    A. Tables, views, stored procedures, indexes, defaults, rules, and triggers

    B. Tables, views, stored procedures, defaults, rules, and triggers

C. Tables, views, stored procedures, defaults, constraints, rules, and triggers

D. Tables, views, stored procedures, triggers, and constraints

24. Server configuration options are stored in:

    A. *sysconfigures*

    B. *syssettings*

    C. *sysoptions*

    D. *sysconfigures* and *syscurconfigs*

25. For which type of configuration option must the server be stopped and restarted?

    A. Dynamic

    B. Static

    C. Basic

    D. Advanced

26. Which command line parameter(s) start SQL Server in a minimal configuration?

    A. –f

    B. –m

    C. –c –m

    D. –t

27. What is the purpose of the RECONFIGURE command in SQL?

    A. It forces a shutdown and restart of the SQL Server.

    B. It causes dynamic options to be reset to their defaults.

C. It causes dynamic options set with sp_configure to take effect.

D. It causes static options set with sp_configure to take effect.

28. In which database do the system stored procedures reside?

    A. *master*

    B. *model*

    C. *msdb*

    D. *tempdb*

29. What are characteristics of an extended stored procedure?

    A. Most begin with the letters sp_.

    B. They provide functionality not native to SQL Server.

    C. They increase the size of devices, databases, and segments.

    D. They are a way to call a function in a DLL.

30. What is the purpose of the sp_help stored procedure?

    A. It launches the Transact-SQL help file.

    B. It provides a user-friendly way to read the database catalog.

    C. It returns information about most database objects.

    D. It lists the objects in a database.

Answers to Review Questions

1. A,C

2. B

3. A,E

4. C

5. B,C,D

6. C,D

7. D

8. A

9. B

10. A,C,D

11. A,C,D

12. D

13. B

14. B

15. A

16. D

17. A,D

18. C,E

19. B,D,E

20. B,C,D,E

21. A,C,E

22. A,B,C,D. Changing the data in the database affects the transaction log, which is a system table.

23. B

24. D

25. B

26. A

27. C

28. A

29. B, D

30. B,C,D

Answers to Test Yourself Question at Beginning of Chapter

1. The *master* database is the database that SQL Server uses to store information about all databases on the server, and it stores the server configuration. See "System Databases."

2. The *model* database acts as a template for all new user databases; SQL Server copies the information in the master database when a new database is created. See "System Databases."

3. The *msdb* database stores information used by the SQL Executive service. See "System Databases."

4. *Tempdb* is the database used by SQL Server to store intermediate results created when executing a query or cursor. See "System Databases."

5. The system catalog contains information about the operation of the SQL Server as a whole. A database catalog contains the database definition and information needed by SQL Server to manage a database. See "System Tables."

6. A *page* is the smallest unit of storage management in SQL Server. It is always 2 kilobytes (KB) in size. An *extent* is composed of eight pages, for a total size of 16 KB. Extents are used to store tables and indexes. An *allocation unit* is composed of 32 extents, or 256 pages, for a total size of 1/2 MB. Allocation units are used to create a database. See "Units of Storage in SQL Server."

7. A *device* is the physical operating system file used to store data in SQL Server. See "Managing Database Devices."

8. DISK INIT, sp_dropdevice, and DISK RESIZE. See "Managing Database Devices."

9. Databases are created on one or more devices; devices may be created on different physical disks, so databases may span multiple physical disks. A device also can hold multiple databases. See "Units of Storage in SQL Server."

C h a p t e r

Data Definition

3

This chapter helps you prepare for the exam by covering the following objectives:

 Objectives

▶ Increase transaction log size

▶ Create and modify tables

▶ Apply an IDENTITY property to a table definition

▶ Identify appropriate uses for the different types of constraints

▶ Apply REFERENCE constraints to enforce referential integrity

Test Yourself! Before reading this chapter, test yourself to determine how much study time you will need to devote to this section.

1. What are the benefits of placing a database's transaction log on a separate device?

2. What command is used to increase the size of a database or transaction log? To decrease the size?

3. What is the purpose of the *seed* and *increment* values when creating an IDENTITY column?

4. Name the three main commands used to manage tables in a database.

5. Name the two main categories of constraints.

6. What are the advantages of using constraints instead of triggers, defaults, or rules?

Answers are located at the end of the chapter...

In Chapter 2, "System Databases and Tables," you were introduced to SQL Server's methods of physical storage. The first half of this chapter continues where the previous chapter left off, and discusses how databases are implemented in SQL Server. Once you have implemented a database, you can create tables and other objects in SQL Server.

Chapter 1, "Data Modeling," focused on taking real-world concepts and modeling them as entities, relationships, and attributes. In that chapter, you were introduced to database tables as a way to implement entities and attributes, and referential integrity constraints to implement relationships. The second half of this chapter discusses the implementation of tables and constraints in more detail.

In order to prepare you for these areas of the exam, this chapter covers the following topics:

▶ Understanding databases and transaction logs

▶ Managing databases

▶ Understanding data types

▶ Managing tables

▶ Using constraints

 Tip

The test objectives for this chapter are somewhat misleading. To best prepare for the exam, be sure you are familiar with *all* of the concepts discussed in this chapter. In addition, make sure you know the Transact-SQL commands used to manage databases and tables. While Enterprise Manager can be used to manage databases and tables, the test focuses on the SQL commands.

Understanding Databases and Transaction Logs

In SQL Server, the database is at the top of the hierarchy of physical storage. Databases reside on one or more devices, which may reside on multiple physical disks. Databases in SQL Server are composed of different *segments*, or database fragments. A segment is used to partition the information stored in a database, and may share a device with other segments. A database in SQL Server initially consists of three segments: the system segment, the default (or data) segment, and the log segment.

Note

It is possible to define additional segments in a database to improve performance. However, this is a rarely used feature of SQL Server, so it is not discussed in this chapter. See the SQL Server Books Online for more information about segments.

As the name implies, the system segment is where the database's system tables (the database catalog) are stored. The default (or data) segment is where all of the database's information is actually stored; tables, indexes, and other objects are created on the default segment. The log segment stores the database's transaction log. SQL Server uses the transaction log to record all changes made to a database.

How the Transaction Log Works

The transaction log is the heart of SQL Server's ability to recover a database in the event of a system crash. SQL Server uses a *write-ahead* log, which means that database changes are logged before they are applied. If the server fails because of a power outage or other problem, SQL Server automatically recovers the database by applying committed transactions and rolling back incomplete transactions.

Here is a step-by-step overview of how SQL Server uses the transaction log:

1. Some sort of change to the database is made. Except for a few cases, every modification to a database is logged. Some examples of logged modifications follow:

    ▶ Direct changes to the data caused by the execution of an INSERT, UPDATE, or DELETE statement

    ▶ Creation of a database object

    ▶ Page and extent allocations caused when information is added to a table or index

 **Note**

Non-logged operations operate significantly faster than logged operations because SQL Server does not have the additional overhead of writing log records. Bulk-copy and SELECT INTO operations can be non-logged, and are usually used for handling large amounts of data.

Non-logged operations make the transaction log useless for database recovery, so the database should be fully backed up after performing a non-logged operation.

2. The pages to be modified are loaded into memory from disk.

3. As each modification is made, the change is written to the transaction log before the change is applied to the data. Transaction log changes are written immediately to disk, but modified data pages are just modified in memory.

4. About once a minute, the SQL Server CHECKPOINT process looks at the database and flushes any modified pages in memory to the disk. The checkpoint marks the transaction log to indicate which transaction was last written to disk.

In the event of a system failure, SQL Server performs automatic recovery on startup. SQL Server looks at the transactions in the transaction log after the last CHECKPOINT because these are database changes that have not been written to disk. Completed transactions are applied to the database (rolled forward), and incomplete transactions are backed out (rolled back).

 Warning

For this recovery process to work, SQL Server must accurately know when log changes have been written to disk. Disk controllers that perform write caching can destroy the usefulness of the transaction log by making SQL Server believe that log changes have been written to disk when they have not. In this situation, SQL Server's copy of the log and the copy of the log on disk are out of sync, and automatic recovery may fail.

Because write caching almost always improves disk performance, many high performance servers have write caching controllers. Most of the better controllers have a battery backup that maintains the cache in event of a power failure. Using write-caching controllers with a battery backup is acceptable because cached information can be written to disk on startup, and the SQL Server log will remain intact. If your server has a write caching controller, make sure it also has a battery backup.

Write caching software cannot guarantee that cached information will be written to disk in event of a system failure. Therefore, you should never use write-caching software with SQL Server.

Placement of the Transaction Log

The transaction log should be placed on a separate device from the rest of the database. Doing so provides the following benefits:

▶ The transaction log size may be explicitly defined, and the log will not compete with the data for storage space.

▶ The size of the transaction log may be monitored by using performance monitor or the DBCC command.

▶ The transaction log may be backed up independently of the database, which increases the speed of backups and allows incremental backups of the database. Volatile databases may have their transaction logs dumped several times a day to provide up to the minute recovery. For more information on backing up the transaction log, see the SQL Server Books Online or the SQL Administration study guide.

▶ Placing the database and transaction log on separate physical disks can greatly improve the performance of SQL Server because data and log writes do not compete for disk time.

Managing Databases

 Objective ▶

For the test, you need to know the various commands used to manage databases in SQL Server. This section covers the creation and deletion of databases, as well as the commands used to change the size of a database. In addition, you will learn about the various configuration options available for a database. As noted, the test focuses mainly on the Transact-SQL commands used to manage databases, though you should familiarize yourself with the Enterprise Manager tools as well.

Creating a Database

Before implementing a data model in SQL Server, you must create a database to store the various tables and other objects required to store the information. By default, only the system administrator can create databases, though this permission may be transferred to other users. When you create a database, you give it a name, define which device(s) it will reside on, and specify the size for the data and log. When you are creating a database keep the following in mind:

▶ The database name can be up to 30 characters in length, and must be unique on the server.

▶ The minimum size of a database is 1 MB, although if you do not specify a size, the database will default to 2 MB.

▶ If you do not specify the device(s) for the database, the database will be created on any default devices on the server.

▶ The transaction log should be placed on a separate device. Generally, the log size should be about 10 to 25 percent of the size of the data.

▶ Databases are allocated in 1/2 MB increments. If you specify a database size that is larger than the available space on the device(s), SQL Server rounds to the nearest 1/2 MB.

To create a database using the Transact-SQL CREATE DATABASE command, implement the following steps:

1. From SQL Enterprise Manager, select the server on which you wish to create the new database. From the main menu, select Tools, SQL Query Tool. The Query dialog box appears, as shown in figure 3.1.

Figure 3.1

The Query dialog box in SQL Enterprise Manager.

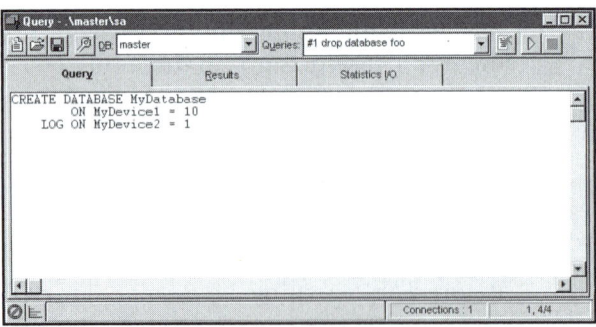

2. You must be in the *master* database to create a database. Use the DB combo box to select the master database.

3. The syntax for the CREATE DATABASE command is as follows:

```
CREATE DATABASE database_name
    [ON {DEFAULT | database_device} [=size]
        [, database_device [=size]] ...]
    [LOG ON {DEFAULT | database_device} [=size]
        [, database_device [=size]] ...]
    [FOR LOAD]
```

▶ The ON keyword is used to specify which device(s) the database is created on. If this is omitted, the database is created on the default device(s). If a device is specified, but no size is specified, 2 MB is allocated on that device.

▶ The LOG ON keyword is used to specify which device(s) the log is created on. If this is omitted, the log is shared with the data on the data device(s). If a device is specified, but no size is specified, 2 MB is allocated on that device.

▶ When specifying the size of the database on a device, express the size in megabytes. Note that this is different than creating a device, where you specify the device size in number of 2-K pages.

▶ Use the FOR LOAD keyword if you intend to immediately load the database from a backup dump. Doing so prevents any users from accessing the database until after the load is complete. In addition, no data pages in the database will be initialized, so creating the database takes much less time.

Following are some examples of the CREATE DATABASE statement:

This statement creates a database named MyDatabase on the default device(s) with a default size of 2 MB:

```
CREATE DATABASE MyDatabase
```

This statement creates MyDatabase with 4 MB of data space, 2 MB on DataDevice1, and 2 MB on DataDevice2. The log is 2 MB in size and located on LogDevice1.

```
CREATE DATABASE MyDatabase
    ON DataDevice1, DataDevice2
    LOG ON LogDevice1
```

This statement creates a database named MyDatabase that is 100 megabytes in size, with a ten-megabyte log. The data resides on DataDevice and the log resides on LogDevice.

```
CREATE DATABASE MyDatabase
    ON DataDevice = 100
    LOG ON LogDevice = 10
```

4. Execute the query by typing Alt-X or clicking on the Execute Query button. The database is created. SQL Server reports the actual size of the database it created (and the log, if it is on a separate device) in 2 K pages.

To create a database from Enterprise Manager:

1. From the Server Manager window, select a server, and expand the tree view by clicking the plus sign to the left of the stoplight icon (which represents the server). Select the Databases folder, right-click so that the context menu appears, and select the New Database option. The New Database dialog box appears, as shown in figure 3.2.

Figure 3.2

The New Database dialog box.

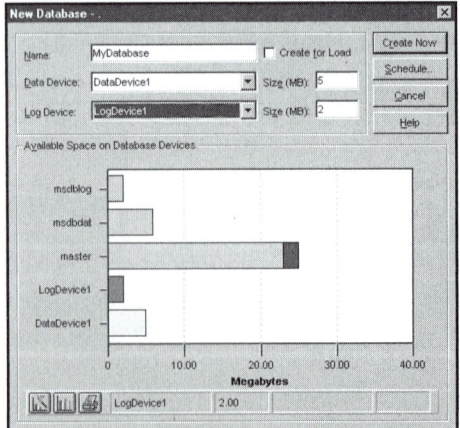

Note

You also can get to a Manage Databases dialog box by selecting Manage, Databases from the Enterprise Manager menu. This dialog box has commands that enable you to add, resize, and delete databases on the server.

2. Enter the name of the database in the Name box.

3. If this database is loaded from a backup dump, check the Create For Load check box.

4. Select the data device for this database by using the Data Device combo box. If you would like to create a new device for this database, you may select the <new> option from the list of devices. Note that you cannot specify multiple data devices for a database created with this dialog box.

5. Enter the size of the database in the Size box next to the Data Device combo box. The database cannot be less than 1 MB in size.

6. If the log is to be on a different device than the data, select the log device from the Log Device combo box. If you would like to create a new device for the log, select the <new> option from the list of devices. Note that you cannot specify multiple log devices from this dialog box.

7. Enter the size of the log in the Size box next to the Log Device combo box.

8. You have now entered all of the information required to create a database. Clicking the Create Now button creates the database and returns you to the Server Manager window. Clicking the Schedule button enables you to schedule the database's creation for a later time. The SQL Executive must be running to schedule the creation.

 **Tip**

If you are creating a very large database, schedule the database creation even if you want it created immediately. Schedule the command for immediate execution, and Enterprise Manager starts the task in the background and returns control to you immediately. If you do not schedule the database creation, Enterprise Manager is totally unresponsive while the database is being created.

**Note**

SQL Server enables you to create databases on removable media, such as a floppy disk, CD-ROM, or ZIP drive. This feature is most useful for distributing read-only databases on CD-ROM. To create a database of this type, use the sp_create_removable system stored procedure.

For more information about creating and using databases on removable media, see the SQL Server Books Online.

Changing the Size of a Database

Databases in SQL Server may be resized if they are too small or too large. Databases are resized in 1/2 MB increments, just like when they are created. Both resizing commands are fully logged, so it is possible for the database to be recovered in the event of a system failure. Nevertheless, it is a good idea to backup both the *master* database and the database being resized before and after the database is resized.

**Warning**

Take special care not to resize a database more than necessary. Resizing a database affects its recoverability in the event of a *master* database corruption. This is because (except in a few circumstances) a database backup must be loaded into a database of the same size and structure as the original.

Every time a database is resized, the database's structure is changed and the changes are recorded in *master*. If the *master* database is lost or corrupted, and no backup is available, then any user databases must be recreated. For the backup dumps to work properly, user databases must be created at their original size and changes must be applied *in the correct order.*

Fortunately, SQL Server 6.5 added a system stored procedure, sp_help_revdatabase, that creates a script that can properly recreate a database in the event of a *master* failure. Another stored procedure, sp_coalesce_fragments, can reduce the number of database fragments created by multiple resizings.

For more information about the effects of resizing a database and these stored procedures, see the SQL Server Books Online.

Expanding a Database

A database may be expanded by using the Transact-SQL ALTER DATABASE command or by using Enterprise Manager. Permissions to expand a database are transferred along with permissions to create a database (these permissions default to the system administrator only). The minimum amount to expand a database is 1 MB, and the default amount to expand a database is 1 MB.

To expand a database using Transact-SQL:

1. From SQL Enterprise Manager, select the server on which the database to be expanded resides. From the main menu, select Tools, SQL Query Tool. The Query window appears (refer again to figure 3.1).

2. You must be in the *master* database to expand a database. Use the DB combo box to select the *master* database.

3. The syntax for the ALTER DATABASE command is as follows:

```
ALTER DATABASE <database_name>
   [ON {DEFAULT | database_device} [=size]
      [, database_device [=size]] ...]
   [FOR LOAD]
```

   ▶ The ON keyword is used to specify which device(s) the database will be expanded on. If this is omitted, the database is expanded on the default device(s). If a device is specified, but no size is specified, the database is expanded by 1 MB on that device.

   If one of the specified devices contains only the database log, then the log is expanded by the specified amount.

   ▶ The size parameter is the size by which the database should be expanded, expressed in megabytes.

   ▶ Use the FOR LOAD keyword if you intend to immediately load the database from a backup dump. Doing so prevents any users from accessing the database until after the load is complete. The FOR LOAD keyword is only effective if the database was also created FOR LOAD.

Following are some examples of the ALTER DATABASE statement:

This statement expands MyDatabase by 1 MB on an available default device:

```
ALTER DATABASE MyDatabase
```

This statement expands MyDatabase by 3 MB on Data-Device1 and expands the log by 2 MB on LogDevice1:

```
ALTER DATABASE MyDatabase
    ON DataDevice1 = 3, LogDevice1 = 2
```

4. Execute the query by typing Alt-X or clicking the Execute Query button. The database is expanded, and SQL Server reports the number of 2-K pages used on each device for the expansion.

To expand a database using Enterprise Manager, do the following:

1. From the Server Manager window, select a server, and expand the tree view by clicking the plus sign to the left of the stoplight icon (which represents the server).

2. Select the Databases folder and expand the tree view by clicking the plus sign next to the folder icon.

3. Select the database you wish to expand from the list, and right-click so the context menu appears. Click the Edit option. The Edit Database dialog box appears, as shown in figure 3.3.

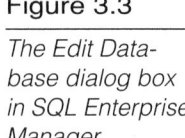

Figure 3.3

The Edit Data-base dialog box in SQL Enterprise Manager.

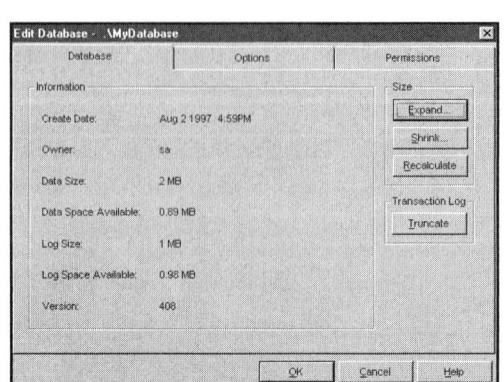

4. Click the Expand button on the right side of the Database tab. The Expand Database dialog box appears, as shown in figure 3.4.

Figure 3.4

The Expand Database dialog box in SQL Enterprise Manager.

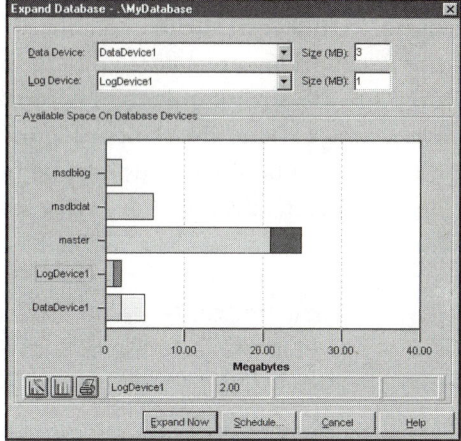

5. Select the data device for the expansion from the Data Device combo box. Enter the size by which to expand the data segment in the size box to the right of the Data Device combo box. You may select (none) if you do not wish to expand the data segment. You also can select <new> to create a new device for the expansion.

6. Select the log device for the expansion from the Log Device combo box. Enter the size by which to expand the log segment in the size box to the right of the Log Device combo box. You may select (none) if you do not wish to expand the log segment. You also can select <new> to create a new device for the expansion.

7. You have now entered all of the information required to expand the database. Clicking the Expand Now button expands the database and returns you to the Server Manager window. Clicking the Schedule button enables you to schedule the database's expansion for a later time.

Shrinking a Database

A database may be shrunk by using the Transact-SQL Database Consistency Checker (DBCC) SHRINKDB command or by using Enterprise Manager. Only the system administrator or database owner (DBO) can shrink a database. When a database is shrunk, the data and log are *both* shrunk to bring the database to the specified size. To shrink only the log or data, shrink the entire database, then expand the data or log to the desired size. Before a database can be shrunk, it must be placed in single-user mode. Setting this database option is discussed later in the chapter.

 Note

> To shrink the *master* or *tempdb* database, you need to place the server in single-user mode. See the SQL Books Online for more information.

To shrink a database using DBCC SHRINKDB:

1. From SQL Enterprise Manager, select the server on which the database to be shrunk resides. From the main menu, select Tools, SQL Query Tool. The Query window appears (refer to figure 3.1).

2. You must execute the SHRINKDB command from the database to be shrunk. Select the appropriate database from the DB combo box.

3. The database must be in single user mode before executing the SHRINKDB command. Use sp_dboption or Enterprise Manager, described later in the chapter, to set this option.

4. The syntax of the SHRINKDB command is:

```
DBCC SHRINKDB (database_name [,new_size])
```

   ▶ The database_name is the name of the database to shrink.

   ▶ The new_size parameter is the new size for the database, expressed in the number of 2-K pages. If this parameter is omitted, then DBCC reports the minimum size to which the database may be shrunk. Note that the database may not be shrunk past the size of the *model* database or the default size for a database.

For example, to shrink the MyDatabase database to 5 mega-bytes, execute the following query:

```
DBCC SHRINKDB (MyDatabase,2560)
```

 **Note**

Remember that to obtain the number of 2-K pages used for the size of a database, multiply the size of the database in megabytes by 512. For more information on sizing databases, see Chapter 2.

5. Execute the query by typing Alt-X or clicking the Execute Query button. The database is shrunk to the requested size.

6. Turn off the Single User option for the database by using sp_dboption or Enterprise Manager.

To shrink a database from Enterprise Manager, implement the following steps:

1. From the Server Manager window, select a server, and expand the tree view by clicking the plus sign to the left of the stoplight icon (which represents the server).

2. Select the Databases folder, and expand the tree view by clicking the plus sign next to the folder icon.

3. Select the database you wish to shrink from the list, and right-click so the context menu appears. Click the Edit option. The Edit Database dialog box appears (refer to figure 3.3).

4. Click the Shrink button on the right side of the Database tab. A dialog box appears, alerting you that the database will be placed in single user mode. Click Yes, and the Shrink Database dialog box appears, as shown in figure 3.5.

Figure 3.5

The Shrink Data-base dialog box in SQL Enterprise Manager.

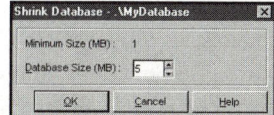

5. The dialog box shows the minimum size for the database. In the Database Size box, type the new size for the database, in megabytes, or use the spinner buttons to change the database size.

6. Click OK to shrink the database.

Deleting a Database

Deleting (or dropping) a database completely removes the database from the server. All data in the database is deleted. However, the devices used by the database remain intact.

To drop a database using the Transact-SQL DROP DATABASE command, do the following:

1. From SQL Enterprise Manager, select the server on which the database to be deleted resides. From the main menu, select Tools, SQL Query Tool. The Query window appears (refer to figure 3.1).

2. To drop a database, you must execute the command from the *master* database. Use the DB combo box to select the *master* database.

3. The syntax of the DROP DATABASE command is:

```
DROP DATABASE <dbname>
```

For example, this statement drops the MyDatabase database:

```
DROP DATABASE MyDatabase
```

4. Execute the query by typing Alt-X or clicking the Execute Query button. The database is deleted.

To drop a database from Enterprise Manager, do the following:

1. From the Server Manager window, select a server, and expand the tree view by clicking the plus sign to the left of the stoplight icon (which represents the server).

2. Select the Databases folder, and expand the tree view by clicking the plus sign next to the folder icon.

3. Select the database from the list, and right-click so the context menu appears. Select the Delete option, as shown in figure 3.6. A confirmation message asks you if you really want to delete the database. Click Yes, and the database is dropped.

Figure 3.6

Dropping a database from SQL Enterprise Manager.

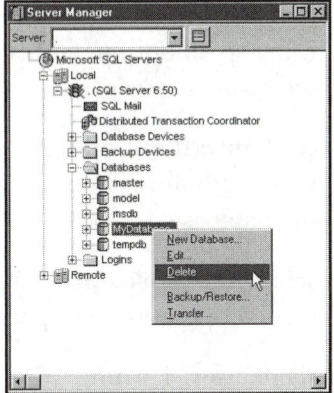

Database Options

You may recall from the last chapter that each SQL Server has a number of configuration options that may be set by the administrator. In turn, each database has a number of configuration options specific to that database. Only the system administrator or DBO can set these options, which follow:

▶ **ANSI null default:** Specifies whether columns are NULLable by default. If this option is turned on, then columns that do not have their NULL option explicitly defined during a CREATE TABLE or ALTER TABLE statement default to allowing NULLs.

▶ **dbo use only:** If this option is turned on, then only the database owner (DBO) or users aliased to the DBO may access the database.

▶ **no chkpt on recovery:** Determines whether a checkpoint record is added to the log after auto-recovery is performed at startup.

- ▶ **offline:** This option is primarily used for databases stored on removable media. When a database is offline, no users can access the database. SQL Server does not open the files containing the database's devices, and the database is not automatically recovered at server startup. This option can only be set by using sp_dboption.

- ▶ **published:** Determines if a database is allowed to provide publications for replication. This option can only be set by using sp_dboption, and is usually only set when replication is set up on a server.

- ▶ **read only:** If this option is turned on, users (including the system administrator and DBO) cannot modify any data in the database.

- ▶ **select into/bulkcopy:** If this option is turned on, then non-logged operations are permitted in the database.

- ▶ **single user:** Turning this option on restricts the number of connections into the database. Only one user may access the database at a time. This option is used with the DBCC SHRINKDB command described previously.

- ▶ **subscribed:** Determines if a database is allowed to subscribe to publications from other databases involved in replication. This option can only be set by using sp_dboption, and is usually only set when replication is set up on a server.

- ▶ **trunc. log on chkpt.:** If set, then committed transactions are removed from the transaction log every time the CHECKPOINT process occurs. This option is useful in databases where transaction log dumps are not needed, such as a database under development, because it reduces the likelihood of the transaction log filling up.

 Tip

Setting a database option in the *model* database causes that option to be set in all newly-created databases.

Database options can be set by using the sp_dboption system stored procedure, or through Enterprise Manager. A few of the options can only be set using sp_dboption. To use sp_dboption to set a database option, do the following:

1. From SQL Enterprise Manager, select the server on which the database resides. From the main menu, select Tools, SQL Query Tool. The Query window appears (refer to figure 3.1).

2. The syntax of the sp_dboption stored procedure is:

```
sp_dboption [dbname] [, 'optname' [ , {TRUE | FALSE } ]]
```

3. sp_dboption behaves differently when different options are specified. Consider the following examples:

   1. Calling sp_dboption without any parameters causes all database options to be listed:

   ```
   sp_dboption
   ```

   2. Calling sp_dboption with only a database name returns a list of all enabled options in that database:

   ```
   sp_dboption pubs
   ```

   3. Calling sp_dboption with a database name and option name returns the current setting for that option:

   ```
   sp_dboption pubs,'read only'
   ```

   4. Calling sp_dboption with a database name, option name, and setting value turns the option on or off:

   ```
   sp_dboption pubs, 'read only', true
   ```

4. Execute the query by typing Alt-X or clicking the execute button on the toolbar of the query window. The database option will be changed.

To set database options from Enterprise Manager, implement the following steps:

1. From the Server Manager window, select a server, and expand the tree view by clicking the plus sign to the left of the stoplight icon (which represents the server).

2. Select the Databases folder, and expand the tree view by clicking the plus sign next to the folder icon.

3. Select the database for which you wish to change an option, and right-click so the context menu appears. Click the Edit option. The Edit Database dialog box appears. Select the Options tab, as shown in figure 3.7.

4. Turn an option on or off by checking or unchecking its check box. Click the OK button to save your changes.

Figure 3.7

The Database Options tab on the Edit Database dialog box in Enterprise Manager.

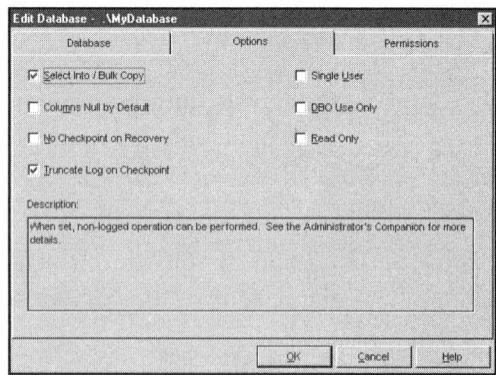

Understanding Data Types

Before creating tables in a database, it is helpful to understand what kinds of data can be stored in SQL Server. SQL Server uses nineteen different *data types* to identify the type of information (be it numeric, character based, or some other type) stored in a column. In addition, database users can define their own data types based on the system supplied data types.

Data types also are used to define the type of data passed as a parameter to a stored procedure or the type of data used in a local variable.

System Data Types

The nineteen system data types can be grouped into seven broad categories. For more information about each specific data type, see the SQL Server Books Online.

Binary: The *binary* and *varbinary* types are used to store up to 255 bytes of binary information.

Character: The *char* and *varchar* types store up to 255 alphanumeric characters. The *char* type is fixed length, while the *varchar* type is variable length. Use the *char* data type when you expect each value to be roughly the same size; use the *varchar* type if a character field can contain NULLs or will have data of widely varying lengths.

Date & Time: The *datetime* and *smalldatetime* types both store date and time values. The difference between the two is the range of dates each can store.

Exact Numeric: The *decimal, numeric, money,* and *smallmoney* types can all store decimal numbers exactly. In SQL Server 6.5, there is no difference between the *decimal* and *numeric* types.

Floating Point (approximate numeric): The *float* and *real* types both provide for the approximate storage of decimal numbers, the main difference between the two being the range of values each can store.

Integer: The *int, smallint,* and *tinyint* types all store integer data in varying ranges.

Special: The *bit* data type can store 0 or 1; it is often used for Boolean flags, and cannot be NULLable. The *timestamp* data type provides a value unique to the database every time a column is inserted or updated. The *text* data type stores about two billion characters, and the *image* type stores about two billion bytes of binary information. Both the *text* and *image* types have special considerations when used; see the SQL Books Online for more information.

User-Defined Data Types

SQL Server allows custom data types to be defined. User-defined data types help ensure that similar columns have the same data type, NULL option, default, and rule, and help document the database. A user-defined data type has the following characteristics:

▶ **Base Type:** This defines the main SQL Server data type for the user-defined type (UDT).

▶ **Null Option:** Specifies the default NULL option for columns that use this user-defined type. The UDT NULL option may be overridden when a table is created or changed.

▶ **Rule:** A UDT may have a rule bound to it that defines a range of values acceptable for the column. For more information about rules, see Chapter 8, "Using Views, Defaults, and Rules."

▶ **Default:** A UDT may have a default bound to it that defines an initial value for the column. Default values are most often used with columns that do not allow NULLs. For more information about defaults, see Chapter 8.

UDTs may be added and deleted through Enterprise Manager, or by using the sp_addtype and sp_droptype system stored procedures.

Managing Tables

 Objective ▶

Once you are finished with defining the physical storage for a database, you will add tables and other objects to your database to implement the data model. Tables are used to store all of the data in a database and are the most structurally complex of all the database objects. The remainder of this chapter covers how tables are implemented in SQL Server, and how data integrity is maintained.

When working with tables, it is helpful to remember these facts:

▶ Table names may be up to thirty characters in length, and must be unique in a database.

▶ A table may contain up to 250 columns, and the combined row length (sum of all of the bytes of storage for all columns) may not be more than 1,962 bytes.

▶ Column names must be unique within a table.

▶ A SQL Server database may contain up to two billion tables (although a database with this many tables would be difficult to administer!)

Each column in a table has four important characteristics. The first is the column name—this identifies the column in the table. Next, the column data type specifies the type of information stored in the column. The column's NULL option defines whether the column can contain NULLs. Finally, the column may have one or more constraints associated with it. Constraints are discussed later in the chapter.

Creating a Table

When you create a table, you are really defining the table's structure in terms of its columns. This can be done by using the Transact SQL CREATE TABLE statement, or by using Enterprise Manager.

To create a table using Transact-SQL, use these steps:

1. Open the SQL Query window in Enterprise Manager.

2. Select the database that contains the new table from the DB combo box.

3. Type the CREATE TABLE command. The simplified syntax is:

```
CREATE TABLE [database.[owner].]table_name
(
 {col_name datatype [null_option]
    [[, next_col_name datatype [null_option]]...]}
)
```

Constraints also can be defined in the CREATE TABLE statement—the syntax is covered later in the chapter. Every column must be named and have a data type defined. If no NULL option is specified, then the column defaults to disallow NULLs.

 **Note** Enabling the ANSI Null Default database option causes table columns to allow NULLs if no NULL option is specified for the column.

4. In this example, a table named MyTable is created in the MyDatabase database with three columns. Note that the second column has no NULL option set, so it defaults to NOT NULL.

```
CREATE TABLE MyDatabase..MyTable
(
  ID        int         NOT NULL,
  LastName  varchar(30),
  FirstName varchar(30) NULL
)
```

5. Execute the query by typing Alt-X or by clicking the Execute button on the toolbar. The table is added to the database.

To create a table in Enterprise Manager, do the following:

1. In the Server Manager window, select the server that contains the database to which you wish to add the table. Expand the tree view by clicking on the plus sign to the left of the server name.

2. Expand the Databases folder by clicking the plus sign to the left of the folder icon. A list of all of the server's databases appears.

3. Select the database to which you wish to add the table. Click the plus sign to the left of the database icon to expand the tree view. Click the plus sign next to the Objects folder to show a list of all database objects. The resulting display looks similar to the one shown in figure 3.8.

4. Right-click the Tables folder so that the context menu appears. Select the New Table option. You are presented with the Manage Tables window, similar to the one presented in figure 3.9.

Figure 3.8

Navigating to the Tables folder for a database in Enterprise Manager.

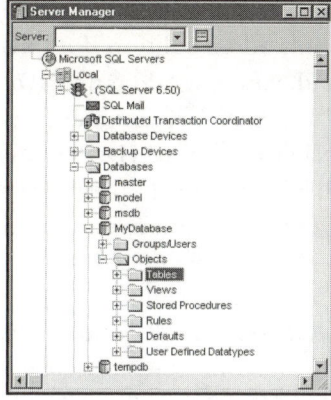

Figure 3.9

The Manage Tables window in Enterprise Manager.

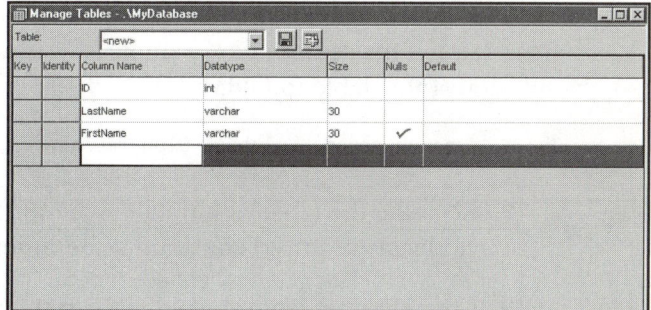

5. Define each column for the table by typing a column name in the grid, selecting a data type, entering a data type size (for some data types), entering a NULL option, and entering a default.

6. When you are done entering the columns for the table, click the Save Table button on the window's toolbar. The Specify Table Name dialog box appears and prompts you to name the new table.

7. Enter the name of the new table and click OK. The table is added to the database.

Modifying a Table

After you create a table, you may modify its structure by adding columns, and adding, changing, or removing constraints (constraints are covered in more detail later in the chapter). Be aware of two restrictions when altering the columns in a table. First, you may only add a column if its NULL option is set to allow NULLs. Second, you may add a new IDENTITY column to the table if one does not exist, but you may not change an existing column to an IDENTITY column (IDENTITY columns are covered in more detail later in the chapter). If you need to add a non-NULL column to a table, you must drop and re-create the table.

Tip

If you need to add a non-NULL column to a table that contains data, follow these steps:

1. Rename the existing table by using the sp_rename system stored procedure. For example, this code renames the MyTable table to OldMyTable:

```
exec sp_rename MyTable, OldMyTable
```

2. Recreate the table with the new column(s). Be sure to include any required constraints and indexes.

3. Copy the data from the old table to the new table.

4. Recreate any triggers or stored procedures that depended on the old table.

Tip

Microsoft's Visual InterDev product contains a number of database utilities. One helpful feature of the product is that it automatically scripts the preceding process when you make a change to a table that requires it to be dropped and re-created.

The Transact-SQL ALTER TABLE statement is used to modify an existing table, as follows:

1. Open the SQL Query window in Enterprise Manager.

2. Use the DB combo box to select the database that contains the table to be modified.

3. Type the ALTER TABLE command. The simplified syntax is:

```
ALTER TABLE [database.[owner].]table_name
(
 ADD {col_name datatype [null_option]
     [[, next_col_name datatype [null_option]]...]}
)
```

Constraints also can be defined in the ALTER TABLE statement—the syntax is covered later in the chapter. Every column must be named and have a data type defined. Columns added using the ALTER TABLE statement must allow NULLs.

4. In this example, the MyTable table is modified to add two columns:

```
ALTER TABLE MyDatabase..MyTable
   ADD
   SocialSecurityNumber   varchar(11)   NULL,
   BirthDate              datetime      NULL
```

5. Execute the query by typing Alt-X or clicking the Execute button on the toolbar. The table will be modified.

Columns and constraints also can be added from the Manage Tables window in Enterprise Manager (refer to figure 3.9.)

Dropping a Table

A table may be dropped (deleted) from a database by its owner, the system administrator, or the DBO. When a table is dropped, all data, indexes, triggers, and constraints associated with the table also are deleted.

To drop a table using Transact-SQL, implement the following steps:

1. Open the SQL Query window in Enterprise Manager.

2. Select the database that contains the table from the DB combo box.

3. Type the DROP TABLE command. The syntax is:

```
DROP TABLE <tablename>
```

For example, to drop a table named MyTable, type the following:

```
DROP TABLE MyTable
```

4. Execute the query by typing Alt-X or clicking the Execute button on the toolbar. The table is dropped from the database.

To drop a table by using Enterprise Manager:

1. Navigate to the Tables folder for the database containing the table to drop, as explained under the heading "Creating a Table."

2. Expand the Tables folder by clicking the plus sign to the left of the folder icon.

3. Select the table you want to drop, and right-click so the context menu appears. Select the Drop option, and the Drop Objects dialog box appears, as shown in figure 3.10.

4. Click the Drop All button. The table is dropped from the database.

Figure 3.10

The Drop Objects dialog box in Enterprise Manager.

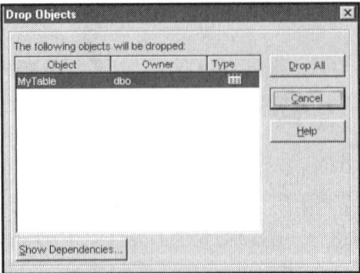

Using Constraints

Objective

Data integrity is an important concept to keep in mind when designing a database. *Data integrity* is a broad term that simply refers to the correctness of data in a database. One of the benefits of using SQL Server is that all of the data integrity rules can be defined in a central location—namely, the database. There are three main types of data integrity:

▶ **Entity Integrity:** Recall from Chapter 1 that one of the requirements in a relational database design is the ability to distinguish different instances of an entity. This concept is known as entity integrity, and it is accomplished by creating a primary key in a table.

▶ **Domain Integrity:** Domain integrity is concerned with ensuring that column values fall within an acceptable range of values (the *domain*). Domain integrity also refers to the data type and NULLability of a column.

▶ **Referential Integrity:** Referential integrity refers to the requirement that primary and foreign keys remain synchronized between parent and child tables.

SQL Server supports two different implementations of data integrity. *Procedural* data integrity, which is available in all versions of SQL Server, relies on views, triggers, stored procedures, defaults, and rules to enforce domain and referential integrity. Procedural data integrity is the most flexible, but incurs the most execution overhead and can be error-prone.

SQL Server 6.0 introduced constraints as a way to maintain *declarative* data integrity. Constraints provide a concise, consistent way to manage all three types of data integrity by extending the SQL syntax used to create and modify tables. In other words, the data integrity is declared when a table is created. Constraints are less error-prone and incur less execution overhead than procedural methods; however, constraints are less flexible.

There are no clearly defined rules for when one type of data integrity should be used over another. Usually, a mix of methods is used. The remainder of the chapter covers the different types of constraints and how they enforce each type of data integrity.

Managing Table Constraints

As mentioned previously, constraints may be created on a table when the table is initially defined. Another benefit of constraints is that they may be added or removed from the table without the need to drop or modify the table itself. Using the Transact-SQL

CREATE TABLE and ALTER TABLE statements gives you the most flexibility in defining constraints, though you may find that using Enterprise Manager's Manage Tables window is easier.

When using constraints in a database implementation, be aware that constraint names must be unique in the database. If you do not explicitly assign a name to a constraint, SQL Server provides one, such as PK__mytable__2CD2B24E. These system supplied names can make administering constraints more difficult.

 **Tip**

Use the system stored procedure sp_help or sp_helpconstraint to see each constraint placed on a table.

Adding and Dropping Constraints with Transact-SQL

The previous discussions of the CREATE TABLE and ALTER TABLE statements excluded the syntax used to manage table constraints. This section shows you the full syntax diagram for each statement and gives examples of adding and dropping constraints on a table. More detailed Transact-SQL syntax is shown for each constraint type later in the chapter.

When using Transact-SQL statements to manage constraints, you either declare constraints at the column level or the table level. Where you declare the constraint has no bearing on how it functions; the syntax is merely different. Constraints that involve more than one column must be declared at the table level.

Constraints are usually first declared when a table is created with the CREATE TABLE statement. Here is the full syntax for CREATE TABLE:

```
CREATE TABLE [database.[owner].]table_name
(
  {col_name column_properties [col_constraint [col_constraint
[...col_constraint]]]
    ¦ [[,] table_constraint]}
  [[,] {next_col_name | next_table_constraint}...]
)
```

Note that constraints may be declared in-line with the column definition, such as:

```
EmployeeSalary  money  not null CHECK (EmployeeSalary > 0)
➡DEFAULT 50000
```

This example defines both a CHECK constraint and a DEFAULT constraint on the EmployeeSalary column. Both constraints are said to be defined at the column level.

 **Tip**

> Typically, column level constraints are used when possible, because they make the CREATE TABLE statement easier to read.

Constraints declared at the table level may be interspersed with the column definitions, or may be included at the end of the column definitions in the statement. This example shows a PRIMARY KEY constraint and a UNIQUE constraint both declared at the table level:

```
CREATE TABLE Employee (
  EmployeeID      int  IDENTITY,
    PRIMARY KEY (EmployeeID),
  FirstName       char(30),
  LastName        char(30),
  SocialSecNumber char(11),
    CONSTRAINT UQ_EmployeeSSN
    UNIQUE (SocialSecNumber)
)
```

Typically, all table-level constraints are included at the end of the column list to improve readability. Note that in the preceding example, a name was explicitly assigned (UQ_EmployeeSSN) to the UNIQUE constraint on the social security number column.

You may use the ALTER TABLE statement to add or drop constraints after a table has been created. The full syntax of ALTER TABLE follows:

```
ALTER TABLE [database.[owner].]table_name
[WITH NOCHECK]
```

```
[ADD
    {col_name column_properties [column_constraints] | [[,]
table_constraint]}
        [, {next_col_name | next_table_constraint}]...]
|
[DROP [CONSTRAINT]
        constraint_name [, constraint_name2]...]
```

You have already seen how to add columns by using the ALTER TABLE statement. When you add new columns with constraints, or add new table-level constraints, the syntax used to describe columns and constraints is exactly the same as the CREATE TABLE syntax. Dropping a constraint is straightforward. Executing the following statement drops the unique constraint defined earlier on the Employee table.

```
ALTER TABLE Employee
    DROP CONSTRAINT UQ_EmployeeSSN
```

Note

The WITH NOCHECK option in the ALTER TABLE statement disables constraint checking for FOREIGN KEY and CHECK constraints during the table's modification. This enables these constraints to be added even if the existing data violates these constraints.

This option is typically used when a table is large and the data is already known to be accurate. Disabling constraint checking when modifying the table improves the speed of the modification.

The NOCHECK option has no effect on PRIMARY KEY, UNIQUE, or DEFAULT constraints.

Adding and Dropping Constraints with Enterprise Manager

Constraints may be added and removed from the Manage Tables window in Enterprise Manager. When this window is first opened, it simply shows the columns in the table and their various properties. Clicking the Advanced Features button on the window's toolbar opens a set of index tabs at the bottom of the window, as shown in figure 3.11.

Figure 3.11

The Advanced Features tab in the Manage Tables window.

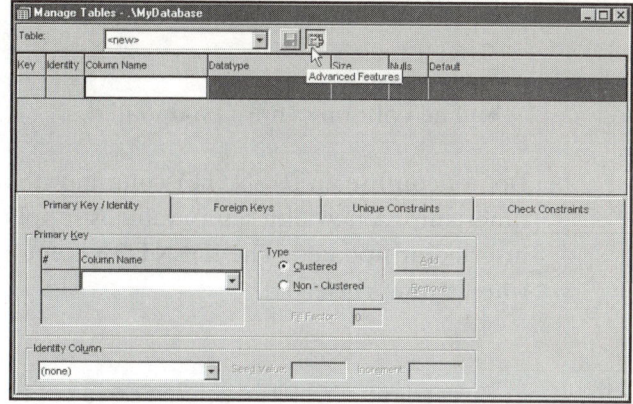

The Advanced Features tabs are used to manage every constraint type, except for DEFAULTS, which are managed from the grid containing the table columns and their properties. Note that when you use Enterprise Manager to modify a table's constraints, you may not name PRIMARY KEY or DEFAULT constraints, and you do not need to make a distinction between constraints declared at the column level or the table level.

Using an IDENTITY Column

 Objective

Technically, the IDENTITY property for a column is not a constraint, it is a third setting for a column's NULL option. Nevertheless, IDENTITY columns are often used to provide entity integrity, so they are included in this section.

An IDENTITY column is a special column in a table that provides a sequential, auto-incrementing number generated every time a record is inserted into the table. The number for a new row is determined by taking the last value in the column and adding an *increment* value supplied during the column's definition. Keep the following characteristics in mind when using IDENTITY columns:

▶ A table can only have one IDENTITY column.

▶ The column must use an integer data type (*int, smallint,* or *tinyint*) or an exact numeric data type (*numeric, decimal*) with no fractional component. In other words, the column must contain only whole numbers.

▶ The column is automatically restricted from containing NULLs.

▶ The column cannot be updated.

Do not confuse an IDENTITY column with a column containing a timestamp. A new timestamp value is supplied when a column is inserted or updated. The IDENTITY column only supplies values when a row is inserted.

 **Note**

By itself, an IDENTITY column does not enforce entity integrity. The IDENTITY property just causes a column to supply auto-incrementing numbers useful as surrogate key values. However, placing a PRIMARY KEY or UNIQUE constraint on the column enables it to enforce entity integrity.

Creating an IDENTITY Column

An IDENTITY column is created when a table is created with the CREATE TABLE statement, or when a table is modified via an AL-TER TABLE statement. Recall that the syntax for creating a column in either one of these statements takes on the following form:

```
column_name data_type [null_option]
```

Adding the IDENTITY option into the syntax diagram gives you the following:

```
column_name data_type [ {null_option | IDENTITY
[(seed,increment)]} ]
```

The *seed* and *increment* values are optional. If one is specified, both must be specified. The seed value indicates what the value of the IDENTITY column will be when the first row is inserted into the table. The increment value specifies the step used to increment to the next value in the column. If these values are omitted, then seed and increment both default to 1.

Here are some examples of CREATE TABLE statements using IDENTITY columns:

1. This example creates a table with several columns. The first column, ID, is an IDENTITY column with seed and increment of 1:

```
CREATE TABLE IdentityEx1 (
    ID          int          IDENTITY,
    FirstName   varchar(30)  NOT NULL,
    LastName    varchar(30)  NOT NULL
)
```

2. This example shows how the seed and increment values are explicitly defined:

```
CREATE TABLE IdentityEx2 (
    ID          int          IDENTITY(100,5),
    FirstName   varchar(30)  NOT NULL,
    LastName    varchar(30)  NOT NULL
)
```

3. This example shows that the increment can be a negative number:

```
CREATE TABLE IdentityEx3 (
    ID          int          IDENTITY(0,-1),
    FirstName   varchar(30)  NOT NULL,
    LastName    varchar(30)  NOT NULL
)
```

An IDENTITY column also can be added to a table by using the advanced features tabs in the Manage Tables window in SQL Enterprise Manger.

Special Considerations for IDENTITY Columns

Tables with IDENTITY columns require some special considerations when inserting data. When inserting information into the table by way of the INSERT statement, the identity column should be omitted from the list of columns to insert. For example, to insert data into any of the three preceding sample tables, the syntax would be:

```
INSERT IdentityEx1 (FirstName,LastName) VALUES ('John','Smith')
```

Note how the ID column is omitted from the INSERT statement. SQL Server automatically provides the value for this column when the row is inserted. See Chapter 6, "Modifying Data," for more information about the INSERT statement.

 Tip

> It is possible to explicitly provide a value for an identity column when using the INSERT statement. Turning on the IDENTITY_INSERT option for the table enables you to explicitly enter values in an identity column. For more information about the IDENTITY_INSERT option, see the SQL Server Books Online.

It is possible to query a table to determine the last identity value inserted into that table. This information is obtained by querying the value of the @@IDENTITY global variable, as in this example:

```
SELECT @@IDENTITY from IdentityEx1
```

This query returns the last identity value used in the IdentityEx1 table.

Declarative Referential Integrity (DRI) Constraints

The DRI constraints are used by SQL Server to enforce both entity and referential integrity. All referential integrity enforced with DRI constraints is restrictive; in other words, updates to key values are not permitted, parent records may not be deleted if child records exist, and a child record may not be inserted if its foreign key value does not match a parent's primary key value.

PRIMARY KEY Constraint

The PRIMARY KEY constraint is used to enforce entity integrity because the primary key can be used to uniquely identify any row in a table. A PRIMARY KEY constraint may be created as a column level constraint (for single column keys) or as a table level constraint (for multiple column keys). Keep the following facts in mind when using a PRIMARY KEY constraint:

- ▶ Only one PRIMARY KEY constraint may be created per table.

- ▶ The column(s) participating in a primary key cannot enable NULLs. The key may be composed of up to 16 columns.

- ▶ A PK is enforced by creating a unique index on the key column(s). The type of index (clustered or non-clustered) may be specified when the constraint is defined; the default is a clustered index. The index cannot be dropped without dropping the constraint.

- ▶ A PK constraint is required if the table will be referenced by a FOREIGN KEY constraint or if the table will be replicated.

The simplified syntax of the PRIMARY KEY constraint, when used with the CREATE TABLE or ALTER TABLE statement, is as follows:

```
[CONSTRAINT pk_name]
  PRIMARY KEY [CLUSTERED | NONCLUSTERED]
  (column1 [,column2 [,...column16]])
```

Following are some examples of the syntax used to create this constraint:

1. This example creates a table with a column-level PK constraint on the ID column. SQL Server provides a system name for the constraint, and the resulting index is clustered:

```
CREATE TABLE Employee
(
    EmployeeID  int          IDENTITY PRIMARY KEY,
    FirstName   varchar(30)  NOT NULL,
    LastName    varchar(30)  NOT NULL,
    HireDate    datetime     NULL
)
```

2. This example creates a table with a table-level PK constraint on two columns. The name of the constraint is PK_EmployeeReview. The resulting index is clustered:

```
CREATE TABLE EmployeeReview
(
    EmployeeID      int       NOT NULL,
    ReviewDate      datetime  NOT NULL,
```

```
PerformanceRank   tinyint       NOT NULL,
Comments          text          NULL,
CONSTRAINT PK_EmployeeReview
   PRIMARY KEY (EmployeeID, ReviewDate)
)
```

3. This example is similar to example 2, except the resulting index is non-clustered:

```
CREATE TABLE EmployeeReview
(
    EmployeeID      int       NOT NULL,
    ReviewDate      datetime  NOT NULL,
    PerformanceRank tinyint   NOT NULL,
    Comments        text      NULL,
    CONSTRAINT PK_EmployeeReview
       PRIMARY KEY NONCLUSTERED (EmployeeID, ReviewDate)
)
```

A PK constraint also can be added from the Manage Tables window in SQL Enterprise Manger. The first of the Advanced Features tabs is used to define a primary key for the table.

FOREIGN KEY Constraint

 Objective

The FOREIGN KEY constraint is used to enforce referential integrity between tables. An FK constraint may be created as a column level constraint (for single column foreign keys) or as a table level constraint (for multiple column foreign keys). Keep these facts in mind when using an FK constraint:

▶ A foreign key must reference a PRIMARY KEY or UNIQUE constraint in the referenced table. The FK may reference the same table (a recursive relationship) or another table in the same database. For cross-database referential integrity, use a trigger.

▶ The number of columns in the FK must match the number of columns in the referenced PK or UNIQUE constraints. In addition, the data types of each column must match.

▶ No index is created on the column(s) participating in a foreign key. You should build an index on the FK column(s) to improve the performance of queries using the FK in a join.

Here is the simplified syntax of the FOREIGN KEY constraint as it is used with the CREATE TABLE or ALTER TABLE statement:

```
[CONSTRAINT fk_name]
  [FOREIGN KEY (column1 [,column2 [,...column16]])]
  REFERENCES referenced_table (ref_column1 [,ref_column2
[,...ref_column16]])
```

The following are examples of the syntax used to create this constraint:

1. This example creates the EmployeeReview table shown previously and adds the foreign key reference back to the Employee table. The foreign key constraint has a system-supplied name:

```
CREATE TABLE EmployeeReview
(
    EmployeeID      int       NOT NULL REFERENCES Employee
    ➥(EmployeeID),
    ReviewDate      datetime  NOT NULL,
    PerformanceRank tinyint   NOT NULL,
    Comments        text      NULL,
    CONSTRAINT PK_EmployeeReview
        PRIMARY KEY (EmployeeID, ReviewDate)
)
```

(This example assumes the Employee table has a PK or UNIQUE constraint on the EmployeeID column.)

2. This example shows how to define the same FK constraint shown in #1 as a table level constraint:

```
CREATE TABLE EmployeeReview
(
    EmployeeID      int       NOT NULL,
    ReviewDate      datetime  NOT NULL,
    PerformanceRank tinyint   NOT NULL,
    Comments        text      NULL,
```

```
        CONSTRAINT PK_EmployeeReview
           PRIMARY KEY (EmployeeID, ReviewDate),

        FOREIGN KEY (EmployeeID)
           REFERENCES Employee (EmployeeID)
     )
```

3. This example shows how a recursive relationship is implemented. The Employee table self-references itself to model the employee-manager relationship. The constraint is given a name (FK_ManagerID) in this example:

```
CREATE TABLE Employee
(
    EmployeeID int          IDENTITY PRIMARY KEY,
    FirstName  varchar(30)  NOT NULL,
    LastName   varchar(30)  NOT NULL,
    HireDate   datetime     NULL,
    ManagerID  int          NULL,

    CONSTRAINT FK_ManagerID
    FOREIGN KEY (ManagerID)
       REFERENCES Employee (EmployeeID)
)
```

An FK constraint also can be added from the Manage Tables window in SQL Enterprise Manger. The second of the Advanced Features tabs enables you to define a table's foreign key(s).

UNIQUE Constraint

UNIQUE constraints are very similar to PRIMARY KEY constraints in that both are used to enforce entity integrity. There are a number of subtle differences between the two types of constraints, however:

▶ Only one PK constraint may exist on a table, but multiple UNIQUE constraints may exist. UNIQUE constraints are usually used to define alternate keys (AKs) on a table.

▶ UNIQUE constraints create an index just like PK constraints, but the index defaults to being non-clustered.

▶ Columns participating in a UNIQUE constraint may contain NULLs.

The syntax to create a UNIQUE constraint is very similar to that of a PRIMARY KEY constraint:

```
[CONSTRAINT unique_constraint_name]
  UNIQUE [CLUSTERED | NONCLUSTERED]
  (column1 [,column2 [,...column16]])
```

The above syntax is used in the same manner as when creating a PK constraint. UNIQUE constraints also can be added from the Manage Tables window in SQL Enterprise Manger. The third of the Advanced Features tabs enables you to define UNIQUE constraints for the selected table.

Data Validation Constraints

Data validation constraints are used to enforce domain integrity in SQL Server by ensuring that columns have valid values. This is accomplished in one of two ways: by checking the column's value against a predefined rule (on insert and update), and by providing a default value for a column if a value is not specified (on insert).

CHECK Constraint

A CHECK constraint is very similar to a rule (for more information about rules, see Chapter 8. A CHECK constraint provides a way for SQL Server to validate the value in a column (or columns) when a row is inserted or updated. For instance, a CHECK constraint may be used to enforce the entry of a phone number field as (###) ###-####. Keep the following in mind when using CHECK constraints:

▶ The CHECK constraint's data validation rule must evaluate to a Boolean expression.

▶ CHECK constraints can only reference a single table, and they may not use subqueries.

▶ Unlike rules, CHECK constraints may reference other columns in the table.

▶ CHECK constraints may be created at the column or table level.

▶ Unlike rules, CHECK constraints are automatically bound to a column when they are created.

CHECK constraints may be created from the Manage Tables window in Enterprise Manager—use the fourth Advanced Features tab to define CHECK constraints. CHECK constraints also can be defined with Transact-SQL; the following is the simplified syntax of the CHECK constraint as it is used with the CREATE TABLE or ALTER TABLE statement:

```
[CONSTRAINT check_constraint_name]
   CHECK (check_expression)
```

For example, this CREATE TABLE statement shows a data validation rule that forces the user to enter a formatted phone number. The CHECK constraint is declared at the table level and named CK_ValidPhone:

```
CREATE TABLE Employee
(
   EmployeeID  int          IDENTITY,
   FirstName   varchar(30)  NOT NULL,
   LastName    varchar(30)  NOT NULL,
   HireDate    datetime     NULL,
   HomePhone   char(14)     NOT NULL,

   CONSTRAINT CK_ValidPhone
      CHECK (@value LIKE '([0-9][0-9][0-9]) [0-9][0-9][0-9]-[0-
9][0-9][0-9][0-9]')
)
```

DEFAULT Constraint

A DEFAULT constraint is very similar to an object-based default. (For more information about defaults, see Chapter 8.) A DEFAULT constraint is used when rows are inserted into a table. If a column has a DEFAULT constraint, and the user does not explicitly specify a value for the column, then the constraint's value is used instead. DEFAULT constraints are useful for providing values for columns that do not enable NULLs. Keep the following in mind when using DEFAULT constraints:

▶ Only one DEFAULT constraint may be defined per column.

▶ This constraint may not be placed on an IDENTITY column, or a column that has a *timestamp* data type.

▶ DEFAULT constraints may be created at the column or table level.

▶ Unlike object-based defaults, DEFAULT constraints are automatically bound to a column when they are created.

DEFAULT constraints may be created in the Transact-SQL CREATE TABLE or ALTER TABLE statements. The basic Transact-SQL syntax for a DEFAULT constraint is as follows:

```
[CONSTRAINT default_constraint_name]
   DEFAULT {constant_value I niladic-function I NULL}
   [FOR column_name]
```

The constraint name is optional, and the FOR keyword need only be used when the constraint is declared at the column level. A default may consist of a constant value (such as the number 42 or the string 'abc'), a NULL, or the result of a *niladic* function. A niladic function returns a value without accepting any parameters; examples include user_name() and getdate(), which return the database user's name and the current date, respectively.

You also can use the Manage Tables window in Enterprise Manager to add DEFAULT constraints to columns. The grid containing the table columns and their properties has a place to enter a default value for each column. Simply enter the default value in the space provided.

Summary

The first half of this chapter discussed how databases are implemented and managed in SQL Server. As you learned, once you have implemented a database, you can create tables and other objects in SQL Server. The second half of this chapter discussed the implementation and management of tables and constraints in some detail.

Exercises

Note   The exercises in this chapter build on each other, and so are best done in sequential order.

Exercise 3.1:   Creating a Database

Exercise 3.1 walks you through the process of creating a database on two devices. The first device contains the data, and the second device contains the log.

This exercise and Exercise 3.2 assume that you have two devices named DataDevice and LogDevice on your system that are at least 10 MB in size. In addition, these exercises assume the devices are empty. See Chapter 2 for examples of creating devices.

1. Load SQL Enterprise Manager. From the Server Manager window, select the server on which you wish to create the new database.

2. Load the SQL Query tool by selecting Tools, SQL Query Tool from the application's main menu.

3. Use the DB combo box to select the *master* database.

4. In the query window, type:

```
CREATE DATABASE Exercise3
   ON    DataDevice = 5
   LOG ON LogDevice = 2
```

5. Execute the query by typing Alt-X or clicking the Execute Query button on the query window's toolbar.

A 7-megabyte database named Exercise3 is created. 5 MB of the database stores data and is located on the DataDevice device. The other 2 MB of the database is allocated to the transaction log, which resides on the device LogDevice.

Exercise 3.2: Expanding a Database and Transaction Log

In Exercise 3.2, you expand the database you created in Exercise 3.1. You expand the database in two steps: the log, then the data.

1. If it is not already loaded, open the SQL Query tool by selecting Tools, SQL Query Tool from the application's main menu.

2. Use the DB combo box to select the *master* database.

3. In the query window, type:

```
ALTER DATABASE Exercise3 ON LogDevice = 5
```

4. Execute the query by typing Alt-X or clicking the Execute Query button on the query window's toolbar. The database's log is expanded by 5 MB, for a total log size of 7 MB.

5. In the query window, type:

```
ALTER DATABASE Exercise3 ON DataDevice = 5
```

6. Execute the query. The database's data area is expanded by 5 MB, for a total data size of 5 MB.

Note

The two preceding queries could have been executed as a unit by using this query:

```
ALTER DATABASE Exercise3 on LogDevice = 5, DataDevice = 5
```

7. In the query window, execute the query:

```
exec sp_helpdb Exercise3
```

Note how the total size of the database has been increased, and how the database is located in four fragments on two devices.

Exercise 3.3: Creating a Table

In Exercise 3.3, you create a table to store a company's employee information. This table is created in the database you created in Exercise 3.1.

1. If it is not already loaded, open the SQL Query tool by selecting Tools, SQL Query Tool from the application's main menu.

2. Use the DB combo box to select the *Exercise3* database. If the database does not show up in the list, choose the <refresh> option to refresh the list of databases. Then, choose the *Exercise3* database.

3. Type the following query in the query window:

```
CREATE TABLE Employee
(
    FirstName               varchar(30) NOT NULL,
    LastName                varchar(30) NOT NULL,
    MiddleInitial           char(1)  NULL,
    SocialSecurityNumber    char(11) NOT NULL,
    HireDate                datetime NULL
)
```

4. Execute the query by typing Alt-X or clicking the Execute Query button on the query window's toolbar. The Employee table is created.

5. In the query window, execute this query:

```
exec sp_help Employee
```

Check to see that the columns were created with the proper data types and NULL options.

Exercise 3.4: Adding an IDENTITY Column to a Table

Exercise 3.4 walks you through the steps required to add an IDENTITY column (EmployeeID) to the Employee table you created in Exercise 3.3.

1. If it isn't already loaded, open the SQL Query tool by selecting Tools, SQL Query Tool from the application's main menu.

2. Use the DB combo box to select the *Exercise3* database.

3. Type the following query in the query window:

```
ALTER TABLE Employee
ADD    EmployeeID    int    IDENTITY
```

4. Execute the query by typing Alt-X or clicking the Execute Query button on the query window's toolbar. A new column called EmployeeID is added to the Employee table. The column is an IDENTITY column with a *seed* and *increment* of 1.

5. In the query window, execute this query:

```
exec sp_help Employee
```

Check to see that the IDENTITY column has been added.

Exercise 3.5: Adding Constraints to a Table

In this exercise, you add three constraints to the Employee table you created in Exercise 3.1. EmployeeID will have a PRIMARY KEY constraint, and SocialSecurityNumber will have a DEFAULT constraint and a UNIQUE constraint.

1. If it is not already loaded, open the SQL Query tool by selecting Tools, SQL Query Tool from the application's main menu.

2. Use the DB combo box to select the *Exercise3* database.

3. Type the following query in the query window:

```
ALTER TABLE Employee
ADD
    CONSTRAINT PK_Employee
        PRIMARY KEY (EmployeeID),
    CONSTRAINT UQ_SSN
        UNIQUE (SocialSecurityNumber),
    DEFAULT '000-00-0000' FOR SocialSecurityNumber
```

4. Execute the query by typing Alt-X or clicking the Execute Query button on the query window's toolbar. The constraints are added to the table.

5. In the query window, execute this query:

```
exec sp_help Employee
```

Notice that the three constraints show up in the results. The PRIMARY KEY and UNIQUE constraints show the names specified in step 3, and the DEFAULT constraint have a system-supplied name. Note also that the table has two new indexes to enforce the PK and UNIQUE constraints.

Exercise 3.6: Implementing a Relationship Using a REFERENCE Constraint

Exercise 3.6 walks you through the steps to build a new table, EmployeeCertification, that will store information about an employee's professional certifications. The table is a child of the Employee table, and has a relationship enforced by a REFERENCE constraint.

1. If it is not already loaded, open the SQL Query tool by selecting Tools, SQL Query Tool from the application's main menu.

2. Use the DB combo box to select the *Exercise3* database.

3. Type the following query in the query window:

```
CREATE TABLE EmployeeCertification
(
    EmployeeID                   int       NOT NULL REFERENCES
    ➥Employee(EmployeeID),
    CertificationTestNumber      char(5)   NOT NULL,
    DateTestPassed               datetime  NOT NULL,
    PRIMARY KEY (EmployeeID, CertificationTestNumber)
)
```

4. Execute the query by typing Alt-X or clicking the Execute Query button on the query window's toolbar. The new table is created. The first two columns are the primary key, and the EmployeeID column references the EmployeeID column in the Employee table.

5. In the query window, execute this query:

```
exec sp_help EmployeeCertification
```

Notice the two constraints on the table. Because the preceding query did not specify constraint names, system-supplied names will be used.

Review Questions

1. How many segments exist in a new database?

    A. Four

    B. One

    C. Five

    D. Three

2. The purpose of the transaction log is to:

    A. audit users' changes to the database

    B. ensure the integrity of the database in event of a system failure

    C. improve the performance of database changes

    D. keep track of changes made to the database so incomplete changes may be rolled back.

    E. allow up to the minute database recoverability

3. SQL Server uses what kind of transaction log?

    A. Read-ahead

    B. Write-ahead

    C. Fail-safe

    D. Write-cached

4. Which database option allows non-logged operations to occur?

    A. select into / bulkcopy

    B. IDENTITY_INSERT

    C. nolog

    D. CHECKPOINT

5. Placing the transaction log on a device separate from the data device(s) gives the following benefits: (select all that apply)

    A. Log size may be monitored.

    B. Incremental backups of the database may be created.

    C. Performance of logged operations may be improved.

    D. Non-logged operations are allowed.

    E. The transaction log will not compete with data for storage space.

6. Which of the following are true about databases and devices?

    A. Databases may contain more than one device.

    B. Different devices can reside on separate physical disks.

    C. Devices may contain more than one database.

    D. Databases may reside on more than one device.

    E. Databases may not reside on devices that are on different physical disks.

7. When using the CREATE DATABASE statement, the size of the database is expressed in:

    A. number of 2-K pages

    B. megabytes

    C. number of allocation units

8. What is the purpose of the FOR LOAD keyword in the CREATE DATABASE and ALTER DATABASE statements?

    A. It prevents changes to the database size until after the database is loaded from a backup.

    B. It forces all data pages in the new database to be zeroed out in preparation for a database load.

    C. It loads the specified database dump into the newly created database.

    D. It prevents users from accessing the database until after the database is loaded from a backup.

9. What is/are the effects of multiple database resizings?

    A. Database backups can be less reliable.

    B. Multiple database fragments make recoverability more difficult in the event of a master database corruption.

    C. Multiple database fragments have a negative performance impact.

    D. No adverse effects occur.

10. While adding a table to the database, you receive the following error message: "Can't allocate space for object 'tablename' in database 'dbname' because the 'default' segment is full. What is the best course of action?

    A. Expand the current data device, or create a new data device. Use ALTER DATABASE to expand the database log into the new space.

    B. Run DBCC SHRINKDB (dbname) to reclaim fragmented pages in the database.

    C. Expand the current data device, or create a new data device. Use ALTER DATABASE to expand the database into the new space.

    D. Expand the current log device, or create a new log device. Use ALTER DATABASE to expand the database log into the new space.

11. While adding a table to the database, you receive the following error message: "Can't allocate space for object 'tablename' in database 'dbname' because the 'logsegment' segment is full. What is the best course of action?

    A. Expand the current data device, or create a new data device. Use ALTER DATABASE to expand the database log into the new space.

    B. Run DBCC SHRINKDB (dbname, LOGONLY) to reclaim fragmented pages in the database transaction log.

C. Expand the current data device, or create a new data device. Use ALTER DATABASE to expand the database into the new space.

D. Expand the current log device, or create a new log device. Use ALTER DATABASE to expand the database log into the new space.

12. Which user(s) may run the CREATE DATABASE and ALTER DATABASE commands?

   A. The system administrator

   B. The database owner (DBO)

   C. Users granted permission to use CREATE DATABASE

13. Which database must you be in to execute the CREATE DATA-BASE, ALTER DATABASE, or DROP DATABASE command?

   A. *tempdb*

   B. *master*

   C. *model*

14. Which command is used to change database options?

   A. ALTER DATABASE

   B. RECONFIGURE

   C. sp_configure

   D. sp_dboption

15. What is/are the effect(s) of turning on the 'trunc. log on chkpt.' option?

   A. Committed transactions are removed from the log about once a minute.

   B. The transaction log may be dumped quickly for recovery purposes.

   C. Users may perform non-logged operations.

   D. The transaction log is less likely to fill up.

16. What are the Transact-SQL commands used to create and delete user-defined data types?

    A. CREATE UDDT and DROP UDDT

    B. sp_bindtype and sp_droptype

    C. sp_addtype and sp_droptype

    D. sp_addtype and sp_unbindtype

17. What are some benefits of user-defined types?

    A. UDTs give SQL Server the flexibility to store future data types.

    B. UDTs help document a database.

    C. UDTs provide consistent column properties for similar columns.

    D. UDTs help enforce column naming conventions.

18. Data types are used to define:

    A. the type of information stored in a table's column

    B. the type of information used in a local variable

    C. the type of information passed between triggers and tables

    D. the type of information used in a stored procedure's parameters

19. SQL Server maintains what types of information about a column in the table definition?

    A. Name, NULL option, and constraints

    B. Name, data type, and NULL option

    C. Name, data type, NULL option, and bytes of overhead

    D. Name, data type, NULL option, and constraints

20. What statement(s) are NOT true about tables and columns?

   A. A table may contain up to 250 columns.

   B. Column names must be unique within the database.

   C. Table and column names can be up to thirty characters in length.

   D. A table definition is really just a collection of column definitions.

21. When altering the structure of a table, which of the following rules apply (choose two)?

   A. New columns may be added with either NULL option.

   B. New columns may be added only if they allow NULLs.

   C. An existing column may be converted to an IDENTITY column.

   D. Columns of the *timestamp* data type cannot be added.

   E. A new IDENTITY column may be added if one does not already exist.

22. What is the purpose of the WITH NOCHECK option in the ALTER TABLE statement?

   A. All constraint checking is disabled to improve performance.

   B. Constraint checking is turned off for the table until turned back on with the WITH CHECK keyword.

   C. PRIMARY KEY and UNIQUE constraints are not checked for the duration of the table modification.

   D. CHECK and FOREIGN KEY / REFERENCE constraints are not checked for the duration of the table modification.

23. What are the three main types of data integrity implemented by SQL Server constraints?

    A. Domain integrity

    B. Attribute integrity

    C. Entity integrity

    D. Referential integrity

    E. Data type integrity

24. What is the syntax for defining a column in the CREATE TABLE statement?

    A. column_name, data_type [,{null_option | IDENTITY}]

    B. column_name [data_type [{null_option | IDENTITY}]]

    C. column_name data_type {null_option | IDENTITY}

    D. column_name data_type [{null_option | IDENTITY}]

25. How is a NOT NULL column added to an existing table?

    A. By using the ALTER TABLE statement

    B. By dropping and recreating the table

    C. By using ALTER TABLE to add a NULLable column, then using sp_changenull to change the column's NULL option

26. What are the benefits of procedural data integrity implemented using views, triggers, rules, and defaults?

    A. Less error-prone than constraints

    B. Lower execution overhead than constraints

    C. Cross-database referential integrity

    D. Maximum flexibility in handling data integrity violations

27. Which of the following statements about PRIMARY KEY constraints are true?

    A. They are implemented via a unique index.

    B. The constraint's index may be dropped and rebuilt independently of the constraint.

    C. The key column(s) may allow NULLs.

    D. They enforce entity integrity.

    E. The constraint's index is clustered by default.

28. A FOREIGN KEY constraint requires what type of constraint(s) in the referenced table?

    A. PRIMARY KEY

    B. CHECK

    C. FOREIGN KEY

    D. UNIQUE

29. When a constraint is declared at the column level (choose two):

    A. it has a lower execution overhead than a constraint declared at the table level

    B. it only applies to that column

    C. the syntax is to separate it from the column definition by a comma, such as:

    ```
    Column_name column_type [{null_option | IDENTITY}],
    constraint_definition
    ```

    D. the syntax is to separate it from the column definition by a space, such as:

    ```
    Column_name column_type [{null_option | IDENTITY}]
    constraint_definition
    ```

    E. no other constraints may be defined for that column

30. How does an administrator replace a missing row in a table with an IDENTITY column?

    A. By turning on the IDENTITY_INSERT option for the table and inserting a record with an explicit IDENTITY value

    B. By executing sp_insert_identity on the table

    C. By using sp_dboption to configure the database so that identity columns may be updated

    D. By dropping and recreating the table, then inserting the old records in the correct order

Answers to Review Questions

1. D

2. B,D,E

3. B

4. A

5. A,B,C,E

6. B,C,D

7. B

8. D

9. B

10. C

11. D

12. A,C

13. B

14. D

15. A,D

16. C

17. B,C

18. A,B,D

19. D

20. B

21. B,E

22. D

23. A,C,D

24. D

25. B

26. C,D

27. A,D,E

28. A,D

29. B,D

30. A

Answers to Test Yourself Questions at Beginning of Chapter

1. Keeping the transaction log on a separate device improves the recoverability of the database, prevents competition between the database and log for space, and can improve the performance of the database. See "Placement of the Transaction Log."

2. ALTER DATABASE, DBCC SHRINKDB. See "Changing the Size of a Database."

3. The *seed* value specifies the starting number for the auto-increment, and the *increment* value specifies the step used to increment to the next value. See "Using an IDENTITY Column."

4. CREATE TABLE, ALTER TABLE, DROP TABLE. See "Managing Tables."

5. Declarative Referential Integrity (DRI) constraints, which are used to enforce entity integrity and referential integrity, and Data Validation constraints, which are used to enforce domain integrity. See "Declarative Referential Integrity (DRI) Constraints" and "Data Validation Constraints."

6. Constraints have lower execution overhead than triggers, defaults, or rules, and tend to be less error-prone. See "Using Constraints."

Chapter

Retrieving Data

4

This chapter helps you prepare for the exam by covering the following objectives:

 Objectives

- ▶ Write SELECT statements to retrieve specified columns

- ▶ Write SELECT statements that use system functions

- ▶ Manipulate numeric, character, and datetime data using TSQL functions

- ▶ Select specific rows based on comparisons, ranges, lists, character strings, and search arguments

- ▶ Select rows using wildcards with the LIKE statement

- ▶ Format and sort query results

Test Yourself! Before reading this chapter, test yourself to determine how much study time you will need to devote to this section.

1. What is the syntax for a simple SELECT statement?

2. You want to return all the names and addresses of everyone in the Authors table. What statement would you use to accomplish this task?

3. You want to return every column from the Authors table, except one, without having to name every column. What statement would be the best way to accomplish this task?

4. You want to return all of the names from the Authors table in a single column with a heading of 'Names'. What statement would you use to accomplish this task?

5. Write a SELECT statement to return from the Titles table all the titles and what the price would be if discounted 10%.

6. Write a SELECT statement to return from the Titles table all the titles and the price, where the price is less than $15.

7. Write a SELECT statement to return all the names from the Authors table where the last name ends in 'ger'.

8. Write a SELECT statement that returns all the titles of books that have no price from the Titles table.

9. Write a SELECT statement that returns all the names and states, ordered by the state and last name from the Authors table.

Answers are located at the end of the chapter...

Retrieving data may be the most important function of a database. All the data in the world is worthless if it cannot be accessed. The basis for retrieving data in the SQL language is the SELECT statement. This chapter introduces you to the SELECT statement and describes how to retrieve formatted output from a single table. In this chapter you learn about the following:

▶ The general syntax of the SELECT statement

▶ How to choose columns for output

▶ Formatting and manipulating data for output

▶ How to choose rows for output using specific operators and wildcards

▶ Sorting result rows

Writing SELECT Statements: An Overview

Objective

SELECT statements tell SQL Server what data you are interested in. In the statement, you must describe to SQL Server what information you want, and where to go to get it. The rigid syntax of a SELECT statement is simply the way that you and SQL Server agree to communicate. If you properly form a SELECT command, the syntax forces you to put key information exactly where SQL Server expects to find it. Some of the information you must provide consists of the following: the tables where the data can be found, the columns of interest in those tables, the criteria that the data must meet to qualify for being returned, and the order and format that you want the data to be returned in.

You will see that you must know how to get the information you want yourself before you can tell SQL Server how to get it. This is why a clear, appropriately normalized data model is so important. SQL Server will never have a problem finding the tables where the information you need is kept, because you will always have to provide a clear plan to access the data yourself.

You are the one who must understand the data model and know how to use it. SQL Server does determine the optimal method of following your plan. SQL Server doesn't use any tables you don't tell it to or follow any criteria you don't provide. However, it tries to determine for itself how best to read the tables and what indexes, if any, it should use. If you consider your data model a roadmap, you must tell SQL Server where to go, but it decides what path to take to get there.

Here is the basic syntax for the SQL SELECT statement.

```
SELECT [ALL | DISTINCT] select_list
  [INTO [new_table_name]]
[FROM {table_name | view_name}[(optimizer_hints)]
[WHERE {search_conditions}]
[ORDER BY {column_name}]
```

Because the square brackets denote optional parameters, you can see that very little is actually required for a proper SELECT statement. A legitimate statement can consist of nothing more than the 'SELECT' keyword and a 'select_list'.

There are four clauses that are used most often in SELECT statements. They are:

▶ SELECT—specifies columns to be returned

▶ FROM—specifies the table

▶ WHERE—specifies the rows to be returned

▶ ORDER BY—specifies a sorting order

These four clauses together can allow data to be retrieved from tables and formatted to your needs. There are other keywords that can be used to build more powerful queries, and they are described in Chapter 5, "Retrieving Data (Advanced Topics)."

Here is an example of a simple SELECT statement executed in the sample database Pubs that comes with SQL SERVER.

```
SELECT *
FROM authors
WHERE au_lname >= 'Smith'
ORDER BY au_lname
```

This statement returns all the rows from the Authors table where the author's last name is greater than or equal to 'Smith' in alphabetical order.

Choosing Columns

A SELECT * command is perhaps the simplest possible statement for retrieving data. It simply returns all the columns from the table specified in the order in which the table was originally created. This allows a statement to be written very quickly, with minimal knowledge about the structure of the table you are querying.

The ease of this command is offset, however, by its inflexibility. Most often you will want to specify exactly what columns to retrieve and what order they should be in. Specifying columns also enables you to add formatting commands to each column to perform arithmetic operations, capitalize strings, and many other operations to improve the appearance of your data.

Specifying Columns and Column Order

It is the asterisk, '*', following the keyword SELECT that commands SQL Server to return all columns. To return specific columns, you include a list of all the columns you want to see, in the order that you want to see them. To do this, simply replace the '*' with the names of the specific columns you want to return, separated by commas.

 Tip

Explicitly entering every column from a table in the SELECT list can be tedious and more likely to lead to spelling and typing errors. To quickly obtain a list of all columns, start by running a SELECT * statement in Enterprise Manager. The result set you get back has all of the column names of the table in the first line of the heading. This line can be copied right over the '*' in your SELECT statement, giving you an automatic list of all the column names. You still need to put commas between each column name, and you will almost certainly want to eliminate the extra spaces you end up with, but for a table containing ten or more columns, this can be a real timesaver.

If you only wanted to see the names of the authors, you could rewrite the example like this:

```
SELECT au_fname, au_lname
FROM Authors
WHERE au_lname >= 'Smith'
ORDER BY au_lname
```

Notice that in this example, not only is the output limited to just the name fields, the order in which the columns are returned is changed by specifying au_fname first.

 Note

Specifying the columns in your queries serves a greater purpose than just formatting. It also enables you to limit the amount of data that needs to be returned to you from the server. The transfer of data over a network to a local machine can often be the slowest portion of issuing a query. For the best response, you should always try to limit your results to only the columns needed.

Specifying Column Headings

When you specify the columns you want to see, you also have the opportunity to change the headings that SQL Server returns. By default, the heading of each column is the name of the column itself in the table. You can change that heading in either of two ways. The first is by including the keyword AS after the column name, followed by our own label. Or you can include the label before the column name with an equal sign between the two.

The syntax for each is as follows:

```
SELECT column_name [AS] column_heading [, column_name…]
FROM table_name
```

-OR-

```
SELECT column_heading = column_name [, column_name…]
FROM table_name
```

Note that the keyword AS in the first form of the syntax is optional and can be omitted. Your column headings may include spaces if you desire, but to do so the entire heading must then be surrounded by quotes. The syntax is shown below, followed by an example.

```
Column_heading = 'string literal' | string_literal
```

An example:

```
SELECT au_fname 'first name', au_lname 'last name'
FROM Authors
```

Using Literals as Columns

It is also possible to specify literals in the returned columns. These can be in the form of literal strings, essentially labels inserted into the result set, or constant arithmetic expressions. Both expressions are inserted into the column list as though they were columns themselves. Literal strings are surrounded by quotes to distinguish them from column names, but arithmetic expressions are automatically recognized without special delimiters.

The syntax is as follows:

```
SELECT column_name | 'string literal' | arithmetic_expression [,
➡column_name...]
FROM table_name
```

 **Note**

Note that string literals and arithmetic expressions don't automatically receive column headings in the result set returned by SQL Server. This is because there is no column name for the heading to default to. If a heading is needed, it can be supplied in the same fashion as you saw earlier.

Using string literals in columns can enable you to embed labels into your result sets. The value of using numeric literals can be as simple as using SQL Server as an overpriced calculator. See the following examples:

```
SELECT 'The book ', title, ' costs $', price
FROM Titles
SELECT 2+2
```

Formatting and Manipulating Data for Output

 Objective

SQL Server supplies many functions to aid in formatting, and manipulating data for output. There are special string and date functions, all the basic arithmetic operators, and more complex numeric functions. There also are special system functions that return information about the SQL Server environment.

Using String Functions

String functions allow detailed formatting of character data. There are functions to capitalize strings, trim leading or trailing spaces, even functions to search strings for a specified pattern. All these functions can accept a column name or a string literal for the char_expr, but note that string literals must be enclosed by quotes. These functions listed in table 4.1 also can be found with greater detail in the Transact-SQL Reference included with the SQL Server client tools, by searching for String Functions.

Table 4.1

String Functions		
Functions	Parameters	Result
+	(expression + expression)	Concatenates two character strings, binary strings, column names, or a combination of them.
Ascii	(char_expr)	Indicates the ASCII code value of the leftmost character of a character expression.
Char	(integer_expr)	Converts a character from an ASCII code. Returns NULL if code is out of range.

Functions	Parameters	Result
Charindex	('pattern', expression)	Returns the starting position of the specified pattern. A pattern is a char_expr.
Difference	(char_expr1, char_expr2)	The difference function compares two strings and evaluates the similarity between them, returning the value from 0 through 4. The value 4 is the best match.
Lower	(char_expr)	Converts character data to lowercase.
Ltrim	(char_expr)	Removes leading blanks.
Patindex	('%pattern%', expression)	Returns the starting position of the first occurrence of pattern in the specified expression.
Replicate	(char_expr, integer_expr)	Repeats a character expression a specified number of times.
Reverse	(char_expr)	Returns the reverse of char_expr.
Right	(char_expr, integer_expr)	Returns the rightmost integer expr characters.
Rtrim	(char_expr)	Removes trailing blanks.
Soundex	(char_expr)	Returns a four-digit (SOUNDEX) code to evaluate the similarity of two strings.
Space	(integer_expr)	Returns integer_expr number of spaces.
Str	(float_expr [, length [, decimal]])	Returns character data converted from numeric data.

continues

Table 4.1 Continued

String Functions

Functions	Parameters	Result
Stuff	(char_expr1, start, length, char_expr2)	Deletes length characters from char_expr1 at start and then inserts char_expr2 into char_expr1 at start.
Substring	(expression, start, length)	Returns length number of characters from expression beginning at start position.
Upper	(char_expr)	Converts lowercase character data to uppercase.

The following are examples and the resulting output of a few of the functions in the preceding table.

```
SELECT 'Answer is: ' + Substring('123456',2,3)
```

Result—Answer is: 234

```
SELECT 'Name is: ' + Upper('john')
```

Result—Name is: JOHN

```
SELECT 'Name is: ' + Rtrim('john    ') + 'doe'
```

Result—Name is: johndoe

Date Functions

There also are several functions provided by SQL Server for working with date fields. These functions enable dates to be added and subtracted, and even broken down into days, months, years, and times. These functions can be used in the SELECT clause to allow date columns to be formatted, but they also are often useful in the WHERE clause, for example, to specify all rows in the month of January. The date parameter of these functions can take a date column or a date literal. When passing a date literal, remember to enclose the string in quotes. Table 4.2 lists all the date functions and a brief description.

Table 4.2

Date Functions

Function	Parameters	Results
Dateadd	(datepart, number, date)	Adds the number of dateparts to the date.
Datediff	(datepart, date1, date2)	Returns the number of dateparts between date1 and date2.
Datename	(datepart, date)	Returns the datepart of the date in character format. (Ex. 'January' or 'Monday').
Datepart	(datepart, date)	Returns the datepart of the date in numeric format. (Ex. 7 or 2).
Getdate	()	Returns the current system date.

Table 4.3 describes the codes SQL Server recognizes as dateparts, and the values for each:

Table 4.3

Dateparts

Datepart	Abbreviation	Values
Year	Yy	1753–9999
Quarter	Qq	1–4
Month	Mm	1–12
Day of Year	Dy	1–366
Day	Dd	1–31
Week	Wk	1–53

continues

Table 4.3   Continued

Dateparts		
Datepart	Abbreviation	Values
Weekday	Dw	1–7 (Sun.–Sat.)
Hour	Hh	0–23
Minute	Mi	0–59
Second	Ss	0–59
Millisecond	Ms	0–999

An example of using dateparts and their values follows.

```
SELECT 'Date is: ' + Dateadd(MM,4,'Jan 1 1900')
```

Result—Date is: May 1 1900 12:00AM

Numeric Operations

SQL Server supports five common mathematical operations for working with numeric data. These operators can be used wherever an expression is allowed in a SELECT statement. Each operator is listed in table 4.4.

Table 4.4

Mathematical Operators	
Symbol	Operation
+	Addition
–	Subtraction
/	Division
*	Multiplication
%	Modulo (remainder of integer division)

These operations are all familiar mathematical functions except, perhaps, for the modulo function. Modulo only operates on integers. It returns the remainder of division between the two integers.

This remainder is always an integer between zero and one less than the divisor.

One simple trick of the modulo function is to test a number as even or odd. If you take any number modulo two, the result is always zero or one. So by taking the modulo two of any number, the result of zero or one indicates if the original number is even or odd, respectively.

All of the preceding functions can be used with any numeric datatype, except modulo, which can only be used with integer types.

When processing mathematical formulas, SQL Server evaluates multiplicative expressions first, then additive expressions. Expressions with equal precedence are evaluated from left to right. This default precedence can be overridden by using parentheses to group operations that should be evaluated first in the expression. Expressions that are grouped in parentheses are always evaluated first in the statement.

For more powerful mathematical operations, SQL Server provides the following functions listed in table 4.5:

Table 4.5

More Powerful Mathematical Operators

Function	Parameters	Result
Abs	(numeric_expr)	Absolute value of the numeric expression.
Acos	(float_expr)	Angle (in radians) whose cosine is the specified approximate numeric (float) expression.
Asin	(float_expr)	Angle (in radians) whose sine is the specified approximate numeric (float) expression.

continues

Table 4.5 Continued

Function	Parameters	Result
Atan	(float_expr)	Angle (in radians) whose tangent is the specified approximate numeric (float) expression.
Atn2	(float_expr1, float_expr2)	Angle (in radians) whose tangent is (float_expr1/ float_expr2) between two approximate numeric (float) expressions.
Ceiling	(numeric_expr)	Smallest integer greater than or equal to the numeric expression.
Cos	(float_expr)	Trigonometric cosine of the specified angle (in radians) in an approximate numeric (float) expression.
Cot	(float_expr)	Trigonometric cotangent of the specified angle (in radians) in an approximate numeric (float) expression.
Degrees	(numeric_expr)	Degrees converted from radians of the numeric expression.
Exp	(float_expr)	Exponential value of the specified approximate numeric (float) expression.
Floor	(numeric_expr)	Largest integer less than or equal to the specified numeric expression.
Log	(float_expr)	Natural logarithm of the specified approximate numeric (float) expression.
Log10	(float_expr)	Base-10 logarithm of the specified approximate numeric (float) expression.

Function	Parameters	Result
Pi	( )	Constant value of 3.141592653589793.
Power	(numeric_expr, y)	Value of numeric expression to the power of y, where y is a numeric datatype (decimal, float, int, money, numeric, real, smallint, smallmoney, or tinyint).
Radians	(numeric_expr)	Radians converted from degrees of the numeric expression.
Rand	([seed])	Random approximate numeric (float) value between 0 and 1, optionally specifying an integer expression as the seed.
Round	(numeric_expr, length)	Numeric expression rounded off to the length (or precision) specified as an integer expression.
Sign	(numeric_expr)	Returns the positive (+1), zero (0), or negative (−1) sign of the numeric expression.
Sin	(float_expr)	Trigonometric sine of the specified angle (measured in radians) in an approximate numeric (float) expression.
Sqrt	(float_expr)	Square root of the specified approximate numeric (float) expression.
Tan	(float_expr)	Trigonometric tangent of the specified angle (measured in radians) in an approximate numeric (float) expression.

In the following example the value of Pi is rounded to four decimal places.

```
SELECT Round(Pi(), 4)
```

Results in—3.1416

 **Note**   Note that not all operations can accept all data types.

Using the Convert Function

SQL Server also provides a special CONVERT function that is used specifically for converting one data type to another. With the CONVERT function you can perform comparisons between character columns that contain numeric information and numeric data types, and vice versa.

The CONVERT function also provides many options for date formats. Date columns are stored internally as numbers, but are most commonly converted to character types for display, so the CONVERT function includes the ability to format the information during the conversion. This function can be used anywhere in a SELECT statement that expressions are used.

The syntax for the CONVERT function is as follows:

```
CONVERT (datatype[(length)], expression [,style])
```

The style parameter in the preceding syntax includes the forms outlined in table 4.6.

Table 4.6

Style Parameters			
Without Century (yy)	With Century (yyyy)	Standard	Output
–	0 or 100	Default	Mon dd yyyy hh:mi AM (or PM)

Without century (yy)	With century (yyyy)	Standard	Output
1	101	USA	mm/dd/yy
2	102	ANSI	yy.mm.dd
3	103	British/French	dd/mm/yy
4	104	German	dd.mm.yy
5	105	Italian	dd-mm-yy
6	106	–	dd mon yy
7	107	–	Mon dd, yy
8	108	–	hh:mm:ss
–	9 or 109	Default + milliseconds	Mon dd yyyy hh:mi:ss:mmm AM (or PM)
10	110	USA	mm-dd-yy
11	111	JAPAN	yy/mm/dd
12	112	ISO	Yymmdd
–	13 or 113	Europe default + milliseconds	dd mon yyyy hh:mm:ss:mmm (24h)
14	114	–	hh:mi:ss:mmm (24h)

 **Note**   The default values (style 0 or 100, 9 or 109, and 13 or 113) always return the century (yyyy).

System Functions

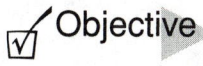 **Objective**   There are many functions provided by SQL Server that do not readily fit into any one of the categories just discussed. These functions are all grouped together as System Functions (see table 4.7). Many of these functions provide a shortcut to looking up common information from system tables. For example, the User ID can be found for a user name, or the Object ID can be found

for an object name. Other functions provide information about a given piece of data, such as the length of a string. Two functions in particular, IsNull and NullIf, provide powerful methods of handling NULL data.

Table 4.7

System Functions

System Function	Parameters	Result
Coalesce	(expression1, expression2, ... expressionN)	Returns the first non-NULL expression. For details, see the CASE statement.
Col_Length	('table_name', 'column_name')	The defined length of a column.
Col_Name	(table_id, column_id)	The name of the column.
Datalength	('expression')	The actual length of an expression of any datatype. Because varchar, varbinary, text, and image datatypes can store variable-length data, Datalength is especially useful with those datatypes.
Db_ID	(['database_name'])	The database identification number.
Db_Name	([database_id])	The database name.
Getansinull	(['database_name'])	The default nullability for the database. This function returns 1 when the nullability is the ANSI NULL default.
Host_ID	( )	The workstation identification number.
Host_Name	( )	The workstation name.
Ident_Incr	('table_name')	The increment value (returned as numeric (@@MAXPRECISION,0)) specified during creation of an identity column.

System Function	Parameters	Result
Ident_Seed	('table_name')	The seed value (returned as numeric (@@MAXPRECI-SION,0)) specified during creation of an identity column.
Index_Col	('table_name', index_id, key_id)	The indexed column name.
IsNull	(expression, value)	Replaces NULL entries with the specified value.
NullIf	(expression1, expression2)	The resulting expression is NULL when expression1 is equivalent to expression2. For details, see the CASE statement.
Object_ID	('object_name')	The database object identification number.
Object_Name	(object_id)	The database object name.
Stats_Date	(table_id, index_id)	The date that the statistics for the specified index (index_id) were last updated.
Suser_ID	(['login_name'])	The user's login identification number.
Suser_Name	(['server_user_id'])	The user's login identification name.
User_ID	(['user_name'])	The user's database identification number.
User_Name	(['user_id'])	The user's database user name.

This following is an example of the syntax using Datalength from the preceding table in a query (see fig. 4.1).

```
SELECT 'Number of characters in ' + rtrim(au_lname) + ' is: ',
Datalength(au_lname)
FROM Authors
```

Figure 4.1

Example of Datalength function.

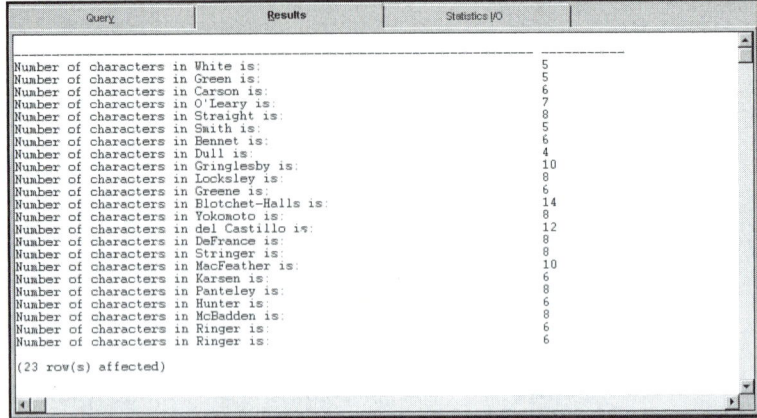

```
                              Query              |        Results         |     Statistics I/O
Number of characters in White is:                                5
Number of characters in Green is:                                5
Number of characters in Carson is:                               6
Number of characters in O'Leary is:                              7
Number of characters in Straight is:                             8
Number of characters in Smith is:                                5
Number of characters in Bennet is:                               6
Number of characters in Dull is:                                 4
Number of characters in Gringlesby is:                           10
Number of characters in Locksley is:                             8
Number of characters in Greene is:                               6
Number of characters in Blotchet-Halls is:                       14
Number of characters in Yokomoto is:                             8
Number of characters in del Castillo is:                         12
Number of characters in DeFrance is:                             8
Number of characters in Stringer is:                             8
Number of characters in MacFeather is:                           10
Number of characters in Karsen is:                               6
Number of characters in Panteley is:                             8
Number of characters in Hunter is:                               6
Number of characters in McBadden is:                             8
Number of characters in Ringer is:                               6
Number of characters in Ringer is:                               6

(23 row(s) affected)
```

Using DISTINCT and ALL Keywords

There are two optional keywords that can be used in the SELECT clause of a SELECT statement. DISTINCT and ALL specify whether to include duplicate rows in the result set.

ALL is the default assumed if neither option is specified. ALL indicates that all rows meeting the SELECT criteria should be returned to the user regardless of duplicate information.

DISTINCT indicates that of all rows in the result set that are exact duplicates, only one should be returned. This does not mean that the rows filtered out by the DISTINCT keyword are duplicates in the table from which they were retrieved, only that the data included in the columns returned formed duplicates. If a column with a unique index is part of the result set of a query on a single table, the DISTINCT keyword will have no effect.

The following example illustrates the use of the ALL keyword in the SELECT statement and its effect on the resulting output (see fig. 4.2).

```
SELECT ALL State
FROM Authors
```

Figure 4.2

Result of the ALL keyword example.

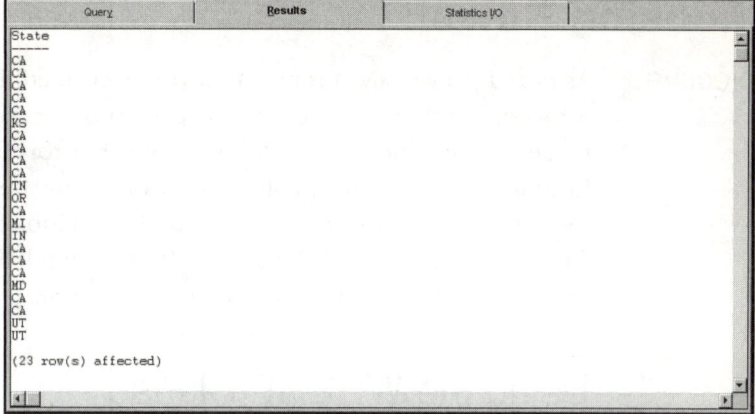

The following example illustrates the use of the DISTINCT keyword in the SELECT statement and its effect on the resulting output (see fig. 4.3).

```
SELECT DISTINCT State
FROM Authors
```

Figure 4.3

Result of the DISTINCT keyword example.

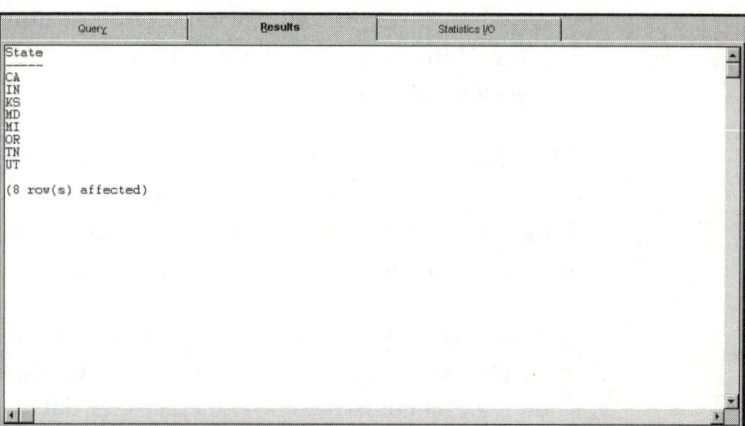

 **Note**

Note that the DISTINCT keyword refers to the entire row of data being returned. It is not possible to use DISTINCT to eliminate duplicates in just one column. The GROUP BY clause explained in the next chapter can be used to group multiple rows together based on specific columns.

Choosing Rows

 Objective

As noted previously, it is rare that you ever need to return all the information that is in a table. Most often there is a particular piece or a specific set of entities for which information is needed. Limiting the number of columns isn't the only option. Instead of returning the entire contents of a table and looking for the rows you need, the WHERE clause enables you to tell SQL Server exactly what rows you are looking for in the table.

Using the WHERE Clause

The WHERE clause of a SELECT statement enables you to filter out certain rows from a table. The most common operations to perform for making row selections are simple comparisons. These operations enable you to specify rows that are equal to, greater than, or less than values you supply. All of these operations rely heavily on the sort order that your server is using to determine what values are "greater than" others. The idea of greater and lesser values is very straightforward when dealing with numbers. The very nature of a number system makes comparisons of this type very simple.

With character data things are not so clear. For example, what value is less than the other when comparing 'A' and 'a'? SQL Server uses the sort order defined at installation to make the judgement as to which characters have precedence in comparisons.

The sort order defines a ranking of all the possible characters to make comparisons easy. This ranking lets you know what to expect when making comparisons with character data.

 Note

To determine the sort order that your server is using, issue the command sp_helpsort. This stored procedure is supplied by SQL Server to briefly describe the sort order and to show all the allowable characters in order. Note that some characters are considered equal to each other even though they are different characters. This is especially true for case-insensitive orders, where lowercase and uppercase characters are not differentiated. The results of the command are seen in figure 4.4.

Figure 4.4

Result of stored procedure sp_helpsort.

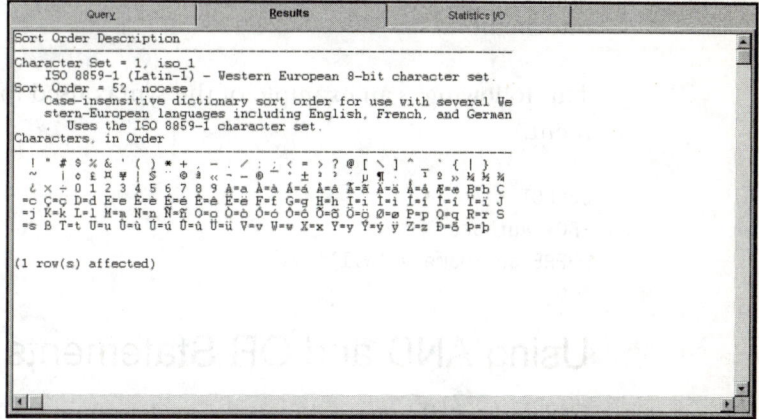

Using Comparison Operators

The complete set of comparison operators is as follows:

- ▶ = Equal to
- ▶ > Greater than
- ▶ < Less than
- ▶ >= Greater than or equal to
- ▶ <= Less than or equal to
- ▶ <> Not equal to
- ▶ != Not equal to
- ▶ !> Not greater than
- ▶ !< Not less than

Comparisons to Literals

Row selection is most commonly done by comparisons to literal values. For example, you can return all the books that cost less than $15.00, or all the authors with the last name of 'Williams'. Using comparisons like this enables you to quickly locate specific information.

This following is an example of the syntax used for a literal statement.

```
SELECT *
FROM Authors
WHERE au_lname = 'Williams'
```

Using AND and OR Statements

It also is possible to make selections based on multiple criteria. This is done by using the keywords AND and OR between each of the selection expressions. The conjunction AND specifies that all selection criteria must be met for a row to be returned, whereas the OR specifies that either of the joined expressions is enough to make a selection.

Parentheses should be used to group AND and OR conjunctions together to avoid ambiguity over which expressions should be evaluated first and subsequently performed in the query. If parentheses are not used, SQL Server evaluates AND clauses first.

This following is an example of the syntax used for AND and OR statements.

```
SELECT rtrim(au_fname) + ' ' + rtrim(au_lname) 'Author Name',
➥state, city
FROM Authors
WHERE (state = 'CA' AND City != 'Oakland')
OR   (City = 'Salt Lake City')
```

Figure 4.5 provides the data you would expect from the example.

Figure 4.5

Result of a SELECT statement with multiple criteria.

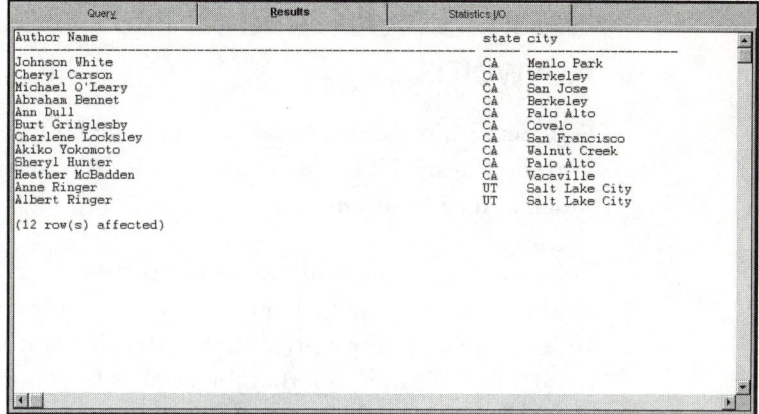

```
Query              Results              Statistics I/O
Author Name                                    state city
-------------------------------------------------------------
Johnson White                                  CA    Menlo Park
Cheryl Carson                                  CA    Berkeley
Michael O'Leary                                CA    San Jose
Abraham Bennet                                 CA    Berkeley
Ann Dull                                       CA    Palo Alto
Burt Gringlesby                                CA    Covelo
Charlene Locksley                              CA    San Francisco
Akiko Yokomoto                                 CA    Walnut Creek
Sheryl Hunter                                  CA    Palo Alto
Heather McBadden                               CA    Vacaville
Anne Ringer                                    UT    Salt Lake City
Albert Ringer                                  UT    Salt Lake City

(12 row(s) affected)
```

Using the BETWEEN and NOT BETWEEN Keywords

SQL Server provides a useful tool for specifying data within a set range of values by supporting the BETWEEN keyword. BETWEEN specifies an inclusive range of values in a shorthand notation.

The following examples are exactly equivalent statements.

```
SELECT *
FROM Titles
WHERE Price BETWEEN 5.00 AND 20.00
SELECT *
FROM Titles
WHERE Price >= 5.00
AND Price <= 20.00
```

Note

Note that the BETWEEN keyword does not provide any unique functionality, it only allows for shortened notation of statements that could be built without the use of BETWEEN.

It is possible to find all values that do not fall in the range specified by including the NOT keyword before BETWEEN.

Using IS NULL and IS NOT NULL Keywords

SQL Server provides the special value of NULL to represent unknown values. NULL does not so much indicate any value as much as it indicates no value.

For example, if you didn't know the price of a certain book, you could set a price of $0.00, but that isn't very clear because $0.00 isn't a legal value for a price. It is better that you specify the price as NULL, indicating not that the book is free, but that you don't know the value.

Because NULL indicates the lack of any value, it behaves differently in comparison statements. In a comparison a NULL value is not greater, nor less than any other value. Comparing any value to be greater or less than NULL always returns false.

Equal and not equal comparisons can be expressed against the keyword NULL with expected results, but these comparisons between columns do not return NULL records. Returning all the rows from a table where the Price column equals itself, for example, does not return any rows with a price of NULL. Returning all the rows from a table where the Price does not equal itself does not return any rows whatsoever. In either case, the NULL values were excluded from the results. This behavior of the keyword NULL, acting as it does in one manner, but acting differently with column values of NULL, can be very confusing.

For this reason, SQL Server provides the IS keyword. Using IS NULL is the preferred method of specifying that you want to return NULL values. The NOT keyword can be used in conjunction with the IS keyword to specify that you want to return rows where a field IS NOT NULL. By always using the IS keyword to compare a value to the keyword NULL, this confusing behavior of NULL comparisons can be avoided. Always use the IS keyword, and otherwise expect NULL values to be excluded from equal comparisons.

The following statement does not return any records where the price is NULL.

```
SELECT Title, Price
FROM Titles
WHERE Price = Price
```

The following is an example of the syntax used for the IS NULL statement to return all the books that have not had a price set yet. Figure 4.6 depicts the results of the query.

```
SELECT Title, Price
FROM Titles
WHERE Price IS NULL
```

Figure 4.6

Result of IS NULL keyword example.

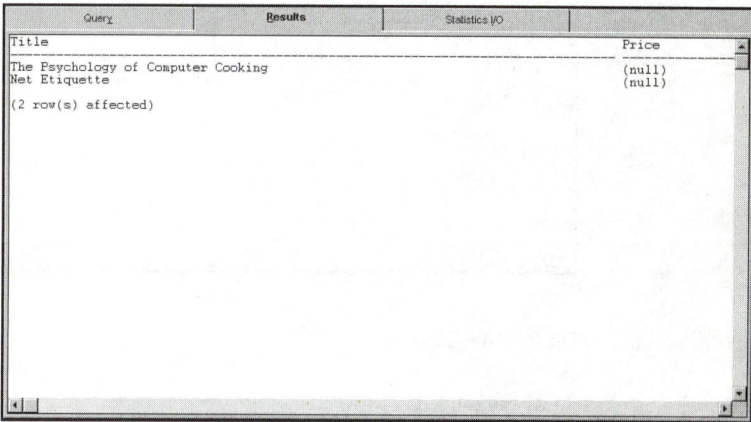

This following is an example of the syntax used for the IS NOT NULL statement. Here, you are trying to assemble a list of only those titles that have a price set. Figure 4.7 depicts the results of the query.

```
SELECT Title, Price
FROM Titles
WHERE Price IS NOT NULL
```

NULL values always sort first regardless of the server's sort order.

Using IN and NOT IN Statements

Instead of comparing columns to individual values, it also is possible to find where a column value is equal to any single member of a list. This enables a much more compact syntax than multiple 'equal to' expressions chained together by OR clauses. By comparing in lists, SQL Server also is able to optimize its search, giving better performance than evaluating multiple OR clauses. Comparing to lists is accomplished with the IN keyword, by evaluating where the values of a column are 'IN' a parenthetical list of values separated by commas.

Figure 4.7

Result of the IS NOT NULL example.

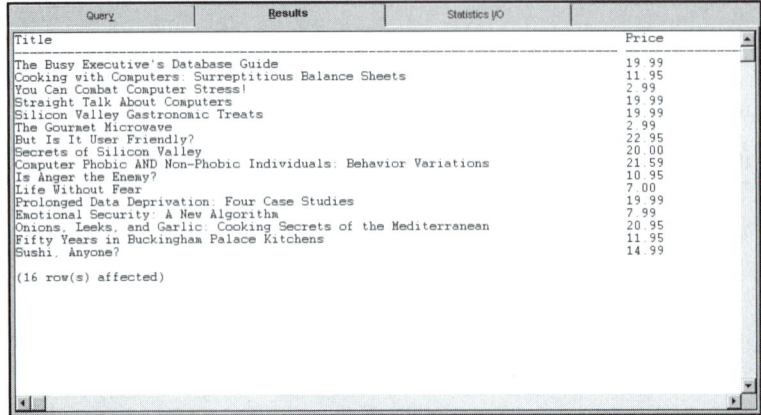

```
Title                                                              Price
The Busy Executive's Database Guide                                19.99
Cooking with Computers: Surreptitious Balance Sheets               11.95
You Can Combat Computer Stress!                                    2.99
Straight Talk About Computers                                      19.99
Silicon Valley Gastronomic Treats                                  19.99
The Gourmet Microwave                                              2.99
But Is It User Friendly?                                           22.95
Secrets of Silicon Valley                                          20.00
Computer Phobic AND Non-Phobic Individuals: Behavior Variations    21.59
Is Anger the Enemy?                                                10.95
Life Without Fear                                                  7.00
Prolonged Data Deprivation: Four Case Studies                      19.99
Emotional Security: A New Algorithm                                7.99
Onions, Leeks, and Garlic: Cooking Secrets of the Mediterranean    20.95
Fifty Years in Buckingham Palace Kitchens                          11.95
Sushi, Anyone?                                                     14.99

(16 row(s) affected)
```

The syntax follows:

```
SELECT select_list
FROM table_list
WHERE [NOT] expression [NOT] IN (value_list)
```

Note

Note that there are two possible locations for the NOT keyword allowed by the syntax. While the statement can be negated by including the NOT keyword in either location, using NOT in both locations results in the two canceling each other's effects.

Using LIKE Statements

Objective

It also is possible to do wildcard matching on strings. The key word LIKE is used in place of the equal sign to indicate a wildcard matching expression.

SQL Server provides four different wildcards for pattern matching expressions, as shown in table 4.8.

Table 4.8

Wildcard Expressions

Wildcard	Meaning
%	Any string of zero or more characters
_ (underscore)	Any single character
[ ]	Any single character within the specified range ([a–f]) or set ([abcdef])
[^]	Any single character not within the specified range ([^a–f]) or set ([^abcdef])

When constructing a pattern string, remember that every character in that string is significant, including spaces. While trailing spaces are usually ignored in comparisons, if they are explicitly stated in the pattern string, then they must exist in the data string found.

The following is an example of the syntax for the LIKE keyword, with the results shown in figure 4.8

```
SELECT rtrim(au_fname) + ' ' + rtrim(au_lname) 'Author Name',
state, city
FROM Authors
WHERE au_lname LIKE '%ger'
```

Figure 4.8

Result of the LIKE keyword example.

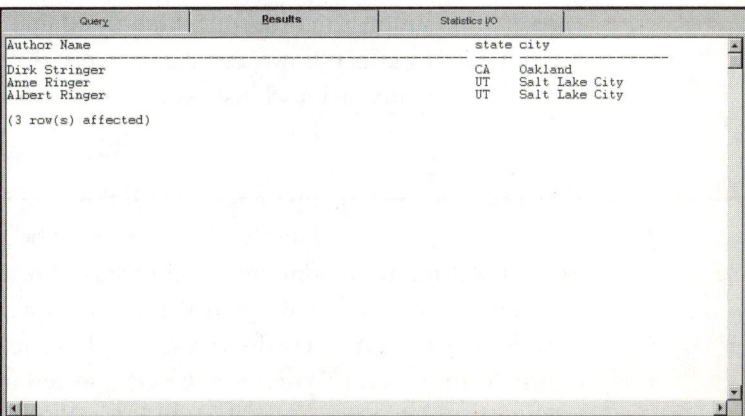

```
Author Name                                          state city
------------------------------------                 ----- -----
Dirk Stringer                                        CA    Oakland
Anne Ringer                                          UT    Salt Lake City
Albert Ringer                                        UT    Salt Lake City

(3 row(s) affected)
```

The LIKE operator is extremely useful when comparing a specific time or date. The datetime data type holds many different parts including, month, day, year, hour, minute, and more. Very often, only a specific date is needed and the time is considered irrelevant. Using the LIKE operator, a pattern can be easily constructed that specifies the date, but will accept any time. This method is usually easier than specifying a range of dates and times to search on.

```
SELECT Title
FROM Titles
WHERE Title LIKE '%ix %'
```

Sorting Result Rows

 Objective

In addition to choosing the rows to return in a result table, you may want to exercise control over the order in which those rows appear in the table. SQL Server provides a straightforward means for sorting result rows.

The Importance of Sorting

The ORDER BY clause enables you to specify that SQL Server should return the data in a specific order. Order can be crucial to efficient and accurate interpretation of large result sets. By default, the data you request is returned in what is called *database order*. This is simply the order in which the data happens to reside in the table. In effect, however, you have no guarantees that the data will be in any order whatsoever if no ORDER BY clause is specified.

Very often, when a database is created, the data is first loaded into it in large loads. This data that is loaded may be sorted by some value, resulting in the data residing in sorted order in the tables. When this data is queried it may therefore appear in the order desired naturally. As records are modified, however, this order gradually disappears. When the data is queried in the future, it may seem to be in the order desired but with several records scattered randomly throughout or even miscellaneous records gathered together at the end of the list. Thus, key information being sought may be missed.

Using the ORDER BY Statement

The ORDER BY statement has the following syntax:

```
SELECT select_list
FROM table_list
WHERE search_conditions
ORDER BY column_name | select_list_number | expression [ASC | DESC]
[,column_name | select_list_number | expression [ASC | DESC] ..]
```

The items in the ORDER BY clause determine the ordering of the results in decreasing importance. The listed items are normally columns in the SELECT list. In this case the first column listed is sorted throughout the result set, the second column is sorted within duplicates of the first, and so on.

The items in the sort list should be referenced by column heading if one is given. If a function is used on a table column, SQL Server supplies no name for that result column unless a column heading is given. If a column heading is not supplied, the entire result column description, function name and all, can be used in the ORDER BY. Alternately, the columns in the SELECT list can be referenced by their ordinal position. Though it is less clear to anyone reading your query later, it can be much faster to simply list the number of the column to sort by, instead of entering a long formula as a column identifier. Finally, SQL Server enables you to sort by a table column that is not even returned by the query.

 Note

Note that many SQL databases do not allow sorting on columns not included in the SELECT list. In these systems, when a user-supplied heading is given to a column, that heading, or the ordinal position of the column in the SELECT list, must be how the column is referenced in the ORDER BY clause, because the actual column name is not recognized. It is SQL Server's ability to sort on non-returned columns that enables you to use the original table column name rather than an explicit heading.

The following examples are all equivalent and would produce the results found in figure 4.9.

```
SELECT rtrim(au_fname) + ' ' + rtrim(au_lname) 'Author Name',
state, city
FROM Authors
ORDER BY state, rtrim(au_fname) + ' ' + rtrim(au_lname)

SELECT rtrim(au_fname) + ' ' + rtrim(au_lname) 'Author Name',
state, city
FROM Authors
ORDER BY 2, 1

SELECT rtrim(au_fname) + ' ' + rtrim(au_lname) 'Author Name',
state, city
FROM Authors
ORDER BY state, 'Author Name'
```

Figure 4.9

Result of the ORDER BY clause examples.

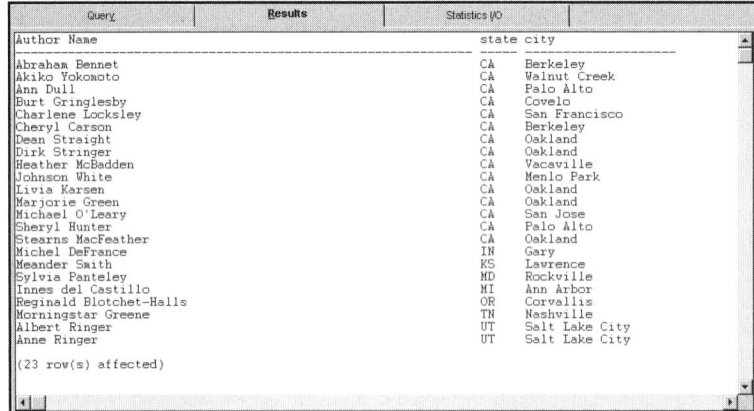

Summary

In summary, this chapter covered several objectives that assist in retrieving information from a selected table. These objectives included writing a SELECT statement and selecting specific rows based on many different operators. You have learned how to manipulate character, numeric, and date data using Transact SQL functions, and you have written SELECT statements that use system functions. You can format and sort the query results.

Using these concepts, you can retrieve information from any single table, format the results, and restrict the amount of data brought back, so that only the necessary information is returned in the result set. Once this is accomplished, you should be ready to expand the selections to multiple tables, knowing that the information is easily restricted so as not to be overwhelming and that the data can be presented in the clearest format possible.

In the next chapter you will learn how to join multiple tables in a single statement, how to use the GROUP BY, HAVING, and COMPUTE clauses to return summary data, and how to use subqueries to help perform certain complex data retrievals.

Exercises

Pubs, the sample database that comes with SQL Server, is used throughout these exercises.

Exercise 4.1: Executing a Simple Query

The purpose of this exercise is to use the Query tool in Enterprise Manager to execute a simple query.

1. Load Enterprise Manager and open a Query Window by choosing SQL Query Tool from the Tools menu.

2. From the DB drop-down box choose Pubs.

3. Type in the following SELECT statement to retrieve all columns and all rows from the Titles table.

```
SELECT *
FROM Titles
```

4. Run the query by hitting the Execute Query button, or by typing Ctrl-E.

5. The Query Tab switches to the Results Tab and the screen quickly fills with the results of your query.

Exercise 4.2: Retrieving Data from a Table

The purpose of this example is to write several simple SELECT statements to retrieve data from the Titles table.

1. Write a query to return only the Title, Price, and Year-to-Date sales from the Titles table (columns title, price, and ytd_sales).

2. Modify your query to change the column heading of ytd_sales to Copies Sold.

3. Add a column to your query results that returns Price multiplied by ytd_sales and label the result Dollar Sales.

4. Use the IsNull function to change NULLs from the Copies Sold column to 0.

5. Add the Str function to the Copies Sold column to format the results to a length of 10 with 2 decimals.

The final query should look something like the following:

```
SELECT Title, Price, ytd_sales 'Copies Sold', Str(IsNull(Price *
ytd_sales, 0.0), 10, 2) 'Dollar Sales'
FROM Titles
```

Exercise 4.3: Returning Selected Rows from a Table

The purpose of this exercise is to return only selected rows from the Titles table.

1. Write a query to return all the titles (title column) from the Titles table where the Price is greater than $15.00.

2. Use the BETWEEN keyword to modify your query to return all the titles where the Price is greater than $15.00 and less than $22.00.

3. Modify your query to further restrict the rows returned to those with Year-to-Date sales (ytd_sales column) greater than 1,000.

The final query should look something like the following:

```
SELECT Title
FROM Titles
WHERE Price BETWEEN 15.00 AND 22.00
  AND ytd_sales > 1000
```

Exercise 4.4: Using the LIKE Statement

This exercise gives you practice using the LIKE statement.

1. Write a query to return all the titles (title column) that begin with the word The from the Titles table, using the LIKE statement with the % wildcard.

2. Write a similar query to return all the titles that have the word Computer anywhere in them.

continues

Exercise 4.4: Continued

3. Finally, use the square brackets along with the % wildcard to find all the titles that have either a comma, or a semicolon anywhere in them.

The three queries should look something like the following:

```
SELECT Title
FROM Titles
WHERE Title LIKE 'The %'

SELECT Title
FROM Titles
WHERE Title LIKE '% Computer %'

SELECT Title
FROM Titles
WHERE Title LIKE '%[,;]%'
```

Exercise 4.5: Using System Functions

This exercise familiarizes you with several system functions.

1. Use the Col_Length system function to return the length of the notes column in the Titles table.

2. In a different statement use the Col_Name system function to return the name of the second column of the Titles table.

Note

Col_Name requires the ID of a table rather than the table name. Use the Object_ID function to pass the ID of the Titles table to Col_Name.

3. Write a statement using the Datalength function that returns the length of the note column for every row in the Titles table.

4. Have SQL Server return the name of your workstation by using the Host_name function.

5. Use Suser_Name and User_Name functions together to return your login name and database user name.

The five queries should look something like the following:

```
SELECT Col_Length('Titles', 'Notes')

SELECT Col_Name(Object_ID('Titles'), 2)

SELECT Datalength(Notes)
FROM Titles

SELECT Host_Name()

SELECT sUser_name(), User_name()
```

Exercise 4.6: Using Order BY Keywords

Use the **ORDER BY** keywords to format the output of a query in sorted order.

1. Return all the rows from the Titles table where the titles are sorted within types.

The final query should look something like the following:

```
SELECT *
FROM Titles
ORDER BY Type, Title
```

Review Questions

1. Which of the following are parts of a SELECT statement?

    A. FROM

    B. SORT BY

    C. WHERE

    D. SELECT

2. Choose all the SELECT clauses that will return the au_fname columns as 'Name'.

    A. SELECT au_fname as 'Name'

    B. SELECT 'Name' = au_fname

    C. SELECT Name

    D. SELECT au_fname 'Name'

3. What statement would you use in the WHERE clause to select all the names beginning with 'B' from a table?

    A. WHERE name = 'B%'

    B. WHERE name = 'B*'

    C. WHERE name LIKE 'B%'

    D. WHERE name LIKE 'B*'

4. What statements could you use in the WHERE clause to select all of the rows in a table where price is greater than $10 and less than $25?

    A. WHERE price > 10

    B. WHERE price BETWEEN 10 and 25

    C. WHERE price >10 and <25

    D. WHERE price BETWEEN 10,25

5. What statement could you use in the WHERE clause to select all the rows in a table where no price is defined?

    A. WHERE price IS NOT NULL

    B. WHERE price IS < 0

    C. WHERE price != 0

    D. WHERE price IS NULL

6. Choose all the statements that you could use in the WHERE clause to find only the rows where the first name is "Bobby" or "Bobbi".

    A. WHERE name = "Bobby" or name = "Bobbi"

    B. WHERE name LIKE "Bobb_"

    C. WHERE name LIKE "Bobb%"

    D. WHERE name LIKE "Bobb[iy]"

7. What statement could you use in the WHERE clause to select all the rows in a table where the DueDate column is in July?

    A. WHERE Datepart("MM", DueDate) = 7

    B. WHERE Datepart("MM", DueDate) = "July"

    C. WHERE DueDate in "July"

    D. WHERE Datepart("July", DueDate) IS TRUE

8. Which statements will return the value of two squared?

    A. SELECT 2 * 2

    B. SELECT 2^2

    C. SELECT Power(2, 2)

    D. SELECT Sqr(2)

9. Which statements will concatenate "string1" and "string2"?

    A. SELECT "string1", "string2"

    B. SELECT "string1" + "string2"

    C. SELECT Concat("string1" + "string2")

    D. SELECT Concat("string1", "string2")

10. Which queries will return all the names in the Authors table sorted by first name, then last?

    A. SELECT au_fname, au_lname

        FROM Authors

        SORT BY 1, 2

    B. SELECT au_fname, au_lname

        FROM Authors

        ORDER BY au_fname, au_lname

    C. SELECT au_fname, au_lname

        FROM Authors

        SORT BY au_fname, au_lname

    D. SELECT au_fname, au_lname

        FROM Authors

        ORDER BY 1, 2

Answers to Review Questions

1. A,C,D

2. A,B,D

3. C

4. B

5. D

6. A,D

7. A

8. A,C

9. B

10. B,D

Answers to Test Yourself Questions at Beginning of Chapter

1. SELECT select_list
   FROM *table_name*
   WHERE *search_conditions*
   ORDER BY *sort_list*
   See "Writing SELECT Statements: An Overview."

2. SELECT au_fname,au_lname,address,city,state
   FROM Authors
   See "Writing SELECT Statements: An Overview."

3. You would have to explicitly name every column that you intend to return. There is no method to exclude a single column from a SELECT * statement. See "Choosing Columns."

4. SELECT au_fname + ' ' + au_lname Names
   FROM Authors
   See "Specifying Column Headings."

5. SELECT title, price * .90
   FROM Titles
   See "Numeric Operations."

6. SELECT title, price
   FROM Titles
   WHERE price < 15.00
   See "Using Comparison Operators."

7. SELECT au_fname, au_lname
   FROM Authors
   WHERE au_lname LIKE '%ger'
   See "Using LIKE Statements."

8. SELECT title, price
   FROM Titles
   WHERE price IS NULL
   See "Using IS NULL and IS NOT NULL Keywords."

9. SELECT au_fname, au_lname, state
   FROM Authors
   ORDER BY state, au_lname
   See "Using the ORDER BY Statement."

Chapter

Retrieving Data
(Advanced Topics)

5

This chapter will help you prepare for the exam by covering the following objectives:

 Objectives

- ▶ Generate summary data by using aggregate functions

- ▶ Generate summary data by using the COMPUTE clause and COMPUTE BY clause

- ▶ Generate summary data by using the GROUP BY clause

- ▶ Generate summary data by using the HAVING clause

- ▶ Correlate data by using outer joins

- ▶ Correlate data by using self-joins

- ▶ Recognize and apply subqueries that use nested SELECT statements

Test Yourself! Before reading this chapter, test yourself to determine how much study time you will need to devote to this section.

1. Write a SELECT statement to return the number of records in the Title-Author table from the Pubs database.

2. John wants to know the highest Price of any book in the Titles table. What statement would return this value?

3. Sandy wants to know the total amount of Advances paid out by each publisher for the books in the Titles table. Write a statement that would return this information.

4. Carol would like to find the average Price of the books from each category (of each Type) in the Titles table. Write a statement to find this information.

5. Bill needs to find out how many Authors who are under Contract live in each State. What statement could he write involving the Authors table to find this information?

6. Bill later finds that it would be helpful to include a total of all the Authors under Contract from every State in his query. How could he accomplish this?

7. Sandy would like to be able to see a listing of all Titles and the name of the Publisher for each title. Write a statement that could return this list from the Titles and Publishers tables.

8. Peter needs a list of names of all the authors in the Authors table and the IDs of the books they have written, if any. He knows that the TitleAuthor table contains a listing of every Author ID (Au_ID) with the ID of the book they wrote (Title_ID). What statement could return the list he needs?

9. Laura needs to be able to see the Author and Title of every book in the Titles table. Write a statement that will return every Title along with its Author(s).

Answers are located at the end of the chapter...

This chapter expands on the features of the SELECT statement. Familiarity with retrieving data from at least a single table is assumed in the way this information is presented. The focus of this chapter is on the more advanced features of SQL for retrieving data. The topics covered include:

▶ Generating summary data about a result set using aggregate functions

▶ Joining data from multiple tables together into a result set

▶ Utilizing subqueries using nested SELECT statements

Generating Summary Data

 Objective

There are many methods of deriving summary data from the results of a query. SQL Server supports functions that report aggregate information such as a count of the rows returned, the sum or average of a column, or even the minimum or maximum values from a column. There also are two clauses, GROUP BY and HAVING, which enable you to group together similar rows and restrict your results to only those having a specific criteria. Finally, you'll be introduced to the COMPUTE clause that enables you to perform summaries of your summaries, such as the sum of sums.

SQL Server supports many functions that report *aggregate* information about a column. That is, information is derived from all the rows in a column. Aggregate functions all share a similar syntax, as shown in the following example:

```
aggregate_function ([ALL | DISTINCT] expression)
```

In this syntax, the expression is almost always a column name. The function then operates on all the rows in that column to return the information requested. A listing of all the aggregate functions with a description of each is contained in table 5.1.

Table 5.1 Aggregate Functions

Aggregate Function	Description
Avg	Returns the average of all the values, or only the DISTINCT values, in the expression. Avg can be used with numeric columns only. NULL values are ignored.
Count	Returns the number of non-NULL values in the expression. When DISTINCT is specified, Count finds the number of unique non-NULL values. Count can be used with both numeric and character columns. NULL values are ignored.
Count(*)	Returns the number of rows. Count(*) takes no parameters and cannot be used with DISTINCT. All rows are counted, even those with NULL values.
Max	Returns the maximum value in the expression. Max can be used with numeric, character, and datetime columns, but not with bit columns. With character columns, Max finds the highest value in the collating sequence. Max ignores any NULL values. DISTINCT is available for ANSI compatibility, but it is not meaningful with Max.
Min	Returns the minimum value in the expression. Min can be used with numeric, character, and datetime columns, but not with bit columns. With character columns, Min finds the value that is lowest in the sort sequence. Min ignores any NULL values. DISTINCT is available for ANSI compatibility, but it is not meaningful with Min.
Sum	Returns the sum of all the values, or only the DISTINCT values, in the expression. Sum can be used with numeric columns only. NULL values are ignored.

Normally, an aggregate function returns a single value based on all the rows dictated by the WHERE clause (or the entire table if the WHERE clause is omitted). In these circumstances an aggregate function cannot be combined in a SELECT list with simple column names because the single value returned by the aggregate function cannot be combined with the multiple values that would be returned from the column named in the table. The following is an example of such an invalid statement:

```
SELECT title, sum(price)
FROM title
```

Aggregate functions also cannot be used in a WHERE clause. The aggregation is performed on all the rows in a result set, whereas the WHERE clause is used to compile that result set. Therefore, because the aggregate function is computed after the WHERE clause is applied, its value does not exist to be used in the WHERE clause.

Used by themselves, aggregate functions are most useful when a quick answer is needed about a table. Just by replacing the SELECT list of a query, the Count(*) function can be used to get a feel for how much data may be returned by a query before actually executing the full statement. Before inserting a new row into a table, the highest current ID can be determined with the Max function so the new row can use the next highest value. Application developers therefore use queries with such simple aggregations most often when they experiment with the data, rather than being used in reporting tools.

These limitations on the use of aggregate functions make them seem to be of only limited use. However, you will see that aggregate functions are central to the concept of grouping together similar rows using the GROUP BY clause. In this way, aggregate functions take on tremendous power and versatility.

Using the GROUP BY Clause

 Objective

The GROUP BY clause enables you to group together similar rows from a result set. That is, by specifying columns in the GROUP BY clause, SQL Server takes all the rows in the result set where the values in those columns, taken as a whole, are identical and combines them into a single row. In its simplest case, the GROUP BY does nothing more than the DISTINCT keyword. The following statement returns all the values of the Pub_ID and Type columns of the Title table in the Pubs database, with identical values of

Pub_ID and Type grouped together. The results of the query are shown in figure 5.1.

```
SELECT pub_id, type
FROM title
GROUP BY pub_id, type
```

Figure 5.1

An example of a SELECT statement with a GROUP BY clause.

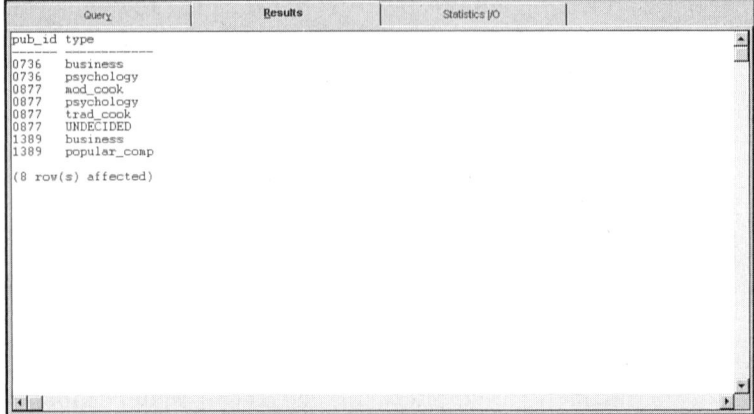

The example results exemplify the simplest case mentioned previously; the query returns results no different than what can be done through the DISTINCT keyword. Note that when used this way, all the columns named in the SELECT list must also be included in the GROUP BY clause. This is because there is no way to return the distinct values of one column, while multiple distinct values exist in another column. To illustrate this point, consider adding titles to the SELECT list of the above example without including it in the GROUP BY clause. If all the titles were shown for a given Pub_id/Type pair, there would be no grouping of Pub_id and Type at all, except, perhaps, an ordering that would more properly be done by an ORDER BY clause.

Although all the items in the SELECT list must exist in the GROUP BY clause, the reverse is not true. It would be perfectly acceptable to not show pub_id in the SELECT list of the example above. It may be that not having the information listed would result in your result set being less clear and more difficult to understand, but it is legitimate to do so.

> **Note**
> It is important to always remember the order in which SQL Server expects to see each clause in a statement. Note that any of these clauses can be omitted (except the SELECT clause itself), as long as the rest maintain the same relative order.
>
> ```
> SELECT select_list
> FROM table_name
> WHERE clause
> GROUP BY clause
> HAVING clause
> ORDER BY clause
> COMPUTE clause
> ```

The GROUP BY clause shows its true value when it is combined with the use of aggregate functions in the SELECT list. When used in a statement containing a GROUP BY clause, an aggregate function operates on all the rows that were grouped to form a single result row. When used this way, summary results can be returned for groups of rows in a result set. The following code based on the titles table of the Pubs database returns the total year-to-date sales for all the titles of similar subject matter released by each publisher. Those results are presented in figure 5.2.

```
SELECT pub_id, type, sum(ytd_sales)
FROM titles
GROUP BY pub_id, type
```

Figure 5.2

An example of returning summary data with a GROUP BY clause.

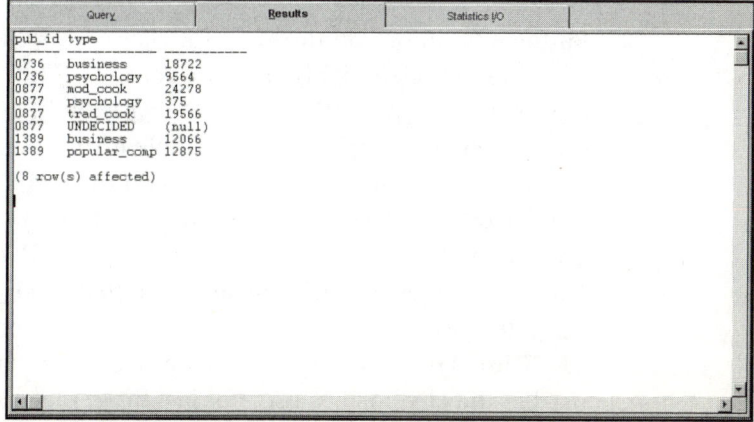

Using the HAVING Clause

 Objective

As stated earlier in this section, aggregate functions cannot be used in the WHERE clause of a SELECT statement. Instead, along with the GROUP BY clause, SQL Server supports the HAVING clause. The HAVING clause works just like the WHERE clause, except that it operates after aggregate functions have been calculated. Therefore, if you wanted to return only those rows in the above example where the year-to-date sales where greater than $10,000, you could use the following statement:

```
SELECT pub_id, type, sum(ytd_sales)
FROM titles
GROUP BY pub_id, type
HAVING sum(ytd_sales) > 10000.00
```

Although the HAVING clause specifically is needed to support filtering rows based on the values of aggregate functions, it also can be used for more mundane selections. In the preceding example, we could also have stated in the HAVING clause not to include any books about business. These kinds of standard conditions can be included in either the HAVING or the WHERE clause with no effect on the query results. It is better, however, to use the WHERE clause wherever possible. By operating on the results first, the WHERE clause can eliminate unnecessary data from the result set before SQL Server has to perform aggregate functions on those results. Any work that you can spare SQL Server from doing naturally improves its—and your—performance.

Putting conditions on the WHERE clause wherever possible is not only more efficient, it also is more versatile. The conditions that can be put in a WHERE clause are nearly limitless, in that they can reference any column of any table involved in the query. The HAVING clause, because it operates on the results determined by the rest of the query, can only contain conditions relating to aggregate functions, or columns named in the GROUP BY clause. Note that this is not the same as saying that the HAVING clause can reference only those columns that are contained in the SELECT list. The difference is that any aggregate function can be used in the HAVING clause, not just those that are in the SELECT list. The aggregate functions used in a HAVING clause may even

reference columns that are not referred to in any way by the SE-
LECT list.

Although the HAVING and the WHERE clauses have many similarities, they each fill a specific role, and care should be taken to
use each properly. The WHERE clause, you have seen, is to be
used to create a result set. The WHERE clause should therefore
be designed to return the smallest result set possible to minimize
the work that SQL Server must do. The HAVING clause is used to
make selections on the result set after it has been grouped according to the GROUP BY list. Therefore, the HAVING clause should
always contain conditions that can only be accomplished after the
initial result set is compiled. Because non-aggregate functions on
columns in the GROUP BY clause also can be operated on by the
WHERE clause, they should only be used in the HAVING clause
in conjunction with conditions on an aggregate function.

Using the COMPUTE and COMPUTE BY Clauses

√ Objective ►   You have seen that aggregate functions can be used alone in a
SELECT list to provide summary information on an entire result
set. In this case, however, no other information can be brought
back that could show the data that made up the total. This appar-
ent drawback is resolved by using the COMPUTE clause. Aggregate functions can be included in a COMPUTE clause that will
cause an extra line to be included in the result set that corresponds to the result of the aggregation specified.

In this chapter you have learned that aggregate functions could
not be used in a SELECT list with non-aggregated columns without using a GROUP BY clause. In a preceding example you saw
that you could not return a list of all the titles in the Title table of
the Pubs database along with the sum of the individual prices.
Now the COMPUTE clause can enable you to write the query you
wanted. The results of the query are listed in figure 5.3.

```
SELECT title, price
FROM title
COMPUTE sum(price)
```

Figure 5.3

An example of returning summary data with COMPUTE clause.

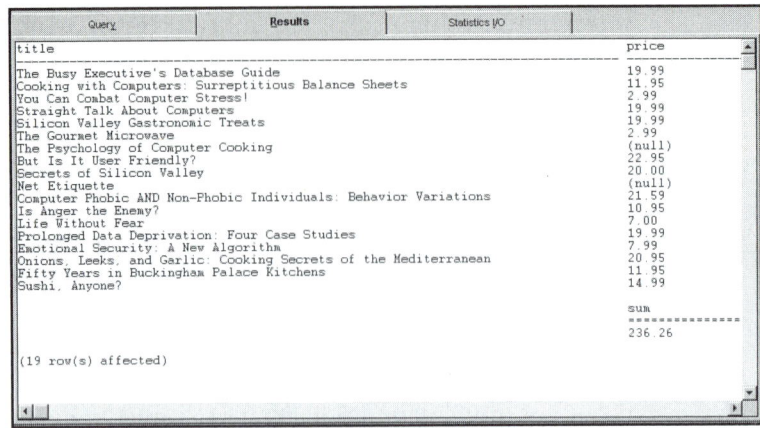

There are limitations to what can be done with the COMPUTE clause. Aggregate functions in the COMPUTE clause can only be used on columns that exist in the SELECT list. In the preceding example, in order to show the sum of all the prices, the price column itself had to be a part of the SELECT list.

The COMPUTE clause may operate on a column in the SELECT list more than once. In the preceding example, it would have been possible to compute both the sum and the average price for all titles. To compute both aggregations, simply include both statements after the COMPUTE keyword, and separate the two functions with a comma.

```
SELECT title, price
FROM title
COMPUTE sum(price),avg(price)
```

When COMPUTE is used in a statement containing a GROUP BY clause, it behaves in its normal fashion. Remember that COMPUTE must follow the GROUP BY or HAVING clause if one exists. COMPUTE can be used to provide aggregates of aggregate functions in the SELECT list. To specify an aggregate of an aggregate in the SELECT list, simply enclose the entire aggregate function, including column reference, in the parenthetical COMPUTE aggregate function. An example of this follows.

```
SELECT pub_id, type, sum(ytd_sales) 'Total Sales'
FROM titles
GROUP BY pub_id, type
ORDER BY pub_id, type
COMPUTE avg(sum(ytd_sales))
```

In the preceding example COMPUTE behaves just as it would with a statement that did not contain a GROUP BY, that is, it calculates a single total encompassing all rows in the result set. In this particular example the COMPUTE clause returned the average year-to-date sales of titles grouped by publisher, and subject type.

SQL Server also provides a way to calculate the average sales of all subjects for each publisher. This is done by modifying the same COMPUTE clause with a BY modifier, which follows after the complete COMPUTE clause. The BY modifier to the COMPUTE clause acts very much like a second GROUP BY clause. The COMPUTE BY modifier consists of a list of columns from the GROUP BY clause, which directs SQL Server to again group the results after the GROUP BY has been completed, and then perform the COMPUTE actions on those groups. This can best be illustrated though an example and the results listed in figure 5.4.:

```
SELECT pub_id, type, sum(ytd_sales) 'Total Sales'
FROM titles
GROUP BY pub_id, type
ORDER BY pub_id, type
COMPUTE avg(sum(ytd_sales))
BY pub_id
```

It is important to note that the ORDER BY clause that has been included in both of the previous examples is in fact necessary when using the COMPUTE BY modifier. In order for the COMPUTE BY modifier to be able to perform its grouping by publisher, the ORDER BY clause was necessary to ensure that the publisher IDs were gathered together. The COMPUTE BY modifier may contain fewer column names than the ORDER BY statement, but the columns that it does contain must match the beginning of the ORDER BY.

Figure 5.4

An example of returning summary data with the COMPUTE BY clause.

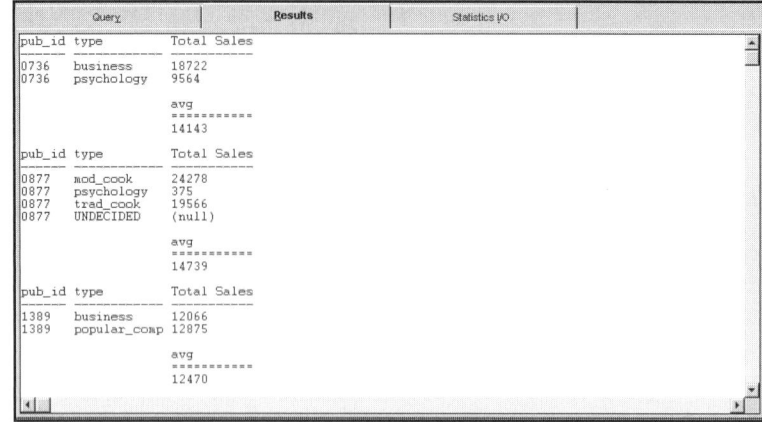

By using the COMPUTE BY clause to calculate totals for individual groups in the query, the average of the grand total of year-to-date sales across all publishers was lost. Fortunately SQL Server provides a method of calculating such a grand total even in this situation. The COMPUTE clause is allowed to appear multiple times in a single SELECT statement. Therefore, to accomplish the average of the grand total across all publishers, in addition to the average sales calculations for each publisher individually, add a second COMPUTE clause after the COMPUTE BY clause, as is shown in the following example and figure 5.5.

```
SELECT pub_id, type, sum(ytd_sales) 'Total Sales'
FROM titles
GROUP BY pub_id, type
ORDER BY pub_id, type
COMPUTE avg(sum(ytd_sales))
BY pub_id
COMPUTE avg(sum(ytd_sales))
```

Figure 5.5

An example of a query with multiple COMPUTE clauses.

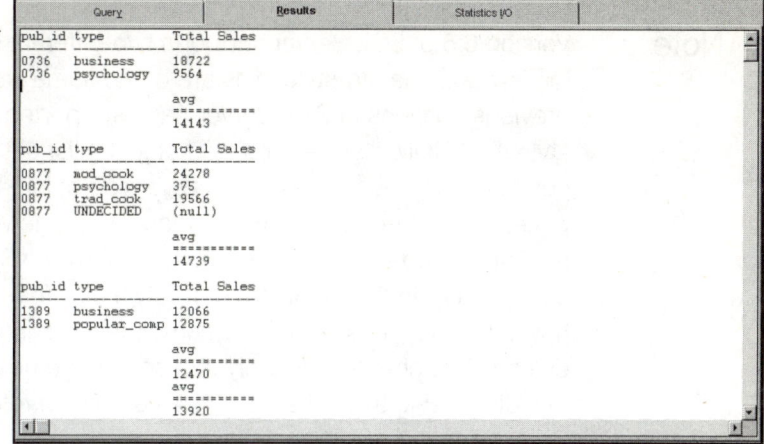

Using Joins

Perhaps the most fundamental ability of a Relational Database Management System such as SQL Server is its ability to store data in multiple logical units (in other words, tables), and then relate those tables to each other through joins. A join is a single query that accesses data from multiple tables. It is this ability to correlate data from many different tables into a single result set that makes the Relational Database Model so powerful.

The SQL language supports three distinct kinds of joins. These are:

▶ inner joins

▶ outer joins

▶ cross joins

In addition, there are self-joins that are special cases of each of these. All of these join types are discussed in depth in the following sections.

 Note

Version 6.5 of SQL Server supports two different styles of the join syntax. The old-style joins are of the same kind that all previous versions of SQL Server have supported. In the old style the FROM clause consisted of just a list of tables. The conditions for the join, as well as the type of join, were completely contained in the WHERE clause. The new-style joins are introduced in SQL Server 6.5 to achieve ANSI standard compliance. In the ANSI standard style all information about how tables relate is contained completely within the FROM clause. This chapter primarily focuses on the new ANSI syntax, discussing the old style only as a point of reference.

Using Inner Joins

An inner join, also known as an equi-join, is the most common type of join. In an inner join, the rows from two tables are combined wherever data in specified columns from each table are equal. In other words, an inner join returns results that contain the instances that the two tables have in common. It is possible in an inner join for a single row from one table to be matched to multiple rows in another table. In an inner join, if any rows in either table do not match any rows in the other table, they are not returned. The only rows that are returned in an inner join are those that have an exact match, according to the specified criteria, in the other table. It is worth noting that in a true inner join at least one criterion must be specified to relate the two tables.

The syntax of the ANSI standard inner join is contained entirely in the FROM clause. In the FROM clause, both tables are specified with the keywords INNER JOIN between them, and the keyword ON follows. The conditions of the join follow the keyword ON, and may contain any number of individual criteria chained together with the standard conjunctions AND and OR. The following is an example of a simple ANSI style INNER JOIN that returns all the author IDs for every title in the Titles table.

```
SELECT Au_ID, Title
FROM TitleAuthor
  INNER JOIN Titles
    ON Titles.Title_ID = TitleAuthor.Title_ID
```

Figure 5.6

An example of an ANSI standard INNER JOIN.

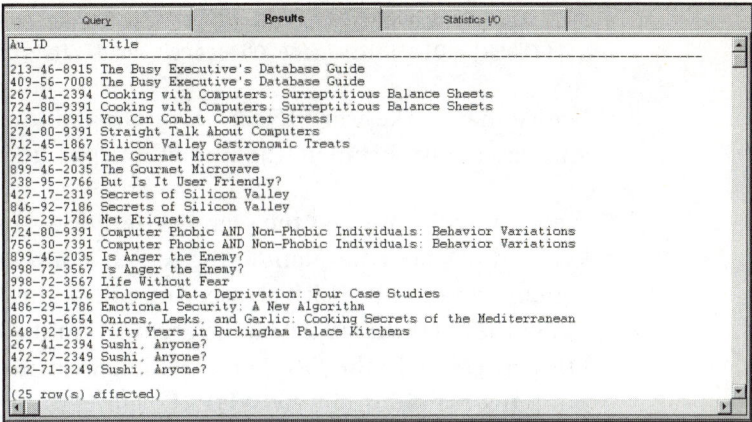

```
        Query              Results              Statistics I/O
Au_ID        Title
-------------------------------------------------------------------
213-46-8915 The Busy Executive's Database Guide
409-56-7008 The Busy Executive's Database Guide
267-41-2394 Cooking with Computers: Surreptitious Balance Sheets
724-80-9391 Cooking with Computers: Surreptitious Balance Sheets
213-46-8915 You Can Combat Computer Stress!
274-80-9391 Straight Talk About Computers
712-45-1867 Silicon Valley Gastronomic Treats
722-51-5454 The Gourmet Microwave
899-46-2035 The Gourmet Microwave
238-95-7766 But Is It User Friendly?
427-17-2319 Secrets of Silicon Valley
846-92-7186 Secrets of Silicon Valley
486-29-1786 Net Etiquette
724-80-9391 Computer Phobic AND Non-Phobic Individuals: Behavior Variations
756-30-7391 Computer Phobic AND Non-Phobic Individuals: Behavior Variations
899-46-2035 Is Anger the Enemy?
998-72-3567 Is Anger the Enemy?
998-72-3567 Life Without Fear
172-32-1176 Prolonged Data Deprivation: Four Case Studies
486-29-1786 Emotional Security: A New Algorithm
807-91-6654 Onions, Leeks, and Garlic: Cooking Secrets of the Mediterranean
648-92-1872 Fifty Years in Buckingham Palace Kitchens
267-41-2394 Sushi, Anyone?
472-27-2349 Sushi, Anyone?
672-71-3249 Sushi, Anyone?

(25 row(s) affected)
```

Theoretically, any number of tables could be joined together in one query. To join more than two tables, the first join structure, including all conditions following the keyword ON, is simply followed by the keywords INNER JOIN again, then the third table name and the ON expression. In each ON expression, any column from any preceding table may be referenced. Optionally, each join phrase of two tables and an ON expression can be surrounded by parentheses to indicate that each such join can be considered a single combined table that each successive table then joins to.

With inner joins, this grouping is not significant because inner joins are commutative. That is, they can be performed in any order equivalently. SQL Server obeys the parenthetical order where such order would affect the outcome of the query. Where such grouping is irrelevant (such as with inner joins), SQL Server optimizes the query as it sees fit, regardless of the parentheses. Explicitly grouping joins becomes important when outer joins are discussed later in this chapter.

Note

Although there is no limit inherent in the syntax, SQL Server imposes a limit of 16 tables that can be joined in one query.

The syntax diagram for the SELECT statement, including the ANSI standard INNER JOIN, follows:

```
SELECT select_list
```

```
FROM table_name [INNER] JOIN table_name ON search_conditions
  [[INNER] JOIN table_name ON search_conditions]
```

Notice that the keyword INNER is optional in the syntax. Inner joins are always assumed when no other specifier is present.

It also is significant that the search_conditions that follow the keyword ON are equivalent to the search_conditions that can be contained in the WHERE clause. Any condition that can be written in the WHERE clause can be included in the conditions in an ON expression in the FROM clause. Likewise, it is permissible to put JOIN conditions in the WHERE clause, though some expression for the search_conditions must be present in the ON phrase to fulfill the syntax requirements.

This may seem to imply that the WHERE clause is irrelevant, and can be ignored. While it is true that any kind of a condition can be included in the FROM clause, it is extremely poor practice to do so. The FROM clause should be used to state all the tables that are to participate in the join, and specifically how those tables relate to each other. Then any filtering of data to specify exactly what rows in each table may participate in the query should be contained in the WHERE clause. Adhering to this style vastly improves the readability of a query.

With the old style, joins are primarily conducted in the WHERE clause. After the keyword FROM, a list of tables follows, with each table name separated by a comma. All search conditions, including the relations between tables, are contained in the WHERE clause.

This old-style join syntax is much more difficult to read and maintain. No distinction is made between join criteria and row restrictions, often resulting in a seemingly random ordering of conditions. With no guidance offered though the syntax to order the join conditions and separate out row restricting criteria, complicated queries joining multiple tables can be very difficult to decipher. It is for this reason that the newer ANSI standard joins are preferred. The following code illustrates the old-style join syntax and the results of the query are displayed in figure 5.7.

```
SELECT TitleAuthor.Au_ID, Titles.Title
FROM TitleAuthor, Titles
WHERE Titles.Title_ID = TitleAuthor.Title_ID
```

Figure 5.7

An example of an old-style INNER JOIN.

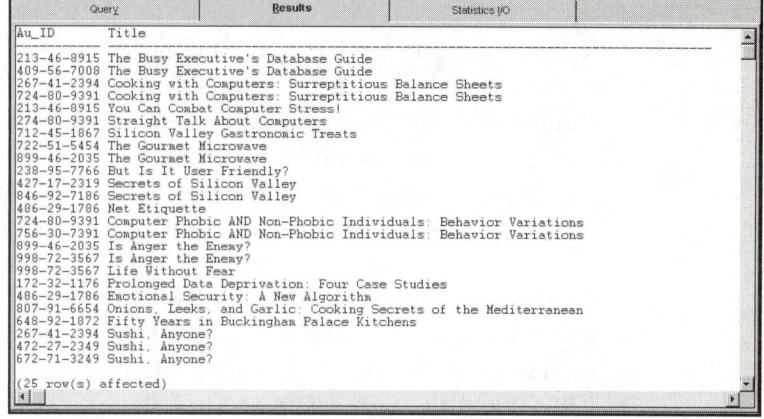

```
| Query |           | Results |              | Statistics I/O |
Au_ID       Title
-----------------------------------------------------------------------------
213-46-8915 The Busy Executive's Database Guide
409-56-7008 The Busy Executive's Database Guide
267-41-2394 Cooking with Computers: Surreptitious Balance Sheets
724-80-9391 Cooking with Computers: Surreptitious Balance Sheets
213-46-8915 You Can Combat Computer Stress!
274-80-9391 Straight Talk About Computers
712-45-1867 Silicon Valley Gastronomic Treats
722-51-5454 The Gourmet Microwave
899-46-2035 The Gourmet Microwave
238-95-7766 But Is It User Friendly?
427-17-2319 Secrets of Silicon Valley
846-92-7186 Secrets of Silicon Valley
486-29-1786 Net Etiquette
724-80-9391 Computer Phobic AND Non-Phobic Individuals: Behavior Variations
756-30-7391 Computer Phobic AND Non-Phobic Individuals: Behavior Variations
899-46-2035 Is Anger the Enemy?
998-72-3567 Is Anger the Enemy?
998-72-3567 Life Without Fear
172-32-1176 Prolonged Data Deprivation: Four Case Studies
486-29-1786 Emotional Security: A New Algorithm
807-91-6654 Onions, Leeks, and Garlic: Cooking Secrets of the Mediterranean
648-92-1872 Fifty Years in Buckingham Palace Kitchens
267-41-2394 Sushi, Anyone?
472-27-2349 Sushi, Anyone?
672-71-3249 Sushi, Anyone?

(25 row(s) affected)
```

Note

Although the old-style join syntax is supported for backward compatibility, Microsoft makes no promise to maintain this backward compatibility in the future. In fact, the "joins" topic in the Transact SQL Help file explicitly states that the old style will NOT be supported in a future release of SQL Server, although it is not disclosed what release will discontinue this syntax.

Exam Tip

Although Microsoft has re-released the Implementation test for version 6.5, the questions and examples in the test are still based on the older style, 6.0 joins. Although the newer style has many benefits, you should still acquire a familiarity with the old style.

When multiple tables are joined together, all of the columns from each of the tables can be referenced throughout the query. If any of the tables happen to have columns with the same name, such as two tables that each have a "Change_Date" column for example, it would be unclear which table was being referred to wherever that column name is used. To avoid this ambiguity, the column name can be preceded by the table name with a dot notation. Thus the

"Change_Date" column for a table named "Sales" could be referenced as "Sales.Change_Date". This kind of notation can be used even where no ambiguity exists—making the query easier to read and maintain.

Regardless of the syntax used, SQL Server provides a method of renaming tables for the purpose of a query. This feature, known as aliasing, enables long or obscure table names to be aliased to short, clear names within a query. This feature does not in any way affect the actual naming of the table, it only has meaning within a single query where such aliasing is used.

To alias a table, simply follow the table name in the FROM clause with the keyword AS and the alias name desired. The keyword AS, used in aliasing, is in fact optional and can be omitted. When a table name is replaced with an alias, that replacement spans the entire query. An alias must be used everywhere in the query that the table name would otherwise go.

```
SELECT TA.Au_ID, T.Title
FROM TitleAuthor AS TA
  JOIN Title AS T
    ON T.Title_ID = TA.Title.ID
```

 **Note**   It is worth pointing out that when a table name is aliased in a query, the replacement extends even to the SELECT list, which precedes the FROM clause. If a column name needs to be clarified by a table name in the SELECT list, any alias that exists for that table must be used. SQL Server parses the query in such a way that it can identify aliases in the SELECT list even though the FROM clause defines those aliases after the fact.

Using Outer Joins

 **Objective**   Outer joins differ from inner joins in that even rows that do not have matches in a joined table can be returned. In an outer join, the conditions are specified in the same manner as they are for the inner join. The only difference is that the keyword JOIN is

preceded by one of the outer qualifiers. The qualifier used with the keyword JOIN specifies which table retains all of its rows, and which table must have matches. Therefore the outer join syntax comes in three varieties, left, right, and full outer joins. In a left outer join, all rows are shown from the table to the left of the JOIN keyword, whereas in a right outer join all rows are retained from the right. In a full outer join, all rows are retained from both tables.

In an outer join, when a row from the specified table has no matching row from the other table, NULL values are returned for the missing column values.

The following code listing demonstrates the same query, written as both a LEFT OUTER JOIN and as a RIGHT OUTER JOIN by reversing the order of the tables in the FROM clause. Figure 5.8 displays the results (although not in their entirety as some of them have scrolled below the bottom of the window).

```
SELECT Au_Fname + ' ' + Au_Lname, Title_ID
FROM Author
  LEFT JOIN TitleAuthor
    ON TitleAuthor.Au_ID = Author.Au_ID

SELECT Au_Fname + ' ' + Au_Lname, Title_ID
FROM TitleAuthor
  RIGHT JOIN Author
    ON TitleAuthor.Au_ID = Author.Au_ID
```

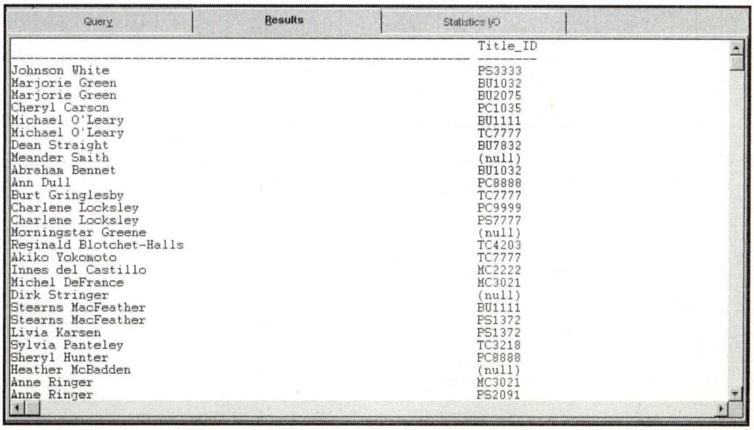

	Title_ID
Johnson White	PS3333
Marjorie Green	BU1032
Marjorie Green	BU2075
Cheryl Carson	PC1035
Michael O'Leary	BU1111
Michael O'Leary	TC7777
Dean Straight	BU7832
Meander Smith	(null)
Abraham Bennet	BU1032
Ann Dull	PC8888
Burt Gringlesby	TC7777
Charlene Locksley	PC9999
Charlene Locksley	PS7777
Morningstar Greene	(null)
Reginald Blotchet-Halls	TC4203
Akiko Yokomoto	TC7777
Innes del Castillo	MC2222
Michel DeFrance	MC3021
Dirk Stringer	(null)
Stearns MacFeather	BU1111
Stearns MacFeather	PS1372
Livia Karsen	PS1372
Sylvia Panteley	TC3218
Sheryl Hunter	PC8888
Heather McBadden	(null)
Anne Ringer	MC3021
Anne Ringer	PS2091

Figure 5.8

An example of ANSI standard LEFT and RIGHT OUTER JOINs.

 Note

The keywords LEFT, RIGHT, and FULL, are not required to be accompanied by the keyword OUTER. OUTER is assumed when any of these qualifiers are present.

In a full outer join all the rows from both tables are returned. Where a row in either table has no match in the other table, that row is returned with NULL values filling the fields from the table with no match. This full outer join has no equivalent in the old syntax.

The old-style outer join syntax is quite different from the ANSI standard style. In the old style, the expressions that relate the two tables are joined with a "*=" for a left outer join and "=*" for a right outer join. This kind of syntax is inferior to the new style. With the old style, there could be ambiguities about whether limiting criteria should be applied before or after the join operation. In an outer join this ambiguity could cause serious limitations.

Using an example from the Pubs database, say that you want to keep all records from the Authors table while you join to the Title-Author table to match all authors with the IDs of the books they have written, if any. This query can be written in either style equally well. Say, however, that you want to eliminate all the Californians from the join, though you still want to see all authors regardless of their home state. The following query can accomplish this task using the new syntax. The result table follows in figure 5.9.

```
SELECT au_fname, state, title_id
FROM authors A
  LEFT JOIN titleauthor TA
    ON A.au_id = TA.au_id
    AND  A.state <> 'ca'
```

Figure 5.9

An example of new outer join syntax applying criteria before a join.

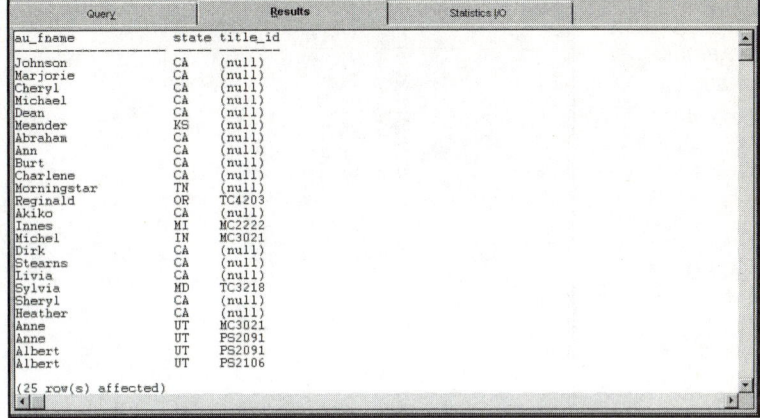

```
  au_fname        state title_id
  -----------     ----- --------
  Johnson         CA    (null)
  Marjorie        CA    (null)
  Cheryl          CA    (null)
  Michael         CA    (null)
  Dean            CA    (null)
  Meander         KS    (null)
  Abraham         CA    (null)
  Ann             CA    (null)
  Burt            CA    (null)
  Charlene        CA    (null)
  Morningstar     TN    (null)
  Reginald        OR    TC4203
  Akiko           CA    (null)
  Innes           MI    MC2222
  Michel          IN    MC3021
  Dirk            CA    (null)
  Stearns         CA    (null)
  Livia           CA    (null)
  Sylvia          MD    TC3218
  Sheryl          CA    (null)
  Heather         CA    (null)
  Anne            UT    MC3021
  Anne            UT    PS2091
  Albert          UT    PS2091
  Albert          UT    PS2106

  (25 row(s) affected)
```

The preceding syntax specifies that the Authors from California should not participate in the join. It does not, however, state that they should be left out of the results. The WHERE clause specifies what rows to leave out, and there was no WHERE clause used in this example. Therefore *all* authors were returned, but those from California were simply not connected to their books. This same query cannot be written using the old syntax. The old syntax performs joins in the WHERE clause along with filtering criteria. The following code samples in the new and old syntax are equivalent, and as can be seen in figure 5.10, they both eliminate all authors from California from the results.

```
SELECT au_fname, state, title_id
FROM authors A
   LEFT JOIN titleauthor TA
     ON A.au_id = TA.au_id
WHERE A.state <> 'ca'


SELECT au_fname, state, title_id
FROM Authors A, TitleAuthor TA
WHERE A.au_id *= TA.au_id
   AND A.state <> 'ca'
```

Figure 5.10

An example of new and old syntax applying criteria after a join.

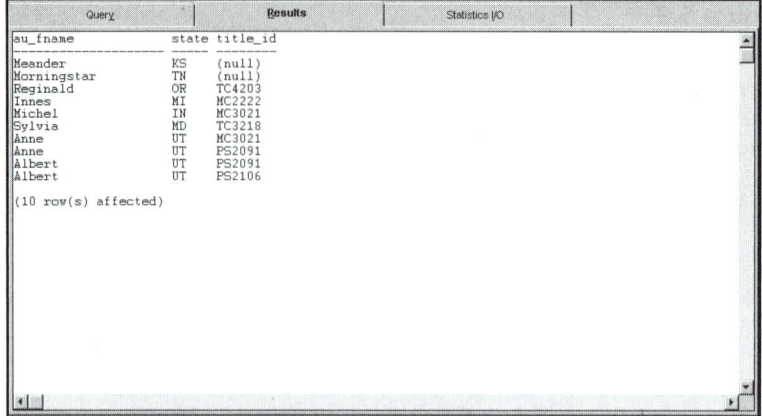

```
au_fname                state title_id
---------------------   ----- --------
Meander                 KS    (null)
Morningstar             TN    (null)
Reginald                OR    TC4203
Innes                   MI    MC2222
Michel                  IN    MC3021
Sylvia                  MD    TC3218
Anne                    UT    MC3021
Anne                    UT    PS2091
Albert                  UT    PS2091
Albert                  UT    PS2106

(10 row(s) affected)
```

This simple example may not be very practical, but it does quickly show the differences between the two syntax styles. The greater clarity provided by the new ANSI standard syntax has made it preferred over the old.

The third distinct join form is the cross join. In a cross join, all rows in the left table are matched with all rows in the right table. The result of a cross join is known as a Cartesian Product of the two tables. A cross join can be thought of as an inner join where there are no restrictions defined.

To perform a cross join, the first table name is followed by the keywords CROSS JOIN, which is followed by the second table name. The keyword ON is not included in the syntax, and there are no conditions specified in the FROM clause.

Note

Cross joins tend to return an extreme amount of data. Where there are X number of rows in the first table and Y rows in the second, a cross join returns X*Y rows. On tables of any significant size at all, this can quickly overload a system. Extreme care should be used with cross joins.

Using a Self-Join

 Any of the preceding join types can be written as a self-join. In a self-join a table is joined to itself. When this is done one of the two tables must be aliased so the two versions of the table can be distinguished. In a self-join the table is treated as though two different copies exist. Once one or both tables are aliased to avoid the obvious name conflict, the join is written as though there were two entirely different tables being joined. The fact that the two tables just so happen to have an identical structure is completely irrelevant.

 Use a self-join to find duplicate values in a table.

When performing a self-join, column names from the table involved are always ambiguous. It is important to specify which alias of the table is intended along with the column name. Always use the following syntax to reference columns in a self-join:

```
Table_Alias_Name.Column_Name
```

Using Subqueries

 Subqueries are an extremely powerful feature of the SQL language. Subqueries enable you to embed a query inside of another query. This allows queries to retrieve data with a single step that would otherwise require several steps.

Subqueries Used in Joins as Tables

There are two distinct types of subqueries: those that return a single column and a single row, and those that return a single column but multiple rows. Notice that all subqueries may return only a single column. Subqueries that return only a single row can be used in a query wherever an expression is allowed. Subqueries returning multiple rows may exist only in the WHERE or HAVING clause.

To include a subquery in a SELECT statement, simply enclose the subquery in parentheses. Subqueries may be used wherever expressions are allowed. However, different restrictions are placed on subqueries based upon where they are used.

Subqueries that return a single column from a single row may be used anywhere in a query that an expression may be used. These subqueries are executed before the rest of the main query and are checked to verify that only one row is returned. After the subquery is executed, SQL Server treats it as a single, constant value equal to the result. Subqueries of this type should be written carefully to ensure that they will never return more than one row. If the data in the table changes such that the subquery will then return multiple rows, the including query will suddenly stop returning the expected results when it is run. This kind of error can be quite frustrating to a user who has come to rely on the results of your query.

These subqueries are commonly used in the SELECT list of a query, or in the WHERE or HAVING clause. One use for such a subquery is to get around some of the limitations of aggregate functions. As discussed earlier in this chapter, an expression in the WHERE clause cannot contain an aggregate function. However, a subquery could be written that would retrieve the value that the aggregate function would return. This value from the subquery could then be used in the WHERE clause, or even included in a SELECT list.

The following is an example of the use of a subquery in the SELECT list of a SELECT statement. The results are displayed in figure 5.11.

```
SELECT Title, (SELECT Count(*) FROM Titles)
FROM Titles
```

Figure 5.11

An example of subquery return-ing one value.

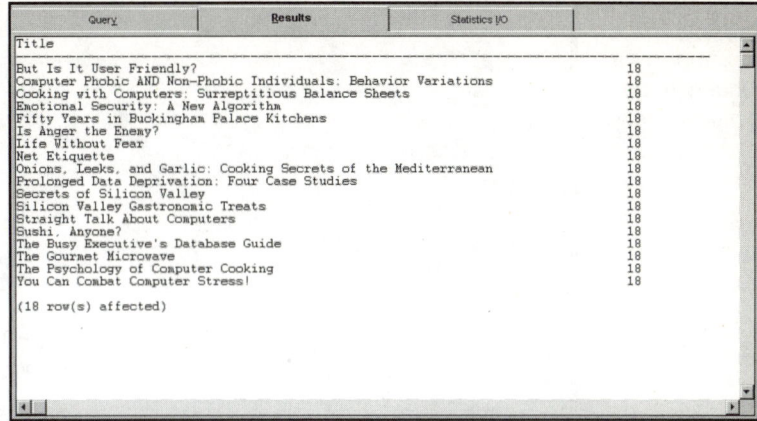

Subqueries that return multiple rows are more limited in where they can be used. Such subqueries are used in the WHERE or HAVING clause to compare a column value to all the values re-turned by the subquery. The list returned by a subquery is intro-duced by the keyword IN or a comparison operator used with the keywords ANY, ALL, or SOME. A subquery returning a list of val-ues also can be used alone in an expression introduced by the EXISTS keyword.

The following is an example of a subquery used in the WHERE clause of a statement. The subquery returns the IDs of only the lead authors from the TitleAuthor table.

```
SELECT au_fname + ' ' + au_lname
FROM Authors
WHERE au_id IN (
        SELECT au_id
        FROM TitleAuthor
        WHERE au_ord = 1
)
```

Figure 5.12

An example of a subquery returning multiple rows.

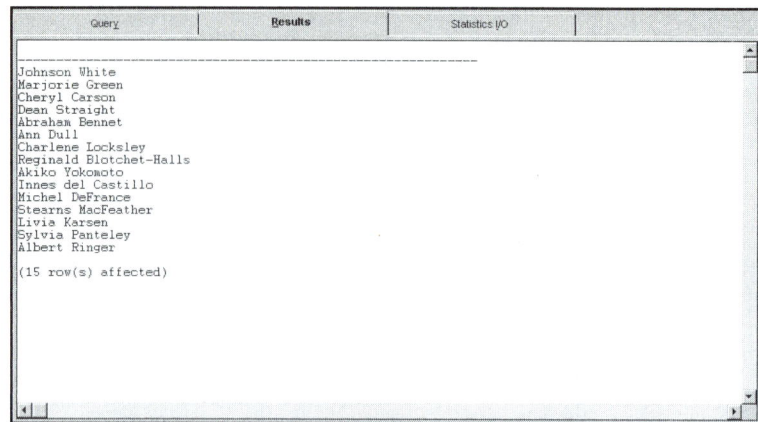

```
|    Query    |   Results   |  Statistics I/O  |
```
```
-------------------------------------------------
Johnson White
Marjorie Green
Cheryl Carson
Dean Straight
Abraham Bennet
Ann Dull
Charlene Locksley
Reginald Blotchet-Halls
Akiko Yokomoto
Innes del Castillo
Michel DeFrance
Stearns MacFeather
Livia Karsen
Sylvia Panteley
Albert Ringer

(15 row(s) affected)
```

Note   These subqueries also can be used in the ON phrase of the FROM clause as well as the WHERE or HAVING clause. Because a subquery like this would not be a part of defining the relationship between two tables in a join, however, such a subquery should not be used in that context.

The value of a column can be compared to all the values of a list returned by a subquery. This is accomplished with a standard comparison operator modified by one of the keywords ANY, ALL, or SOME. In this kind of expression, the value of the column is compared to each of the values in the list to find if the comparison is true for ANY, ALL, or SOME of the individual expressions. The ANY and SOME keywords are equivalent, and cause the expression to return true if the comparison is true in at least one case. The ALL keyword specifies that the comparison must be true for all values in the list. It is also possible to test if the values of a column equal any value in a list with the IN keyword. Using the IN keyword is equivalent to using the equal comparison with the ANY or SOME modifying keywords.

The following is an example of using a subquery to show a Publisher's name where all of their books have a price greater than $10.00.

```
SELECT Pub_Name
FROM Publishers
WHERE Pub_id = '1389'
  AND 10.00 < ALL (
        SELECT Price
        FROM Titles
        WHERE Pub_id = '1389'
          AND Price IS NOT NULL
)
```

> **Note** The previous section describes using subqueries to provide lists to compare with. All the operations described also work with static lists you can provide in the query. To create such a list, simply enter any number of values separated by commas inside parentheses.

A subquery returning multiple values also can be used to test for the existence of a value. This is done by preceding a query that could return any number of values with the keyword EXISTS. If the subquery returns any rows the expression returns true. If no rows are returned by the subquery the expression returns false. By convention, the subquery used with the EXISTS operator should use the asterisk "*" for its SELECT list. It is allowed to name a column explicitly and even multiple columns do not cause an error, but this is not considered good practice.

The following is an example of using EXISTS in a query:

```
SELECT au_fname + ' '+ au_lname
FROM Authors
WHERE Au_ID = '172-32-1176'
  AND EXISTS (
        SELECT *
        FROM TitleAuthor
          JOIN Titles
            ON Titles.Title_ID = TitleAuthor.Title_ID
        WHERE Title.Price > 15.00
          AND TitleAuthor.Au_ID = '172-32-1176'
)
```

Subqueries Used in WHERE for Correlated Subqueries

So far all the subqueries discussed could be run as stand-alone queries in their own right. In these simple cases SQL Server could theoretically substitute the result of the subquery directly into the main statement before its own independent execution. SQL Server provides for a more flexible type of subquery, however, known as correlated subqueries. Correlated subqueries reference columns in the outer query inside themselves. Such queries could not be run independently because they reference columns that are undefined within the context of the subquery.

Any column from any table in the outer query can be referenced in the WHERE clause of the subquery. When this happens the subquery is evaluated for every value of the column in the outer query. Thus the subquery is executed repeatedly with different values in the WHERE clause each time.

```
SELECT Authors.Au_ID, au_fname + ' ' + au_lname
FROM Authors
  JOIN TitleAuthor
    ON Authors.Au_ID = TitleAuthor.Au_ID
WHERE EXISTS (
        SELECT *
        FROM Titles
        WHERE Titles.Title_ID = TitleAuthor.Title_ID
)
```

A correlated subquery can be a very powerful tool. However, it carries a significant price in speed. Because it has to be executed repeatedly, this kind of a query takes many times as long as a similar query would take. Such a similar query, however, could not retrieve the same kind of data as a correlated subquery.

There is a special use for subqueries that is introduced by the ANSI standard syntax supported by SQL Server 6.5. In the FROM clause, the results from a subquery can be joined into the rest of the query as though that result set were a table itself. Such a subquery is called a derived table. It is always necessary to alias this derived table because it has no inherent name of its own. This is the only time it is acceptable for a subquery to return multiple columns. All of the columns returned in a derived table must have column headings that can serve as column names for the table. A subquery used as a table itself cannot refer to columns in other tables it is joining with to form a correlated subquery. A correlated subquery is run multiple times for every value of the external column it references, yet a derived table must return a single set of values to join to. Such a query and its results are illustrated in the following statements and figure 5.13.

```
SELECT Au_fname, State, Title
FROM Authors
  LEFT JOIN (
        SELECT Au_id, Title
        FROM TitleAuthor
          JOIN Titles
            ON Titles.Title_ID = TitleAuthor.Title_ID
 ) AS AuthorTitles
    ON Authors.au_id = AuthorTitles.au_id
```

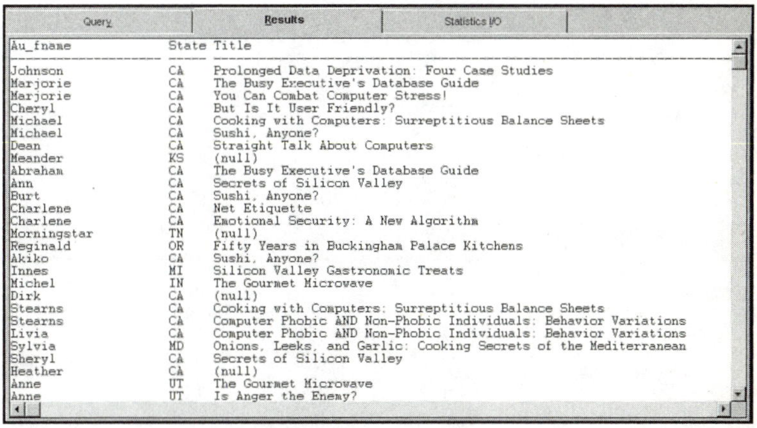

Au_fname	State	Title
Johnson	CA	Prolonged Data Deprivation: Four Case Studies
Marjorie	CA	The Busy Executive's Database Guide
Marjorie	CA	You Can Combat Computer Stress!
Cheryl	CA	But Is It User Friendly?
Michael	CA	Cooking with Computers: Surreptitious Balance Sheets
Michael	CA	Sushi, Anyone?
Dean	CA	Straight Talk About Computers
Meander	KS	(null)
Abraham	CA	The Busy Executive's Database Guide
Ann	CA	Secrets of Silicon Valley
Burt	CA	Sushi, Anyone?
Charlene	CA	Net Etiquette
Charlene	CA	Emotional Security: A New Algorithm
Morningstar	TN	(null)
Reginald	OR	Fifty Years in Buckingham Palace Kitchens
Akiko	CA	Sushi, Anyone?
Innes	MI	Silicon Valley Gastronomic Treats
Michel	IN	The Gourmet Microwave
Dirk	CA	(null)
Stearns	CA	Cooking with Computers: Surreptitious Balance Sheets
Stearns	CA	Computer Phobic AND Non-Phobic Individuals: Behavior Variations
Livia	CA	Computer Phobic AND Non-Phobic Individuals: Behavior Variations
Sylvia	MD	Onions, Leeks, and Garlic: Cooking Secrets of the Mediterranean
Sheryl	CA	Secrets of Silicon Valley
Heather	CA	(null)
Anne	UT	The Gourmet Microwave
Anne	UT	Is Anger the Enemy?

Figure 5.13

An example of a derived table in a JOIN.

Summary

This chapter has discussed many advanced features of the SELECT statement. With these features you can now generate summary data on a result set using both aggregate functions and the COMPUTE and COMPUTE BY clause. The use of the GROUP BY and HAVING clauses along with these summary features was discussed as well.

In addition, you can now retrieve data from any number of tables through joins. You can use joins to get only matching data through INNER JOINs, data with or without matches through OUTER JOINs, or you can even do full matches between two tables without any regard to matches by using CROSS JOINs.

Finally, subqueries were discussed. With subqueries you can embed single results anywhere in a query, or perform comparisons against the results of another query. You also can use correlated subqueries to return comparison results unique to each row in the outer query.

With this information, you are ready to write any variety of queries to pull back any kind of data. You can see now how to exploit the relations in any data model to join results in whatever fashion is necessary to get the information you need. You can include summary data in your queries to provide the most meaningful results possible to the end user.

Exercises

The Pubs sample database that comes with SQL Server is used throughout these exercises.

Exercise 5.1: Use of Aggregate Functions to Return Simple Summary Data

The purpose of this exercise is to use the various aggregate functions to return simple summary data.

1. Load Enterprise Manager and open a Query Window by choosing SQL Query Tool from the Tools menu.

2. Write a single statement to return the number of rows in the Titles table.

3. Write another statement to return both the Minimum and Maximum Prices from the Titles table.

4. Write a statement to find the sum total of all Advances paid for every book in the Titles table.

5. Write a statement to return the number of books that have a price defined using the DISTINCT keyword with the Count function.

Your queries should look similar to the following:

```
SELECT count(*)
FROM Titles
```

```
SELECT min(Price), max(Price)
FROM Titles
```

```
SELECT sum(Advance)
FROM Titles
```

```
SELECT count(DISTINCT Price)
FROM Titles
```

Exercise 5.2: Generate Summary Data with the GROUP BY Clause

The purpose of this exercise is to demonstrate the use of the GROUP BY clause for generating summary data.

1. First write a query to return the Publisher ID and the Type from the Titles table.

2. Now you can eliminate the duplicates by adding the GROUP BY clause to your statement. You must group by both of the columns in your result set.

3. To find the average price of all the books by a publisher in each category, simply add the Avg aggregate function to your SELECT list.

Your final query should look much like the following:

```
SELECT Pub_ID, Type, Avg(Price)
FROM Titles
GROUP BY Pub_ID, Type
```

Exercise 5.3: Generating Summary Data Using the HAVING Clause

In this exercise you use the HAVING clause to restrict the data brought back by a SELECT statement containing a GROUP BY clause.

1. Duplicate the solution to Exercise 5.2 to produce a statement to show the Average Price of the books by each Publisher in every category.

2. Add a HAVING clause to the statement to restrict the results to only show publishers and categories where the Average Price is NOT NULL.

Your resulting query should be similar to the following:

```
SELECT Pub_ID, Type, Avg(Price)
FROM Titles
GROUP BY Pub_ID, Type
HAVING Avg(Price) IS NOT NULL
```

Exercise 5.4:   Generate Summary Data Using the COMPUTE Clause

In this exercise you further modify the query from Exercises 5.2 and 5.3 to generate summary data for the group summaries.

1. Using the solution from 5.3 as a basis, show both the Average Price for all books in a category for a publisher, and the sum of the Year to Date Sales (ytd_sales column).

2. Add titles to both of the aggregate fields. Appropriate titles might be "Avg Price" and "Total Sales".

3. Use a COMPUTE clause to find the Average Price, and Average Sales of all the rows.

4. Add another condition to your COMPUTE clause to find the highest Average Price as well. (Hint: use the Max aggregate function.)

You should end up with a query similar to the following:

```
SELECT Pub_ID, Type, Avg(Price) 'Avg Price', Sum(ytd_Sales)
'Total Sales'
FROM Titles
GROUP BY Pub_ID, Type
HAVING Avg(Price) IS NOT NULL
COMPUTE Avg(Avg(Price)), Avg(Sum(ytd_Sales)), Max(Avg(Price))
```

Exercise 5.5:   Generate Summary Data Using the COMPUTE BY Clause

This Exercise helps familiarize you with the COMPUTE BY clause. It also demonstrates the use of multiple COMPUTE clauses in a single statement.

1. Again, this exercise builds upon the previous solution. Using the solution from Exercise 5.4 as a guide, write a query to return the Pub_ID, Type, Average Price, and sum total of year to date Sales from the Titles table, grouped by the Publisher's ID and the Type of each book. Filter out any rows that have no Average Price defined. Note that this is the same as the previous exercise without the COMPUTE clause.

2. Sort these results by the Publisher's ID and Type of book.

3. Now you can use a COMPUTE BY clause to show the Average, Average price, and the Total of the sum total of Year to Date Sales, for each Publisher. (Hint: use the Avg, and Sum functions in the COMPUTE clause, then specify to perform those computations BY Pub_ID.)

4. You can continue this example by computing summaries of the Publisher summaries. Add a final COMPUTE clause to the end of the statement to find the Average, Average Price, the Average Year to Date Sales total, and the highest Average Price of all rows. Note that this is identical to the COMPUTE clause that was used in Exercise 5.4.

Here is an example of what your final query might look like:

```
SELECT Pub_ID, Type, Avg(Price) 'Avg Price', Sum(ytd_Sales)
'Total Sales'
FROM Titles
GROUP BY Pub_ID, Type
HAVING Avg(Price) IS NOT NULL
ORDER BY Pub_ID, Type
COMPUTE Avg(Avg(Price)), Sum(Sum(ytd_Sales))
BY Pub_ID
COMPUTE Avg(Avg(Price)), Avg(Sum(ytd_Sales)), Max(Avg(Price))
```

Exercise 5.6: Correlate Data Using INNER JOIN

This exercise is a simple introduction to writing joins. It is recommended that you complete this exercise using the old-style join syntax first, because that is what you can expect to see on the Certification Test.

1. Before attempting the join, write a query to return just the Publisher ID and the Title (Pub_ID, Title) of every book in the Titles table.

2. Now you can use a join to the Publisher table to include the name of the Publisher (Pub_name) to your results. To do this you need to pull all the rows where the Titles table's Publisher ID equals the Publishers table's Publisher ID. Remember to specify the table name before the Publisher ID field name to avoid ambiguity.

Here are examples of the final query, shown in both the new ANSI standard and the old style of the syntax.

```
SELECT Publishers.Pub_ID, Pub_Name, Title
FROM Titles, Publishers
WHERE Titles.Pub_ID = Publishers.Pub_ID

SELECT Publishers.Pub_ID, Pub_Name, Title
FROM Titles
  JOIN Publishers
    ON Titles.Pub_ID = Publishers.Pub_ID
```

Exercise 5.7:   Correlate Data Using OUTER JOIN

This exercise gives you practice writing an OUTER JOIN. Again, it is recommended that you complete this exercise using the old-style join syntax first, because that is what you can expect to see on the Certification Test.

1. This Exercise borrows from Exercise 5.6 to demonstrate using an OUTER JOIN to return all the Publishers, and whatever Titles match. Copy the query from Exercise 5.6 to give you a statement that returns all the books from the Titles table and the name of the Publisher for each.

2. In the old style, modify the equal comparison between the Publisher IDs to use the "*=" or "=*" outer join comparison. Remember that the "*" is on the side where you want to keep all the rows.

3. If you're using the new-style joins, modify the JOIN keyword to perform a LEFT OUTER or RIGHT OUTER join. Remember that the LEFT or RIGHT specifies which side should retain all the rows.

What follows is an example of both styles of joins to solve the exercise.

```
SELECT Publishers.Pub_ID, Pub_Name, Title
FROM Titles, Publishers
WHERE Titles.Pub_ID =* Publishers.Pub_ID
```

continues

Exercise 5.7: Continued

```
SELECT Publishers.Pub_ID, Pub_Name, Title
FROM Titles
  RIGHT JOIN Publishers
    ON Titles.Pub_ID = Publishers.Pub_ID
```

Exercise 5.8: Correlate Data Using a Self-Join

One of the most useful features of a self-join is that it can be used to find duplicate records in a table. This exercise demonstrates a self-join by finding all the duplicate Author IDs in the TitleAuthor table.

1. Write a query that joins the TitleAuthor table to itself. Alias the first instance of the table to T1 and the second instance to T2. Return the Author ID (Au_ID) from the T1 table in the SELECT list. Furthermore, add a condition that the Title ID (Title_ID) from the two tables should not equal. This prevents the same row matching itself.

2. Enhance the query by specifying the DISTINCT keyword in the Select List so that we see only the Author IDs we need.

3. The query can be further enhanced by joining in the Authors table to the TitleAuthor table aliased T1 and displaying the first and last name of the Authors.

The following statements demonstrate first the old, then the new syntax style solutions to the problem.

```
SELECT DISTINCT T1.Au_ID, A.au_fname + ' ' + A.au_lname
FROM TitleAuthor AS T1, TitleAuthor AS T2, Authors AS A
WHERE T1.Au_ID = T2.Au_ID
  AND T1.Title_ID <> T2.Title_ID
  AND A.Au_ID = T1.Au_ID

SELECT DISTINCT T1.Au_ID, A.au_fname + ' ' + A.au_lname
FROM TitleAuthor AS T1
  JOIN TitleAuthor AS T2
    ON T1.Au_ID = T2.Au_ID
    AND T1.Title_ID <> T2.Title_ID
  JOIN Authors AS A
    ON A.Au_ID = T1.Au_ID
```

Review Questions

1. Which of the following are aggregate functions?

    A. Sum

    B. ABS

    C. Max

    D. Count

2. What is a valid GROUP BY clause for the following SELECT list?

    SELECT Pub_ID, Type, Max(Price)

    A. GROUP BY Pub_ID, Type, Max(Price)

    B. GROUP BY Pub_ID, Type, Price

    C. GROUP BY Pub_ID, Type

    D. GROUP BY Max(Price)

3. Which of the following statements are true of the HAVING clause?

    A. The HAVING clause can be used in any statement instead of the WHERE clause.

    B. The HAVING clause can restrict rows based on the values of aggregate functions.

    C. The HAVING clause must be accompanied by the GROUP BY clause.

    D. The HAVING clause can refer to fields not in the GROUP BY clause.

4. The COMPUTE BY clause requires the following clauses to exist.

    A. GROUP BY

    B. HAVING

C. ORDER BY

D. WHERE

5. Which one of the following statements will return *all* the Author IDs from the Authors table along with any Title IDs on matching rows from the TitleAuthor table?

A. SELECT Authors.Au_ID, TitleAuthor.Title_ID

FROM Authors, TitleAuthor

WHERE Authors.Au_ID = TitleAuthor.Au_ID

B. SELECT Authors.Au_ID, TitleAuthor.Title_ID

FROM Authors, TitleAuthor

WHERE Authors.Au_ID *= TitleAuthor.Au_ID

C. SELECT Authors.Au_ID, TitleAuthor.Title_ID

FROM TitleAuthor, Author

WHERE Authors.Au_ID =* TitleAuthor.Au_ID

D. SELECT Authors.Au_ID, TitleAuthor.Title_ID

FROM TitleAuthor, Author

WHERE Authors.Au_ID *= TitleAuthor.Au_ID

6. Which of the following statements will return all the Au_ID fields that appear more than once in the TitleAuthor table?

A. SELECT DISTINCT T1.Au_ID

FROM TitleAuthor T1, TitleAuthor T2

WHERE T1.Au_ID = T2.Au_ID

AND T1.Title_ID <> T2.Title_ID

B. SELECT DISTINCT Au_ID

FROM TitleAuthor

C. SELECT DISTINCT T1.Au_ID

FROM TitleAuthor AS T1, TitleAuthor AS T2

WHERE T1.Au_ID = T2.Au_ID

    D. SELECT DISTINCT T1.Au_ID

       FROM TitleAuthor AS T1, TitleAuthor AS T2

       WHERE T1.Au_ID = T2.Au_ID

       AND T1.Title_ID = T2.Title_ID

7. Which of the following statements are true of subqueries?

    A. A subquery must be enclosed in parentheses.

    B. A subquery always returns multiple columns.

    C. A subquery in the WHERE clause can refer to fields from the outer query.

    D. A subquery can always be run as an independent statement.

8. Which of the following statements are true of correlated subqueries?

    A. A correlated subquery is any subquery that includes a join operation.

    B. A correlated subquery can be used to make a derived table in the ANSI join syntax.

    C. A correlated subquery always includes a join.

    D. A correlated subquery can only be executed once.

9. Which of the following SQL features are used to generate summary data?

    A. Outer joins

    B. COMPUTE clause

    C. Derived tables

    D. Aggregate functions

10. What do JOINs enable you to do?

    A. Correlate data from multiple tables

    B. Generate summary information on a table

C. Return result columns that are derived from multiple columns in a table

D. Identify unmatched rows between two tables

Answers to Review Questions

1. A,C,D

2. C

3. B,C,D

4. A,C

5. B

6. A

7. A,C

8. C

9. B,D

10. A,D

Answers to Test Yourself Questions at Beginning of Chapter

1. SELECT count(*)
   FROM TitleAuthor
   See "Generating Summary Data."

2. SELECT max(Price)
   FROM Titles
   See "Generating Summary Data."

3. SELECT Pub_id, sum(Advance)
   FROM Titles
   GROUP BY Pub_id
   See "Using the GROUP BY Clause."

4. SELECT Type, avg(Price)
   FROM Titles
   GROUP BY Type
   See "Using the GROUP BY Clause."

5. SELECT State, count(State)
    FROM Authors
    WHERE Contract = 1
    GROUP BY State
    See "Using the GROUP BY Clause."

6. SELECT State, count(State)
    FROM Authors
    WHERE Contract = 1
    GROUP BY State
    COMPUTE sum(count(State))
    See "Using the COMPUTE and COMPUTE BY Clauses."

7. SELECT Publishers.Pub_Name, Titles.Title, Price
    FROM Publishers
      JOIN Titles
        ON Titles.Pub_ID = Publishers.Pub_ID

OR

    SELECT Publishers.Pub_Name, Titles.Title, Price
    FROM Publishers, Titles
    WHERE Titles.Pub_ID = Publishers.Pub_ID
    See "Using Inner Joins."

8. SELECT au_fname + ' ' + au_lname, title_id
    FROM TitleAuthor
      RIGHT JOIN Authors
        ON Authors.Au_ID = TitleAuthor.Au_ID

OR

    SELECT au_fname + ' ' + au_lname, title_id
    FROM TitleAuthor, Authors
    WHERE Authors.Au_ID *= TitleAuthor.Au_ID
    See "Using Outer Joins."

9. SELECT au_fname + ' ' + au_lname, title
    FROM (TitleAuthor
      JOIN Titles
        ON Titles.Title_ID = TitleAuthor.Title_ID)
      JOIN Authors
        ON Authors.Au_ID = TitleAuthor.Au_ID

OR

    SELECT au_fname + ' ' + au_lname, title
    FROM TitleAuthor, Authors, Titles
    WHERE Authors.Au_ID = TitleAuthor.Au_ID
      AND TitleAuthor.Title_id = titles.Title_ID
    See "Using Inner Joins."

Chapter

Modifying Data

6

This chapter helps you prepare for the exam by covering the following objectives:

 Objective ▶

- ▶ Manipulate data by using INSERT statements

- ▶ Manipulate data by using UPDATE statements

- ▶ Manipulate data by using DELETE statements

- ▶ Import and export data

Test Yourself! Before reading this chapter, test yourself to determine how much study time you will need to devote to this section.

1. What are the purposes of the INSERT, UPDATE, and DELETE statements?

2. How many rows may be modified by using the above statements?

3. How many tables may be modified by using the above statements?

4. What is the purpose of the Bulk Copy Program (BCP)?

5. What is the difference between a slow BCP and a fast BCP?

Answers are located at the end of the chapter...

This chapter introduces you to the Structured Query Language (SQL) commands used to modify data in a database. These three commands are known collectively as the Data Manipulation Language (DML) statements. A number of examples are shown for each SQL command to explain the syntax. If you have access to a SQL Server, these commands work on the Pubs database. By the end of this chapter, you will be able to insert, modify, and delete rows in a table by using these commands.

This chapter also covers the bulk transfer of data into and out of SQL Server. The Bulk Copy Program (BCP) and the Database Transfer tool in Enterprise Manager are both used to efficiently move large amounts of data into and out of a table. The Transfer tool copies database objects in addition to transferring data.

In order to prepare you for the exam, this chapter covers the following topics:

- ▶ The INSERT statement
- ▶ The UPDATE statement
- ▶ The DELETE statement
- ▶ Importing and Exporting Data with BCP
- ▶ Using the Transfer Tool in Enterprise Manager

The INSERT Statement

 Objective

The INSERT statement is used to add a single row or multiple rows of data to a table or a view. For more information on views, see Chapter 8, "Using Views, Defaults, and Rules." By default, only the table owner may insert rows into a table, although this permission may be transferred to other users. When using the INSERT statement, keep the following in mind:

- ▶ Because of the rules SQL Server imposes on batches of SQL statements, the maximum amount of data that may be inserted in a single batch is around 128K. The actual amount will be slightly less, because SQL Server requires some memory for the query plan.

▶ Attempting to insert data of the incorrect data type into a column causes an error, and the INSERT statement will be rolled back. Likewise, explicitly inserting a NULL value into a column that does not accept NULLs causes an error.

▶ When inserting data into a view based on more than one table, data may only be inserted into one base table at a time. For more information on the restrictions placed on views, see Chapter 8 and the SQL Server Books Online.

▶ If the inserted data violates a rule or constraint, then the INSERT fails and returns an error message.

▶ When inserting characters into a column of type *varchar*, or into a *char* column that accepts NULLs, all trailing spaces are removed from the string. Inserting an empty string ('') into columns of this type inserts a single space.

▶ When inserting data into a *char* column, all strings (even empty strings) are right-padded to the defined length of the column.

Typically, INSERT statements are executed from the Query Tool in SQL Enterprise Manager or from the ISQL application. However, INSERT statements may also be executed from other front-end applications written in Visual Basic or Visual C++.

Basic Syntax

The syntax of the INSERT statement is as follows:

```
INSERT [INTO] {table_name | view_name}
   [(column_list)]
   {DEFAULT VALUES | VALUES (values_list) | select_statement |
   ➥stored_procedure}
```

The INSERT command consists of three basic parts. The first is the INSERT keyword itself, followed by the name of the table or view to which data is being added. Note that the INTO keyword is always optional. Next, the columns that data will be inserted into are listed. If this column list is omitted, SQL Server assumes that you will be inserting a value in every column. The last part of the INSERT statement defines where the column values will come from for the data row(s).

The table name or view name may be fully qualified in the form [database.[owner].]tablename or [database.[owner].]viewname. This enables you to insert records into a table or view that resides in another database or that is owned by another user.

Note that when you omit the column list, you must provide a value for every column in the table. When you use a column list, you need only provide values for the columns you list in the INSERT statement. The columns in the column list can appear in any order. Some rules apply to the column(s) omitted from the column list:

▶ If the omitted column(s) does not allow NULLs, and does not have a default or default constraint, the insert statement will fail.

▶ If the omitted column(s) does not allow NULLs, but has a default bound to it (or a default constraint defined), then the default value will be used for the column.

▶ If the column permits NULL values, then a NULL will be inserted (unless a default exists for that column).

Column values may come from four different sources. The DE-FAULT VALUES and VALUES keywords are used to specify column values when inserting a single row. A SELECT statement or stored procedure may be used to provide column values for one or more rows. Let's look at some examples of inserting a single row; the multiple row inserts are covered a bit later in this section.

1. This statement attempts to insert a row into the authors table in the Pubs database by using all default values:

```
INSERT authors DEFAULT VALUES
```

However, the DEFAULT VALUES keyword only works if all columns that disallow NULLs have a default defined. In this case, the au_id, au_lname, au_fname, and contract columns disallow NULLs, and have no defaults. The result of this query is a set of error messages:

```
Msg 233, Level 16, State 2
The column au_id in table authors may not be null.
Msg 233, Level 16, State 2
The column au_lname in table authors may not be null.
Msg 233, Level 16, State 2
The column au_fname in table authors may not be null.
Msg 233, Level 16, State 2
The column contract in table authors may not be null.
```

2. A single row may be inserted by specifying column values with the VALUES keyword. The list of values must be enclosed in parentheses; character strings and date/time values must be enclosed in single quotes ('). This example inserts a new row and provides a value in every column:

```
INSERT authors
    (au_id, au_lname, au_fname, phone, address, city, state,
zip, contract)
    VALUES ('111-22-3333','Davies','Joshua','302 444-
1515','14 N. Bluff','Atlanta','GA','55111',1)
```

Note that the preceding example explicitly lists all the columns in the table. If a value is to be inserted in every column, a shorthand way of writing the INSERT is to omit the column list, as shown here:

```
INSERT authors
    VALUES ('111-22-3333','Davies','Joshua','302 444-
➡1515','14 N. Bluff','Atlanta','GA','55111',1)
```

3. The first example showed that only four columns in the authors table prohibit NULLs and have no default. All other columns either allow NULLs or have a default defined. Thus, we may insert a record for this table by specifying values only for those four columns:

```
INSERT authors
    (au_id, au_lname, au_fname, contract)
    VALUES ('111-22-4444','Cook','Fergus',1)
```

The address columns all allow NULLs, so they will contain NULL values. The phone number column defaults to 'UN-KNOWN'. Note that because the columns in the column list may appear in any order, this statement is equivalent to the previous one:

```
INSERT authors
    (contract, au_id, au_fname, au_lname)
    VALUES (1,'111-22-4444','Fergus','Cook')
```

4. A special keyword, DEFAULT, may be used in the values list to indicate that you want the default value (if one exists) to be used for that column:

```
INSERT authors
    (au_id, au_lname, au_fname, phone, address, contract)
    VALUES ('111-33-4444','Cook','Angus', DEFAULT, DEFAULT, 1)
```

The column for which you use the DEFAULT keyword must have a default if it prohibits NULLs. Otherwise, SQL Server provides a NULL value for a column that does not allow NULLs, and an error will occur. In this example, the phone column contains the value 'UNKNOWN', because that is the default for the column, and the address column contains a NULL, because it has no default.

Using INSERT on a Table with an IDENTITY Column

There are some special considerations you need to keep in mind when inserting rows into a table that contains an identity column. These examples use the jobs table in the Pubs database.

1. When omitting the column list, do not specify a value for the IDENTITY column in the VALUES list, like so:

```
INSERT jobs
    VALUES ('Mailroom Clerk',20,30)
```

2. When using a column list, do not include the IDENTITY column in the column list or the VALUES list:

```
INSERT jobs
    (job_desc, min_lvl, max_lvl)
    VALUES ('Mailroom Clerk',20,30)
```

Including the IDENTITY column in the list will cause an error, because an IDENTITY column normally cannot have a value explicitly defined for it. This statement:

```
INSERT jobs
    (job_id, job_desc, min_lvl, max_lvl)
    VALUES (42, 'Mailroom Clerk',20,30)
```

Causes this error:

```
Msg 544, Level 16, State 1
Attempting to insert explicit value for identity column in
table 'jobs' when IDENTITY_INSERT is set to OFF
```

3. If an explicit value must be supplied for an IDENTITY column, a special option (IDENTITY_INSERT) must be turned on for the table, and a column list must be used.

**Note**   The IDENTITY_INSERT option may only be turned on for one table at a time.

For example, if the 'Editor' job (with a job_id of 12) was deleted accidentally, the following SQL batch would re-insert the row:

```
SET IDENTITY_INSERT jobs ON

INSERT jobs
    (job_id, job_desc, min_lvl, max_lvl)
    VALUES (12, 'Editor',25,100)

SET IDENTITY_INSERT jobs OFF
```

Using a Nested SELECT Statement with INSERT

It is possible to use a SELECT statement to provide column values for the INSERT statement. The columns returned by the SELECT statement must match the columns in the inserted table or in the column list of the INSERT statement. In addition, the data types of the columns returned by the SELECT must match the data types for the inserted column(s). Using a nested SELECT also allows multiple rows to be inserted in a single statement. For more information about the SELECT statement, see Chapters 4, "Retrieving Data," and 5, "Retrieving Data (Advanced Topics)."

If you want to experiment with the examples presented in this section, first execute this SQL statement in the Pubs database to create the authors_examples table:

```
CREATE TABLE authors_examples (
    au_id      smallint      NOT NULL,
    au_lname   varchar (40)  NOT NULL ,
    au_fname   varchar (20)  NOT NULL ,
    phone      char (12)     NOT NULL DEFAULT ('UNKNOWN'),
    address    varchar (40)  NULL ,
    city       varchar (20)  NULL ,
    state      char (2)      NULL ,
    zip        char (5)      NULL ,
    contract   bit           NOT NULL
)
```

Note

The primary key for the authors_examples table is intentionally omitted so that rows from the authors table may be inserted multiple times. This omission is only used for demonstrating the various forms of the INSERT SELECT syntax. Generally, every table should have a primary key.

1. This example shows the most basic form of the INSERT SE-LECT syntax. It copies all columns and all rows from the authors table to the authors_examples table:

```
INSERT authors_examples
    SELECT * FROM authors
```

 **Tip**

To check the rows returned by the SELECT statement, you can use a trick in the Query Tool that enables you to execute a small portion of the query. Use the Shift-arrow keys or the mouse to highlight only the portion of the query you want to execute (in this case, the SELECT statement without the IN-SERT). Then, type Alt-X or click the Execute Query button. Only the highlighted portion of the query will be executed.

2. To copy only a subset of the rows from one table to another, a WHERE clause may be used with the SELECT statement. This example only inserts the authors from California into the authors_examples table:

```
INSERT authors_examples
    SELECT *
    FROM authors
    WHERE state LIKE 'CA'
```

3. The SELECT statement may also use a join to filter rows based on values in a related table, or pull column values from a related table. In this example, only those authors having a royalty percentage of 100% are added to the authors_examples table:

```
INSERT authors_examples
    SELECT authors.*
    FROM authors INNER JOIN titleauthor
        ON authors.au_id = titleauthor.au_id
    WHERE titleauthor.royaltyper = 100
```

4. The columns receiving inserted data may be restricted by using a column list in the INSERT statement. The selected columns must match the columns inserted. In this example, only the author ID, first name, last name, and contract are

copied into the authors_examples table. The phone column for every inserted author will default to 'UNKNOWN'; all other columns will be NULL:

```
INSERT authors_examples
    (au_id, au_fname, au_lname, contract)
        SELECT au_id, au_fname, au_lname, contract
          FROM authors
```

5. Constant values may be used in the SELECT portion of the statement to give all inserted rows the same value in a particular column. This example is similar to #4, except that every author's phone number is set to '800 555-1212':

```
INSERT authors_examples
    (au_id, au_fname, au_lname, contract, phone)
        SELECT au_id, au_fname, au_lname, contract, '800
        ➡555-1212'
          FROM authors
```

You may recall from Chapter 3, "Data Definition," that adding a NOT NULL column to a table requires the table to be dropped and recreated. Any data in the old table is lost unless it is first copied to the new table. The INSERT SELECT is especially useful for copying information from one table to another.

Using a Stored Procedure with INSERT

In SQL Server 6.5, Microsoft added a feature that enables you to write INSERT statements that insert rows into a table based on the results of a stored procedure. This syntax has basically the same restrictions and advantages as using a nested SELECT statement; the columns returned by the stored procedure must match the inserted columns, and the stored procedure may return multiple rows to be inserted. All types of stored procedures (user, system, and extended) may be used to supply values to the INSERT statement.

For example, this SQL batch creates a new table called dboptions as it inserts the results of the stored procedure sp_dboption into the table:

```
CREATE TABLE dboptions (option_name varchar(255) NOT NULL)
GO

INSERT dboptions
    EXECUTE  sp_dboption pubs
```

The main advantage of using a stored procedure in place of a SELECT statement is that it gives you the ability to fetch information from a remote server. For example, this statement pulls information from another server to populate a table in the local database:

```
INSERT employees
    EXECUTE  remoteserver.employeesdb.dbo.sp_getemployeeinfo
```

For more information on using stored procedures in the INSERT statement, see the SQL Server Books Online.

The UPDATE Statement

 Objective
The UPDATE statement is used to modify one or more rows of data in a single table or view. The table owner is granted the permission to update rows and may grant this permission to other database users. The UPDATE statement has some restrictions that are very similar to those of the INSERT statement:

> ► Because of the rules SQL Server imposes on batches of SQL statements, the maximum amount of data that may be updated in a single batch is around 128K. The actual amount is slightly less, because SQL Server requires some memory for the query plan.

> ► If a column is updated in such a way that its new value violates the data type, NULL option, rule, or CHECK constraint on that column, the UPDATE fails and the changes are rolled back.

> ► When updating a view based on more than one table, only the data from a single table may be updated at a time. For more information about the restrictions placed on views, see Chapter 8 and the SQL Server Books Online.

▶ *Char* and *varchar* columns behave as described in the "Insert" section in this chapter.

As with all DML statements, UPDATEs may be executed from the Query Tool in SQL Enterprise Manager, the ISQL application, or other front-end applications written in Visual Basic or Visual C++.

Basic Syntax

The abbreviated syntax of the UPDATE statement is as follows:

```
UPDATE {table_name | view_name}
SET
  { column_name = {NULL | DEFAULT | expression} }
  [,{ column_name = {NULL | DEFAULT | expression}...]
[WHERE {search_conditions | CURRENT OF cursor_name}]
```

The SET keyword defines which columns to update in the table or view. The column name is specified, along with the new value for the column. Using the NULL keyword explicitly updates the column to a NULL value. Using the DEFAULT keyword updates the column to its default value, or NULL if no default exists. Otherwise, the column may be updated to a constant value, the results of a function, or the results of a subquery.

The WHERE clause may be omitted entirely, in which case all rows in the table or view are updated. If a WHERE clause is used, then rows may be updated based on standard search criteria or a single row may be updated in a cursor. For more information about using WHERE clauses, see Chapters 4 and 5); for more information about cursors, see Chapter 9, "Programmability."

The preceding syntax is simplified for clarity. It is possible to update variables in the UPDATE statement as well. See the SQL Server Books Online for the full syntax.

The following are some examples of using simple UPDATE statements:

1. This example updates the authors table and sets each author's phone number back to the default value:

```
UPDATE authors
   SET phone = DEFAULT
```

This example has no WHERE clause, so it affects all rows in the table. The phone column could also have been set to a constant value, as shown in this example:

```
UPDATE authors
   SET phone = 'NO PHONE'
```

2. A column may also be updated based on an arithmetic expression. This example updates the titles table to give each author a well-deserved 10 percent increase on their book advances:

```
UPDATE titles
   SET advance = advance * 1.1
```

3. To update only certain rows in a table, use a WHERE clause. This example gives all authors of computer books an additional 10 percent increase on their book advances:

```
UPDATE titles
   SET advance = advance * 1.1
   WHERE title LIKE '%computer%'
```

4. To update the current row of a cursor, use the WHERE CURRENT OF keywords, as shown here:

```
UPDATE jobs
    SET min_lvl = 20
    WHERE CURRENT OF jobs_cursor_to_update
```

Examples #2 and #3 above showed how it is possible to update a column based on an arithmetic expression that involves columns from the same table. It is also possible to use a subquery to provide a value for a column. The WHERE clauses in the prior examples use criteria from the table being updated. It is possible to update rows in a table based on information stored in another table by using a subquery.

Using Subqueries with the UPDATE Statement

Recall from Chapter 5 that subqueries are queries that are embedded in another query. Subqueries may be used with the UPDATE statement in two different ways:

▶ A subquery may be used to provide a value for a column in the SET statement. The subquery must return zero or one value. This example shows how a subquery is used to raise the salary level of all employees hired on or before June 30, 1990, to the maximum salary for their job:

```
UPDATE employee
   SET job_lvl =
      (SELECT max_lvl FROM JOBS WHERE employee.job_id =
      ➥jobs.job_id)
   WHERE hire_date <= '6/30/1990'
```

Note that because the subquery is correlated (the subquery references the outer query—see Chapter 5 for more information), and every employee has a matching job in the jobs table, this subquery always returns one value.

▶ A subquery may be used in the WHERE clause of the UPDATE statement to update records based on records in other tables. A criteria value in the WHERE clause may be matched exactly to a subquery that returns one value, or the criteria value may be matched to a subquery returning multiple values by the use of the IN or EXISTS keywords. As an example, consider the following query, which adds $10,000 to the salary of every employee that works for a publisher that publishes computer books:

```
UPDATE employee
    SET job_lvl = job_lvl + 10
    WHERE pub_id IN
       (SELECT publishers.pub_id FROM publishers INNER JOIN
       ➥titles
        ON publishers.pub_id = titles.pub_id
        WHERE type LIKE 'popular_comp'
       )
```

Subqueries are the ANSI standard way to reference other tables in an UPDATE statement. However, Microsoft has extended the syntax of the UPDATE statement to make referencing other tables easier, as shown in the next section.

Transact-SQL Extensions to the UPDATE Statement

The Transact-SQL UPDATE statement features a FROM clause that allows other tables to be referenced and joined without using a subquery. The extended syntax is as follows:

```
UPDATE {table_name | view_name}
SET
  { column_name = {NULL | DEFAULT | expression} }
  [,{ column_name = {NULL | DEFAULT | expression}...]
[FROM {table_list}]
[WHERE {search_conditions | CURRENT OF cursor_name}]
```

The new FROM clause is used just like the FROM clause on a SELECT statement. Joins may be created between tables by using the old TSQL syntax or the new ANSI-standard syntax. (Chapter 5 discusses joins in more detail.)

 Note

This syntax is specific to SQL Server and may not work with other relational database systems. The subquery syntax presented previously works with all databases that comply with the ANSI SQL syntax.

These examples show how the queries presented in the previous section may be rewritten to use the Transact-SQL syntax:

1. This query updates the employee table to give employees hired on or before June 30, 1990 the maximum salary for their job:

```
UPDATE employee
    SET job_lvl = jobs.max_lvl
    FROM employee INNER JOIN jobs ON employee.job_id =
    ➥jobs.job_id
    WHERE employee.hire_date <= '6/30/1990'
```

2. This query updates the employee table to give the employees of publishers of computer books a $10,000 raise:

```
UPDATE employee
    SET job_lvl = job_lvl + 10
    FROM employee INNER JOIN
        (publishers INNER JOIN titles
            ON publishers.pub_id = titles.pub_id)
        ON employee.pub_id = publishers.pub_id
    WHERE titles.type LIKE 'popular_comp'
```

Note how the query syntax is more consistent when the TSQL extension is used. Many people find that queries with joins are easier to read and write than queries with subqueries. Use whichever you are most comfortable with, with the understanding that the Transact-SQL syntax is specific to SQL Server.

Direct and Deferred Updates

SQL Server may use one of two different methods to update the columns specified in an UPDATE statement. Although these methods are not explicitly mentioned on the test, knowing about them can help you optimize update queries, especially when a large number of rows are updated in a single query.

When SQL Server performs a direct update (or an update-in-place, as it is also known), it simply modifies the data page to reflect the new value in the column. A single log record is written that notes the change in the data. When SQL Server performs a deferred update, it actually deletes the old row and inserts a row with the new values. In a deferred update, at least two log records are written (one for the delete, one for the insert), and other log records may be written to reflect the changes in the table's index(es). Because a direct update writes fewer records to the transaction log, it performs much better than a deferred update.

For a direct update to occur, three basic conditions must be met:

▶ The table cannot have an UPDATE trigger.

▶ The table cannot be marked for replication to other databases.

▶ The UPDATE cannot affect the columns that are used in a clustered index.

In addition, other conditions must be met, depending on whether the UPDATE statement modifies one or many rows:

▶ For updates that modify a single row, the following conditions must be met for a direct update to occur:

   ▶ The updated columns may be variable length (this includes columns of the *varchar* or *varbinary* types, or columns that allow NULLs), but the updated row must fit on the same data page as the original row.

   ▶ The updated column(s) can be part of a unique, non-clustered index if the column(s) are fixed-width and the criteria in the WHERE clause produces an exact match *using that index*. (Remember that any time columns in a clustered index are updated, a deferred update is guaranteed.)

   ▶ If the updated column(s) participate in a non-unique, non-clustered index, then they must be fixed-width for the direct update to occur.

   ▶ No more than 50 percent of the original row may be modified.

▶ For updates that modify multiple rows, the following conditions must be met for a direct update to occur:

   ▶ The updated column(s) cannot be variable length; columns of type *varchar* or *varbinary* fall into this category, as do columns that allow NULLs.

   ▶ The updated column(s) cannot be part of a unique, non-clustered index. (Remember that any time columns in a clustered index are updated, a deferred update is guaranteed.)

   ▶ If the updated column(s) participate in a non-unique, non-clustered index, then they must be fixed-width for the direct update to occur.

> ▶ The table being updated cannot have a column with a *timestamp* data type.

SQL Server does not automatically report which update method it will use for a query. In order to see this information, you must turn on the SHOWPLAN option. This option causes SQL Server to print information about the query plan it will use for the query. The results from a SHOWPLAN can be difficult to interpret, and a discussion on SHOWPLAN is outside the scope of this book. See the SQL Server Books Online for more information—an entire appendix is devoted to this topic.

The DELETE Statement

 Objective ▶ The DELETE statement is used to delete one or more data rows from a table or view. By default, only the table owner may delete rows from a table, although this permission may be granted to other database users. The DELETE statement can only affect a single table at a time, so it may not be used with views that are based on more than one table. DELETE reclaims the database space used by the deleted data rows and any corresponding index rows.

As with all DML statements, DELETEs may be executed from the Query Tool in SQL Enterprise Manager, the ISQL application, or other front-end applications written in Visual Basic or Visual C++.

 Tip

If you execute the examples in this section, data is deleted from the Pubs database. To restore this database, you may execute the script found in the file \MSSQL\INSTALL\ INSTPUBS.SQL. Execute this script while in the *master* database, and Pubs is restored to its original state.

Basic Syntax

The syntax of the DELETE statement is as follows:

```
DELETE [FROM] [[database.][owner].]{table_name | view_name}
    [WHERE {search_conditions | CURRENT OF cursor_name}]
```

The FROM keyword is always optional, and is usually just included for readability. The WHERE clause may be omitted entirely, in which case all rows are deleted from the table or view. If a WHERE clause is used, then rows may be deleted based on standard search criteria or a single row may be deleted from a cursor. For more information on using WHERE clauses, see Chapters 4 and 5; for more information on cursors, see Chapter 9.

Here are some examples of using simple DELETE statements:

1. These examples delete all rows in the discounts table:

   ```
   DELETE discounts
   DELETE FROM discounts
   ```

2. This example deletes the sales records prior to January 1, 1994:

   ```
   DELETE Sales
       WHERE ord_date < '01/01/1994'
   ```

3. This example deletes the current row of the cursor named employee_service:

   ```
   DELETE Sales
       WHERE CURRENT OF employee_service
   ```

Note that in the preceding examples, rows were deleted based on criteria from the table containing the deleted rows. It is possible to delete rows from a table based on information stored in another table, as shown in the next two sections.

Using a Subquery in the WHERE Clause

Subqueries may be used in the WHERE clause of a DELETE statement in much the same way that they are used in a SELECT statement. In the WHERE clause, a criteria value may be matched against a set (by using the IN or EXISTS keywords), or a criteria may be matched to a subquery that returns a single value. Subqueries may be *correlated*, which means that they reference a value in the main, or "outer" query. For a more thorough discussion of subqueries, see Chapter 5.

The following are examples of how subqueries may be used to delete records from a table based on the records present in another table or tables:

1. To delete the employees that have a salary range of $25,000 to $100,000, a subquery is used to first select the job_id for every job that matches this description. The DELETE statement then deletes those employees whose job_id falls within the set of job_id's returned by the subquery:

```
DELETE employee
    WHERE job_id IN
        (SELECT job_id FROM jobs WHERE
        min_lvl = 25 AND max_lvl = 100)
```

This is an example of matching a criteria value to a set of values returned by a subquery. The subquery may return zero or more values.

2. This query deletes the royalty schedule records for book titles that feature information about traditional cooking:

```
DELETE roysched
    WHERE title_id =
        (SELECT title_id FROM titles
        WHERE title_id = roysched.title_id
        AND type LIKE 'trad_cook')
```

This is an example of a criteria value being matched to a subquery that returns a single value. The subquery must return zero or one value. The example also shows the use of a correlated subquery; the subquery selects information from the titles table based on the title_id in the roysched table.

Subqueries are the ANSI standard way to reference other tables in a DELETE statement. However, another syntax exists, as discussed in the next section.

Transact-SQL Extension to the DELETE Statement

Microsoft has extended the syntax of the DELETE statement to make delete queries based on multiple tables easier to read and write. An additional FROM clause is added to the DELETE statement so that multiple tables may be referenced and joined:

```
DELETE [FROM] [[database.][owner].]{table_name | view_name}
    [FROM {table_list}]
    [WHERE {search_conditions | CURRENT OF cursor_name}]
```

The new FROM clause is used just like the FROM clause on a SELECT statement. Joins may be created between tables by using the old TSQL syntax or the new ANSI-standard syntax. (Chapter 5 discusses joins in more detail.)

 Note

Again, this syntax is specific to SQL Server and may not work with other relational database systems. The subquery syntax presented previously works with all databases that comply with the ANSI SQL syntax.

The two examples presented previously are rewritten here using the Transact-SQL syntax:

1. This query deletes those employees with a salary range of $25,000 to $100,000:

```
DELETE employee
    FROM employee INNER JOIN jobs
        ON jobs.job_id = employee.job_id
    WHERE jobs.min_lvl = 25 AND jobs.max_lvl = 100
```

2. This query deletes the royalty schedules for books on traditional cooking:

```
DELETE roysched
    FROM roysched INNER JOIN titles
        ON roysched.title_id = titles.title_id
    WHERE titles.type LIKE 'trad_cook'
```

 **Tip**

> If you want to see which rows will be deleted by these queries, you may comment out the "DELETE <tablename>" portion of the query and replace it with "SELECT * FROM <tablename>". This turns the DELETE statement into a SELECT statement so you may verify that the correct rows will be deleted.

Using the TRUNCATE TABLE Statement

The TRUNCATE TABLE statement is very similar to an unrestricted DELETE in that it removes all rows from a table, but is usually much faster. When a DELETE statement is executed, every row deletion is logged in the transaction log. When a TRUNCATE TABLE statement is executed, whole data pages are deallocated, and only the page deallocations are logged. While the TRUNCATE TABLE and unrestricted DELETE are basically the same, there are some subtle differences you need to be aware of:

▶ Because TRUNCATE TABLE does not log each individual row deletion, it cannot be rolled back if executed from within a transaction.

▶ TRUNCATE TABLE does not activate the DELETE trigger on a table.

▶ TRUNCATE TABLE may not be used on a table that is referenced by a FOREIGN KEY constraint.

▶ If an IDENTITY column exists on the truncated table, it will be reset to its original *seed* value.

The syntax of the TRUNCATE TABLE statement is:

```
TRUNCATE TABLE [[database.[owner].]table_name
```

For example, this statement removes all rows from the authors_examples table used in the "Insert" section:

```
TRUNCATE TABLE pubs..authors_examples
```

Importing and Exporting Data with BCP

 Objective

The Bulk Copy Program (BCP) is a utility that ships with SQL Server that does exactly what its name implies—it moves large amounts of data into and out of a SQL Server database. Data may be imported from or exported to a text or native-format file. (For more information about the BCP file types, see "BCP Terminology" later in this section.)

BCP is a command line utility that is executed from a DOS window within Windows NT. For this reason, developers often complain about its cryptic commands and error messages. However, BCP is perhaps the most powerful tool available to the SQL Server database developer, so it deserves careful study. Here are some of the more common uses for the BCP utility:

▶ Importing ISAM or VSAM data from a mainframe into SQL Server tables.

▶ Importing flat-file information from other sources, such as other databases or electronic data services.

▶ Exporting information in a database for use in other data analysis tools, such as a spreadsheet.

▶ Transferring data from one SQL Server to another.

 Tip

BCP is built around several API calls in the DB-Library interface to SQL Server. This means that you can write applications in C or C++ that use DB-Lib to transfer large amounts of data. For more information on the DB-Library API, see Chapter 12, "Application Development and Open Data Services (ODS)" or the SQL Server Books Online.

BCP Terminology

Before you begin using BCP, you should learn about the jargon surrounding the use of this utility. Following are some of the more common terms you will encounter when using BCP:

▶ **Data File:** This is the operating system file that contains the data to be imported into SQL Server, or the file that contains exported data. You will often see this called a *source file* when the data is to be imported. The data may be in either native or character format.

▶ **Character Format:** BCP can import from or export to a *character* (or text) file. These files use the standard ASCII character set to store information, and are often used when transferring data between heterogeneous sources (such as a SQL Server and a mainframe). Columns in a character file are divided by delimiters (such as a comma or a Tab character) or defined to be of a certain size (a fixed-width file). You may use a text editor such as Notepad to view the contents of a character file.

▶ **Native Format:** BCP also can import from or export to a *native* file. Native files are binary files that contain the data in the same format that SQL Server uses to internally store data. Native files are generally used to transfer data between SQL Servers.

▶ **Format File:** When transferring data into or out of a character data file, you may use a *format file* to specify the column and row delimiters used in the data file. Format files also are useful for importing only parts of the data file into a table. The format file is covered later in this section.

▶ **Batch Size:** By default, BCP loads all rows from the data file into SQL Server in a single transaction. By specifying a batch size, you can tell BCP to load the data in smaller "chunks." See "Command-Line Syntax" later in this chapter for more information.

▶ **Source Table/Destination Table:** These terms are often used to describe the table from which data will be exported or the table to which data will be imported, respectively.

Permissions Required to Use BCP

To use the BCP utility, you must have a valid logon ID on the SQL Server and a valid user ID in the database involved in the data transfer. In addition, you must have the following permissions:

- ▶ If the data file resides on an NTFS partition, you must have permissions to read from the file (for imports) and create or modify the file (for exports).

- ▶ When importing data, you must have INSERT permission on the destination table. If you own the table, you will automatically have INSERT permission; otherwise, the table owner needs to grant this to your database user ID.

- ▶ When exporting data, you must have SELECT permission on the source table. The table owner has this permission to select data and may grant this permission to other database users. In addition, you must have SELECT permission on three tables in the database's catalog: *sysobjects, syscolumns,* and *sysindexes.*

BCP Data Transfer Behavior

Knowing about how BCP transfers data into and out of SQL Server can save you hours of frustration. The first thing to remember is that when importing data into a table, rows are appended to the end of the table; existing rows are left intact. Alternately, when exporting to a file, the file is overwritten if it already exists.

When BCP is importing data into a table, other users in the database may be using that table. The rows inserted by BCP become visible after a batch has been completed. (Remember that by default, the entire contents of the data file are loaded in a single batch.) When BCP is exporting data from a table, other users may be using the table as well. However, BCP exports a "snapshot" of the table as it existed when the BCP was started. Data modifications made by users after the BCP has started are not reflected in the data file. For this reason, it is often a good idea to prevent users from accessing the database (or at least the table) while data is being exported.

When BCP is importing data into a table, two different methods may be used: fast BCP or slow BCP. Keep in mind that BCP, whether it be fast or slow, is many times faster than any other SQL Server data transfer method. Regardless of the transfer speed, column data types and NULL options are always enforced. Attempting to import data of the incorrect type, or attempting to import a NULL value into a column that forbids NULLs will cause the BCP batch to fail. Fortunately, any default constraints are honored during a BCP import.

Fast BCP

Fast BCP is the preferred method for transferring very large amounts of data because it is (as the name implies) extremely fast—several thousand rows may be inserted per second. In a fast BCP, SQL Server only logs the extent allocations used to increase the size of the destination table. (Recall from Chapter 2 that tables are expanded by 16K extents when data is inserted.)

For a fast BCP to take place, a number of conditions must be met:

▶ The "Select Into/Bulkcopy" option for the database must be turned on. This allows non-logged operations to occur, and fast BCP is basically a non-logged operation. (The log writes due to page allocations are built-in to the normal operations of SQL Server; thus, fast BCP is considered non-logged.)

 **Warning**

Permitting non-logged operations in a database means that you lose the ability to perform up-to-the-minute recovery with the transaction log; only the full database may be backed up and restored. (SQL Server still performs automatic recovery in the event of a system failure.)

For this reason, you should perform a full backup of a database (if it has data) before importing large amounts of data. After the data load is complete, perform another full backup, and turn off the "Select Into/Bulkcopy" option.

▶ The destination table may not have indexes or constraints defined.

▶ The destination table may have triggers or rules defined; however, rules will not be enforced and triggers will not fire during the data import.

▶ The destination table may not be marked for replication.

If these conditions are not met, a slow BCP takes place.

Slow BCP

During a slow BCP, the inserted data is logged in the transaction log just as if an INSERT statement had been executed. Any constraints on the table are enforced, as are unique indexes. Because the amount of logging increases with a slow BCP, it is often much slower than a fast BCP, often by a factor of ten.

A slow BCP is a fully logged operation, so up-to-the-minute recovery is possible with a current transaction log dump. However, the transaction log may fill up if a large amount of data is imported.

Command-Line Syntax

The syntax of the BCP command line utility follows. The executable file, BCP.EXE, may be found in the BINN subdirectory under the SQL Server installation directory.

```
BCP [[database_name.]owner.]table_name {in | out} datafile
[/m maxerrors] [/f formatfile] [/e errfile]
[/F firstrow] [/L lastrow] [/b batchsize]
[/n] [/c] [/E]
[/t field_term] [/r row_term]
[/i inputfile] [/o outputfile]
/U login_id [/P password] [/T] [/S servername] [/v] [/a
packet_size]
```

Note

Command line options are case sensitive, so /f and /F are different options.

{in | out } specifies whether data will be imported or exported from the table.

datafile specifies the name of the data file.

/m is used to specify the maximum number of errors that may occur before the transfer is canceled. If this option is omitted, BCP fails after ten errors.

/f specifies the name of the format file, if used.

/e specifies the file to which error messages will be logged. By default, error messages are reported on-screen as they are generated.

/F specifies the number of the first row to copy. If omitted, BCP starts transferring with the first row in the data file or source table.

/L specifies the number of the last row to copy. If this option is omitted, BCP ends the transfer with the last row in the data file or source table.

/b enables you to specify the batch size (in # of rows) for the data transfer. If this option is omitted, BCP transfers all rows in a single batch. This option is useful if the entire BCP batch fills the transaction log due to page allocations. Specifying a smaller batch size and turning on the database "trunc. log on chkpt." option can prevent the transaction log from filling up. In addition, reducing the batch size can prevent SQL Server from running out of locks during the import of data.

/n specifies that the data file is a native format file, or that the data file created from an export should be in native format.

/c specifies that a character format data file will be used for the transfer. The default column delimiter is a Tab, and the default row delimiter is a carriage return / linefeed combination (or CRLF).

/E specifies that the BCP transfer will be importing data into a table with an identity column, and that the values for the identity column will be explicitly provided in the data file. This option has no effect if data is being exported.

/**t** specifies the column (or field) terminator for a character format data file.

/**r** specifies the row terminator for a character format data file.

/**i** may be used to specify a file that contains input to redirect to BCP.

/**o** may be used to specify an output file for all BCP messages (other than errors).

/**U** is used when BCP is to log into the SQL Server in mixed or standard security modes. It specifies the name of the database user ID to use for the transfer.

/**P** is used when BCP is to log into the SQL Server in mixed or standard security modes. It specifies the password of the database user ID given with the /U parameter.

/**T** specifies that BCP should log into the SQL Server with a trusted security connection.

/**S** specifies the name of the SQL Server that is participating in the data transfer. This option may be omitted if the data file resides on the actual SQL Server machine. If possible, perform data transfers on the machine that hosts SQL Server—this reduces the overhead generated by sending data across the network.

/**v** prints the DB-Library version information.

/**a** specifies the network packet size used when BCP loads data into a SQL Server over the network. A packet size of 4096 to 8192 gives the best performance.

The following are some examples of using BCP to transfer data into and out of the Pubs database:

1. This example exports data from the authors table into a character file called C:\authors.txt. The file's columns are

tab-delimited, with a new row on each line. A trusted connection is used to connect to the local server.

```
BCP pubs..authors out C:\authors.txt /c /T
```

The results of this command will look something like this:

```
Starting copy...

23 rows copied.
Network packet size (bytes): 4096
Clock Time (ms.): total =     20 Avg =      0 (1150.00 rows
per sec.)
```

2. This example imports the data file from example #1 back into the authors table in the Pubs database:

```
BCP pubs..authors in C:\authors.txt /c /T
```

Because data already exists in the authors table, this import attempts to insert duplicate data. BCP returns the following error message:

```
Starting copy...
Msg 2627, Level 14, State 1:
Line 1:
Violation of PRIMARY KEY constraint 'UPKCL_auidind': Attempt
to insert duplicate key in object 'authors'.
```

3. This example exports the contents of the authors table into a native format file called C:\authors.dat:

```
BCP pubs..authors out C:\authors.dat /n /T
```

Using Format Files

BCP format files enable you to fine-tune the way data files are imported into a table, or how a table's data is exported into the data file. You may specify different column or row terminators, adjust the length of the data transferred, or rearrange the order in which table columns are transferred. You will most often create a format file when importing a mainframe text file into SQL Server. Figure 6.1 shows a sample format file that might be used to import data into the jobs table in the Pubs database. Each part of the format file is marked so you may distinguish between the different parts used.

Figure 6.1

Annotated format file for the jobs table.

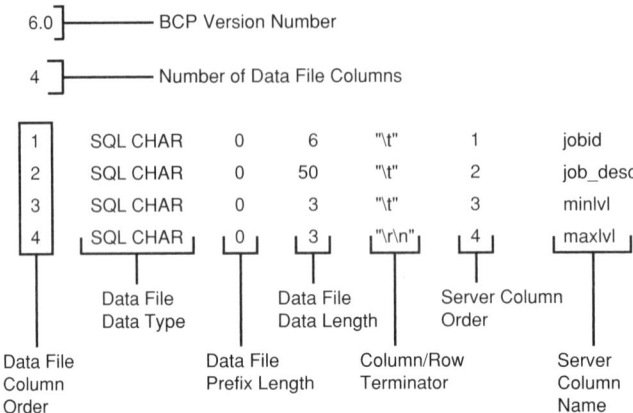

The purposes of each part of the format file are detailed in the following list:

Version: This is version number of the BCP program. This is always "6.0" for SQL Server versions 6.0 and later.

Number of Columns: This is the number of columns in the data file.

Data File Column Order: This is the order in which the columns appear in the data file. These are usually just listed in sequential order.

Data Type: Specifies the data type of the column in the data file. For text files, always use SQLCHAR. For native format files, use the name of the table column's data type, such as SQLSMALLINT for a smallint column.

Prefix Length: This value is used with native format files to specify a storage area in the file used to hold the length of the data in the column. For text files, always use 0.

Data Length: This value specifies the actual length of the data in the data file for a particular column. For text files, this is the maximum length of a column—for instance, when the max_lvl column is represented as characters, the number may range from 0 to 255. The maximum length for this field would be 3 characters.

Terminator: The terminator column is used to specify column terminators for all but the last column and a row terminator for the last column. Typically, tabs (\t) or commas are used to delimit columns, and a CRLF (\r\n) is used to delimit rows.

Server Column Order: This specifies the column that SQL Server should insert into or retrieve from in the destination or source table.

Server Column Name: The name of the column in the source or destination table. SQL Server does not actually use this to determine which column data will be inserted to or retrieved from, so you may enter any value here. However, you cannot leave this column blank.

See the SQL Server Books Online for more in-depth information about how format files may be used in a data transfer.

Using the Transfer Tool in Enterprise Manager

Prior to SQL 6.0, a separate tool called SQL Transfer Manager shipped with SQL Server. This tool provided a graphical interface that enabled you to easily transfer data between SQL Servers. In SQL 6.5, Microsoft eliminated this separate application and added its functionality to SQL Enterprise Manager. This section introduces you to the new transfer tool in Enterprise Manager.

The transfer tool is used to move data between different databases residing on the same SQL Server or different SQL Servers. In addition, objects and data may be transferred from a Sybase SQL Server to a Microsoft SQL Server. Unlike BCP, which just transfers data, the transfer tool also can transfer objects (such as tables, indexes, triggers, stored procedures, and so on) between databases.

To use the transfer tool, follow these steps:

1. Load the SQL Enterprise Manager application. In the server manager window, select the server that contains the source database for the transfer.

2. From the main menu, select Tools, Database/Object Transfer... The Database/Object Transfer dialog box appears, as shown in figure 6.2.

Figure 6.2

The Database/Object Transfer dialog box.

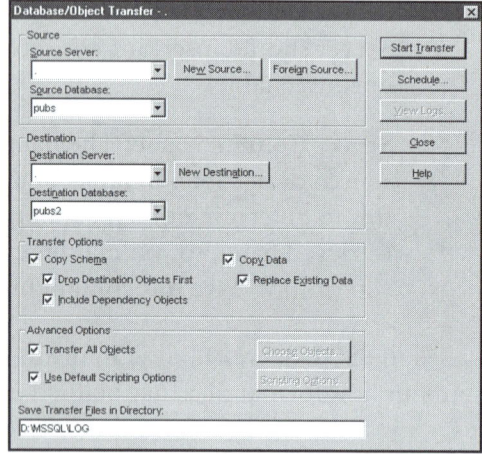

3. In the Source frame, select the source server and database by using the Source Server and Source Database combo boxes, respectively. The objects transferred come from this server and database.

   You may use the New Source button to register a new SQL Server in Enterprise Manager. Alternately, you may use the Foreign Source button to log into a Sybase SQL Server.

4. In the Destination frame, use the Destination Server and Destination Database combo boxes to specify the server and database to which you wish to transfer the data. If the destination server isn't already registered in Enterprise Manager, use the New Destination button to register it.

 **Note** The destination database must already exist; there is no way to create a new database from the transfer tool.

5. In the Transfer Options frame, you may set options for the transfer:

   ▶ **Copy Schema:** By checking this box, you tell the transfer tool to copy database objects from the source database to the destination database. If the objects being transferred already exist in the destination database, choosing the Drop Destination Objects option removes and re-creates these objects. If you would like SQL Server to transfer objects dependent on other objects (such as a table's triggers along with the table), enable the Include Dependency Objects option.

   ▶ **Copy Data:** By checking this box, you tell transfer manager to copy the data from the source tables to the destination tables. If you want to replace any existing data in existing destination tables, click the Replace Existing Data box.

      If you choose the Copy Data option without choosing the Copy Schema option, the destination tables must exist, or transfer manager will not be able to move the data.

6. In the Advanced Options frame, you may set additional options to govern the transfer:

   ▶ **Objects to Transfer:** This option enables you to specify which objects in the source database you wish to transfer to the destination database.

   ▶ **Scripting Options:** This option enables you to specify which parts of the database schema you wish to transfer. You may control scripting for table indexes and constraints, and security permissions.

7. To start the transfer, click the Start Transfer button in the upper-right corner of the dialog box. The transfer begins

immediately, with a progress indicator to keep you apprised of the status of the transfer.

 **Note**

You also may click the Schedule button to schedule the transfer for a later time, perhaps during off-hours.

In addition, you may schedule the transfer for immediate execution, which has the advantage of returning control immediately to Enterprise Manager. Otherwise, you will be unable to use Enterprise Manager while the transfer is taking place.

The transfer tool is very useful for moving databases between servers, or creating copies of databases for backup or testing purposes. It eliminates much of the busywork involved in generating scripts, running the scripts in the new database, and manually transferring data using BCP.

Summary

This chapter introduced you to the INSERT, UPDATE, and DELETE commands, the Structured Query Language (SQL) keywords used to modify data in a database. These commands allowed you to insert, modify, and delete rows in a table. This chapter also covered the bulk transfer of data into and out of SQL Server. The Bulk Copy Program (BCP) and the Database Transfer tool in Enterprise Manager can both be used to efficiently move large amounts of data into and out of a table. As noted in the chapter, the Transfer tool copies database objects in addition to transferring data.

Exercises

Exercise 6.1:   Inserting a Record into the Authors Table

This exercise walks you through the steps required to insert a record into the authors table in the Pubs database. You can insert a record that makes you an author.

1. Start the SQL Enterprise Manager application. In the Server Manager window, select a SQL Server that contains the Pubs database.

2. From the application's main menu, select Tools, SQL Query Tool. The Query window appears.

3. Select the Pubs database from the DB combo box.

4. Type the following query:

```
INSERT INTO authors (au_id, au_lname, au_fname, phone,
➥address, city, state, zip, contract)
VALUES ('<your ssn>','<your last name>','<your first
➥name>','<your phone number>', '<your address>','<your
➥city>','<your state>','<your zip code>',1)
```

Your query should look something like the following:

```
INSERT INTO authors (au_id, au_lname, au_fname, phone,
➥address, city, state, zip, contract)
VALUES ('111-22-9999','Author','Joe','816 555-1212',
        '123 anystreet','Kansas City','MO','64114',1)
```

5. Type Alt-X or click the Execute Query button on the query window toolbar to execute the query. The following message should appear:

```
(1 row(s) affected)
```

Exercise 6.2:   Modifying Records in the Titles Table

In this exercise, you update all of the computer titles in the titles table to increase the advance amount by 10%.

1. Start the SQL Enterprise Manager application. In the Server Manager window, select a SQL Server that contains the Pubs database.

2. From the application's main menu, select Tools, SQL Query Tool. The Query window appears.

3. Select the Pubs database from the DB combo box.

4. Type the following query:

```
UPDATE titles
    SET advance = advance * 1.1
    WHERE type LIKE 'popular_comp'
```

5. Type Alt-X or click the Execute Query button on the query window toolbar to execute the query. A message similar to the following should appear:

```
(3 row(s) affected)
```

Exercise 6.3:   Deleting a Record from the Authors Table

In this exercise, you delete the record you inserted in Exercise 6.1 from the authors table in the Pubs database.

1. Start the SQL Enterprise Manager application. In the Server Manager window, select a SQL Server that contains the Pubs database.

2. From the application's main menu, select Tools, SQL Query Tool. The Query window appears.

3. Select the Pubs database from the DB combo box.

4. Type the following query:

```
DELETE authors
    WHERE au_id = '111-22-9999'
```

If you used your own social security number when inserting the record, use that in the preceding query. If you used the example INSERT statement in Exercise 6.1, this query deletes the sample record:

```
DELETE authors
    WHERE au_id = '<your ssn>'
```

5. Type Alt-X or click the Execute Query button on the query window toolbar to execute the query. The following message should appear:

```
(1 row(s) affected)
```

Exercise 6.4: Exporting the Contents of the Employee Table

In this exercise, you export the rows in the employee table to a text file and a native file.

1. Open a DOS window, and change to a directory in which you wish to create the data files.

2. At the command prompt, type the following command to export the employee table to a text file. This example assumes that your SQL Server is using trusted security. If it is not, specify a user name and password by using the /U and /P command line parameters.

```
BCP pubs..employee out empl.txt /T /c
```

BCP should give a message similar to the following:

```
Starting copy...

34 rows copied.
Network packet size (bytes): 4096
Clock Time (ms.): total =     90 Avg =     2 (377.78 rows
per sec.)
```

3. Examine the contents of the empl.txt file by issuing the following command:

```
type empl.txt
```

4. Export the employee table again, this time in native format:

```
BCP pubs..employee out empl.dat /T /n
```

5. Examine the contents of the empl.dat file by issuing this command at the DOS prompt:

```
type empl.dat
```

Note that the file is difficult, if not impossible, to read as straight text. This is because the file is stored in a more efficient binary format. If you compare the size of the two files, the native file will be smaller.

Exercise 6.5: Importing the Contents of the Employee Table

In this exercise, you delete the contents of the employee table and load the contents of one of the data files you created in Exercise 6.4.

1. Start the SQL Enterprise Manager application. In the Server Manager window, select a SQL Server that contains the Pubs database.

2. From the application's main menu, select Tools|SQL Query Tool... The Query window appears.

3. Select the Pubs database from the DB combo box.

4. Type the following query:

```
DELETE employee
```

5. Execute the query by typing Alt-X or clicking the Execute Query button on the query window toolbar. The contents of the employee table are deleted.

6. Open a DOS window, and change to the directory that contains the data files you created in Exercise 6.4.

7. Now, import one of the data files into the employee table. If you want to import the text file, use *empl.txt* as the data file name and use the /c command line switch. If you want to

import the native file, use *empl.dat* as the data file name and use the /n command line switch. The following command imports the character-based file:

```
BCP pubs..employee in empl.txt /T /c
```

BCP should return messages similar to the following:

```
Starting copy...

34 rows copied.
Network packet size (bytes): 4096
Clock Time (ms.): total =    110 Avg =      3 (309.09 rows
per sec.)
```

8. Switch back to the Query window in Enterprise Manager and execute this query to verify that the contents of the data file have been imported into the table:

```
SELECT * FROM employee
```

Review Questions

1. When using an INSERT statement, data to be inserted may come from:

   A. The VALUES clause

   B. A stored procedure

   C. Another database

   D. A SELECT statement

2. What is the purpose of the column list in the INSERT statement?

   A. It provides values to be inserted into each column.

   B. It lists which columns will have data inserted into them.

   C. It lists which columns will be excluded from having data inserted in them.

   D. SQL Server does not use the column list; it is used only as a means for the developer to document the columns used in the INSERT statement.

3. You want to insert data into the jobs table of the Pubs database, which has an IDENTITY column. Which statement(s) enable you to insert a row into this table?

   A. INSERT jobs (job_id, job_desc, min_lvl, max_lvl) VALUES (42,'Temp Employee',10,10)

   B. INSERT jobs (job_desc, min_lvl, max_lvl) VALUES ('Temp Employee',10,10)

   C. INSERT jobs VALUES (42,'Temp Employee',10,10)

   D. SET IDENTITY_INSERT ON

      INSERT jobs (job_id, job_desc, min_lvl, max_lvl) VALUES (42,'Temp Employee',10,10)

      SET IDENTITY_INSERT OFF

4. If the column list is omitted from the INSERT statement, which columns must be provided in the VALUES clause? Assume IDENTITY_INSERT is turned off.

    A. All columns

    B. Only those columns that do not allow NULLs

    C. Only the columns without defaults defined

    D. All columns except the identity column

5. What is the purpose of the DEFAULT keyword when used in the VALUES clause of the INSERT statement?

    A. To define a default value for a column

    B. To explicitly use the default value of a column

    C. To specify a default value for that column if the SELECT statement provides a NULL value

    D. To explicitly use the column's default value if the column allows NULLs

6. If the DEFAULT keyword is used in the INSERT or UPDATE statement, and no default exists for that column, what is/are the result(s)?

    A. A NULL value will be provided for the column.

    B. The query will fail.

    C. The query may fail if the column does not allow NULLs.

    D. A value of 'UNKNOWN' is placed in the column.

7. In the SET portion of an UPDATE statement, where may the new value for a column come from?

   A. Another table by way of a single-result subquery or table join in the FROM clause

   B. An arithmetic expression or constant value

   C. Values for multiple rows in the update may come from a subquery that returns more than one value

   D. Another column within the table itself

   E. An explicit NULL value may be specified

8. An UPDATE statement may modify how many tables?

   A. One or more tables, provided the UPDATE statement is not operating on a view

   B. Only one, except when updating a view based on multiple tables

   C. One

   D. Up to sixteen

9. Omitting the WHERE clause of an UPDATE or DELETE statement has what effect?

   A. All rows in the specified table are affected.

   B. The query returns an error because the WHERE clause is required.

   C. Only the current row of the specified cursor is affected.

10. A subquery that returns multiple values may be used in what parts of an UPDATE statement?

    A. The SET clause only

    B. The SET and WHERE clauses

    C. The WHERE clause only

11. What is/are the purpose(s) of the additional FROM clause in the extended Transact-SQL syntax for the UPDATE and DELETE statements?

    A. Allows data modifications to more than one table

    B. Allows data modifications based on data in other tables

    C. Allows column values in the UPDATE statement to come from columns in other tables

    D. Provides an alternative way to perform subqueries

12. If a table has an UPDATE trigger, how does this affect the update method used on the table?

    A. A direct update will occur.

    B. A deferred update will occur.

    C. Triggers are ignored when determining the update method.

13. How does a TRUNCATE TABLE statement differ from an unrestricted DELETE?

    A. A TRUNCATE TABLE cannot be rolled back, even if it occurs within a transaction.

    B. An unrestricted DELETE resets an IDENTITY column to its original seed, while the TRUNCATE TABLE will not.

    C. If the table is referenced by a FOREIGN KEY constraint, only the DELETE may be used.

    D. The TRUNCATE TABLE causes a DELETE trigger to be fired, while the DELETE will not.

    E. A TRUNCATE TABLE is often much faster than an unrestricted DELETE.

14. What utilities may be used to transfer large amounts of data in SQL Server 6.5?

   A. Bulk Copy Program (BCP)

   B. SQL Transfer Manager

   C. Transfer tool in Enterprise Manager

   D. DB-Library functions called from Visual Basic or C++

15. How do BCP and the Enterprise Manager Transfer tool differ?

   A. Both offer the same features.

   B. The Transfer Tool can copy database objects, not just data.

   C. BCP can copy database objects, not just data.

16. When using BCP to copy data into a table, which of the following statement(s) apply?

   A. Database users will not be able to access the table because BCP will lock it.

   B. Database users will see the rows inserted by BCP after each batch is complete.

   C. You must have INSERT permission on the table.

   D. Existing rows in the table are replaced by BCP.

   E. A fast BCP may occur even if the table has triggers or rules defined.

17. When using BCP to transfer data out of a table, which of the following statement(s) apply?

   A. Database users will not be able to access the table because BCP will lock it.

   B. You must have SELECT permission on the table.

    C. Data changes made by other users during the BCP will not be reflected in the data file.

    D. The contents of the data file are replaced if the data file already exists.

18. For a fast BCP to occur, which conditions must be met?

    A. The destination database must have its "Select Into/ Bulkcopy" option turned on.

    B. The table may not have constraints or indexes defined.

    C. The data file must be in native format.

    D. The destination table may not be marked for replication.

    E. The destination table may not have triggers or rules defined.

19. Why would you use the /E command line switch during a BCP?

    A. Because the destination table has an identity column defined

    B. To enable the enhanced features of BCP

    C. Because the destination table has an identity column defined, and the source file explicitly provides values for that column

    D. Because the source table has an identity column, it will not be exported

20. What are the main reasons for using a format file?

    A. To provide alternative row and column terminators

    B. To provide column names for a new table created during an import

    C. To rearrange the order in which columns are imported into a table

    D. To parse a text file in a non-standard format

Answers to Review Questions

1. A,B,C,D. Data may come from another database by means of a remote stored procedure.

2. B

3. B,D

4. D

5. B

6. A,C

7. A,B,D,E

8. C

9. A

10. C

11. B,C,D

12. B

13. A,C,E

14. A,C,D. Transfer Manager was available prior to version 6.5.

15. B

16. B,C,E

17. B,C,D

18. A,B,D

19. C

20. A,C,D

Answers to Test Yourself Questions at Beginning of Chapter

1. The INSERT statement adds row(s) to a table; see "The INSERT statement." The UPDATE statement modifies existing row(s) in a table; see "The UPDATE Statement." The DELETE statement removes row(s) from a table; see "The DELETE Statement."

2. Zero or more rows may be affected by the three data modification statements. See "The INSERT Statement," "The UPDATE Statement," or "The DELETE Statement."

3. Only one table may be affected at a time by using the data modification commands. See "The INSERT State-ment," "The UPDATE Statement," or "The DELETE Statement."

4. BCP is used to transfer large amounts of data into SQL Server from a file, or transfer large amounts of data out of SQL Server into a file. See "Importing and Exporting Data with BCP."

5. A fast BCP is a non-logged operation, while a slow BCP logs all data inserted into a table. A slow BCP is used if the table has indexes or constraints, if the table is marked for replication, or if non-logged operations are not permitted in the table's database. A fast BCP is many times faster than a slow BCP. See "BCP Data Transfer Behavior."

Chapter

Indexes

7

This chapter helps you prepare for the exam by covering the following objectives:

 Objectives

- ▶ Identify appropriate uses of indexing

- ▶ Differentiate between clustered and non-clustered indexes

- ▶ Create unique and composite indexes

- ▶ Identify performance considerations when using indexes

- ▶ Use index management options

Test Yourself! Before reading this chapter, test yourself to determine how much study time you will need to devote to this section.

1. What is the *main* difference between a clustered and non-clustered index?

2. What are the advantages and disadvantages of using indexes?

3. What is a unique index?

4. What is a composite index?

5. What are the two main Transact-SQL commands used for managing indexes?

6. Which index characteristic does SQL Server use to determine if an index should be used in a query?

Answers are located at the end of the chapter...

Indexes are an important part of any database implementation. Properly indexed tables allow SQL Server to quickly and efficiently access the data in a database. On the other hand, improperly indexed tables, while they may not slow SQL Server, can consume unnecessary space in the database. Understanding and applying the indexing options available to you is therefore vital not only for passing the test, but also for having a well-functioning database.

This chapter covers the information you need to know for the test and for effectively implementing indexes in a database. It starts with several sections that introduce you to indexes and how they work, then progresses to discussions on implementing indexes. The topics include:

- ▶ Introduction to indexes

- ▶ Characteristics of indexes

- ▶ Guidelines for indexing

- ▶ SQL Server's use of indexes

- ▶ Managing indexes with Transact-SQL

- ▶ Managing indexes with Enterprise Manager

Introduction to Indexes

 Indexes are extremely beneficial if they are used properly in a database. Following are some of the advantages of using indexes.

- ▶ Indexes give SQL Server a much quicker path to any particular row in a table. Without an index, SQL Server would need to perform a search through all of the rows in a table. (See "SQL Server's Use of Indexes," later in this chapter.)

- ▶ Indexes can enforce entity integrity (see Chapter 1, "Data Modeling") by guaranteeing that rows are not duplicated in a table.

▶ Indexes can improve the performance of queries that use joins to retrieve data from two or more tables. (see Chapter 5, "Retrieving Data (Advanced Topics)" for more information on joins.)

▶ Indexes are always created in ascending order, based on the sort order of the database (The sort order is determined when the SQL Server is installed. See New Riders's *MCSE Training Guide: SQL Server 6.5 Administration* for more information). Because the rows are indexed in ascending order, they can be used to physically sort the rows in a table and greatly improve the performance of queries that use the ORDER BY clause.

Because indexes are so helpful, you may ask why don't we index every column in every table? Well, the primary reason is that indexes can actually slow down the performance of queries that update data. SQL Server dynamically updates the index(es) on a table whenever the data in that table is changed. Indexes also consume space in the database, and take time to create. Maintaining many indexes on a large table can be impractical.

So, what exactly is an index? Indexes serve much the same purpose as a library's card catalog. A card catalog provides multiple ways to look up a book in a library. Books are listed alphabetically by title or author on index cards for easy searching, then the card provides a Dewey decimal number that enables you to quickly find the book in the library's stacks.

Indexes in SQL Server are implemented in much the same way; SQL Server maintains an ordered list of the rows in a table so it may look them up quickly. The arrangement of the index information is based on the index's *key*—this is the column or columns in the table that SQL Server uses to perform the lookup. A card catalog also has a key; books may be indexed by title or author name, for instance.

SQL Server indexes differ from a card catalog in structure if not in function. Information in an index is arranged in a tree-like structure to increase the speed of searches performed with the index. At the top of the index tree is the *root* of the index. Starting at the root, SQL Server follows a path down through the levels of the index (the *non-leaf* pages) to get to the *leaf* pages, which then reference the actual data rows. A library card catalog can be thought of as an index with two levels. The first level is the labeling on the drawers of the catalog, which enables you to pick the correct drawer, say for author names beginning with the letter B. You then refine your search by browsing through the index cards in the drawer. The card you are looking for then points you to the correct book.

Characteristics of Indexes

 Objective

SQL Server has two major types of indexes, clustered and non-clustered, that differ slightly in the way they are implemented. Indexes also may be created to permit only unique key values or may be created on more than one column.

Clustered Indexes

In a clustered index, the data pages of the table and the leaf pages of the index are one and the same. This reduces an extra jump that SQL Server must make from the leaf page of the index to the appropriate data page in the table and has the added effect of physically sorting the rows by the index's key. Figure 7.1 shows a graphical representation of a clustered index.

Figure 7.1

A clustered index.

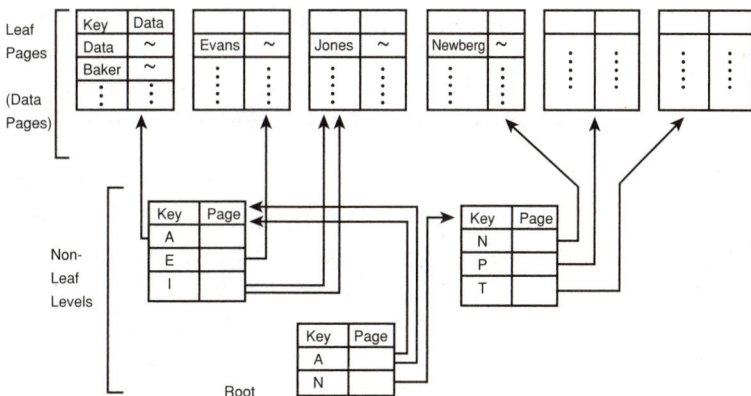

The figure shows how a table of authors might be indexed by author last name. At the top of the diagram are the table's data pages, which show several rows of data, keyed by authors' last names. Remember that because this is a clustered index, these pages also are the leaf pages of the index. On the next few levels of the index, the index pages contain key values and pointers to the next level of the index. Note how the index tapers off to the root index page.

To find the author *Jones*, SQL Server would follow these steps:

1. *Jones* begins with a J, so SQL Server follows the left branch of the index. (The index is created in ascending order, and J comes before N).

2. The next page contains three values: A, E, and I. J comes after I, so SQL Server follows the rightmost branch from that page.

3. This path takes it to the data page, where it can look through the rows until it finds Jones.

Note that (unless the table is small) SQL Server looks at fewer pages when using an index than when scanning through every row in the table.

When you are creating a clustered index, keep the following in mind:

1. Only one clustered index may be created per table.

2. The leaf pages are the table's data pages, and the rows are physically stored in order according to the index key.

3. Because the physical order of the rows is changed when a clustered index is built, create a clustered index before creating any non-clustered indexes. Otherwise, all non-clustered indexes need to be rebuilt.

4. Clustered indexes are smaller than non-clustered indexes. However, you need enough room in the database (about 1.2 times the original table's size) to initially create a clustered index.

For more information about when a clustered index should be chosen over a non-clustered index, see the section later in this chapter, "Guidelines for Indexing."

Non-Clustered Indexes

In a non-clustered index, the leaf pages maintain a set of pointers into the appropriate *rows* on the data pages. (This differs slightly from a clustered index. In a clustered index, the last index level points to the data pages, not individual rows.) For this reason, the card catalog example mentioned previously is more like a non-clustered index than a clustered index. The index cards have pointers that tell you where to find a particular book. Figure 7.2 shows a graphical representation of a non-clustered index.

Figure 7.2

A non-clustered index.

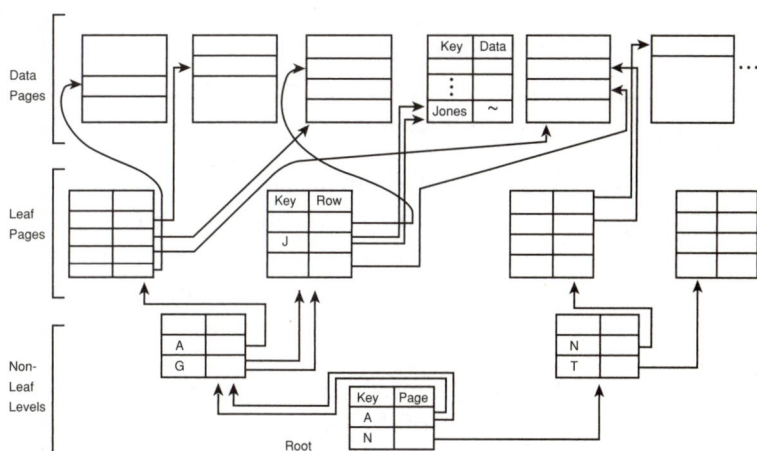

The figure shows how a table of authors might be indexed by author last name. At the top of the diagram are the table's data pages, which show several rows of data. Note that the authors' names do not appear in any particular order. The next level is the leaf level of the index. Every row in the leaf level pages points to a row in the data pages. Below the leaf pages are the additional pages of the index, which just maintain pointers to other index pages. Again, the index tapers to a single root page.

In this example, to find the author *Jones*, SQL Server would follow these steps:

1. Jones begins with a J, so SQL Server follows the left branch of the index.

2. The next page contains two values: A and G. J comes after G, so SQL Server follows the right branch from the page.

3. The right branch takes it to a leaf page. By looking through the leaf page, it finds J and follows the pointer to the row containing Jones.

When you are creating a non-clustered index, keep the following in mind:

1. Up to 249 non-clustered indexes may exist on a table. Remember that some constraints create indexes, and these count against that total.

2. The leaf pages point to the appropriate data pages in the table. The logical order of the rows as defined by the index's key is different than the physical order.

3. Because the physical order of the rows is changed when a clustered index is built, create a clustered index before creating any non-clustered indexes. Otherwise, all non-clustered indexes will need to be rebuilt so that the leaf page pointers point to the correct data pages.

4. Non-clustered indexes are larger than clustered indexes because of the extra set of leaf pages. However, building a non-clustered index requires significantly less space than building a non-clustered index.

For more information about deciding which index should be clustered and which should be non-clustered, see the section titled "Guidelines for Indexing."

Composite Indexes

A *composite index* is simply an index that has more than one column in its key. Composite indexes are helpful when you plan to write queries that search for rows based on all of the values in multiple columns, such as an author's last name and first name.

Keep the following in mind when building and using composite indexes:

▶ Up to 16 columns may be used in an index. The combined size of the columns may not exceed 900 bytes.

▶ The order in which the columns are used in the index is very important. An index on authors' last names and first names is not the same as an index on authors' first names and last names.

▶ SQL Server doesn't use the composite index unless the first column in the key is specified. So, specifying only an author's first name as criteria on a table with a last/first name index will not use the index. For this example, the index is used if you specify a last name as criteria, or both the last name and first name as criteria.

▶ When building a composite index, use the column with the widest range of values (the most unique) as the first column. This helps SQL Server narrow a search faster.

Unique Indexes

A *unique index* has an additional requirement placed on its key values—namely, that they must be unique within a table. Unique indexes are how SQL Server enforces PRIMARY KEY and UNIQUE constraints for entity integrity (Chapters 1 and 3 discuss entity integrity in more detail).

When you insert into a table with a unique index or update a table with a unique index, SQL Server checks the new key value against all other key values in the table. If the new key value duplicates an existing value, then SQL Server disallows the insert or update.

Unique indexes are fairly self-explanatory. However, there is one thing to keep in mind when creating an index on a column or columns that permit NULL values. A NULL value counts as a distinctly unique value when used in an indexed column. Refer to figure 7.3, which shows a composite unique index on a table where both columns in the index key allow NULLs.

Figure 7.3

A unique index on columns that allow NULL values.

Unique Index On These Columns

Key Column 1	Key Column 2	Other Columns
1	1	~
1	< Null >	~
< Null >	1	~
< Null >	< Null >	~

All four rows shown in figure 7.3 are unique. Remember that in a composite unique index, the combination of values in all key columns must be unique. Because NULL counts as a distinct value, the four rows shown have unique key combinations. Attempting to insert a record into this table with a NULL value in any of the key columns causes SQL Server to reject the row.

Guidelines for Indexing

 Objective

There are no hard and fast rules for when you should or should not create an index, but there are some pretty good rules of thumb that you can follow. Before we get into specifics, probably the best rule you can remember is that indexes should be *selective*.

SQL Server works best with indexes that narrow its search quickly. For example, if you were to index a table containing a listing of Kansas City's residents, indexing on last name would probably be a good idea. Even for a common name like Jones, the number of rows returned (say 25,000) would be small in comparison to the total number of rows in the table (say, 1.3 million). The selectivity in this example is around 2 percent—finding all people with the surname Jones returns only about 2 percent of the table.

On the other hand, indexing on a column that is not very unique (such as gender) is useless to SQL Server. If we assume that Kansas City's distribution of women and men is roughly equal, then about half of the table will be returned if SQL Server tries to narrow its search with the index on gender.

For more information on examining an index's selectivity, see the section "Other Index Maintenance," later in this chapter.

Choosing Which Columns to Index

Here are some guidelines for choosing which columns to include in an index:

▶ Primary keys and foreign keys should nearly always be indexed. SQL Server can perform a join much faster if the joined columns are indexed.

▶ Create indexes on columns that you often search on, in other words, columns often used in the WHERE clause of a query.

▶ Create indexes on columns that are often searched for a range of values, like datetime fields.

▶ Create indexes on columns that are often used to sort the results of a query (those columns often included in an ORDER BY clause).

Knowing which columns to index is important. Equally important is knowing what type of index to create.

Choosing an Index's Characteristics

Keep the following in mind when you are choosing the type of index you will be creating:

▶ Create unique indexes on a primary key or alternate key. This allows SQL Server to enforce entity integrity.

 **Tip**

If you create PRIMARY KEY or UNIQUE constraints on a table as described in Chapter 3, SQL Server creates a unique index for you.

▶ If you often retrieve data in sorted order by a particular column, consider putting a clustered index on that column. Because a clustered index physically sorts the rows in a table, SQL Server can retrieve rows very efficiently.

▶ If two or more columns are often searched as a unit, consider placing a composite index on both columns.

▶ Consider using a non-clustered index on the primary key of a table if the table uses an IDENTITY column as its primary key. Placing a clustered index on an IDENTITY column causes all new rows to be inserted at the end of the table, which may cause concurrence problems if many users are inserting data into the table.

Indexes can be created or removed without affecting the data in a table, so feel free to experiment with different types of indexes if you need to.

SQL Server's Use of Indexes

 Objective

Better understanding how and when SQL Server uses indexes will help you create effective indexes. This section introduces you to some of the internal workings of the SQL Server query processor so that you can make well-informed decisions about indexes.

When you execute a query, SQL Server uses one of two methods to find a row or rows in a table. The most basic method is for SQL Server to perform a linear search of all the rows in the table—this is known as a table scan. Although SQL Server now has some optimizations that improve the performance of table scans, this method is still the least efficient because the worst-case possibility is that SQL Server will have to look at every row in the table. This operation can take some time if the table is very large.

If an index is available, SQL Server can find a row by traversing the index tree from the root page to the appropriate leaf page. Unless the table is very small, this reduces the amount of work SQL Server must perform to find a particular row in the table.

When SQL Server executes a query, the query optimizer decides which method will be used to access the rows in a table. This optimization occurs before SQL Server performs the actual work of the query.

The Query Optimizer

The query optimizer is the most sophisticated part of SQL Server's query processor. It may evaluate thousands of possible options to determine the most efficient method for accessing the data required by the query. SQL Server can often parse, optimize, and compile a query plan in less than a second.

The optimizer's goal is to reduce the total number of input/output (I/O) operations that SQL Server has to perform to retrieve the data. I/O operations are relatively time-consuming, so reducing the amount of I/O causes the query to execute faster. The optimizer is cost-based; SQL Server estimates the amount of work (in terms of I/O) required for each access plan, then chooses the plan that results in the least amount of work.

The optimizer's estimates are based on information that SQL Server stores about each table and index. The optimizer knows the approximate size of the table, as well as selectivity information about each index. It can use this information to estimate the number of I/O operations required to retrieve the rows for the query.

Generally, the optimizer chooses an index over a table scan, because indexes are usually the more efficient method for accessing data. However, for small tables, the number of I/O operations required to scan the table may be less than if an index is used. In this case, the optimizer would choose a table scan. Also, if the query will return a large number of rows, a table scan is usually more efficient than retrieving rows through an index.

 **Tip**

Turn on the SHOWPLAN option to see the details of the query optimizer's decisions. SHOWPLAN will show you the access method (table scan or index) used for each table. To turn the SHOWPLAN feature on, add the following statement at the beginning of your query:

```
SET SHOWPLAN ON
```

The results printed from SHOWPLAN can be somewhat difficult to read. However, Chapter 23 in *The SQL Administrator's Companion* is devoted entirely to deciphering the results of SHOWPLAN. The Administrator's Companion is available in printed form or on the SQL Server Books Online.

Using Optimizer Hints

The query optimizer is very good at determining the most efficient access plan for a query. However, in certain rare cases, you might want to fine-tune a query by forcing SQL Server to use a particular index.

 **Note**

> The advantage of the query optimizer is that it dynamically chooses the best access plan based on the current contents of the table. SQL Server chooses the best index, even if the data in the table changes over time. For this reason, it is usually best to let SQL Server choose the access method for a query.

Index optimizer hints are used in the FROM clause of a SQL statement and have the following syntax :

```
(INDEX = {index_name | index_id})
```

Generally, you use the index name instead of an index ID because it is easier to find the name of an index on a table. However, a couple of special values for index_id are supported: specifying 0 for index_id forces a table scan, and specifying 1 for index_id causes the table's clustered index to be used (provided that it exists).

Let's look at an example of using an optimizer hint and why it is a good idea to let SQL Server choose the access method for a query. Consider the following query:

```
SET STATISTICS IO ON

SELECT * FROM titles (INDEX = titleind)
WHERE title LIKE '%computer%'
```

This query returns all titles containing the word "computer" from the titles table. You've forced SQL Server to use the index on the title column. The SET STATISTICS IO ON statement tells SQL Server to show you the amount of I/O performed when the query is run. For this particular query, the results are something like this:

```
Table: titles  scan count 1,  logical reads: 19,  physical reads:
0,  read ahead reads: 0
```

SQL Server performed 19 I/O operations to retrieve 5 rows from the table.

Note

> A logical read is performed whenever SQL Server needs to access a page in the database. If the page is not in memory, then a physical read is performed to retrieve the page from disk. In the preceding example, you can see that the table's pages are in the memory cache because no physical reads were performed.

Now, consider the same query, except without the optimizer hint:

```
SET STATISTICS IO ON

SELECT * FROM titles
WHERE title LIKE '%computer%'
```

The same five rows are returned, but notice that the amount of I/O has gone down significantly:

```
Table: titles  scan count 1,  logical reads: 2,  physical reads:
0,  read ahead reads: 0
```

Without the forced use of the index, SQL Server performs a table scan, which is more efficient in this situation because the table is small.

Managing Indexes with Transact-SQL

Objective

Part of the database designer's role in database implementation is managing the indexes on the database. One of the nicer features of SQL Server is that indexes may be created and dropped independently of their tables, so indexes may be changed without affecting the data in the database. Typically, these changes are accomplished through the use of the Transact-SQL statements covered in this section.

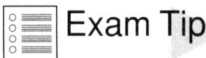**Exam Tip**

The Enterprise Manager application also may be used to manage indexes, as discussed later in the chapter. However, the exam focuses mainly on the Transact-SQL statements used to manage indexes.

Creating Indexes

To create an index on a table, you use the CREATE INDEX statement. There are a few restrictions you should be aware of before using this statement:

- ▶ Only tables may be indexed; you cannot create an index on a view.

- ▶ Only the table's owner or the database owner (DBO) can create an index on a table. This permission may not be transferred to other database users.

- ▶ Columns of *bit, image,* or *text* data types cannot be used as an index's key.

- ▶ If the table is to have a clustered index, create it first before creating any non-clustered indexes. Otherwise, the non-clustered indexes will be rebuilt. See "Clustered Indexes," earlier in this chapter.

The simplified syntax of the CREATE INDEX statement is as follows:

```
CREATE [UNIQUE] [{CLUSTERED | NONCLUSTERED}] INDEX index_name
ON [[database.]owner.]table_name (column_name [, column_name...])
[WITH
    [PAD_INDEX]
    [[,] FILLFACTOR = fill_factor]
    [[,] {SORTED_DATA | SORTED_DATA_REORG}]
]
```

The **UNIQUE** keyword specifies that the new index will disallow duplicate key values. If this keyword is omitted, then the index will be non-unique.

The **CLUSTERED** and **NONCLUSTERED** keywords specify that the new index will be clustered or non-clustered. By default, a non-clustered index is created.

index_name is the name of the new index. This name follows the naming conventions for tables and other objects in the database, and can be up to thirty characters in length.

The **ON** keyword specifies the table and columns on which to create the index. You may create an index on a table in another database, provided that you are the table's owner or the DBO.

The **WITH** keyword is used to specify various options for the new index. These options are discussed later in this section.

Following are some examples of using the CREATE INDEX statement in the Pubs database:

This example creates a non-unique, non-clustered index on the job_desc column in the jobs table:

```
CREATE INDEX idx_job_desc ON jobs (job_desc)
```

These examples create a unique index on the title column in the titles table.

To create a clustered index:

```
CREATE UNIQUE CLUSTERED INDEX uqcidx_title ON titles
(title)
```

To create a non-clustered index, you may use one of the following statements (remember that by default, an index is non-clustered):

```
CREATE UNIQUE NONCLUSTERED INDEX uqncidx_title ON
➥titles (title)
CREATE UNIQUE INDEX uqncidx_title ON titles (title)
```

This example creates a composite index on the au_lname and au_fname columns in the authors table:

```
CREATE INDEX idx_author_name ON authors (au_lname, au_fname)
```

The FILLFACTOR and PAD_INDEX Options

When you create an index, it is possible to fine-tune its performance by using the FILLFACTOR and PAD_INDEX options.

When you create an index without specifying a fill factor, the fill factor value is 0. When SQL Server creates the index, it fills each leaf page full of index entries, and leaves some room on the non-leaf pages. As data is inserted into the table, SQL Server must split the leaf pages (and possibly the non-leaf pages) to make room for the new index entries. This page splitting can cause the performance of data modification queries to suffer. To minimize page splitting, you can use the FILLFACTOR option.

A FILLFACTOR of 1 to 99 fills the leaf pages to the specified percentage of fullness. For example, a fill factor of 50 would leave the leaf pages half-full. The non-leaf pages still leave some empty space for additional entries.

A FILLFACTOR of 100 fills the leaf pages 100 percent full (as does a FILLFACTOR of 0), but the non-leaf pages are also filled to capacity. This results in the smallest possible index, but any inserted data is guaranteed to cause a page split in the index. A 100 percent fill factor is useful for read-only tables.

 **Tip**

SQL Server's FILLFACTOR defaults to 0, but you can change this setting by using sp_configure.

The PAD_INDEX option is used in conjunction with the FILL-FACTOR option. If PAD_INDEX is used, then the non-leaf pages are filled to the percentage specified by the fill factor. Again, a fill factor of 100 percent fills both leaf and non-leaf pages completely full.

This example creates an index on the titles table in which the leaf and non-leaf pages are 25 percent full:

```
CREATE INDEX idx_titles
ON titles (title)
WITH PAD_INDEX, FILLFACTOR = 25
```

The SORTED_DATA and SORTED_DATA_REORG Options

These two options are used when you create a clustered index on data that has already been sorted. Both improve the performance of the CREATE INDEX statement, because SQL Server doesn't physically re-sort the table rows before creating the index. SQL Server does check to see if the data is in sorted order, and the index creation fails if the data is not sorted.

SORTED_DATA_REORG differs from SORTED_DATA in that the data rows are first copied to new data pages before the index is built. This reduces the amount of fragmentation in the table's data pages. Table fragmentation can occur if the table is heavily modified; data pages may become sparsely filled. Fragmentation can decrease query performance.

 **Tip**

You can use the DBCC SHOWCONTIG command to determine if a table is fragmented. See the SQL Server Books Online or Transact-SQL help for more information about this command.

Dropping Indexes

The DROP INDEX statement is used to remove an index from a table. Only the table owner or DBO may use this command. When an index is dropped from a table, only the space used by the index is reclaimed in the database; the table's data remains intact.

This statement may only be used to drop indexes created with the CREATE INDEX statement. Indexes created by PRIMARY KEY or UNIQUE constraints must be dropped by removing the constraint. For information about creating or dropping constraints, see Chapter 3, "Data Definition."

The syntax of the DROP INDEX statement is as follows:

```
DROP INDEX [owner.]table_name.index_name [,
[owner.]table_name.index_name...]
```

Tip

> To determine the name of an index on a table, use the sp_helpindex system stored procedure.

Note that multiple indexes may be dropped in a single statement. Also, there is no database specifier on the table name, so you must execute the DROP INDEX statement from the database containing the index you want to drop.

Here are two examples of the DROP INDEX syntax:

This statement drops the index created in example #1 of the CREATE INDEX examples. The USE statement causes the query to be executed from the specified database, in this case Pubs.

```
USE pubs
DROP INDEX jobs.idx_job_desc
```

Here is an example of dropping multiple indexes in a single statement. This example drops the indexes created in examples #2 and #3 in the CREATE INDEX examples:

```
USE pubs
DROP INDEX titles.uqcidx_title, authors.idx_author_name
```

Other Index Maintenance

Once you have created a table's indexes, you can use a number of commands to retrieve information about the index. In addition, several maintenance commands exist to keep the indexes in good working order.

Checking Index Size

To determine how much space the indexes of a table are consuming in the database, use the sp_spaceused system stored procedure, as follows:

```
EXEC sp_spaceused table_name
```

Here are the results of running sp_spaceused on the titles table in the Pubs database:

```
name        rows    reserved    data    index_size   unused
----------------   ----------   ------------------   --------------
titles      18      48 KB       4 KB    8 KB         36 KB
```

Unfortunately, sp_spaceused is not always accurate, especially if an index has been dropped and recreated. To update this information, you may use the DBCC UPDATEUSAGE command:

```
DBCC UPDATEUSAGE (database_name [, table_name [, index_id]])
```

UPDATEUSAGE can be used in one of three ways:

▶ To update the space used information for every table and index in a database, specify only a database name:

```
DBCC UPDATEUSAGE (pubs)
```

▶ To update the usage information for a particular table in a database, specify both a database and table name:

```
DBCC UPDATEUSAGE (pubs,authors)
```

▶ To update the usage information for a particular index on a table, specify a database name, index name, and index ID:

```
DBCC UPDATEUSAGE (pubs,authors,1)
```

It is a good idea to periodically run the UPDATEUSAGE command for each database to keep this information current. You may then monitor the database's size to determine if the database needs to be expanded.

Checking an Index's Selectivity and Distribution

If you are unsure about the effectiveness of an index, you may view the statistics that SQL Server maintains about the index. When an index is created, SQL Server samples the rows in the table to determine the selectivity of the index. It then creates a page (called the distribution page) that stores the number of rows in the table, the selectivity of the index, and the key values that it sampled to arrive at the selectivity number.

To view the distribution page for an index, use the DBCC SHOW_STATISTICS command. The syntax is as follows:

```
DBCC SHOW_STATISTICS (table_name,index_name)
```

For example, to check the distribution of the titleind index on the titles table, you would execute this query:

```
DBCC SHOW_STATISTICS (titles,titleind)
```

These index statistics should be updated from time to time, as the next section discusses.

Updating Index Statistics

The distribution information for a table is not automatically updated by SQL Server when a table's data changes. This means that it is possible for the distribution information to become out-of-date, especially if many rows in a table have been changed, or if the TRUNCATE TABLE statement has been used on the table. If this information is out of date, SQL Server may not choose the most efficient method to access the table.

To refresh the distribution information for an index, use the UPDATE STATISTICS command. Only the table owner or DBO may execute this command. The syntax is as follows:

```
UPDATE STATISTICS [[database.]owner.]table_name [index_name]
```

▶ If you do not specify an index name, then the statistics for all indexes on the table are updated:

```
UPDATE STATISTICS pubs..titles
```

▶ You also may update the statistics for a single index on a table:

```
UPDATE STATISTICS pubs..titles titleind
```

It is a good idea to set up a scheduled task that periodically updates the statistics for each table's indexes, especially if a database's data changes frequently.

Rebuilding an Index

Recall from earlier in the chapter that an index's fill factor is not maintained after the index is built. As data in the table is added or updated, the index pages are split to accommodate the new index rows on each index page. This means that over time, an index's pages may become only partially full. This can cause data modification queries to take longer to execute.

Table pages also become fragmented over time as data in the table is modified. Rebuilding the table's clustered index physically reorganizes the table's rows and reduces fragmentation.

It is possible for the table owner or DBO to drop and recreate each index manually by using DROP INDEX and CREATE INDEX statements. However, in SQL Server version 6.5, a new DBCC REINDEX command was introduced that has several advantages over the manual method:

- ▶ All indexes on the table may be rebuilt at once, including indexes created by PRIMARY KEY and UNIQUE constraints. This allows a table's indexes to be refreshed without knowing any index names or having to drop and recreate constraints.

- ▶ An index may be rebuilt with a new fill factor.

- ▶ All changes are automatic; the re-indexing is automatically wrapped in a transaction so that all changes may be rolled back in the event of a problem.

As with the other index commands, only the table owner or DBO may issue the DBREINDEX command. The syntax of the command is as follows:

```
DBCC DBREINDEX ('database.owner.table_name' [, index_name
                [, FILLFACTOR [, {SORTED_DATA ¦
➥SORTED_DATA_REORG}]]])
```

 **Note**   The FILLFACTOR and SORTED_DATA options are covered earlier in this section.

Following are some examples of the DBREINDEX command:

To rebuild all indexes on a table, simply specify a table name. This example rebuilds all indexes on the titles table in the Pubs database:

```
DBCC DBREINDEX ('pubs..titles')
```

To rebuild a particular index, specify both the table and index name:

```
DBCC DBREINDEX ('pubs..titles','titleind')
```

A particular index may be rebuilt with an explicit fill factor:

```
DBCC DBREINDEX ('pubs..titles','titleind',80)
```

Or all of a table's indexes may be rebuilt with an explicit fill factor:

```
DBCC DBREINDEX ('pubs..titles','',80)
```

Managing Indexes with Enterprise Manager

The Enterprise Manager application provides an alternate way to manage the indexes in a database. All of the indexes on each table in the database may be managed through the Manage Indexes dialog box.

To get to the Manage Indexes dialog box, perform the following steps:

1. Load the SQL Server Enterprise Manager application if it is not already loaded.

2. From the Server Manager window, select a server on which you wish to manage indexes. Expand the tree view by clicking on the plus sign to the left of the server.

3. Expand the Databases folder by clicking on the plus sign next to the folder icon.

4. Select a database, then choose Manage, Indexes from the application's main menu. The Manage Indexes dialog box will appear, as shown in figure 7.4.

Figure 7.4

The Manage Indexes dialog box in SQL Enterprise Manager.

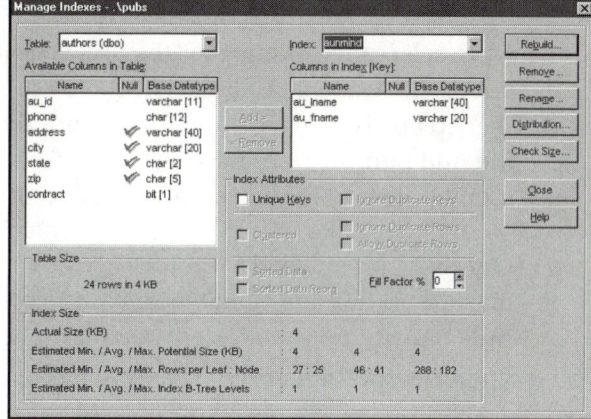

This dialog box has a lot of features for a single screen, so each group of features is discussed separately.

Managing Indexes

The top half of the screen is where you will do the bulk of your work. Before working with a table's indexes, you must first select a table to work with. Use the Table combo box to select the table on which you wish to manage indexes. A list of all columns in the table will appear in the list box labeled Available Columns in Table.

Note

You will be able to view indexes created by PRIMARY KEY or UNIQUE constraints; however, you will not be able to modify or remove these indexes. Instead, use the Manage Tables window or SQL statements to manage the constraints. Constraint management is discussed in Chapter 3.

Creating an Index

To create a new index on the table, first select the (New Index) option from the Index combo box. The box clears so you can type in the name of the new index.

Next, select the columns for the index key by choosing columns out of the Available Columns in Table list box on the left side of the screen. To add a column to the index key, choose it and click the Add button. To remove a column from the index key, choose it in the right-hand list box and click the Remove button.

Once you are satisfied with the key columns for the index, you may specify any additional characteristics for the index in the Index Attributes frame. Here you may specify if the index is unique, clustered, or non-clustered.

Once you are satisfied with the settings for the index, click the Build button. A dialog box appears, as shown in figure 7.5.

Figure 7.5

Scheduling an Index command with the Index Build dialog box.

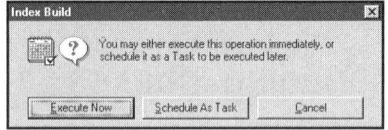

This dialog box is used whenever you execute a command from the Manage Indexes window. It enables you to execute the command immediately, or schedule it for execution at a later time.

 Tip

SQL Enterprise Manager will be unresponsive for the time it takes to execute the index management command if you use the Execute Now button on the scheduling dialog box.

If you want to execute a command immediately, and still use Enterprise Manager, click the Schedule as Task button on the scheduling dialog box. Then, schedule the task for immediate execution. The SQL Executive runs the task in the background, and you may use Enterprise Manager for other tasks.

Dropping an Index

To drop an existing index on the selected table, choose the index from the Index combo box. Then, click the Remove button. The scheduling dialog box appears; usually, dropping an index takes very little time, so it is okay to click the Execute Now button without fear of a long wait. A dialog box appears, asking if you really want to drop the index. Click the Yes button, and the index will be removed.

Modifying and Rebuilding an Index

You may modify an existing index by adding or removing key columns, or changing index attributes. Simply select the index from the Index combo box, make any required changes, and click the Rebuild button.

Renaming an Index

To rename an existing index, first select the index from the Index combo box. Click the Rename button, and the Rename Index dialog box appears, as shown in figure 7.6.

Figure 7.6

The Rename Index dialog box.

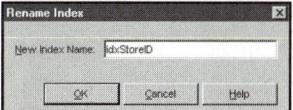

Simply type the new name for the index and click the OK button.

Other Features of the Manage Indexes Dialog Box

The Manage Indexes dialog box has a few other features you should be aware of. First, perhaps the nicest feature is the display at the bottom of the screen that shows you information on the size and structure of the index. You can use this information to determine how much space the index is consuming in the database, and the display is dynamic, so you can see how changing the type and fill factor of the index affects its final size. To update the size information for an existing index, click the Check Size button on the upper-right portion of the screen.

The dialog box also has a feature that enables you to view the distribution and selectivity of an index. Click the Distribution button to show the Index Distribution Statistics screen, as shown in figure 7.7

Figure 7.7

The Index Distribution Statistics screen.

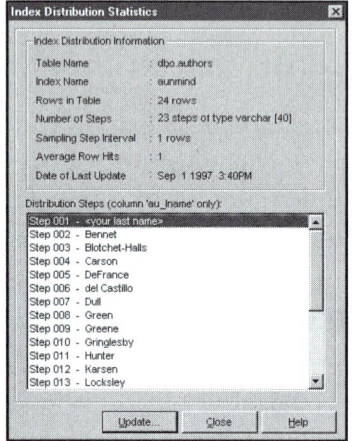

To update the index statistics, click the Update button at the bottom of the screen.

Summary

In this chapter you learned how to use indexes to make for speedier, more efficient access to your databases. You also learned that improperly indexed tables, while they may not slow SQL Server, can consume unnecessary space in the database. Understanding the indexing options available in SQL Server is important to being able to provide an optimally functioning database.

Exercises

Exercise 7.1:   Creating Indexes

In this exercise, you create several indexes on the tables in the Pubs sample database.

1. Open the SQL Enterprise Manager application if it is not already running. From the Server Manager window, select a SQL Server, and expand the tree view by clicking the plus sign to the left of the server name.

2. Expand the Databases folder by clicking the plus sign to the left of the folder icon. Select the Pubs database, and choose Tools, SQL Query Tool from the application's menu. The Query window will appear.

3. First, create an index on the authors table on the au_lname column. Type the following into the query window:

```
CREATE INDEX idx_au_lname on authors (au_lname)
```

4. Execute the query by typing Alt-X or clicking the Execute Query button on the toolbar. The index will be created. The index will be named idx_au_lname, and is a non-clustered, non-unique index.

5. Next, execute the following query to create a unique non-clustered index on the au_id column in the authors table:

```
CREATE UNIQUE INDEX idxuq_au_id on authors (au_id)
```

6. Create a composite index on the au_lname and au_fname columns by executing this query:

```
CREATE UNIQUE INDEX idxcomp_au_name on authors
(au_lname,au_fname)
```

7. Finally, create a clustered index on the roysched table. First, look at the rows in the table by executing this query:

```
SELECT * FROM roysched
```

8. Look at the results of the previous query. Note that the results are sorted in order by the title_id. This is actually because these records were inserted in sorted order and not because a clustered index exists. Now, create a clustered index on the royalty column by executing this query:

```
CREATE CLUSTERED INDEX idxcl_royalty ON roysched (royalty)
```

9. Re-examine the rows in the roysched table by executing this query:

```
SELECT * FROM roysched
```

Note that the results are now sorted according to the values in the royalty column.

Exercise 7.2:   Dropping an Index

This exercise walks you through the steps required to drop one of the indexes you created in Exercise 7.1.

1. Open the SQL Enterprise Manager application if it is not already running. From the Server Manager window, select SQL Server, and expand the tree view by clicking the plus sign to the left of the server name.

2. Expand the Databases folder by clicking the plus sign to the left of the folder icon. Select the Pubs database, and choose Tools, SQL Query Tool from the application's menu. The Query window appears.

3. Drop the unique index you placed on the au_id column in exercise 7.1 by executing this query:

```
DROP INDEX authors.idxuq_au_id
```

Exercise 7.3:   Examining and Updating Index Statistics

In exercise 7.3, you create a new table and examine how the distribution information changes when rows are inserted into the table.

1. Open the SQL Enterprise Manager application if it is not already running. From the Server Manager window, select a

SQL Server, and expand the tree view by clicking the plus sign to the left of the server name.

2. Expand the Databases folder by clicking the plus sign to the left of the folder icon. Select the Pubs database, and choose Tools, SQL Query Tool from the application's menu. The Query window appears.

3. First, duplicate the structure of the publishers table. Type in the following SQL statement:

```
CREATE TABLE publishers_dup (
    pub_id    char(4)     NOT NULL,
    pub_name  varchar(40) NULL,
    city      varchar(20) NULL,
    state     char(2)     NULL,
    country   varchar(30) NULL
)
```

4. Execute the query by typing Alt-X or clicking the Execute Query button on the toolbar. The publishers_dup table will be created, and its structure will be identical to the publisher's table.

5. Insert a row into the publishers_dup table by executing the following query:

```
INSERT publishers_dup VALUES ('1111','New
➥Riders','Indianapolis','IN','USA')
```

6. Now, create a unique clustered index on the publishers_dup table by executing this query:

```
CREATE UNIQUE CLUSTERED INDEX idxuqcl_pub_id ON
➥publishers_dup (pub_id)
```

7. Examine the index statistics by executing this query:

```
DBCC SHOW_STATISTICS (publishers_dup,idxuqcl_pub_id)
```

8. Now, copy the rows from the publishers table into the publishers_dup table by executing this query:

```
INSERT publishers_dup SELECT * FROM publishers
```

9. Re-run the query from step #7. Note that the index statistics have not changed since the index was created.

10. Execute the following query to update the distribution page for the index:

```
UPDATE STATISTICS publishers_dup idxuqcl_pub_id
```

11. Re-run the query from step #7. Note that the index statistics have been updated.

Review Questions

1. What are some of the reasons indexes are used in a database? (Choose all that apply.)

    A. Indexes improve the performance of data retrieval.

    B. Indexes can enforce entity integrity.

    C. Indexes can improve the performance of sorting and grouping queries.

    D. Indexes can reduce the space requirements for a table.

    E. Indexes can improve the performance of joins.

2. In a clustered index,

    A. the leaf pages of the index contain pointers to the data pages of the table.

    B. the leaf pages of the index are the data pages of the table.

    C. the leaf pages of the index contain pointers to the data rows of the table.

    D. the non-leaf pages of the index contain pointers to the data rows of the table.

3. In a non-clustered index,

    A. the leaf pages of the index contain pointers to the data pages of the table.

    B. the leaf pages of the index are the data pages of the table.

    C. the leaf pages of the index contain pointers to the data rows of the table.

    D. the non-leaf pages of the index contain pointers to the data rows of the table.

4. Which of the following statements about clustered indexes are NOT true?

   A. Clustered indexes are smaller than non-clustered indexes.

   B. Clustered indexes physically sort the data rows in a table by the index key.

   C. Clustered indexes require less space to create than non-clustered indexes.

   D. Clustered indexes are best used on IDENTITY columns.

   E. The data pages of the table are the leaf pages of the clustered index.

5. How many clustered indexes may be created on a table?

   A. One

   B. Up to 256

   C. Up to 249

   D. Unlimited, provided there are enough server resources

6. How many non-clustered indexes may be created on a table?

   A. One

   B. Up to 256

   C. Up to 249

   D. Unlimited, provided there are enough server resources

7. A composite index is an index that:

   A. physically sorts the rows in a table

   B. contains multiple keys

   C. logically sorts the rows in a table in both ascending and descending order.

   D. contains multiple columns in its key

8. Which statement(s) is/are true about NULL values in a UNIQUE index?

    A. NULLs are not allowed in a unique index.

    B. NULL values are permitted, provided that the unique index is not created via a **PRIMARY KEY** constraint.

    C. A NULL counts as a distinct value in a key.

    D. Only one column of a composite key may allow NULL values.

9. Which column(s) is/are good candidates for indexing?

    A. Primary keys and foreign keys

    B. Columns used to order the results of a query

    C. Columns that have few distinct values throughout the rows in a table

    D. Columns with high selectivity

10. What are the two basic methods SQL Server may use to find rows in a table?

    A. Searching via a table scan

    B. Searching with an ordered list

    C. Searching with a cross-join

    D. Searching with an index

11. How does the query optimizer decide which method to use to find a row or rows in a table?

    A. The optimizer chooses the method that minimizes logical I/O.

    B. The optimizer chooses the method that minimizes physical I/O.

    C. The optimizer chooses the method that minimizes both logical and physical I/O.

    D. The optimizer always uses an index if one is available.

12. What is the correct syntax for creating a unique, non-clus-
    tered index on the au_id column in the authors table?

    A. CREATE NONCLUSTERED INDEX idxau_id ON
       authors (au_id)

    B. CREATE UNIQUE INDEX idxau_id ON authors
       (au_id)

    C. CREATE UNIQUE CLUSTERED INDEX idxau_id ON
       authors (au_id)

13. Roger wants to create an index on a read-only table. What
    is/are the best option(s) he should use when creating the
    index?

    A. FILLFACTOR = 100

    B. FILLFACTOR = 0

    C. PAD_INDEX, FILLFACTOR = 100

    D. PAD_INDEX, FILLFACTOR = 0

14. Mary would like to minimize page splitting for an index on a
    table that will have many rows inserted. What options/op-
    tions should she use when creating the index?

    A. FILLFACTOR = 100

    B. FILLFACTOR = 0

    C. PAD_INDEX, FILLFACTOR = 50

    D. PAD_INDEX, FILLFACTOR = 1

15. Brian wants to create an index on a table that will have a
    moderate amount of new data inserted into it. He wants to
    reduce page splitting, but also wants the index to be of rea-
    sonable size. Which setting should he use for FILLFACTOR?

    A. FILLFACTOR = 0

    B. FILLFACTOR = 50

    C. FILLFACTOR = 100

16. David ran DBCC SHOWCONTIG on a table and noticed that the table's data pages were heavily fragmented. How should he correct the problem?

    A. Recreate a non-clustered index on the table with the SORTED_DATA option.

    B. Recreate a non-clustered index on the table with the SORTED_DATA_REORG option.

    C. Recreate the table's clustered index with the SORTED_DATA option.

    D. Recreate the table's clustered index with the SORTED_DATA_REORG option.

17. Tiffany is attempting to create a standard clustered index on a table with the SORTED DATA option, but the index creation fails. What is the most likely cause of this problem?

    A. The table's data is not sorted.

    B. There are duplicate values in the index key.

    C. The table is corrupted.

    D. The table is fragmented.

18. Josh is attempting to drop an index on the titles table in the Pubs database with the DROP INDEX statement. However, he is receiving the error message "Cannot drop the index 'titles.titleind', because it doesn't exist in the system catalogs." What are some possible causes of this error?

    A. The index is unique, and he should use DROP UNIQUE INDEX.

    B. The titleind index does not exist on the titles table.

    C. The titles table does not exist in the database.

    D. He is not executing the query from the Pubs database.

19. When should UPDATE STATISTICS be used?

    A. If the TRUNCATE TABLE statement has been used on a table

    B. If any of the table's indexes have been dropped

    C. If the distribution of key values has changed significantly due to data modifications

    D. If the statistics are more than a few days old

20. Chris has noticed that the performance of a SELECT query that worked fine before has suddenly degraded. By using SHOWPLAN he determines that the query processor is using a table scan to retrieve rows from the table, even though an index exists on the column being searched. What is the best course of action for Chris to take?

    A. He should use an optimizer hint to force SQL Server to use the index.

    B. He should run the UPDATE STATISTICS command on the table, then check to see that the indexed column still has a good selectivity.

    C. He should drop and recreate the index with a new FILLFACTOR.

Answers to Review Questions

1. A,B,C,E

2. B. Answer D is not correct because the non-leaf pages of the clustered index contain pointers to the data *pages* of the table.

3. C

4. C,D. Placing a clustered index on an IDENTITY column can cause a *hotspot,* or concurrence problem if many users are inserting rows into a table.

5. A

6. C

7. D. An index only has one key, which may be composed of more than one column.

8. B,C

9. A,B,D

10. A,D

11. C

12. B

13. C

14. D. The options in answer C will reduce page splitting, because the leaf and non-leaf pages will only be partially filled, but answer D will result in the least page splitting.

15. B

16. D

17. A

18. B,C,D

19. A,C

20. B. The problem is most likely caused by the index statistics becoming out of date.

Answers to Test Yourself Questions at Beginning of Chapter

1. In a clustered index, the data pages of the table are the leaf pages of the index, and the rows in the table are physically ordered by the index key. A non-clustered index has leaf pages that point to the table's data pages, and the rows in the table are not physically ordered by the index key. See "Introduction to Indexes."

2. Indexes allow quick retrieval of table rows, and can be used to enforce entity integrity. However, indexes consume space in a database, and can slow data modifications. See "Guidelines for Indexing."

3. A unique index enforces entity integrity by guaranteeing that the index key will be unique in the table. See "Unique Indexes."

4. A composite index is an index whose key is composed of two or more columns. See "Composite Indexes."

5. CREATE INDEX and DROP INDEX. See "Managing Indexes with Transact-SQL."

6. SQL Server examines the selectivity of an index to determine the cost of using the index. If the cost is lower than the other costs for accessing the table, the index will be used. See "SQL Server's Use of Indexes."

Chapter 8

Using Views, Defaults, and Rules

This chapter helps you prepare for the exam by covering the following objectives:

 Objectives

- ▶ Create views
- ▶ Recognize the benefits of using views
- ▶ Create, bind, unbind, and drop defaults
- ▶ Create, bind, unbind, and drop rules

Test Yourself! Before reading this chapter, test yourself to determine how much study time you will need to devote to this section.

1. What is a view?

2. Why can't you index a view?

3. Can a view present data from more than one table at a time?

4. Paul has found that he needs to change the data type of a Social Security Number field from an integer to a character type. To do this he must drop and re-create the table. What should he plan to do to ensure the views he is using to reference the table will still work?

5. Courtney uses a view to present data from the Persons table along with the persons' address information stored in the Addresses table to simplify printing mailing labels. Dan is developing an application that will enable a user to update all of this address information. Is it a good idea for Dan to utilize this view to perform his updates?

6. Courtney wants all middle-initial entries in the Persons table to default to a space if an initial is not entered. Write the command to create a default to do this.

7. Susan wants to ensure that invoice codes, which are used as foreign keys in many different tables, are all exactly 6 characters and that the first and last two characters are numeric, while the rest are alphabetical. How could she use a rule to perform this task?

Answers are located at the end of the chapter...

This chapter introduces two of the concepts that SQL Server supports for administering your database. The first is the idea of a view, which enables you to create a layer of abstraction over tables. This abstraction gives you more control over user access to your data. You will also learn about rules and defaults. These are objects that can be bound to tables to protect against invalid data. With rules and defaults you can put simple business rules in place that will automatically be applied to data modifications.

In summary then, this chapter covers the following topics:

- ▶ Understanding views

  - ▶ Creating views

  - ▶ Recognizing the benefits of using views

  - ▶ Recognizing the limitations of views

- ▶ Understanding rules and defaults

  - ▶ Creating rules

  - ▶ Creating defaults

  - ▶ Binding and unbinding rules and defaults

  - ▶ Dropping rules and defaults

Understanding Views

In order to understand the utility of views, it is best to start with how to create them. Once created, views present certain advantages to the SQL Server administrator. There also are some limitations to the uses of views and those will be discussed as well.

Creating Views

Objective

The following is the syntax for creating views:

```
CREATE VIEW [owner.] view_name
[(column_name [,column_name...])]
[WITH ENCRYPTION]
AS select_statement [WITH CHECK OPTION]
```

The heart of a view is the *select_statement* that follows the keyword AS. The view shows the data returned by the *select_statement* to the user, without the user needing to know about the complexity such a statement might entail.

Creating views should only be done after testing of the SELECT statement to ensure that the result set is returned correctly. Views are created using the SQL Enterprise Manager's Manage Views dialog box, or by writing and executing the full syntax described here in a script. Either way, you will be implementing the same syntax, because the Manage Views dialog box offers only the most basic outline for you to fill out yourself. Figure 8.1 shows the Manage Views dialog box in Enterprise Manager.

Figure 8.1

The Manage Views dialog box from SQL Enterprise Manager.

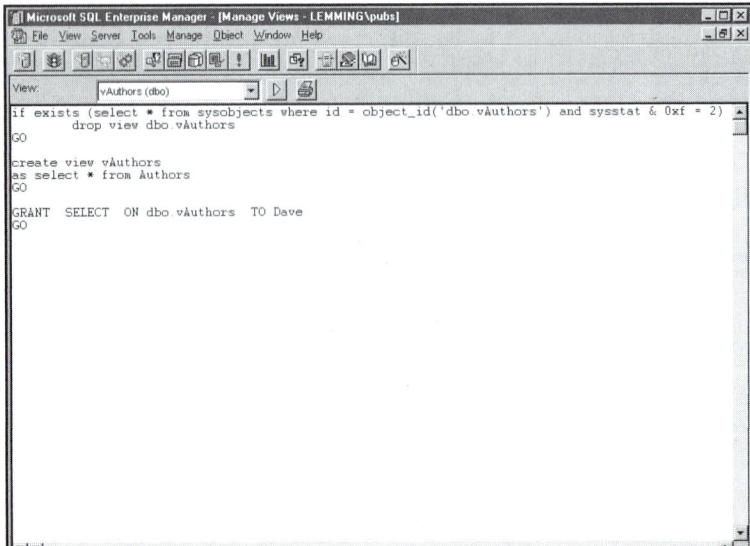

The list of column names in the syntax is optional and can be omitted. This list overlays the column headings that the SELECT statement may contain. If it is omitted, the normal column headings from the SELECT statement become the columns of the view. Whether this column list is included or not, the view must have standard, legal identifiers for all of the columns or an error will occur.

The WITH ENCRYPTION option encrypts the copy of the Create View syntax for your view that SQL Server stores in the *syscomments* table. This prevents anyone from seeing the exact syntax used to create the view. The WITH CHECK OPTION from the syntax causes SQL Server to perform additional checks on data modified through the view. Both of these options are described in greater detail later in the chapter.

The following are several examples of common kinds of views.

```
CREATE VIEW v_ProjectionView
AS
      SELECT Au_fname, Au_lname, City, State, Zip
      FROM Authors

CREATE VIEW v_JoinExample
AS
      SELECT Pub_Name, Title, Price
      FROM Publishers
        JOIN Titles
          ON Titles.Pub_ID = Publishers.Pub_ID

CREATE VIEW v_ComputedColumn
      (Title, Discount, Disc_Price)
AS
      SELECT Title, '10%', Price * 0.90
      FROM Titles

CREATE VIEW v_AggregateExample
      (Category, Avg_Price)
AS
      SELECT Type, Avg(Price)
      FROM Titles
      GROUP BY Type
      HAVING Avg(Price) IS NOT NULL
```

```
CREATE VIEW v_ViewOfView
AS
      SELECT *
      FROM v_ComputedColumn
      WHERE Disc_Price > 15.00
```

The preceding examples illustrate the CREATE VIEW syntax. You can see that views are very flexible. Almost any SELECT statement can be used as the basis of a view. The restrictions on the kinds of views that can be created are discussed later in this chapter.

Recognizing the Benefits of Using Views

 Objective

A view is a structure provided by SQL Server that enables you to represent a standard query in the form of a table. A view, in most ways, can be treated exactly like an actual table. However, it is actually a subset or superset of data from one or more tables. This can allow you to address security issues by restricting users access only to views that show data that is considered appropriate for that user. It also can provide a method of abstracting your data to an unchanging interface. Third-party applications can connect to this interface so that your underlying data model can continue to evolve.

A view is a method of turning the data returned by a single unchanging query into a pseudo-table. That is, a view presents the data returned by a SELECT statement to a user as though that data were contained in a single table.

A view can be used to provide a simplified interface to users. The actual data model may provide for all kinds of information that is not relevant to a particular user. A system of views can be created for that user that provides only the information of interest. Views also can simplify the data access of a user. If a user consistently has to use a complex join to retrieve the information he wants, these joins can be written into a view so that only the qualifying information needs to be supplied each time.

In addition to simplifying the interface to the user, views also can be used to hide or leave out sensitive information that is not necessary to the user. For example, a view can provide access to credit information but filter out actual account numbers and credit card numbers that are considered too sensitive for that user. Then permissions can be granted to the user to access the view rather than the table itself.

Over time a data model may need to be modified to meet a company's changing needs. New tables may be added or existing ones changed to allow for more informative data to be stored. These changes, however, can often cause existing applications to fail. Views can be used to present an unchanging interface to applications so that this problem is avoided. Applications can be written to access only the views, not tables themselves. Then when the data model changes, the views can be changed to retrieve the same information they always have. The application is therefore protected from changes to the underlying data model.

Recognizing the Limitations of Views

There are certain limitations to the kinds of SELECT statements that can be used in creating a view. For example, a view cannot reference temporary tables. Temporary tables are considered too short-lived to make them useful to reference through views. Furthermore, the ORDER BY, COMPUTE, and COMPUTE BY operators cannot be used in the creation of a view, and of course the creator of a view must have sufficient rights to access the data that the view will return.

Information on views is stored in system tables just as is information on user tables, stored_procedures, and other objects. These system tables include *sysobjects, sysprocedures, syscolumns, sysdepends,* and *syscomments.* Experienced users can gain information on a view by examining these tables directly. Alternately, there are two stored procedures that provide useful information on views. The stored procedure sp_helptext outputs the actual SELECT statement used to create the view if the WITH ENCRYPTION option was not used. What sp_helptext does is display the information SQL Server stores in *syscomments* at the time the view is created. The WITH ENCRYPTION option is used for the sole purpose of encrypting that information so it cannot be spied out. To find out what objects the view depends on and what other objects depend on the view, use the system stored procedure sp_depends.

Table 8.1 helps you find where information on views is stored.

Table 8.1

View Information

System Table	Stores Information On...
Sysobjects	View names
Sysprocedures	View normalized query tree
Syscolumns	Columns defined in a view
Sysdepends	View dependencies
Syscomments	Text of view creation statement

If the view is created with the WITH CHECK OPTION statement included, INSERTs and UPDATEs behave differently on that view than they would otherwise. This option causes additional checks to be performed on INSERT and UPDATE statements to ensure that the data affected will be a part of the view, and not be inserted into the underlying table invisible to the view.

Remember that views do not contain any data themselves; the data is stored in the underlying tables. If a view is showing only rows from a table that meet a certain criteria, then it would be possible to write an UPDATE against that view that would cause one or more rows to no longer meet the view's criteria. These rows would still exist in the table. However, they would seem to have disappeared from the view. Similarly, a row could be inserted into the view that would not meet the view's criteria, but would still be allowed into the underlying table. The WITH CHECK OPTION statement causes an error to occur if data updated in or inserted to a view would not appear as part of the view. Table 8.2 runs down the various view options for the WITH CHECK OPTION statement.

Table 8.2

WITH CHECK OPTION View Options

View Definition WHERE Clause Reference Data IN/OUT of Range	WITH CHECK OPTION Not Specified	WITH CHECK OPTION Specified
IN Range (INSERT, UPDATE, & DELETE)	Successful	Successful
OUT of Range (INSERT)	Successful	Error Message (INSERT Fails)
IN Range (UPDATE changes Value out of Range)	Successful	Error Message (UPDATE fails)
OUT of Range (UPDATE)	(0 rows affected)	(0 rows affected)
OUT of Range (DELETE)	(0 rows affected)	(0 rows affected)

It is permissible to write UPDATE and INSERT statements that include views. However there are limitations. The data modified by UPDATE or INSERT must not affect more than one table if the view itself includes a join of multiple tables. So if a view is presenting data obtained from many tables, an UPDATE written against that view could only affect those columns that happen to contain data from a single table. Similarly, an INSERT statement can only cause data to be inserted into one of the tables.

Modifications to data through views are also limited by the fact that views may contain certain columns that cannot be updated or used in an INSERT statement. Any column presented by a view that is a computed value or is the result of a built-in function (such as Trim or Format) cannot be modified. This is simply because such columns do not correspond directly to a column in a table where such modifications must be stored.

INSERT statements have an additional limitation. A view may present only certain columns from its underlying table. If an IN-SERT statement is written for this view, only information contained in that view can be specified. Any additional columns in the table receive default information if any are defined for the column or are left as NULL. If columns exist in the table that do not allow NULL and no default is specified, then no INSERT into a view that does not contain that column can be successful.

Although it is possible to alter data through views, it is generally not advisable to do so. Just as a view is treated like a real table in a SELECT statement, INSERTs, UPDATEs, and DELETEs can be written to affect views the same as they would real tables. However, certain limitations apply to such modifications. It is these limitations that make it bad practice to rely on modifying data through views.

It has already been shown that it is good practice for applications to reference views rather than user tables directly. This practice allows the underlying data model to evolve to meet changing needs while still providing a static interface to the applications that access the database. However, such changes may cause a view that once pulled data from one table to now require a JOIN to collect all the data it needs. Since UPDATEs, INSERTs, and DELETEs can only be written against views such that they cause changes to only one table underlying the view, if a view that once referenced one table now must join two or more, any UPDATEs written against that view will now likely fail. Instead, data modifications should always be done through stored procedures, and views should be used strictly for retrieving data.

Even seemingly simple views can cause problems to UPDATEs and INSERTs. A simple view with no joins and no computed columns may still cause errors when updated if it was built on other views that *do* contain computed columns and joins. In this way views can hide complexity that would otherwise warn the user of such problems.

It is important to keep in mind that views are not tables, despite all their similarities. Views have no user data associated with them at all. In SQL Server, all user data is stored with tables; views merely allow an alternate method of accessing that data. Therefore, views cannot be indexed. Indexes provide information to SQL Server about the physical storage of data to allow quick access to that data. Views have no data, therefore they cannot be indexed.

If queries using views are found to be too slow, the actual data stored in tables should be indexed, and the views written to take advantage of such indexes. Similarly, triggers (see Chapter 10, "Triggers") cannot be created on views. Triggers can only be written to activate when data is modified in a table. Whether the modification is as a result of a statement written using a view or the table itself is irrelevant.

 Note

Because views present themselves to users just like tables, they can often be mistaken for tables until an UPDATE fails because it would modify more than one underlying table, or an index fails to be built against it. Therefore it is a good idea to use a special naming convention with views to set them apart from user tables. A common approach is to preface a descriptive name with "v_".

It is important to know what dependence views have on the tables they reference. Even when a table is dropped and re-created, any view dependent upon it will still reference it correctly, provided the fields referenced by the view still exist. The order in which the table's columns are defined, and even the data types, may be changed. The columns a view references are stored explicitly when the view is created, therefore as long as the view can find those columns when it is executed, the view continues to work. What this also means is that even if a view is created with a SELECT * statement, new columns added to the table aren't automatically added to the view. There is no way to alter an existing view. If a view is to be changed to show additional information, it must be dropped and re-created.

Earlier in this chapter it was stated that even if a table is re-created with a different data type for a column referenced by a view, the view can still reference that column. It is important to note, however, that if the view contains any statement that would fail against the new data type, such as addition on a character field, for example, the next statement executed against that view will fail. This is not because the view was unable to reference that column; it is because SQL Server was unsuccessful at performing the requested operation on the column it found.

Tip

Exporting data out of SQL Server is commonly done with the Bulk Copy program or BCP. Limitations of BCP include that it only exports data from one table, and that it cannot be limited to only certain rows of that table. Views can be used to present a "single" table to BCP even when the data is joined from many tables. By the same token, views can present only rows from a table that meet a certain criteria to BCP.

Summary of Views

Views are an important part of a robust data model. They allow a layer of abstraction between users and the actual data that help provide a level of independence to applications that use your database. They also can provide security benefits for much the same reason. Users aren't seeing the data directly. Finally, they can simplify data access for less experienced users.

Understanding Rules and Defaults

Rules and defaults are independent objects that can be created in a database to help ensure data integrity. Rules allow you to force data that is being inserted or updated into a table to be evaluated against an expression to determine the data's validity. Defaults enable you to specify a value that will be inserted into a column in a table whenever the value is otherwise undefined.

As stated, rules and defaults are objects that exist independently in the database. They are independent because they can exist by themselves with no dependencies whatsoever. They can be found in the *sysobjects* table and therefore have their own unique identifier. This point of the independence of rules and defaults is important because these objects are normally closely tied to a table. Both rules and defaults can easily be mistaken as belonging to a table, even to being a part of that table. Instead, rules and defaults are created as objects, and can then be bound to one or more columns in any number of tables.

It should be noted that rules and defaults enforce the same kinds of data integrity as certain types of constraints (see Chapter 3, "Data Definition"). In fact, constraints are a feature that was added to SQL Server 6.0 for the purpose of providing an enhanced method of accomplishing these tasks. Constraints can operate with less overhead cost to SQL Server than rules and defaults. The checking of data can be done with a constraint before anything gets logged to the Transaction Log, resulting in faster performance. The benefit of rules and defaults, however, is that they are independent objects. A rule or default can be written once, and then bound to any number of columns in the database. Constraints are tied directly to a particular column, so similar functionality must be duplicated where needed.

Creating Rules

 Objective

As independent objects, rules and defaults are created and, when necessary, dropped, each with their own syntax. When they are created, they serve no specific purpose by themselves. First they must be bound to columns, then the rule or default acts upon those columns.

A rule acts upon any data being updated or inserted into any column to which it is bound. A rule consists of one or more expressions that must ultimately result in True or False. Any data being acted upon by a rule is evaluated in that expression. Any data to be inserted or updated through a rule must evaluate to True. Rules can be bound to a user-defined data type or to table columns directly. When a rule is bound to a user-defined data type, it actually acts on columns that are of that data type. Therefore, the rule can be said to be indirectly bound to those columns. This discussion generally refers to rules being bound to columns, even when the binding may truly be to the data type of the columns.

A rule must first be created before it can be used. When a rule is first created, it does not immediately act on any data. Before a rule is used, it must be bound to a column or user-defined data type. Binding must be performed in a separate step from creation. The following is the syntax diagram of the CREATE RULE statement.

```
CREATE RULE [owner.]rule_name
AS@condition_expression
```

The condition_expression referred to by the syntax diagram can consist of any number of expressions conjoined by the AND and OR keywords, and can include any functions that can be found in a WHERE clause. The condition_expression may not refer to any column of any table or any database object. The value of the data being checked by the rule is represented in the condition_expression by an identifier provided in the expression. This parameter can be of any legal identifier type and is prefixed by a"@" symbol. Only one parameter may be used in the condition_expression, but it may be referred to any number of times.

As an alternative to creating rules through a query window, Enterprise Manager provides a graphical interface for this task. From the menu, choose Manage, then Rules. This brings up the Manage Rules dialog box (see fig. 8.2). In the box labeled Rule you can type in the name of a new rule you wish to create or you can choose to examine an existing rule. In the text window at the bottom of the screen, you can view the conditions of an existing rule you chose. For a new rule, you can enter the conditions in exactly the same format as the condition_expression described for the SQL CREATE RULE command.

Figure 8.2

The Manage Rules dialog box from SQL Enterprise Manager.

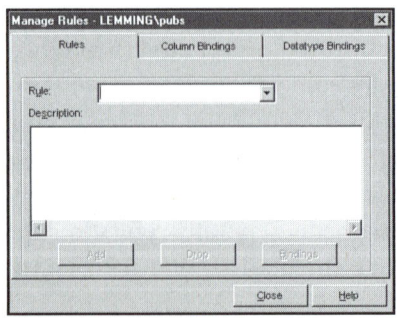

Creating Defaults

 Objective

Defaults act upon INSERTs to the column to which the default is bound. If a row of data is inserted into a table without specifying a value for a column that has a default bound to it, the default supplies a value for that column. Note that if no default is specified for a column that allows NULL values, a NULL is inserted where no specific value is specified. If a column that has no default does not allow NULL values, then an error occurs if no value is specified for that column during an insert. The following table describes this behavior:

Table 8.3

Defaults Relationship to NULL and NOT NULL

Column Definition	No Entry, No Default	No Entry, Default	Enter NULL, No Default	Enter NULL, Default
NULL	NULL	Default	NULL	NULL
NOT NULL	Error	Default	Error	Error

Defaults are created with the CREATE DEFAULT command. When a default is created it still must be bound to whatever columns it should act upon. The syntax for the CREATE DEFAULT statement is as follows:

```
CREATE DEFAULT [owner.]default_name
AS constant_expression
```

The constant_expression referred to in the syntax is simply an expression that will return a value appropriate for the data type of the column for which the default will be used. System functions that don't reference database objects may be used in the constant_expression. No database objects can be referred to in any way from the constant_expression.

Just as rules can be created through the Manage Rules dialog box from Enterprise Manager, defaults are supported by the Manage Defaults dialog box. Choose the Manage menu item, then from the drop-down menu choose Defaults. The dialog box you see should be similar to the one shown in figure 8.3. New defaults can be created or existing ones examined. When creating a new default, the value should be entered following the same rules as the constant_expression.

Figure 8.3

The Manage Defaults dialog box from SQL Enterprise Manager.

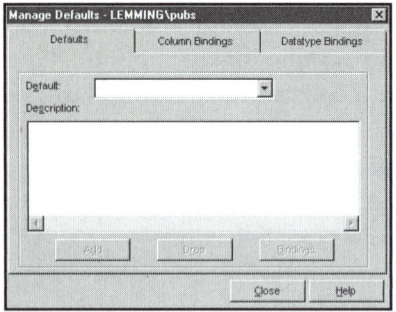

It is very important that the data type of the value that results from the constant_expression matches the column or data type to which the default is bound. When binding to a character field, if the default value is longer than the field, characters are dropped from the right of the string until the value fits. Any value that is supplied by a default has to pass a rule if one applies to the column or data type being inserted to.

Binding and Unbinding Rules and Defaults

 Objective

Rules and defaults must be bound to columns or data types before they can be used. Any data that already exists in the column to which a rule or default is ultimately bound is unaffected by the rule or default. Only future INSERTs or UPDATEs will be acted upon by the rule or default. Both rules and defaults are bound to objects through stored procedures. The syntax for each is described as follows:

```
sp_bindrule rulename, objname [, Future_only]
sp_bindefault defname, objname [, Future_only]
```

The *objname* parameter in the syntax is the name of the user-defined data type or the column that the rule or default should bind to. If a column is specified, the name of the table must also be listed with a period between the two names. It is this "dot" format that indicates a column is being bound, not a data type.

The Future_only parameter is optional and only applies when the rule or default is being applied to a data type. This optional parameter specifies that the rule or default should not be applied to columns that currently have the data type. With the Future_only parameter included, only future table creations with columns of the specified data type will have the rule or default applied.

Bindings also can be performed from the Manage Rules and Manage Defaults dialog boxes in SQL Enterprise Manager. In addition to the initial tab for creating rules and defaults in either the Manage Rules or Manage Defaults dialog boxes, there is a Column Bindings and a Datatype Bindings tab. These two tabs enable you to view the binding of any column of any table or the bindings of any data type. Existing bindings can be dropped and new bindings implemented from these tabs. Figures 8.4 and 8.5 show the Column Bindings and Datatype Bindings tabs of the Manage Rules dialog box.

Figure 8.4

The Column Bindings tab of the Manage Rules dialog box.

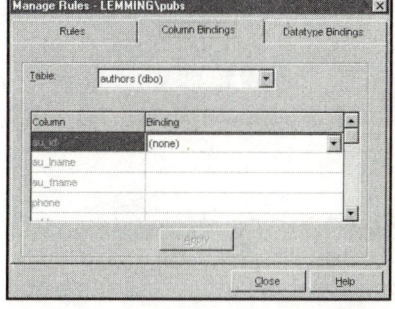

Figure 8.5

The Datatype Bindings tab of the Manage Rules dialog box.

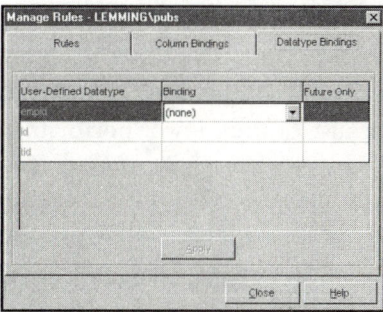

Rules and defaults are unbound through a similar syntax:

```
sp_unbindrule objname [, Future_only]
sp_unbindefault objname [, Future_only]
```

In the unbind procedures the *objname* is used identically to the way it is used in the bind procedures. The optional parameter Future_only again only applies when the rule or default is being unbound from a data type, and it implies that existing bindings be left intact but that new instances of that data type should no longer be bound.

Dropping Rules and Defaults

Objective

Rules and defaults are dropped in similar fashion. The syntax is described as follows:

```
DROP RULE [owner.]rule_name [, [owner.]rule_name …]
DROP DEFAULT [owner.]default_name [, [owner.]default_name …]
```

Note

Rules and defaults must be completely unbound before they may be dropped. Only the owner of the rule or default may drop it. It should be noted that if a table or data type that had a rule or default bound to it is dropped, the rule or default is unbound automatically but not dropped.

Summary of Rules and Defaults

Rules and defaults are similar objects that can be used to enforce data integrity. They can each be bound to multiple objects. As stated, however, their place has been filled by the newer concept of constraints. Although being able to bind a single rule or default to multiple objects can be useful, constraints are preferred because of their lower performance demands.

Summary

With these concepts you will be able to exercise greater control over your database, and you will be in a position to respond more flexibly to your users' requests for data. Successful administration includes rapid and positive responses to changes as well as stable reliability. To successfully implement a manageable database, you need to understand all options at your disposal—and views, rules, and defaults are particularly valuable ones.

Exercises

The sample database "Pubs" that comes with SQL Server is used throughout these exercises.

Exercise 8.1:   Using Enterprise Manager to Create a View

In this function you create a view that joins the Authors, TitleAuthor, and Titles tables.

1. Load Enterprise Manager, and choose the Pubs database from the Server Manager tree view under your server, then the Databases folder.

2. From the Menu at the top of the Enterprise Manager dialog box choose Manage, then views, to load the Manage Views dialog box.

3. The Manage Views dialog box should be ready to accept a new view by default. Delete the text *<VIEW NAME>* and enter **v_AuthorTitles**.

4. On a new line, enter the following SELECT statement to complete the view:

```
CREATE VIEW v_AuthorTitles AS
SELECT Au_fName, Au_lName, Title, Advance
FROM Authors, TitleAuthor, Titles
WHERE Authors.Au_ID = TitleAuthor.Au_ID
  AND TitleAuthor.Title_ID = Titles.Title_ID
```

5. Click the Save Object button that has a green arrow on it to create your view.

Exercise 8.2:   Modifying an Existing View Through the View Manager

Again, you will use the View Manager to modify the view you just created.

1. Open the View Manager dialog box in SQL Enterprise Manager.

continues

Exercise 8.2: Continued

2. From the Views combo box select the view v_AuthorTitles that you created in Exercise 8.1.

3. The full text of your view should be displayed in the window, along with code added at the top to drop the existing version of your view. This code is added because views cannot simply be modified; they must be dropped and re-created. SQL Enterprise Manager generates the code to drop your view if it already exists, and then the actual creation can take place.

4. Combine the Au_Fname field with the Au_Lname field to show the full author name. Replace the two field names in the SELECT list with Au_Fname + ' ' + Au_Lname.

5. Because there is now a derived column in the SELECT list, you must give that column a name. This can be done by providing a column heading in the SELECT list, but instead, enter a list of column names before the keyword AS in the CREATE VIEW statement. Enter a blank line after your view name and before the AS keyword for the column list. Enter three column names, Author, Title, and Cash_Advance, enclosed in parentheses.

6. Create the new view by clicking the Save Object button.

Exercise 8.3: Encrypting a View

In this exercise you see what happens when you encrypt a view.

1. Again, open the View Manager dialog box and choose the v_AuthorTitles view.

2. On a new line after the list of column names, enter the keywords **WITH ENCRYPTION**.

3. Create the view.

Once the view is created, instead of continuing to show the code to create the view as it did the other times, you now see the code to drop the view, followed by the word "<Encrypted>". You are not allowed to see how the view was created after using the WITH ENCRYPTION keywords.

Exercise 8.4: Creating a Rule

In this exercise you create a rule using the Manage Rules dialog box.

1. From the menu of Enterprise Manager, choose Manage, then Rules from the drop-down menu.

2. In the Rule combo box type in the name of your rule, rl_PositiveNumbers.

3. In the Description text box type in the following code:

```
@Number >= 0
```

4. Click on the Add button at the bottom of the dialog box to create this rule.

Exercise 8.5: Creating a Default

In this exercise you use the Manage Default dialog box to create a default.

1. Open a SQL Query dialog box from Enterprise Manager.

2. Type in the following code:

```
Create Default df_ZeroValue
As
        0
go
```

3. Run this query to create the default.

Exercise 8.6: Binding a Rule

In this exercise you bind the rl_PositiveNumbers rule to the Price column of the Titles table.

continues

Exercise 8.6: Continued

1. From the menu of Enterprise Manager, choose Manage, then Rules from the drop-down menu.

2. Click the Column Bindings tab of the Manage Rules dialog box.

3. Choose the Titles table from the drop-down box.

4. Scroll the Column Binding grid at the bottom of the dialog box to find the Price field.

5. Click in the Binding column of the Price row. A drop-down list should contain the choice for rl_PositiveNumbers. Make this selection.

6. Click the Apply button to bind this rule to the Price column.

Exercise 8.7: Binding a Default

In this exercise you bind a default from the Query dialog box.

1. Open the SQL Query dialog box from Enterprise Manager.

2. Type in the following code:

```
sp_bindefault 'df_zerovalue', 'Titles.Price'
```

3. Run this query to bind the default.

Review Questions

1. What does the WITH ENCRYPTION option do when creating a view?

    A. For security reasons, queries accessing this view are encrypted before being sent to the SQL Server.

    B. SQL Server encrypts the entries in the *syscomments* table so that no one but the view owner can see how the view was created.

    C. SQL Server encrypts the entries in the *syscomments* table so that no one, not even the view owner, can see how the view was created.

    D. SQL Server deletes the entries about this view in the *syscomments* table so that no one can see how the view was created.

2. Which of the following statements about views is true?

    A. Modifications can affect only one table in a single statement.

    B. Views can reference Temporary tables.

    C. Creating an index on a view can improve performance.

    D. Views can include computed columns.

3. What statements cannot be used to create a view?

    A. GROUP BY

    B. HAVING

    C. COMPUTE

    D. ORDER BY

4. What can rules be used to enforce?

    A. Values must fall in a specified range.

    B. Values must match a pattern.

    C. Values equal some value in another table.

    D. Values equal some item in a list.

5. Defaults should meet what criteria?

    A. The column should be large enough to hold the default.

    B. The data type of the default should match the column.

    C. The default should adhere to any rule bound to the column.

    D. The default should adhere to Check constraints on the column.

6. When are rules activated?

    A. When data is inserted into the Table.

    B. When the column is updated.

    C. When the table is created.

    D. When data is deleted.

7. When are defaults activated?

    A. When data is inserted into the table.

    B. When the column is updated.

    C. When the table is created.

    D. When data is deleted.

8. Rules are replaced in SQL Server 6.0 by what mechanism?

    A. Unique constraints

    B. Default constraints

    C. Check constraints

    D. Validate constraints

9. Defaults are replaced in SQL Server 6.0 by what mechanism?

    A. Unique constraints

    B. Default constraints

    C. Check constraints

    D. Validate constraints

10. What are the space requirements of views?

    A. Views require as much space as all the tables they are created from.

    B. Views require as much space as would a table that presented the same data.

    C. Views do not store data and therefore use no space.

    D. Views require the space used to store a few records in various system tables.

Answers to Review Questions

1. C

2. A,D

3. C,D

4. A,B,D

5. A,B,C,D

6. A,B

7. A,B

8. C

9. B

10. D

Answers to Test Yourself Questions at Beginning of Chapter

1. A view is an object created in SQL Server to present data derived from one or more tables in the database. A view is referenced just like a table, but it stores no data itself. A view is created with a specific SELECT statement, and the data it shows are the results of that SELECT statement. See "Understanding Views."

2. Views do not store data themselves, they only reference the data from actual tables. Because views do not own data directly, there is nothing to index. See "Recognizing the Limitations of Views."

3. Yes, the SELECT statement used to create the view can join data from any number of tables. (Note that SQL Server actually imposes a limit of 16 tables on any SELECT statement.) See "Creating Views."

4. As long as the view does not perform any integer-based operations on the column being changed, nothing needs to be done. The table can be dropped and recreated, and the view will continue to reference it correctly. See "Recognizing the Limitations of Views."

5. No, any data modifications made to a view may affect only one underlying table, or an error occurs. See "Recognizing the Limitations of Views."

6. Create default def_space As ' '

   See "Creating Defaults."

7. Create Rule rl_invoice_format

   As   @code LIKE '[0-9][A-Z][A-Z][A-Z][0-9][0-9]'

   See "Creating Rules."

C h a p t e r

9

Programmability

This chapter helps you prepare for the exam by covering the following objectives:

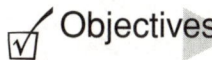 Objectives

> ▶ Identify control-of-flow statements
>
> ▶ Implement cursors
>
> ▶ Recognize the benefits of using stored procedures
>
> ▶ Identify capabilities of SQL Server and MAPI
>
> ▶ Implement string and variable extensions for the EXECUTE statement
>
> ▶ Manage user-defined error messages

Test Yourself! Before reading this chapter, test yourself to determine how much study time you will need to devote to this section.

1. If one of the statements inside a batch causes an error, what happens to the execution of that batch?

2. What happens if a statement in a batch has a syntax error?

3. What is the scope of a local variable?

4. What is a Boolean expression?

5. How many statements can follow an IF statement that returns true?

6. What two statements enable you to interrupt execution of a WHILE loop?

7. Where can the CASE structure be used?

8. What command must be issued before a cursor can be opened?

9. What phrase is used to perform positioned updates and deletes with cursors?

10. How can you register a stored procedure to be executed automatically when SQL Server is started?

11. How can you cause user-defined errors to be written to the SQL Server error log?

Answers are located at the end of the chapter...

Microsoft SQL Server supports the Transact SQL language or TSQL, for interactive queries and scripting. TSQL, in version 6.5, complies with ANSI standards for SQL as well as certain enhancements beyond the ANSI requirements. TSQL is a powerful programming language that can be used to create scripts that can be interpreted at execution time, or TSQL commands can be collected into stored procedures that SQL Server pre-compiles to improve performance. Using the TSQL language to the fullest, you can create batch jobs that evaluate the outcome of individual statements and can adjust the program logic based on the results.

In order to prepare you for the exam, the following topics are covered in this chapter:

- ▶ Control-of-flow Statements

- ▶ The benefits of using stored procedures

- ▶ The capabilities of SQL Server and MAPI

- ▶ Implementing string and variable extensions for the EXECUTE statement

- ▶ Managing user-defined error messages

Control-of-Flow Statements

 Objective

The key to getting started using TSQL is understanding the control-of-flow structures that are available to you. These commands enable you to test conditions and take action based on the results. Examples of control-of-flow statements are IF statements for conditional execution, WHILE statements for looping, and GOTO statements for branching. Proper use of these and other control-of-flow statements gives you tremendous control over SQL Server's execution of your code.

Using Scripts and Batches

When submitting a large group of commands to be executed by SQL Server, it is important to understand how the individual commands are grouped for execution. The group of all commands submitted to SQL Server at one time is called a script. Within a script, commands can be further grouped into logical units known as batches.

A batch is the set of TSQL statements that are executed together. A batch of statements are compiled once as a whole and then executed. If any statement within the batch has a syntax error that prevents it from compiling, the entire batch fails to compile and is not run. Any following batches may still compile and run however. Multiple explicit transactions can exist within a single batch, and a single script submitted to SQL Server for execution can be broken into multiple batches. The keyword GO signifies the end of a batch to SQL Server.

Using Variables

Variables are supported by TSQL to hold single values. In TSQL scripts, variables play less of a role than they do in other languages, such as Visual C++ and Visual Basic. This is because TSQL is a set-based language rather than an iterative one. Common TSQL data manipulation commands such as SELECT, INSERT, UP-DATE, and DELETE normally operate on large sets of data at a time, whereas in many other languages all operations act upon one piece of information at a time. Therefore, in TSQL most data is stored in tables rather than in individual variables. Still, variables are needed to allow iterative programming, and to store return codes and other single pieces of information.

TSQL recognizes two types of variables, local and global. *Local variables* are ones that are created by the user. Local variables are recognized by preceding the name by a single "at" sign (@). These user-defined variables continue to exist until the end of the current batch. *Global variables* are system-defined and are always available. These system variables are preceded by two "at" signs (@@). Global variables are assigned their values by the system and users should not attempt to change these assignments.

Local, user-defined variables are created through the DECLARE statement. Any number of variables can be created together in the same statement, even ones of different data types. The syntax for the DECLARE statement is as follows:

```
DECLARE @variable_name datatype
     [, @variable_name datatype...]
```

After declaring local variables, you generally need to assign them. Assignment of local variables is done with the SELECT statement. In the SELECT list of the statement, local variables are listed, followed by an equal sign and the value to assign. In this way variables can be assigned to constants, function results (such as those from Aggregate or System functions), or even table columns. Variables are generally assigned to a single value, but if a variable is assigned to a column returning multiple values, only the last value in the column is retained in the variable.

SQL Server defines many global system variables. These variables supply information about recent activity on the server, or about your recently executed statements.

The following are common global variables:

- ▶ **@@CURSOR_ROWS.** Specifies the number of rows returned by the cursor that was last opened for this user connection. The values returned are of one of the following forms:

   - ▶ –m if the cursor is being populated asynchronously. The absolute value of the returned value indicates the number of rows currently in the keyset.

   - ▶ n if the cursor is fully populated.

   - ▶ 0 if no cursors have been opened or the last opened cursor has been closed or deallocated.

- ▶ **@@ERROR.** Specifies the last error number generated by the system for the user connection. This variable is normally used immediately after statements in a script or stored procedure to check if the statement succeeded or failed. A value of 0 indicates success.

- ▶ **@@FETCH_STATUS.** Contains the status of the last cursor FETCH command on this user connection. It is set to 0 if the fetch is successful, to –1 if the fetch failed or the row was beyond results set, or to –2 if the row fetched is missing.

▶ **@@IDENTITY.** Indicates the last value that was inserted into an IDENTITY field by this user's connections. The value is NULL if the last INSERT did not change any IDENTITY field. Because many users can INSERT rows into a table at the same time, checking for the highest value of an IDENTITY field may not accurately return the IDENTITY value assigned to the row you just inserted. Use the @@IDENTITY value to indicate what value was assigned to rows you INSERT.

▶ **@@SPID.** Specifies the server process ID number of the current process.

▶ **@@TRANCOUNT.** Specifies the number of transactions that are currently active for the current user.

▶ **@@VERSION.** Specifies the date, version number, and processor type for the current version of SQL Server.

Using BEGIN and END Keywords

The BEGIN and END keywords are used to define a block of statements. A block causes all the statements contained within it to be treated by SQL Server as a single statement. Because all the statements are so grouped together, a block must be completely contained within a batch, as defined earlier. The primary purpose of statement blocks is to define the group of statements that are affected by other control-of-flow statements such as IF, WHILE, and CASE. Each of these control-of-flow statements affect only a single statement, or a statement block.

Using the IF Keyword

The IF statement enables you to control whether statements are executed based on the results of a Boolean expression. The statement following the IF statement is executed only if the Boolean expression returns true. If the Boolean expression returns false, the statement following is skipped. The syntax for the IF statement follows.

```
IF Boolean_expression
      {sql_statement | statement_block}
[ELSE [Boolean_expression]
      {sql_statement | statement_block}]
```

In the preceding syntax listing you can see that either a single statement can follow the Boolean expression, or a block of multiple statements.

The Boolean expression generally consists of some form of a comparison operation. All that is required is that the expression return a single value of true or false. A SELECT statement can be used in a Boolean expression, but it must be contained within parentheses.

The preceding syntax also shows an optional keyword, ELSE. If the initial Boolean expression returns false, then the statement or block following the ELSE statement executes. If the initial expression returns true, however, the ELSE block does not execute. If the ELSE is followed by another Boolean expression, then the statement following only executes if the initial expression is false but the ELSE expression returns true.

The statement blocks following the IF or ELSE expressions can contain almost any kind of statement, including other IF statements. SQL Server does not impose any limits on the number of IF statements that can be nested together. Note that because any statement block must be wholly contained in a batch, the GO command may not be contained in an IF block.

Using the WHILE Statement

A WHILE statement allows for looping in a TSQL script or procedure. The statement following the WHILE expression is repeatedly executed until the expression that follows the WHILE keyword returns false. A description of the WHILE syntax follows:

```
WHILE Boolean_expression
      {sql_statement | statement_block}
      [BREAK]
      {sql_statement | statement_block}
      [CONTINUE]
```

The Boolean expression must follow the same rules as expressions in an IF statement. What is new to the WHILE statement are the two keywords BREAK and CONTINUE. These commands must be contained in a statement block following a WHILE. When either of these commands is encountered in a block, the execution of that block is interrupted. The difference between BREAK and CONTINUE is where execution resumes. The BREAK command causes execution to resume after the WHILE statement block, while the CONTINUE command causes the WHILE expression to be reevaluated immediately, and execution to resume according the result of that expression.

Using the CASE Expression

The CASE expression is a very powerful feature of TSQL. Although in many ways it simply provides the same functionality as nested if...else structures, the CASE expression can actually be used within the body of a SELECT statement. Note however, that CASE is an expression, not a statement like IF. As an expression, CASE cannot be executed by itself, it must be used as a part of another command that can be executed independently.

As stated previously, the CASE expression provides functionality similar to that of an IF statement. A case_expression is specified along with any number of additional expressions. When the case_expression equals one of the additional expressions, an expression associated with the matched expression is returned. The following syntax helps explain this better.

```
CASE expression
     WHEN expression1a THEN expression1b
     [[WHEN expression2a THEN expression2b] [...]]
     [ELSE expressionNb]
END
```

In the preceding syntax, when the expression that follows CASE is equal to expression1a, expression1b is returned as the value of the CASE expression. This comparison is done on all of the WHEN expressions until a match is found. If no WHEN expression equals the CASE expression, then the ELSE expression is returned (if one is provided). If no match is found and no ELSE expression is provided, the CASE expression returns NULL.

There also is an alternate form of the CASE syntax. In this syntax no initial expression is provided for comparison. Instead each WHEN expression must return a Boolean value. Each WHEN expression is evaluated until one returns TRUE, then the related THEN expression is returned. If no WHEN Boolean expression is TRUE, then the ELSE expression is returned. The following syntax illustrates this.

```
CASE
    WHEN Boolean_expression1 THEN expression1
    [[WHEN Boolean_expression2 THEN expression2] [...]]
    [ELSE expressionN]
END
```

Using the GOTO Command

The GOTO command causes the execution of a batch to immediately resume at a label. A label is simply an identifier that is followed by a colon to identify it as an independent entity. Labels can be placed anywhere in your script as a commenting feature, regardless of whether a GOTO refers to it or not.

The GOTO command itself is followed by the name of the identifier without the colon. When the GOTO is executed, the batch continues execution from the label onward. The label referred to by the GOTO may be either before or after the GOTO itself, but it must be within the same batch. It is permissible to use a GOTO within an IF or WHILE command.

Using the RETURN Command

The RETURN command enables you to immediately stop execution of a batch. When the RETURN command is executed, the script execution resumes at the beginning of the next batch in the script. When used in a script, the RETURN command takes no parameters. It is executed as an independent statement all by itself.

The RETURN command also can be used to terminate execution of a stored procedure, which is discussed later in this chapter. When RETURN is used in a stored procedure, it may accept an optional parameter enclosed in parentheses as the value that it returns. If the procedure was called from an EXEC statement, the RETURN value from the procedure can be assigned to a variable and examined for the cause of the procedure's termination. The following syntax shows this use of the RETURN command.

```
RETURN [(integer_expression)]
```

Implementing Cursors

 Objective

Cursors provide you with the ability to work with data in SQL Server iteritively, instead of in sets. SQL is inherently a set-based language. All of its most fundamental data manipulation statements, SELECT, UPDATE, INSERT, and DELETE, normally work with entire sets of data at a time. Cursors enable you to define a set of data and work with that data one row at a time. To work with data in this way, you generally need to use some form of a loop to iterate through the set, which is why using cursors is called an iterative approach.

As a rule, SQL Server can manipulate an arbitrarily large set of data as a set faster than it can respond to an iterative series of commands. Because most iterative solutions can be expressed as set operations with a little work, cursors should generally be avoided. Thinking in terms of whole sets of data instead of individual rows is what makes the SQL language so different from other traditional programming languages. Looking for set-oriented solutions to problems is, however, an important transition to make.

When cursors are found to be necessary, they can be implemented quickly and efficiently in SQL Server. SQL Server supports server-based cursors, where the server maintains the entire set of data that makes up the cursor and keeps track of the current position in the set of the cursor. Before SQL Server 6.0 these operations had to be handled through client libraries, which was much less efficient. By handling all the data itself, SQL Server can process any commands necessary without having to transport data to another application that could possibly be running over a slow network connection.

Declaring Cursors

To use cursors in TSQL you must first define the type of cursor, and the data set it operates on. There are many keywords that can be used in the declaration of a cursor to specify the type of cursor, and the data set to operate on is specified by embedding a SELECT statement in the declaration as well. The following details the syntax for a cursor declaration:

```
DECLARE cursor_name [INSENSITIVE] [SCROLL] CURSOR
FOR select_statement
[FOR {READ ONLY | UPDATE [OF column_list]}]
```

The keyword INSENSITIVE specifies that the result set of the cursor be held in the temporary database, tempdb, so that changes to the underlying tables while the cursor is open will not affect the results of the cursor. These cursors cannot be updated because the only data that is maintained is in tempdb. There is no tie maintained with the underlying table.

The keyword SCROLL specifies that the cursor can be positioned forward or backward and by specified amounts. The different options for scrolling are described by the FETCH command later in this section.

By specifying that the cursor is scrollable, SQL Server needs to maintain a collection of key information about all the rows in the cursor so that it can uniquely identify its position as it moves around. If all the tables involved have unique indexes, then this condition is easily satisfied. If any table does not have a unique index, then the data from that table must be manipulated in the temporary database, tempdb, where each row can be assigned a unique identifier. By storing this information in tempdb however, SQL Server cannot maintain a connection to the real table because there is no way to identify any specific row without a unique index. This is why scrollable cursors cannot be updated if any table does not have a unique index. SQL Server creates the cursor as INSENSITIVE, which is non-updateable.

 **Note**

> Note that if the SCROLL option is not used the cursor only positions itself one row at a time in the forward direction. This is known as a forward-only cursor. Because positioning in this situation is so predictable, no keysets need to be created and stored in tempdb, allowing the cursor to be opened more quickly and positioning speed is much faster. The predictability of scrolling through a forward-only cursor is also why such a cursor can be updateable even if no unique indexes are available.
>
> The benefits of forward-only cursors are only available in SQL Server 6.5. Although version 6.0 demonstrates the same behavior, except for updateability of tables without unique indexes, it did not take advantage of the possibilities forward-only cursors provide. Instead, even forward-only cursors maintained a keyset in tempdb.

The select_statement specified in the DECLARE command is a standard SELECT statement with a few limitations. The keywords COMPUTE, COMPUTE BY, FOR BROWSE, and INTO cannot be used in the declaration of a cursor. If the keywords DISTINCT, UNION, GROUP BY, or HAVING are used in the select_statement, then the cursor is not updateable and declaring it so results in an error. This is because using these options requires SQL Server to store the data in tempdb so that the results can be ordered and otherwise manipulated. Because the data is in tempdb, the cursor is created as INSENSITIVE, which is non-updateable.

The cursor is also INSENSITIVE if the select_statement includes a derived column. This is any column that does not come directly from a single column from some table. The cursor also is INSENSITIVE if one of the tables in the query does not have a unique index and the SCROLL option is used, as was discussed earlier in the SCROLL option.

The READ_ONLY keyword ensures that the cursor allows no modifications. Because non-INSENSITIVE cursors are updateable by default, this option is needed to prevent unintentional updates or deletes.

The UPDATE keyword ensures that the cursor will allow modifications. Because the nature of the tables and the type of SELECT statement that is used can implicitly disallow updates, it is a good idea to explicitly use the UPDATE keyword to ensure that the cursor actually allows data modifications to occur. If the UPDATE demand cannot be honored because of the nature of the rest of the declaration, an error is returned, and the cursor is not declared.

If the UPDATE keyword is used, all columns in the cursor are updateable. Using the OF modifier to UPDATE enables you to explicitly list the columns you intend to modify. Note that the UPDATE keyword does not simply mean that updates are allowed to the rows in the result set, it also indicates that deletions are allowed.

The following are examples of an updateable and an insensitive cursor.

```
DECLARE cur_Update SCROLL CURSOR FOR
      SELECT *
      FROM Authors
FOR UPDATE of au_fname, au_lname

DECLARE cur_Insensitive INSENSITIVE CURSOR FOR
      SELECT *
      FROM Authors
FOR READ_ONLY
```

Using the OPEN Command

The OPEN command requires only the name of the cursor, and no other parameters, to open. The entire definition of the cursor was defined by the DECLARE command. When the cursor is opened, the SELECT statement in the DECLARE command is executed and any results needed for the cursor are collected. If the cursor is INSENSITIVE, this means all the rows are collected and stored in tempdb. If the cursor is forward-only, almost no information is collected. Rather, each successive fetch gathers one more row and information from the previous row is discarded. The OPEN command does not implicitly perform an initial FETCH on the data.

Using the FETCH Command

The FETCH command retrieves requested rows from the cursor's result set. The data from these rows can be stored in variables specified in the FETCH command. The syntax for the FETCH command is as follows:

```
FETCH [[NEXT | PRIOR | FIRST | LAST
      | ABSOLUTE {n | @nvar} | RELATIVE {n | @nvar}]
FROM] cursor_name
[INTO @variable_name1, @variable_name2, ...]
```

The @variable_name parameters each correspond to the columns from the SELECT statement used in the declaration of the cursor. Note that no variables need be provided, and fewer variables may be provided than columns in the SELECT. It is not possible, however, to specify which variable receives data from which column except by position. Therefore, any columns not stored into given variables start from the rightmost in the SELECT list of the declaration. Any variables used in the FETCH command must be declared first.

When positioning the cursor with the FETCH command, you must pay careful attention to the global variable @@FETCH_STATUS. After each FETCH this variable indicates success or failure. A value of zero indicates a successful FETCH. A value of –1 indicates that the position requested was before the beginning or beyond the end of the cursor. A value of –2 indicates that although the position requested existed when the cursor was opened, it has since been deleted. Note that this does not occur in a forward-only cursor or an INSENSITIVE one, because the forward-only cursor keeps no record of membership and so can't say whether any given row used to exist or not, and INSENSITIVE cursors maintain their own data set which cannot be modified.

The NEXT position specifier is the default if no other is provided. This causes the very next row in the result set to be fetched. This is also the only specifier allowed for forward-only cursors.

The PRIOR position specifier fetches the results from the row just before the current row. This does not mean that the row fetched is the one previously fetched, however, because other positioning commands may jump over several rows.

The FIRST and LAST specifiers fetch the results from the very first or the last rows in the result set, respectively. This can be useful to reset the cursor's position to a known point.

The ABSOLUTE and RELATIVE specifiers set the position to a point that could be any distance from the current point. Both of these options require that a distance be specified, either by an integer literal, or by a variable. ABSOLUTE positions the cursor at N number of rows from the FIRST position, where N is the specified distance. RELATIVE positions the cursor N rows away from the current position.

Using the CLOSE and DEALLOCATE Commands

The CLOSE and DEALLOCATE commands each take the cursor name as their only parameter. The CLOSE command releases any data being held by the cursor since it was opened. This may be significant in the case of an INSENSITIVE cursor or relatively minor in the case of a forward-only cursor. No further positioning or editing can be done on a closed cursor.

The DEALLOCATE command removes the definition of the cursor from the server's memory. After a DEALLOCATE command, the cursor cannot be re-opened.

Using the CURRENT OF Keyword

Updateable cursors enable both updates to the individual columns of a cursor and deletions of rows. This is done through UPDATE and DELETE commands, with the CURRENT OF keyword as the only phrase in the WHERE clause. The syntax for each is shown here:

```
UPDATE table_name
    SET column_name1 =
                {expression1 | NULL | (select_statement)}
            [, column_name2 =
                {expression2 | NULL | (select_statement)}...]
WHERE CURRENT OF cursor_name

DELETE FROM table_name
WHERE CURRENT OF cursor_name
```

With these features positioned, updates and deletions through cursors use the same sort of syntax that developers are already familiar with. This makes data modifications through cursors simple and familiar. You will notice that insertions are not supported through cursors, however. Insertions should be made directly to the table where the data belongs, through a normal INSERT statement. If the inserted data then needs to be reflected in the cursor, the cursor must be closed and reopened.

The Benefits of Using Stored Procedures

 Objective

The use of stored procedures is an important part of any database scheme. Stored procedures can be thought of as precompiled scripts. Stored procedures can contain any commands that can be put in a script, including control-of-flow structures, any kinds of data modification or data retrieval statements, cursors, and, of course, error handling. Stored procedures offer many benefits to developers and users alike, as described in this section.

Precompiled Code

One of the major benefits of using stored procedures is that they are precompiled and therefore can run with less overhead than would be experienced by submitting the logic in a script. When a procedure is created, a query tree is created in the system table *sysprocedures*. This query tree is SQL Server's internal representation of the logic behind a stored procedure. The creation of the query tree when the stored procedure is created saves any subsequent calls to the procedure from having to go through that step. Then, when a procedure is run for the first time, it is compiled into an execution plan that is saved into the procedure cache. This execution plan is the optimized set of instructions that tell SQL Server exactly what to do. Because this execution plan is then stored into the procedure cache, subsequent calls to the procedure may not have to do even the work of finding an optimized plan.

It should be understood that although the execution plan stored in the procedure cache is reusable, it is not reentrant. This means that the execution plan can be used by only one process at a time. If the same procedure is executed by another process while the first process is still running, a new execution plan is created, and then two copies of the plan are stored in the procedure cache. Thus, the procedure cache may well contain many different copies of many different stored procedures. This process continues until the procedure cache fills, at which time individual execution plans are removed on a least-recently-used basis.

Sharing Application Logic

Another distinct benefit you get from using stored procedures is that common tasks can be shared between any number of different applications. By writing your stored procedures in small, logical units, the individual pieces can be put together in other stored procedures to accomplish a specific task. Then, some of those same individual units can be reassembled along with other pieces to form a procedure to accomplish a different task. In this way code can be shared among different applications.

Reliability

The approach of using many procedures to each accomplish one specific task also enables you to evaluate the effectiveness of each individual piece of a complicated process so that it can be debugged more effectively. This should result in a much more stable final process. In addition, return codes can be returned from each piece to ensure that if any piece fails for any reason, appropriate actions can be taken. This provides for even further reliability.

Security

Stored procedures also can be used as an integral part of your security system on SQL Server. Stored procedures always run in the security context of their owner. Therefore, anyone granted execute privileges to a stored procedure does not also need to be granted permissions to query or edit every table that stored procedure references. This allows permissions to be set very tightly to allow users only the access they truly need. Then carefully designed stored procedures can be created to allow users to query or edit tables in a controlled manner.

Startup Stored Procedures

It is also possible to register certain stored procedures to be executed whenever SQL Server starts. This ability can enable you to perform routine chores automatically when SQL Server starts. Such routines could be used to update index statistics, or to call the Database Consistency Checker to verify the database integrity, or perhaps you may just want to call several procedures to get them pre-loaded into the cache. Table 9.1 describes stored procedures that can be used to register and unregister procedures to be run at system startup.

Table 9.1

Startup Registration Procedures	
Procedure Syntax	Description
sp_makestartup procedure_name	Makes an existing stored procedure a startup procedure.
sp_unmakestartup procedure_name	Stops a procedure from executing at startup in the future.
sp_helpstartup	Shows a list of all procedures that execute at startup.

The Capabilities of SQL Server and MAPI

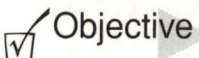 Objective ▶   MAPI is Microsoft's Mail Application Programming Interface. This technology allows applications to send and receive electronic mail. The ability of SQL Server to integrate with MAPI offers a developer powerful tools for working remotely with SQL Server. By using the MAPI based procedures offered with SQL Server you can have SQL Server send messages warning administrators of problems that have occurred. You also can have SQL Server process incoming messages and inform you of the results.

 Note ▶   Configuring a SQL Server to work with MAPI requires someone with administration authority on the machine and the ability to configure your organization's mail system.

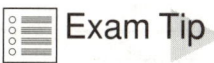 Exam Tip ▶   The SQL Server Implementation exam requires you to be familiar with the capabilities MAPI provides you, but not how to enable MAPI on your server.

Using MAPI to Warn of Server Problems

When errors occur, you can set up SQL Server to respond to those errors by sending mail to people who can identify and correct the problem. This is done by defining alerts that send messages to predefined SQL operators who can take action to correct the problem. It is also possible to use SQL Performance Monitor to monitor conditions in SQL Server and cause alerts when certain conditions are met that indicate an impending problem. Part of MAPI's capabilities include the ability to call an operator's pager or to send mail so that people can be notified immediately.

Talk to your SQL Administrator to find out if your server is configured to use MAPI. Then decide what problems to watch for and who to notify when they occur.

Using MAPI to Process Queries

SQL Server comes with several procedures to send and receive mail messages. With these procedures you can send SQL Server a query and have it mail the results to whomever you need. You also can instruct SQL Server to process mail it receives and mail the results back to the sender. With this ability you can query the status of your database even without a live connection. When your query completes you receive the results in a message, without having to stay on-line waiting for the job to finish.

Table 9.2 lists some of the procedures that you can use and a brief description of the capabilities of each.

Table 9.2

Common MAPI Procedures

Procedure	Description
xp_sendmail	Sends a mail message from SQL Server to any recipient you specify. You can include a query in the call to this procedure that will be executed—the results are sent in the body of the message.
xp_readmail	Reads a mail message that was sent to SQL Server and returns the body of the message in a variable you supply.
xp_findnextmsg	Returns the message ID of the next unread message in SQL Server's mail inbox.
sp_processmail	Uses xp_sendmail, xp_readmail, and xp_findnextmsg to read a new mail message; to execute the body of the message, which is assumed to be a single TSQL statement; and to return the results in another mail message. This procedure can be scheduled to run periodically and handle any new requests that have been sent.

Again, you should talk to your SQL Administrator to have these capabilities implemented on your server. Once the server is configured you can call these procedures from your applications to

take advantage of sending and receiving queries and
messages remotely.

Implementing String and Variable Extensions for the EXECUTE Statement

 Objective

The EXECUTE statement is used to execute either a stored procedure or a TSQL string formed dynamically at run time. When
used to execute a procedure, the EXECUTE command allows a
return code to be accepted from the procedure and stored in a
specified variable. When used to execute a string, EXECUTE allows multiple variables to be concatenated with string literals to
form, in total, a TSQL statement that is then executed. In either
use, the EXECUTE statement allows statements to be executed in
a fashion that is not possible any other way.

Using Procedures

When stored procedures terminate, they normally return some
value to indicate success or failure to the calling routine. The only
way to accept this return value within TSQL, however, is to use the
EXECUTE statement. Stored procedures can be called from a
script simply by specifying the name of the procedure, but with
this approach no return code can be accepted.

The EXECUTE statement also enables you to specify the name of
the stored procedure to be executed within a variable. In this fashion the procedure to be executed can be determined dynamically.

The syntax describing this use of the EXECUTE statement follows:

```
EXEC[ute]
{[@return_status =]
    {[[[server.]database.]owner.]procedure_name[;number] |
        @procedure_name_var}
    [[@parameter_name =] {value | @variable [OUTPUT]]
        [, [@parameter_name =] {value | @variable [OUTPUT]}]...]
    [WITH RECOMPILE]]}
```

This syntax shows how you can declare a variable, referred to as @return_status, that can receive the return value of the procedure. The syntax also shows how you can use a character type variable, referred to as @procedure_name_var, that has been assigned a string representing the name of a procedure to be executed.

Because a stored procedure can be written to accept many different parameters, the EXECUTE statement enables you to optionally specify what parameters you intend to pass data into. You accomplish this by specifying the parameter name just as it appears in the procedure's definition, followed by an equal sign and the value you want to pass. If you do not specify the parameter name, then the values are passed respectively to the parameters in the order in which they appear. The two methods of supplying parameters, named or unnamed, can be used together. However, once a named parameter is used, all subsequent parameters must be named as well.

The final option that can be supplied to the EXECUTE statement is WITH RECOMPILE. If this option is supplied, then precompiled versions of the procedure that may currently exist in the procedure cache are ignored, and a new execution plan is determined and used. If you are passing in parameters that are significantly different from previous executions of the procedure, the optimizer may be able to determine a more efficient method of execution for your particular queries if you specify the WITH RECOMPILE option.

Using Strings

The EXECUTE statement has a very powerful feature that enables you to build ad-hoc queries from strings. Normally, you are not allowed to write a SELECT statement, for example, that uses a variable in place of a table or column name in an effort to write a query that could change dynamically to read from different tables. All objects referred to in a TSQL statement must be referenced directly, not through variables. The EXECUTE statement, however, enables you to assign any values necessary to variables. It will then concatenate those variables together and EXECUTE the resulting string, which presumably will be a fully formed TSQL statement. After putting such a statement together, it is irrelevant where the information to build the string came from or whether table and column names were hard-coded into the strings or derived dynamically.

Managing User-Defined Error Messages

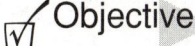 Objective ▶ When writing large TSQL scripts and procedures, you will quickly find situations where errors can occur. You cannot always guarantee that users will enter the kind of data you expect, and this can cause duplicate key violations or other forms of constraint violations. It is often impractical to pre-examine entered data for every possible violation that could occur, and even then it is wise to protect your code against changes to the database structure that could cause errors for which you could not have planned. SQL Server provides the ability to check for and respond to unexpected errors and to respond to bad data by raising errors of your own. You also can embed messages in your code that will be printed out during execution.

Responding to Errors

After the execution of any TSQL statement, the global variable @@ERROR is always set to indicate success or failure. A value of zero indicates success, and any other value means that some error occurred. Good code should always check the value of @@ERROR after any statement. Very often scripts or procedures do their work inside transactions to ensure consistency. In these cases it is especially important to check for errors so that a partially completed transaction is not committed.

As previously stated, any TSQL statement causes @@ERROR to be reset to indicate success or failure of that statement. This means that the very act of checking @@ERROR for a non-zero status causes it to be reset. Therefore, even though you will learn the results of your comparison, you can no longer use @@ERROR to report the error value that occurred. If you need to know the exact error value that was returned by a statement, you must immediately assign @@ERROR to a user-defined variable, and then perform your validation on that variable.

Using the RAISERROR Command

If you detect any condition within your code that you need to warn the user of, you can raise your own custom-defined errors to return. This is done with the RAISERROR command. With the RAISERROR command you can either raise errors that you have defined and registered in the database, or you can create an ad-hoc error message to return. The syntax for RAISERROR follows:

```
RAISERROR ({msg_id | msg_str}, severity, state
[, argument1 [, argument2]] )
[WITH LOG]
```

The severity and state parameters are used by RAISERROR to report additional information to the client application. The severity should be an integer between 1 and 25. Errors with a severity of 1 to 10 are considered informational only—the user may wish to note the occurrence, but should feel safe to ignore it. Errors with a severity of 11 through 16 are those that are generated by the user and can be corrected by the user. These would be constraint violations caused by bad data being sent by the user. Errors with severity 17 through 19 are hardware or software errors. These errors indicate that the user can continue working, though a serious problem exists that may affect the server's performance. Errors returned with a severity of 20 through 25 indicate a fatal problem. Returning these errors causes the client connection to be disconnected.

Only the system administrator may raise an error with a severity of 19 or greater, and then the WITH LOG option must be specified. The error state should indicate the source of the error, if the error can be raised from more than one place. An error state of –1 should be used to indicate no particular state.

The WITH LOG option indicates that the error should be written to SQL Server's error log. This guarantees that the error is recorded where it can be reviewed later. All errors with a severity of greater than 19 are logged.

Either a predefined error or an ad-hoc message can be returned by RAISERROR. A predefined error is one that has been registered in the *sysmessages* system table. You can register and remove errors of your own using the sp_addmessage and the sp_dropmessage stored procedures. The messages RAISERROR uses, whether supplied explicitly or pulled from sysmessages, are subject to parameter replacement so that specific values can be inserted into the string to make the message more relevant. Special format strings are included in the error string to mark the point where the RAISERROR parameters argument1, argument2, and so on, should be inserted. The arguments can be of any data type so long as they match the type required by the format string. The syntax for the format string follows:

```
% [[flag] [width[.precision]] [{h | l}]] type
```

The flag parameter allows the values shown in table 9.3.

Table 9.3

Flag Parameters		
Value	Formatting	Description
– (minus)	Left-justified	Left-justify the result within the given field width.
+ (plus)	+ (plus) or – (minus)	If the output value is of a signed data prefix type, preface the output value with a + or –.
0 (zero)	Zero padding	Pad the result with zeros on the left until the minimum width is reached. The – (minus) code will override this value if both are used together.
# (number)	0x prefix for hexadecimal type of x or X	When used with the o, x, or X format, the # flag prefaces any nonzero value with 0, 0x, or 0X, respectively. This value is ignored with all other formats.
' ' (blank)	Space padding	Preface the output value with blank spaces if the value is signed and positive. This is ignored if included with the + flag.

The width parameter defines the minimum width the replacement argument takes up in the resulting message. Values are normally right-justified within the width specified, though this can be changed by some of the preceding specified values. This parameter can optionally be modified by following it with a decimal point (.) and a precision parameter. The precision specifies a width within the total width that printed characters show. For an integer value, this precision specifies the minimum number of digits to print. For a string the precision specifies the maximum characters to print.

The type parameter indicates the data type that will be embedded into the message string. Note that only integer and character data types are allowed. When this parameter indicates an integer type it can be followed by either the "h" or "l" option to indicate short or long integer types, respectively. Table 9.4 describes the values for this parameter.

Table 9.4

Types

Type Code	Data Type
d or i	Signed integer
o	Unsigned octal
p	Pointer
s	String
u	Unsigned integer
x or X	Unsigned hexadecimal

Using the PRINT Statement

The PRINT statement is used to return a message to the client application. The message can be any kind of text up to 255 characters in length. Either string literals or character variables can be used in a PRINT statement. Although multiple character strings and variables can be concatenated together in a PRINT statement, system functions such as CONVERT cannot be used to allow printing of integer values. Instead, the integer variables must be converted and assigned to character variables before the PRINT statement, and then the character variables can be printed.

Summary

The language of SQL Server, Transact SQL, contains a rich set of commands to enable you to program SQL Server. By utilizing the features of TSQL, you can write complicated scripts that can take action based on conditions found in data and respond to unexpected errors. This kind of logic also can be encapsulated into precompiled procedures that can execute faster than regular scripts that are more accessible to users.

Exercises

These exercises should all be performed in the Pubs database.

Exercise 9.1:   Syntax Errors in Batches

1. Load SQL Enterprise Manager and open a query window. Accumulate the commands that follow into a single script and wait to execute the script until the exercise instructs you to do so. The exercise also indicates where batch separators should go.

2. First you need to create a temporary table to work with in this exercise. Because you may want to run this exercise repeatedly, you also need to be able to drop this table if it already exists. For simplicity, the code to drop and then re-create the table, #MyTable with the single field, myint, is given below. Copy this code into your query window.

```
IF EXISTS (SELECT * FROM tempdb..sysobjects WHERE Name LIKE
➥'#MyTable%')
        DROP TABLE #MyTable
GO

CREATE TABLE #MyTable (
        myint int NOT NULL
)
GO
```

3. To see how batch processing reacts to syntax errors, you can deliberately write a flawed statement followed by a legitimate statement in the same batch. Write an INSERT statement to insert the character 'A' into #MyTable.

4. Now write a statement to select all of the data from #MyTable. Put a column header in the statement to indicate that the SELECT statement is in the flawed batch, such as 'Flawed Batch'. Follow this SELECT with the batch separator GO.

5. In the new batch that follows the error, duplicate the same SELECT statement as in step 4, but change the header to indicate it is executing in the new batch.

6. Now execute the script and examine the results. The table creation should produce no results at all, but the INSERT statement produces an error message indicating that SQL Server could not convert a character to an integer. Following the error message you should see the results from your second query that was in the new batch. The query in the flawed batch never executed at all, demonstrating that all statements in a batch are compiled together and that if any command in the batch fails to compile, the batch is skipped.

7. To further demonstrate the same point, add another SELECT statement before the INSERT and rerun the script. Even though the error follows the first SELECT, the valid SELECT statement does not run because the error occurred at compile time, before any statement in the batch could run.

The following code listing is an example of what your final script should look like.

```
IF EXISTS (SELECT * FROM tempdb..sysobjects WHERE Name LIKE
➥'#MyTable%')
     DROP TABLE #MyTable
GO

CREATE TABLE #MyTable (
     myint int NOT NULL
)
GO

SELECT 'First Batch Results' = myint
FROM #MyTable

INSERT INTO #MyTable (myint)
VALUES ('A')

SELECT 'Batch Results' = myint
FROM #MyTable
GO

SELECT 'New Batch Results' = myint
FROM #MyTable
```

Exercise 9.2: Run-Time Errors in Batches

In Exercise 9.1 you saw how a compile-time error caused a batch not to run. This exercise modifies the results from Exercise 9.1 to show the effect of a run-time error.

1. Load Enterprise Manager and put the script you created from Exercise 9.1 into a Query window.

2. Modify the flawed INSERT statement to insert a NULL value into #MyTable rather than an 'A'. This conflicts with the NOT NULL constraint placed on the column in the table, but unlike data types, constraints are not checked until run time.

3. Execute the script. You should see that although the INSERT statement again generates an error, the three SELECT statements successfully execute.

Exercise 9.3: Control-of-Flow Statements

In this exercise you practice the use of control-of-flow statements.

1. Type the following code into a Query window and guess what output you should expect to see when you execute the code.

```
IF 0 = 1
        Print 'First Print Statement'
        Print 'Second Print Statement'
```

The IF statement causes only one statement following it to run or not to run, depending on the Boolean expression. Therefore, only the second print statement is executed.

2. Now use a WHILE loop to execute a PRINT statement exactly 10 times. Use a variable @Count as an integer to keep track of the number of iterations. Also use a variable of type char(30) named @CharCount. In each iteration of the loop assign the message 'Loop N', where N is the value of @Count, to @CharCount, and print its value. Your results should look something like the following:

```
DECLARE @Count int,
        @CharCount char(30)
SELECT @Count = 1

WHILE @Count <= 10
BEGIN
        SELECT @CharCount = 'Iteration ' + Convert(char,
➥@Count)

        PRINT @CharCount

        SELECT @Count = @Count + 1
END
```

3. To examine the uses of the CASE expression, you can write a SELECT statement to calculate the profitability of the books in the Titles table and display the results in three easy-to-read categories. Your SELECT statement should show all rows from the Titles table. Use the following formula to calculate the profitability of the books: (Price * Ytd_Sales) / (Advance + (Royalty * Ytd_Sales)). Use a CASE expression to evaluate the profitability of each book and print 'Very Profitable' if the result is greater than 1.5, 'Profitable' if the result is equal to or greater than 1.0, or 'Lost Money' if the result is less than 1. Include the title of the book in the results. Your final statement should be similar to this:

```
SELECT      Title,
        'Profitability' = CASE
          WHEN (Price * Ytd_Sales) / (Advance + (Royalty *
➥Ytd_Sales)) > 1.5
          THEN 'Very Profitable'
          WHEN (Price * Ytd_Sales) / (Advance + (Royalty *
➥Ytd_Sales)) >= 1.0
          THEN 'Profitable'
          WHEN (Price * Ytd_Sales) / (Advance + (Royalty *
➥Ytd_Sales)) < 1.0
          THEN 'Lost Money'
        End
FROM Titles
```

Exercise 9.4: Using a Cursor to Repeatedly Execute a Stored Procedure

In this exercise you use a cursor to execute the sp_help stored procedure on every user table in the Pubs database.

1. First, declare a character type variable named @Tablename to hold the names of the tables.

2. Second, declare an INSENSITIVE cursor curTable that will select the Name field of the *sysobjects* table where the Type field is 'U'.

3. Open the cursor and select the first Name into the @Tablename variable.

4. Set up a WHILE loop to execute until the @@FETCH_STATUS variable is not zero, indicating there are no more records. You need to use the BEGIN and END keywords to enclose the body of the loop in a statement block.

5. Immediately inside the loop, use the EXEC statement to execute the string 'SP_HELP' concatenated with the @Tablename variable to execute the stored procedure.

6. Secondly inside the loop, FETCH the next table name from the cursor.

7. After the loop CLOSE and DEALLOCATE the cursor.

Your results should look much like the following:

```
DECLARE @Tablename char(30)
DECLARE curTable INSENSITIVE CURSOR FOR
      SELECT Name
      FROM sysObjects
      WHERE Type = 'U'
FOR READ ONLY

OPEN curTable

FETCH NEXT FROM curTable INTO @Tablename

WHILE @@FETCH_STATUS = 0
BEGIN
```

```
            EXEC ('SP_HELP ' + @Tablename)

            FETCH NEXT FROM curTable INTO @Tablename
    END

    CLOSE curTable
    DEALLOCATE curTable
```

Exercise 9.5: Using a Cursor to Perform Positioned Updates Against a Table

In this exercise you create a table to hold all the Author IDs from the Authors table, then assign each of the rows in the table a unique monotonically increasing value starting at one.

1. First create a temporary table called #HoldAuthors to hold the IDs from the Authors table. Include two fields in the table called Ident, and Au_Id. These should be integer and char(11) types respectively. Note that the Ident field must allow NULLs. Because you may want to re-run the script several times, you should first include code to drop the table if it already exists.

2. Insert the values from the Au_Id field of the Authors table into the Au_Id field from the #HoldAuthors table.

3. Declare a cursor FOR UPDATE that retrieves the Ident column from the #HoldAuthors table.

4. You then need to declare an integer variable @Count and initialize the value to zero.

5. OPEN the cursor, and then FETCH the first record. You do not need to store the value from the FETCH statement.

6. Set up a WHILE loop to execute while the @@FETCH_STATUS global variable remains zero, indicating no problems during the FETCH. You also need to begin a statement block to contain the body of the loop.

7. In the WHILE loop, update the #HoldAuthors table to set the Ident field to the value of @Count, using the CURRENT OF syntax for the UPDATE statement.

continues

Exercise 9.5: Continued

8. Next, increment the value of the @Count variable by one. Then FETCH the next record, and end the statement block of the loop.

9. Finally, select all the values from the #HoldAuthors table to see the results. Your final script should look something like the following:

```
IF EXISTS (SELECT * FROM tempdb..sysobjects WHERE Name LIKE
➥ '#HoldAuthors%')
        DROP TABLE #HoldAuthors
GO

CREATE TABLE #HoldAuthors (
        Ident int NULL,
        Au_ID char(11) Not NULL
)

INSERT INTO #HoldAuthors (
        Au_ID
)
SELECT Au_ID
FROM Authors

DECLARE cur_Author CURSOR FOR
        SELECT Ident
        FROM #HoldAuthors
FOR UPDATE OF Ident

DECLARE @Count int
SELECT @Count = 0

OPEN cur_Author

FETCH NEXT FROM cur_Author

WHILE @@FETCH_STATUS = 0
BEGIN
        UPDATE #HoldAuthors
        SET Ident = @Count
        WHERE CURRENT OF cur_Author
```

```
        SELECT @Count = @Count + 1

        FETCH NEXT FROM cur_Author
END
GO

SELECT *
FROM #HoldAuthors
```

Review Questions

1. What is the lifetime of a user-defined variable?

    A. Duration of the script

    B. Duration of the statement block

    C. Duration of the batch

    D. Duration of the current SQL Server connection

2. What is the significance of the GO statement?

    A. Ends the current transaction.

    B. Causes all commands since the last GO to be compiled and executed.

    C. Ends the current batch.

    D. Causes all commands since the last GO to be compiled and executed, and ends the script.

3. Which of the following commands can be used to interrupt processing of a loop?

    A. BREAK

    B. HALT

    C. EXIT

    D. CONTINUE

4. A GOTO command can cause execution of a batch to resume where?

    A. At a label

    B. At an absolute line number

    C. At a relative line number

    D. Anywhere in the next batch

5. Which of the following are true of stored procedures?

    A. They can be fired by data modifications on tables.

    B. They are precompiled.

    C. They can return only integers and result sets.

    D. They can be executed by only one person at a time.

6. INSENSITIVE cursors provide what functionality?

    A. They enable users to see data inserted since the time the cursor was opened.

    B. They allow faster updates because the data for the cursor is stored in tempdb.

    C. They cannot be scrolled backwards because the data is discarded from the temporary storage once it is fetched.

    D. They ensure an unchanging view of the data as it was when the cursor was opened.

7. User-defined errors can be written to the SQL Server Error Log through what mechanism?

    A. Using the RAISERROR command with a severity of greater than or equal to 19.

    B. Using the PRINT command with the WITH LOG option.

    C. Using the RAISERROR command with the WITH LOG option.

    D. Using the LOGERROR command.

8. What functionality does the EXECUTE statement provide?

    A. It enables you to receive the RETURN value of a stored procedure.

    B. It enables you to write queries that specify table names through a variable.

C. It enables you to UPDATE multiple tables with a single statement.

D. It enables you to execute stored procedures you don't normally have permissions on.

9. Which of the following are true of the abilities of SQL Server working with MAPI?

A. SQL Server can receive mail and act based on the contents of messages.

B. SQL Server can send mail warning of errors that have taken place.

C. Users can write stored procedures that will send mail to operators upon completion.

D. Users can mail queries to SQL Server and receive the results through mail.

10. Which of the following are valid options for a FETCH command?

A. FORWARD

B. BACK

C. ABSOLUTE

D. RELATIVE

Answers to Review Questions

1. B

2. B,C

3. A,D

4. A

5. B,C

6. D

7. C

8. A,B

9. A,B,C,D

10. C,D

Answers to Test Yourself Questions at Beginning of Chapter

1. Execution resumes after the error, and the global variable @@ERROR is set to reflect the error code. See "Using Scripts and Batches."

2. The entire batch fails to compile and execution resumes with the next batch. See "Using Scripts and Batches."

3. A local variable only has duration within the batch it is declared in. See "Using Variables."

4. A Boolean expression is an expression that returns True or False. See "Using the IF Keyword."

5. Only one statement or statement block (defined by a BEGIN/END keyword pair) is executed following an IF statement. See "Using the IF Keyword."

6. The BREAK and CONTINUE statements can be used to interrupt normal execution of a WHILE loop. The BREAK statement exits the WHILE loop and causes execution to resume at the statement following the body of the loop. The CONTINUE statement halts execution of the current loop and causes the Boolean expression to be reevaluated, possibly resuming the WHILE loop. See "Using the WHILE Statement."

7. The CASE structure is used in an expression. CASE does not form a statement that can be executed by itself. See "Using the CASE Expression."

8. A cursor must be declared with the DECLARE CURSOR statement before it can be opened. See "Declaring Cursors."

9. Positioned updates and deletes are performed through otherwise standard UPDATE and DELETE statements using the CURRENT OF phrase in the WHERE clause. See "Using the CURRENT OF Keyword."

10. A procedure can be registered to be executed automatically when SQL Server is started with the sp_makestartup stored procedure. See "Startup Stored Procedures."

11. Errors can be written to the Error Log using the RAISERROR command along with the WITH LOG option specified. See "Using the RAISERROR Command."

Chapter 10

Triggers

This chapter helps you prepare for the exam by covering the following objectives:

Objectives

- ▶ Creating triggers

- ▶ Using triggers for referential integrity

- ▶ Using triggers for data integrity

- ▶ Nesting triggers

- ▶ Using the inserted and deleted tables

Test Yourself! Before reading this chapter, test yourself to determine how much study time you will need to devote to this section.

1. What is a trigger?

2. How can you view the script of a trigger already created in the database?

3. Why might you nest triggers?

4. What are the inserted and deleted tables?

5. What is the proper syntax for creating an insert trigger for the authors table?

6. In general, how could you prevent data in one table, table_1, from being deleted if there is related data in another table, table_2?

7. What are the advantages triggers have over other methods of enforcing data integrity?

Answers are located at the end of the chapter...

Triggers are very similar to stored procedures in that they both are used to batch together sets of related SQL commands. Triggers, however, are only executed by the database engine based on pending inserts, updates, or deletes to a table. They are usually used to enforce business rules for a system. This is referred to as data integrity.

Prior to this version of SQL Server (6.x), triggers were used to enforce referential integrity in the database. But now, SQL Server 6.x contains Primary and Foreign Key constraints that nearly eliminate the need to use triggers for referential integrity. However, as you will see from the rest of this chapter, there are still many data situations that benefit from the use of triggers.

This chapter covers the following topics:

- ▶ Creating triggers

- ▶ Applying the inserted and deleted tables

- ▶ Enforcing referential integrity

- ▶ Nesting triggers

- ▶ Enforcing data integrity

Creating Triggers

 Objective ▶ Triggers are a set of SQL commands that are executed when an UPDATE, INSERT, or DELETE occurs on a table. Each table in the database can have zero to three triggers. A trigger is table-specific and event-specific. So, for example, the authors table could have the following three triggers created for it.

- ▶ authors_ti—an insert trigger, which executes when an insert occurs on the authors table.

- ▶ authors_tu—an update trigger, which executes when an update occurs on the authors table.

- ▶ authors_td—a delete trigger, which executes when a delete occurs on the authors table.

Tip

> You can determine which tables already have triggers assigned to them by using the system stored procedure sp_depends.

The basic syntax for creating a trigger looks like the following:

```
CREATE TRIGGER [owner.]triggername
ON [owner.]tablename
FOR {INSERT, UPDATE, DELETE}
[WITH ENCRYPTION]
AS
/*Trigger text follows */
```

The following sections address this syntax in detail.

CREATE TRIGGER

The CREATE TRIGGER portion of the statement is used to assign a name to the trigger and establish ownership. Ownership is defaulted to the user executing the statement unless otherwise specified. The ownership of the trigger is unchangeable and not transferable. If you need to transfer ownership of the trigger from one user to another, the trigger needs to be dropped and recreated. The DROP TRIGGER syntax resembles the following:

```
DROP TRIGGER triggername
```

Note

> A DROP TRIGGER automatically occurs if you try to create another trigger for the same event on the same table as an existing trigger. The old trigger is dropped and the new trigger becomes active without warning.

ON

The table that you are creating the trigger for is specified using ON. The owner of the table can be specified if necessary. Each trigger is created for a single table only.

FOR

FOR specifies the type of trigger that is to be created: INSERT, UPDATE, and DELETE. Any combination can be specified. In other words, a single trigger can be created to handle INSERT, UPDATE, and DELETE or any combination of those actions.

WITH ENCRYPTION

The WITH ENCRYPTION option is used to hide the contents of a trigger. It prevents a user from using sp_helptext to display the contents of the trigger. Also, the user cannot just select the text column from the *syscomments* table (for example, SELECT text FROM syscomments WHERE name = tablename). The text is encrypted.

AS

Finally, AS is used to lead into the body of the trigger. At this point, the set of SQL statements to be executed should be incorporated. Then the trigger can be created by executing the script you have finished. The following sections feature examples of scripts.

 Caution

> Certain commands cannot be executed from a trigger. You cannot use any CREATE or DROP statements. You cannot GRANT or REVOKE from a trigger. SELECT INTO, TRUNCATE TABLE, ALTER TABLE, ALTER DATABASE, UPDATE STATISTICS, RECONFIGURE, LOAD DATABASE, LOAD TRANSACTION, and all DISK statements are invalid as well.

Using the Inserted and Deleted Tables

The inserted and deleted tables are tables used to hold data changes made to a table that have not yet been committed. They are filled by the system based on the command issued to the database and are made accessible to the programmer with triggers. They have the same structure as the table for which the trigger was created. Triggers can be used to query these tables to determine any further actions that need to occur based on the changes or, if the changes are unacceptable, they can be undone by issuing a ROLLBACK TRANSACTION from the trigger. Each trigger type uses these tables differently.

Insert Triggers

Because an insert is the insertion of an entire row into the database, the deleted table isn't needed. The inserted table holds the rows pending insertion into the table. The following is an example of an insert trigger using the inserted table.

```
CREATE TRIGGER employee_ti
ON employee
FOR INSERT
AS
IF(SELECT count(*)
    FROM inserted
   WHERE inserted.termination_dt is not null) > 0
BEGIN
PRINT 'A new employee cannot have a termination date.'
ROLLBACK TRANSACTION
END
```

Update Triggers

Update triggers use both the inserted and deleted tables. When an update occurs to a table, the old row is placed in the deleted table and the new row is placed in the inserted table. An update trigger can then evaluate these two tables to determine how to proceed. The update trigger can be used to check a single column or the entire table.

Update Triggers for the Table

The following is an example of a table-level update trigger. Here, the table-level trigger is used to keep an audit trail of changes made to the important information in this table.

```
CREATE TRIGGER employee_tu
ON employee
```

```
FOR UPDATE
AS
INSERT employee_history
SELECT  emp_id,
dept_id,
position,
salary
FROM deleted
```

Update Triggers for a Single Column

The following is a sample update trigger showing how to check
for changes to a column. In this case, the goal is to disallow changes to the employee's original date of hire.

```
CREATE TRIGGER employee_tu
ON employee
FOR UPDATE
AS
IF UPDATE(hire_dt)
BEGIN
Print 'The hire date of an employee may not be changed.'
ROLLBACK TRANSACTION
END
```

Delete Triggers

When a DELETE is issued to the database, rows are only deleted
and not inserted, so the inserted table is not used by the delete
trigger. In the following example, the delete trigger on the department table ensures that all employees assigned to the department
being deleted have their dept_id set to NULL.

```
CREATE TRIGGER department_td
ON department
FOR DELETE
AS
UPDATE employee
SET dept_id = NULL
FROM employee e, deleted d
WHERE d.dept_id = e.dept_id
```

Enforcing Referential Integrity

Referential integrity refers to ensuring that the entity referenced in one table actually exists in another table. For example, if you had an employee table and a department table, you would want to make sure that the department you are about to place in the employee table actually exists in the department table. The following exemplifies the use of such a trigger to enforce referential integrity on the tables.

```
CREATE TRIGGER employee_ti
ON employee
FOR INSERT
AS
DECLARE @rows int
SELECT @rows = @@rowcount
IF ( SELECT count(*)
        FROM inserted I, department d
        WHERE insert.dept_id = d.dept_id) <> @rows
BEGIN
        PRINT 'Department does not exist'
        ROLLBACK TRANSACTION
END
```

This trigger first declares a variable to hold the rowcount. The rowcount is the number of rows being effected (inserted in this case). The SELECT statement returns a count of the number of rows being inserted whose dept_id is equal to a dept_id in the department table. If the count from the SELECT statement is equal to the rowcount, then every row being inserted contains a valid dept_id. Otherwise, at least one row does not contain a valid dept_id and therefore the insert is not allowed to continue. ROLLBACK TRANSACTION is used to cancel the insert.

With SQL Server 6.x, referential integrity can now be handled using FOREIGN KEY and REFERENCES constraints. These tell the system that the data in table_b relies on the value from table_a always being there, as shown in the preceding example. Constraints are executed before triggers. So, if a user attempts to delete a value from table_a that is used by table_b, the constraint disallows the deletion and the delete trigger on table_a does not fire.

If, however, you want to delete all the child rows in table_b that correspond to the row being deleted in table_a, you could take one of the following two actions. You could drop the constraint and write a delete trigger on table_a that would delete all the child rows in table_b. Alternately, you could leave the constraint and issue the delete to the child rows in table_b first and then issue the delete to table_a. If you choose to use a trigger, you might find nested triggers to be useful.

Nested Triggers

You can use nested triggers to cascade updates and deletes. Let's say you want to delete all the class registrations from student_classes for a student who decided not to attend your university (delete from student). You could place a delete trigger on both student and student_classes. Then, when the student was deleted, the delete trigger on student would perform a delete on student_class, which could then update the student count in the classes table. See figure 10.1 for an example of the tables involved.

Figure 10.1

Tables involved in the cascading deletes and updates.

Student

Student ID	Last Name	First Name
1	Thompson	Alex
2	Marks	Gary
3	Idle	Eric

Student Class

Class ID	Student ID
1	4
1	3
2	7
2	1
2	3

Class

Class ID	Class Name	Student Count
1	Psychology1	20
2	Literature	18
3	Visual Basic	22

So if student 3, Eric Idle, decides to drop out of his classes for the semester, the application would issue a DELETE statement to the student table to remove this student. The delete trigger on the student table, in this case, would then issue a DELETE to the student_class table of all rows containing student_id 3 to protect referential integrity. When the DELETE is issued to student_class, the delete trigger on this table notices that a student is being removed from a class and issues an UPDATE statement to the class table to subtract one from the class count for each class the student was removed from in the student_class table.

However, if the database was not set up to handle nested triggers, only the delete trigger for the student executes. Nested triggers are enabled by using the system stored procedure sp_configure, as shown in the following:

```
sp_cofigure 'nested_triggers', 1
```

Similarly, nested triggers are disabled with the following statement.

```
sp_configure 'nested_triggers', 0
```

Enforcing Data Integrity

This discussion of data integrity concentrates on user-defined integrity. In many cases, triggers are used to enforce user-defined integrity, also referred to as business rules. Some of the options for enforcement include the following:

- ▶ User-defined data types

- ▶ Defaults and rules

- ▶ Constraints

- ▶ Triggers

If a column is simply not allowed to contain a NULL, this is specified at table creation. If the column's data restrictions can be met using a user-defined data type, this is also specified at table creation time.

When the business rules on a column become more complex, defaults and rules could be used. The default only covers the times when nothing is inserted into the column. The rule can be used to define the bounds the data must conform to, but it cannot reference other columns.

Constraints are like rules in that they specify the bounds to which the data must conform. A column may be assigned more than one constraint, however, and constraints are defined at table creation.

The advantages that triggers give you over the preceding options are the ability to include error checking, looping structures, and access to the values in other columns. The disadvantage of using triggers is that the other options are performed by the system prior to the transaction being logged. Once the information is placed in the transaction log, a ROLLBACK TRANSACTION must be issued to clear the information if it does not meet the requirements. This adds overhead not found with the other options.

Note

> Be aware that when using Bulk Copy Program (BCP) to load large amounts of data into a table, rules, constraints, and triggers are not enforced.

Summary

This chapter covered the creation and use of triggers in a SQL Server database. The use of Primary and Foreign keys in version 6.5 of SQL Server has virtually eliminated the need to utilize triggers to ensure referential integrity in the database. However, as shown in the chapter, triggers can still be profitably used in a variety of data situations.

Exercises

Exercise 10.1: Creating an Update Trigger

In this exercise you create an update trigger that stops the user from changing the column hired_dt in the table employee.

Requirements:

▶ The trigger is an update trigger.

▶ The trigger will be on the employee table.

▶ The trigger will need to determine if the column hired_dt has been changed.

▶ If the user attempted to change hired_dt, then an error needs to be presented to the user.

To create the trigger, use the following steps:

1. Begin the script with the CREATE statement.

```
CREATE TRIGGER employee_tu
ON employee
FOR UPDATE
AS
```

2. Add the check for hired_dt to the script.

```
IF update(hired_dt)
begin
      //Error code goes here
end
```

3. Between begin and end, the error code needs to be added.

```
RAISEERROR ('The employee hire date cannot be changed.', 10, 1)
ROLLBACK TRANSACTION
```

4. Altogether, the script looks like the following:

```
CREATE TRIGGER employee_tu
ON employee
FOR UPDATE
.AS
IF update(hired_dt)
begin
        RAISEERROR ('The employee hire date cannot be
➥changed.', 10, 1)
        ROLLBACK TRANSACTION
end
```

Exercise 10.2: Creating a Delete Trigger

In this exercise you create a delete trigger that prevents the user from deleting rows from the inventory table if the part is referenced in the orders table.

Requirements:

▶ The trigger is a delete trigger.

▶ The trigger is on the parts table.

▶ The trigger needs to check the orders table for references to the part being deleted.

▶ If orders exist, stop the transaction from being processed.

To create the trigger, use the following steps:

1. Begin the script with the CREATE statement.

```
CREATE TRIGGER parts_td
ON parts
FOR DELETE
AS
```

2. Now check the orders table for references to the deleted part.

continues

```
IF (SELECT count(*)
      FROM orders o, deleted d
      WHERE d.part_nbr = o.part_nbr) > 0
begin
      //Error code goes here
end
```

3. Between begin and end, the error code needs to be added.

```
RAISEERROR ('The part has outstanding orders and cannot be
➥deleted.', 10, 1)
ROLLBACK TRANSACTION
```

4. Altogether, the script looks like the following:

```
CREATE TRIGGER parts_td
ON parts
FOR DELETE
AS
IF (SELECT count(*)
      FROM orders o, deleted d
      WHERE d.part_nbr = o.part_nbr) > 0
begin
      RAISEERROR ('The part has outstanding orders and can-
➥not be deleted.', 10, 1)
      ROLLBACK TRANSACTION
end
```

Review Questions

1. How do you find out what triggers have already been created?

    A. Run sp_configure

    B. Run sp_helptriggers

    C. Run sp_depends

2. Why is the option WITH ENCRYPTION useful?

    A. It causes the triggers text to be encrypted when placed in *syscomments* so that any user selecting off *syscomments* or using sp_helptext cannot view the triggers script.

    B. It requires a password to use the trigger.

    C. It gives the user the option of using encryption on the table data via the trigger.

3. Which of the following are valid options in the FOR clause of the CREATE TRIGGER statement? (choose 2)

    A. UPDATE

    B. INSERT, UPDATE

    C. SELECT

    D. SELECT, DELETE

4. Which of the following drops the delete trigger employee_td on the table employee?

    A. DROP DELETE TRIGGER ON employee

    B. DROP TRIGGER employee_td

    C. DROP employee_td

5. Which of following are valid SQL commands in a trigger? (Choose 2)

   A. EXEC

   B. SELECT INTO

   C. GRANT

   D. UPDATE

6. An update trigger typically accesses which of the following?

   A. The updated table

   B. The inserted table only

   C. The inserted and deleted tables

   D. The deleted table only

7. Which of the answers best describe referential integrity?

   A. Maintaining consistency between related data in the same table

   B. The ability to reference data in another table

   C. Maintaining the references established between two tables

8. What is an advantage of triggers over rules and constraints? (Choose 2)

   A. The ability to define the boundaries within which the data must reside

   B. The ability to use looping structures

   C. The ability to reference columns in other tables

   D. The ability to check the data before it is logged

9. If table_a has an insert trigger that performs an update on table_b, in which case will the update trigger on table_b be fired?

A. If 'nested triggers' has a value of 1

B. If 'nested triggers' has a value of TRUE

C. If 'nesting' is set to 0

D. If 'nesting' is set to 1

10. Which of the following are ignored during BCP operations? (Choose 3)

A. User-defined data types

B. Constraints

C. Triggers

D. Rules

Answers to Review Questions

1. C

2. A

3. A,B

4. B

5. A,D

6. C

7. C

8. B,C

9. A

10. B,C,D

Answers to Test Yourself Questions at Beginning of Chapter

1. A trigger is a set of SQL statements that gets executed when an insert, update, or delete occurs on a table. See "Creating Triggers."

2. The system stored procedure sp_helptext can be used to display the script for a trigger unless the trigger was created with the WITH ENCRYPTION option. See "WITH ENCRYPTION."

3. Nesting triggers is useful for performing cascading updates and deletes. See "Nesting Triggers."

4. The inserted and deleted tables are used to hold the data changes that have taken place in a table, but have yet to be committed. See "Using the Inserted and Deleted Tables."

5. The syntax used to create an insert trigger for the authors table would resemble the following.

   CREATE TRIGGER authors_ti

   ON authors

   FOR INSERT

   AS

   See "Creating Triggers."

6. A foreign key constraint on table_2 or a delete trigger on table_1 could be used to prevent the data in table_1 from being deleted while it is still being referenced by table_2. See "Enforcing Referential Integrity."

7. The advantages triggers have over other methods of enforcing data integrity include the ability to include error checking, looping structures, and access to values in other columns. See "Enforcing Data Integrity."

Chapter 11

Replication

This chapter helps you prepare for the exam by covering the following objectives:

 Objectives

- ▶ Apply the appropriate replication model

- ▶ Apply replication appropriately

- ▶ Recognize the roles of the publishing server, distribution server, and subscription server

- ▶ Trace the replication process

Test Yourself! Before reading this chapter, test yourself to determine how much study time you will need to devote to this section.

1. Identify two benefits of replication over other data distribution models.

2. A SQL Server can participate in replication in several functions. Name the three roles that a server can play.

3. Replication may be implemented in many different ways but the models conform to a finite list. Name the six different replication models.

4. The target of the distributed data may or may not have a need for various types of data. Therefore replication enables the publisher to choose how the data is published. What are the three different ways that data may be published in an article?

5. Because of the way the replication processes distribute data, a number of kinds of data cannot be published without extra effort and some cannot be published at all. What type of data cannot be published without this extra effort?

6. Replication subscriptions may be set up in a number of ways. The way that the subscription is set up determines the category it falls in. Identify the two categories that subscriptions fall into and who sets up each type.

7. SQL Executive uses multiple distribution processes to perform replication functions. Name these three subprocesses.

8. When an article is created, the administrator can select from methods of synchronization for the article. What are the three methods of article synchronization?

Answers are located at the end of the chapter...

Introduction

In an enterprise, it is often necessary to distribute data to more than one location. The data may need to be distributed to other people in the same office, or those in other buildings, cities, or even other countries. There are several methods of distributing this data to multiple locations. Some of these methods follow:

▶ Backing up the data to removable media, physically sending the media to the destination, and restoring the data

▶ Exporting the data to a file, transferring the file by some means, and importing the data from the file

▶ Executing remote stored procedures to gather up the data and place it in its appropriate location

▶ Replication

The first option can fail if the media has any errors reading or writing, or if it is lost by the courier. The second option may fail if any data does not conform to a general record format, (that is, image data), if there is a conflict between the data and the delimiter chosen, or if the import and export specifications are not identical. Executing remote stored procedures is a better way to distribute the data, but it is difficult to keep track of exactly what data has changed in order not to retransmit the same set of data repeatedly.

Instead of these options, replication uses safer and more reliable techniques to get the data from one place to another. It is fault tolerant in that instead of actually replicating the data, it recreates the Transact-SQL statements (INSERT, UPDATE, and DELETE) that created the data in the source database.

Because there is no external media, the chance that it will be lost by the courier is eliminated. There is no file to be corrupted or mangled in the process of importing and exporting due to the fact that replication bypasses the import and export specifications and creates the actual statements necessary to create the data.

Replication transfers data in its native format, thereby negating the possibility that the data will have a conflict with the delimiter. It is a method by which data and schema are transferred from a source database to a destination database. Because data modified in the destination database are not transmitted to the source database, the safest way to ensure data integrity is to prevent modifications in the destination database, effectively making it read-only. This allows for the retrieval of various amounts of data without contention in the original database, which is then free to be modified. The data to be replicated can be transferred either at specified intervals or continuously as it is modified, depending upon the manner in which it is set up.

In addition to modifying the frequency with which the data is transferred, the administrator can choose to replicate smaller sets of filtered data or the complete set of data. The source database may replicate its data to any number of destinations, and may also function as a destination database for another source database.

Replication also is a method of data distribution. It corresponds to a data consistency concept referred to simply as loose consistency. *Loose consistency* is defined as a distributed data process that may have a time lag involved between the instant that the data in the original table is modified, and the data in the destination table is updated to make the two copies of data identical. It is not guaranteed that the copies of the data in the source and destination tables are identical at all moments in time in loose consistency models. However, loose consistency models can operate over nearly any communication link, whether it is a modem, local area network (LAN), wide area network (WAN), or databases connected across the Internet that do not always have a constant connection to each other.

The other consistency model is known as *tight consistency*. Although this model has the benefit of identical data in all locations simultaneously, it requires much more intricate hardware. Some of this hardware includes high speed LANs or other connections that allow high volumes of data to be transferred near instantaneously. This approach to consistency comes at the cost of scalability and reduced database availability.

For you to understand replication and do well on that aspect of the exam, the rest of the chapter covers the following topics:

▶ How to apply replication models appropriately

▶ Recognizing the roles of the publishing server, distribution server, and subscribing server

▶ How to trace the replication process

Applying Replication Appropriately

 Replication is a tool for distributing data. As is the case with any tool, some thoughtful analysis must be performed before applying the tool if it is to yield the outcome you desire. It is imperative that the analysis process be done thoroughly to avoid unwanted results. When used correctly replication has several benefits:

▶ Reduced contention in the source database because the data can be retrieved in the destination database

▶ Data is available at multiple locations

▶ Decision support processes become separated from transaction processing

▶ Network traffic at the central location is reduced

However, if you do a poor job of analyzing the role that replication will perform, several unwanted results or side effects may occur. One such side effect is that replication will stop prematurely due to duplicated data being transmitted to a particular location, violating primary keys. Another undesirable side effect is that data from another server may be deleted that is not to be deleted under normal circumstances. These kinds of unwelcome outcomes can be avoided if you understand when and where to use the appropriate replication model.

Applying the Appropriate Replication Model

The six replication models are:

► Central subscriber

► Central publisher

► Central publisher with remote distributor

► Multiple publishers of one table

► Publishing subscriber

► Downloaded data

Each replication model has its own individual characteristics. Applying an incorrect replication model to a situation where replication has been chosen to distribute data can turn the benefits of replication into an implementation and maintenance nightmare. Therefore, you need to understand these models completely before making a model choice or decision.

Replication Model Types

To apply the appropriate replication model to formulating a data distribution solution, the administrator must be aware of the advantages and disadvantages of each replication model. The following discussion addresses only the first four models. They are the most basic and commonly used models, while the last two are utilized less often.

Central Subscriber

The central subscriber model is used in cases where one target database receives data and changes from a number of sites, as shown in figure 11.1. It is normally used to generate corporate data warehouses or other enterprise-wide reporting databases. This model requires a bit more analytical work because the issue of ownership of data comes into play. If the implementation of this type of replication model is not done correctly, data will be overwritten by similar data from other sites.

Figure 11.1

Central subscriber.

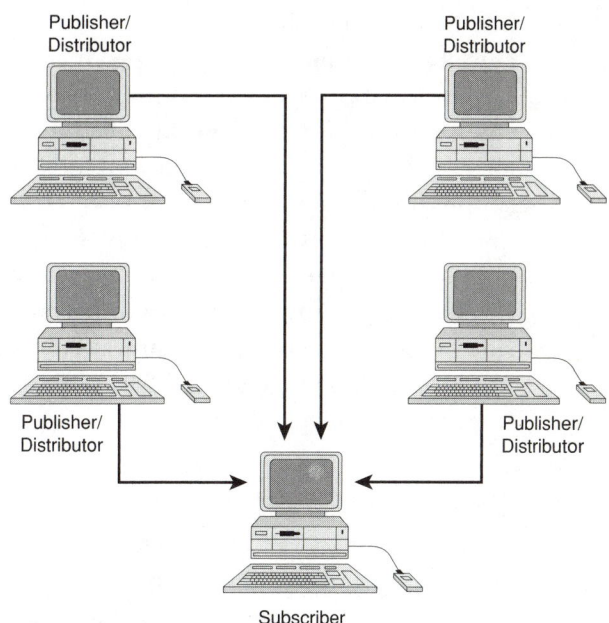

of ownership — Subscriber

**Note**

The destination database should not allow the replicated data to be modified because replication only happens in one direction, from the source to the destination. Data that is changed in the destination has NO effect upon the original data. Changing this read-only data may cause errors to occur if that particular set of data is to be updated by a change in the source database.

**Warning**

Set permissions on the destination database (subscriber) to read-only instead of putting the database in read-only mode. Otherwise the replication processes will not be able to add or modify the data to be replicated!

A good example of this type of replication model is a corporate data warehouse for a manufacturing plant. In this case the individual factories serve the roles of the publishing and distribution servers. As they create their normal products, they use up supplies. A record of the supplies that they use is kept on the server, as well as the amount of pieces produced. When replication runs, this information is sent up to the corporate headquarters to the central subscriber. At corporate headquarters, the individual in charge of ordering supplies takes a look at the amount for each supply. If the amount in inventory is less than a predetermined quantity, this individual calls the plant and reminds them to order additional supplies for that plant. When the supplies arrive, the clerk at the plant updates the number in inventory. On the other side of the central office, executives run reports relating trends in production and usage of supplies. With this information, they can forecast the individual plant's supply and production needs.

Central Publisher

As shown in figure 11.2, in this model only one server is performing the role of the publisher. It serves as the source for all of the data to be distributed and is the default replication option in Microsoft SQL Server. In addition to performing this role, it also performs the task of the distribution server. It distributes the data to any number of subscription servers.

Figure 11.2

Central publisher.

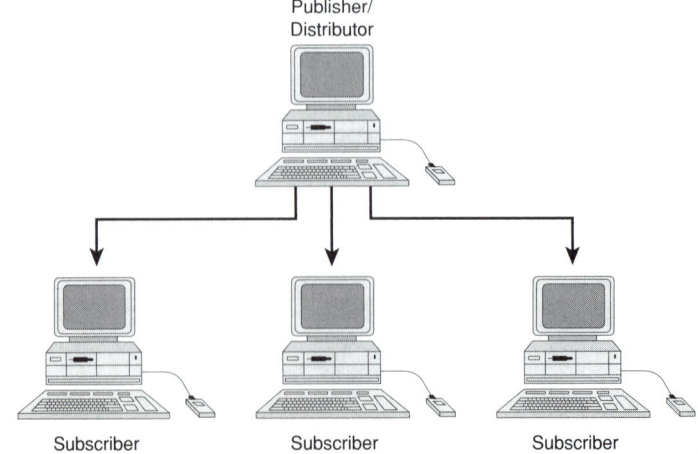

Publisher/
Distributor

Subscriber   Subscriber   Subscriber

Satellite locations like local libraries serve as good examples for the central publisher replication model. When a person is searching through the library catalog for a particular title, chances are good that the search extends beyond the local library. The local library catalog then serves as a subscriber to the Library of Congress, which is the publisher and distributor. The master list of titles is kept on the Library of Congress server and replicated down in parts to the individual library servers. This way the next time the title is the subject of a search, the title is already found on the local catalog.

Central Publisher with Remote Distributor

In some instances the publisher server may have an above average work load. For instance, it may be used concurrently as a file server. In this case, the administrator may choose to offload the work of distributing the data to the subscribing servers to another server (see figure 11.3). This configuration is referred to as central publishing with remote distribution. The distributor may be on the same LAN, on a WAN, or across the Internet. As long as the two servers can communicate, the distribution process proceeds normally. This reduces the amount of storage space required on the publishing server, but it also requires that another complete server be brought online.

Multiple Publishers of One Table

This replication model is the most complicated of the general categories. In this scenario, each server serves all the functions of the three roles: publisher, distributor, and subscriber, as shown in figure 11.4 . The servers are all interconnected and receive as well as send data from a common table. More attention must be paid to defining ownership rules for data in this particular model. Unlike the central subscriber model, the database cannot be placed with read-only permissions because the data can be modified from any of the connected servers. Instead, the design must provide a method for each server to update its own data but leave the remaining data as read-only. This model comes closest to fully implementing a fully distributed data set across all the sites.

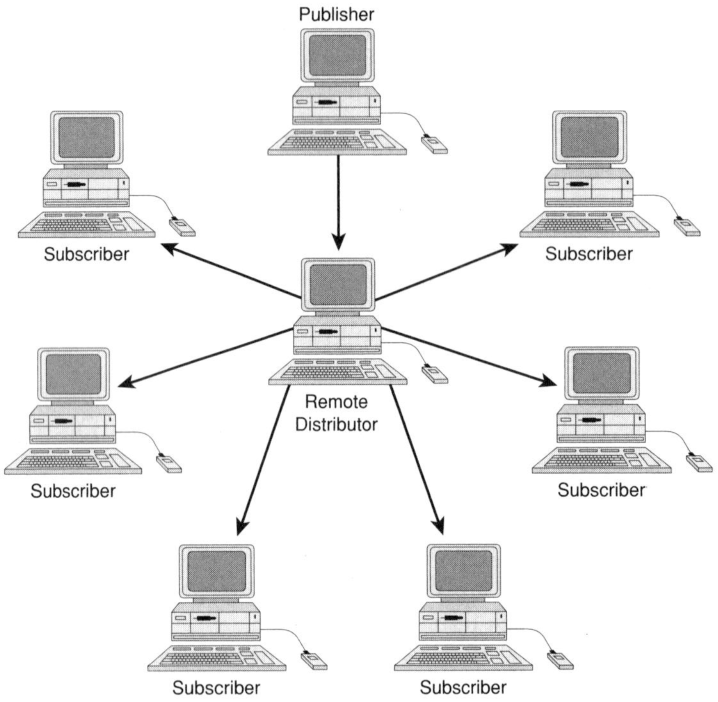

Figure 11.3

Central publisher with remote distributor.

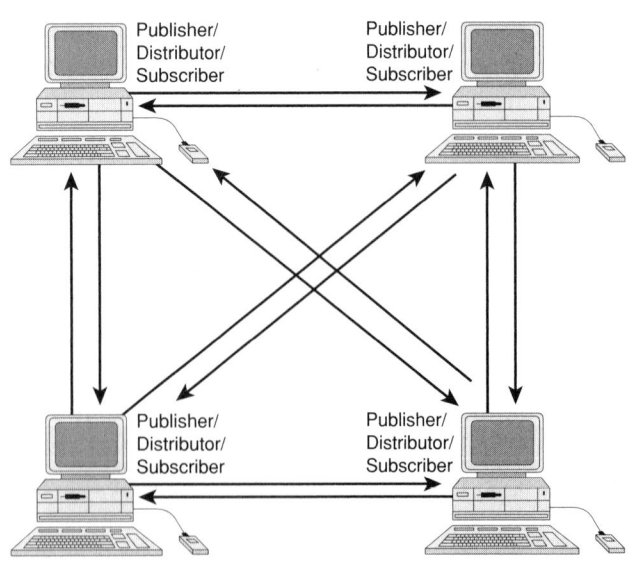

Figure 11.4

Multiple publishers of one table.

The multiple publishers of one table replication model can be appropriately applied to the task of customer maintenance across an enterprise. In this case, each site keeps track of its own customers in a table that is scheduled for replication. This table contains the information about the customer as well as a column identifying the site originating the change. The data is replicated to each site, allowing the same data to be retrieved locally about a customer. When a change is made to a customer's data at the site the customer was created, the change is replicated across the enterprise. Because the column exists with the originating site, code can be written on each server to give only the repl_subscriber process permission to update information with another site_id.

Recognizing Server Roles

 Objective

Replication is implemented using a publisher/subscriber metaphor. Any SQL Server that is set up for replication performs one or more of the following roles:

- ▶ Publication server
- ▶ Distribution server
- ▶ Subscription server

Although replication is commonly tied to a publisher/subscriber metaphor, in order to discuss the other elements of replication it is necessary to also use a tree metaphor with the main branches being the publishing, distributing, and subscribing servers. Along each of these main branches are smaller limbs that correspond to publications, articles, and subscriptions.

Recognizing the Role of the Publication Server (Publisher)

 Objective

A publication server performs several tasks. It contains and maintains the source database for data and schema. It also transfers changes and original data to the distribution server.

Enabling Publishing Servers and Databases

An aspect of setting up the publishing server is choosing what servers it will be replicating to. As shown in figure 11.5, Enterprise Manager provides a dialog box accessible under the Server menu by choosing the options Replication Configuration and then Publishing.

Figure 11.5

Enabling publishing to subscribers.

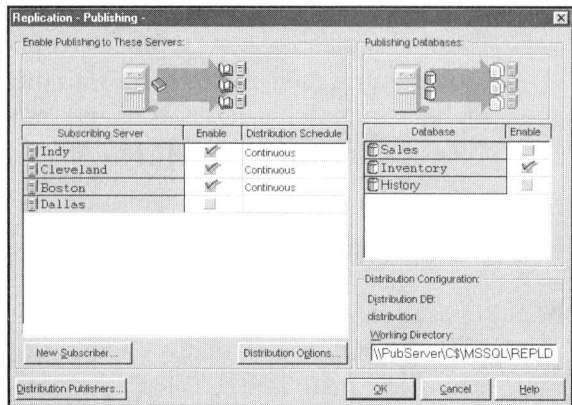

In this example, the servers at Indy, Cleveland, and Boston are permitted to subscribe to PubServer's publications. The check box beside the Inventory database says that publications may be created in the inventory database but not the Sales database. Here, the directory that will be used for synchronization files and special replication commands is set to \\PubServer\C$\SQL65\REPLDATA. Because the field is not long enough to display the entire path, it truncates it at SQL65 in the display but not the actual string.

Modifying Distribution Options for Each Server

After the servers that are permitted to subscribe have been set, each server is defaulted to receive modifications continuously after 100 transactions have occurred. If a different frequency of distribution is needed, the administrator must set the distribution options for each of the subscribers that is different from the default. Figure 11.6 shows the next dialog box that pops up when the Distribution Options button is clicked from the Subscriber dialog box (refer again to figure 11.5).

Figure 11.6

The Distribution Options dialog box.

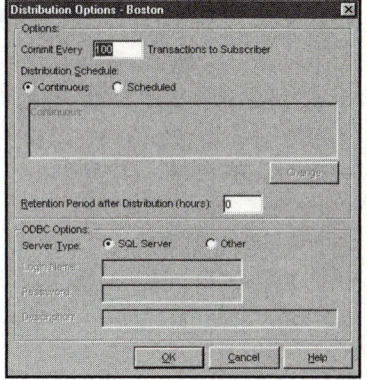

Here the administrator has chosen to transmit data modifications to Boston after every 100 transactions. In addition to modifying the number of transactions to occur before transmission, the administrator may choose to transmit at scheduled intervals rather than continuously. The amount entered in the Retention Period after Distribution (hours) box determines how many hours after the transaction is applied to the subscription database that the transaction information is retained in the distribution database.

Because the replication model can be expressed in terms of publishers, distributors, and subscribers, the model is fleshed out by following the metaphor further and discussing publications and articles.

Managing Publications

The publisher is the source of all the data that will be replicated and as such, it is important to analyze and set up the publication server correctly. Publications are specific to the database in which they are created, therefore multiple publications can be created with the same name in different databases. This allows great flexibility in switching the source of the data simply from the subscriber's side. The price for this flexibility is that a publication may only contain articles from one database. However, in each database on the publication server, multiple publications may be defined. Figure 11.7 shows the dialog box that displays the existing publications for a server.

Figure 11.7

The Manage Publications dialog box.

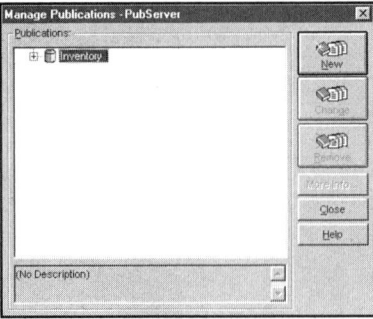

SQL Enterprise Manager provides mechanisms to easily set up publications and articles. These mechanisms are found under the Manage menu by selecting the menu item Replication and then Publications. After a name is entered for the publication, the articles that it contains must be chosen (see figure 11.8).

Figure 11.8

Adding publications.

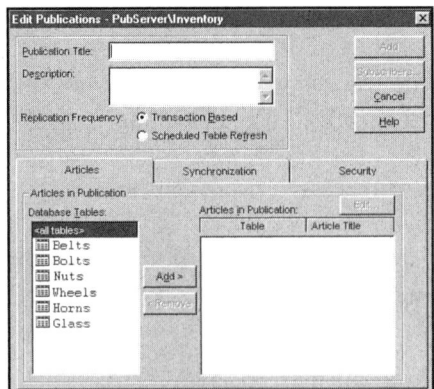

For each of the publications on a publishing database, SQL Enterprise Manager enables an administrator to manage the publication in three different ways:

▶ Security

▶ Replication frequency

▶ Synchronization

Security

At times, the administrator may want to specify that a publication may only be subscribed to by selected servers. In this case the administrator chooses the security method of the publication and marks it Restricted To. This makes the publication invisible to any server that is marked for access. Otherwise, the default security method for publications is Unrestricted, which makes the publication accessible by any server that can communicate with the publication server (see figure 11.9).

Figure 11.9

Publication security.

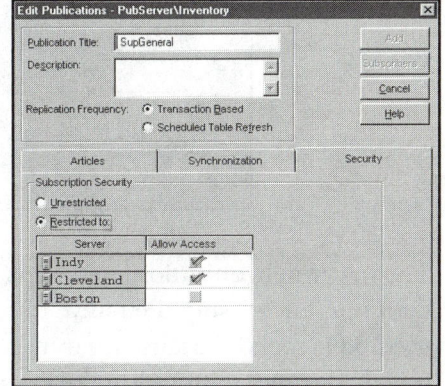

Replication Frequency

The replication frequency method determines when and how data is modified (refer again to figure 11.8). If transaction-based replication is chosen, then each transaction that occurs is retrieved from the transaction log by the log-reader process and sent on to be applied by the distribution process. The other option is to replicate by scheduled table refreshes. As the name suggests, each article contained in the publication transfers its complete set of data to be mirrored in the destination table at scheduled intervals. In addition to the data being replicated, the administrator can choose not to have the actual schema replicated at all. In this case, the server switches to very loose consistency because between the time that a refresh occurs and the next scheduled refresh, no modifications to the publisher's data are replicated.

Synchronization

The initial method of synchronization, as shown in figure 11.10, must be determined before a subscribing server creates a subscription.

Figure 11.10

Publication synchronization.

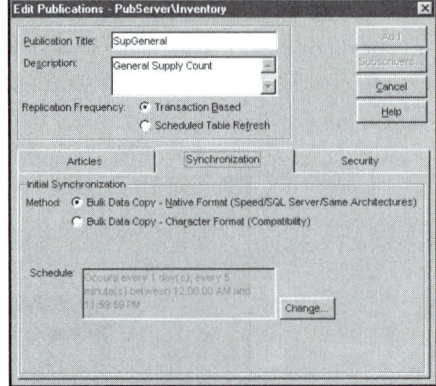

The first synchronization method is implemented as a bulk data copy operation using the native format. The advantage of this method is speed, because no translation is required. However, this speed advantage can only be realized if the architectures are identical and the servers are all SQL Servers. The second method trades speed for compatibility by translating the data to character strings. It is referred to as *character format mode*.

The administrator also can set the synchronization schedule. At the scheduled interval, the publishing table updates each of the subscribers to the most current snapshot of data. This automatic synchronization creates a relatively high level of overhead for the publishing server and the network itself because all of the data must be brought forward. Because of this, administrators would not want a synchronization event to occur in the middle of peak database activity. By scheduling this during low activity periods, such as after normal usage hours, this high load on the server is avoided. This also ensures that at certain intervals the data will be mirrored, tightening up the consistency according to the frequency.

Additional Management Features

In addition to customizing the publication by managing its security, replication frequency, and synchronization options, the publications also can be customized in terms of the ownership of the destination table and in that the commands be executed exactly as they were in the source database.

Some situations may arise where the ownership of a target table is important, perhaps for security. In this case users other than the database owner can publish tables for replication and maintain ownership of their tables. This method is referred to as *owner qualifying the table name.* It allows the data from the table in the publishing server to be replicated in the subscribing server.

In cases where complex operations are to be performed, the administrator setting up the article can choose to use column names in SQL statements. Although it increases network traffic by increasing the length of each INSERT statement generated from the transaction log, it ensures that the data to be inserted fills the appropriate columns in the destination table. Without this option, if the target table's columns are not in the same exact order as the source table, errors may occur, particularly on INSERT operations.

Managing Articles

The base component of the replication model is an article. The article is composed of a table or subset of a table. Although articles have their own properties, they cannot be published for replication by themselves. In addition, the underlying table must have a primary key defined.

 Note

Due to the way that Microsoft SQL Server handles the entries in the transaction log, the replication processes must have a serialized entry point upon which to modify data. The primary key in the table normally fulfills this.

Articles can be created from any set of data in a table and grouped or partitioned in certain ways. If the data is grouped by table columns such that one or more columns are not replicated, the article is referred to as being *vertically partitioned* (see figure 11.11). This is useful when replicating from one table to another table that does not include all of the columns in the source table.

Figure 11.11

Vertical partitioning.

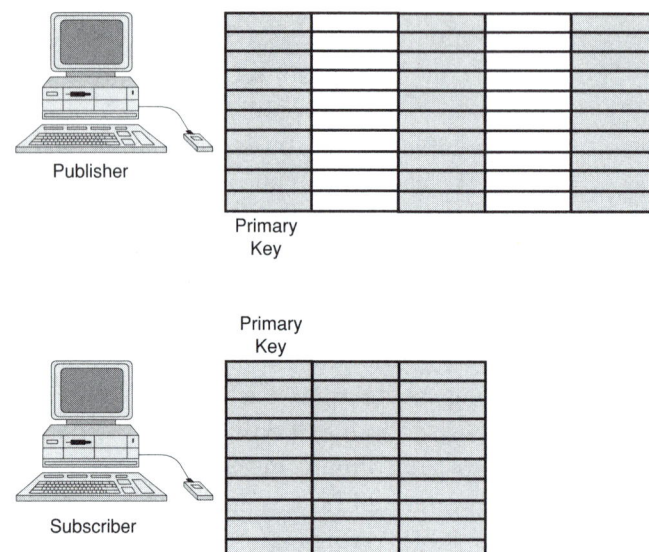

Another method of partitioning is known as horizontal partitioning (see figure 11.12). Servers that subscribe to articles that are horizontally partitioned receive only a subset of the rows. In Microsoft SQL Server T-SQL, a WHERE clause is provided in the filter clause for the article whether it is a SELECT, DELETE, or UPDATE statement.

Because it is sometimes necessary to replicate groups of data that do not conform to vertical or horizontal partitioning, articles may be partitioned both ways. In addition, each manner of grouping can be placed in a separate article in the publication list.

One layer up from the article, the unit is referred to as a publication, which is a group of articles bound together under a common label. In any given database, there can be any number of publications. Publications are the units that subscribing servers use to retrieve and modify the data. When a publication is subscribed to, the subscription server then receives the data from all of the articles bound inside the publication.

Figure 11.12

Horizontal partitioning.

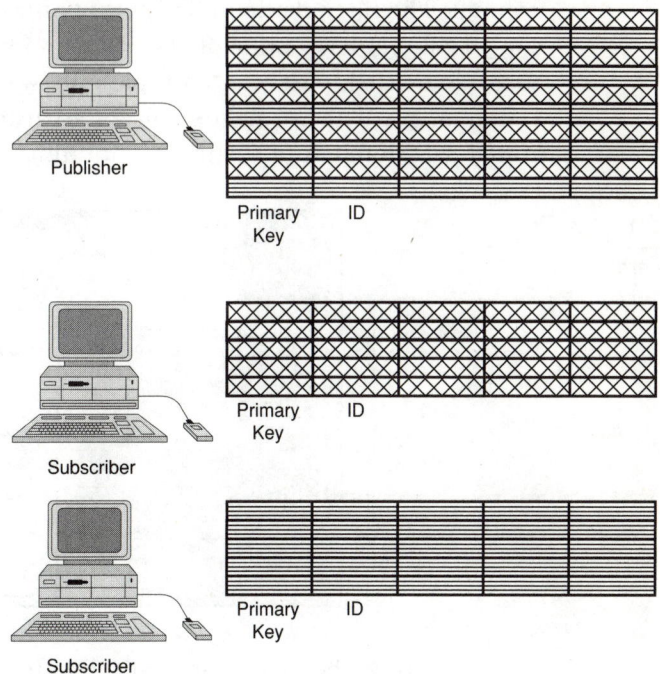

In Microsoft SQL Server, synchronization occurs at the publication level, effectively mirroring all the data from the underlying articles as a group. Therefore it is advisable to group related tables into a single publication so that referential integrity is assured.

Articles have both general options and advanced options to further tune their settings.

General Options

The administrator can define an article by selecting the table that will be replicated. If the data must be filtered by row, some sort of horizontal partitioning must be defined by including a filter clause. Vertical partitioning is used when not all of the columns need to be replicated. In figure 11.13, the Belts_Table article in database Inventory on publisher PubServer is an example of both horizontal and vertical partitioning. The blank box to the right of the length column indicates that the column will not be replicated. This also means that the destination table may not contain this column. The filter clause indicates that only the rows in which the site_id column has a value of 200 will be replicated. This is a clue that this article is part of a "multiple publishers of one table" replication model. The normal default for an article is neither horizontal partitioning nor vertical partitioning.

Figure 11.13

Create article (general).

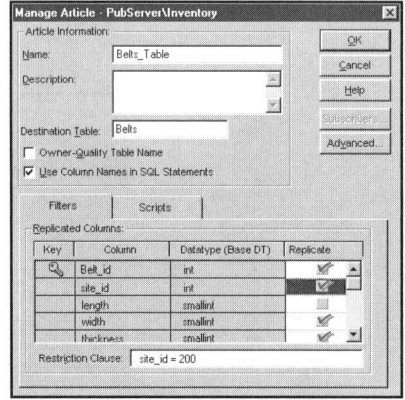

Articles also can be further specialized in terms of what kinds of modifications to the tables will be replicated. The administrator may choose to have any combination of modifications active for replication by changing the status on the Scripts tab of the Articles dialog box.

The default replication mechanism is to replicate on INSERT, UPDATE, and DELETE modifications to the table. In the case where a modification is undesirable, the administrator clicks the diamond next to the custom field of the command and inputs "NONE" (see figure 11.14). This indicates that the article will not replicate these modifications. In addition to specifying a binary replicate/not replicate, the administrator has the option of setting up a stored procedure on the subscribing database that executes when a command is found. The stored procedure takes each of the replicated columns as parameters and may perform any operation that a normal stored procedure is capable of performing. Figure 11.14 shows that a procedure named update_belt_inventory runs when an update modification is applied to the subscribing database.

Figure 11.14

Create article (scripts).

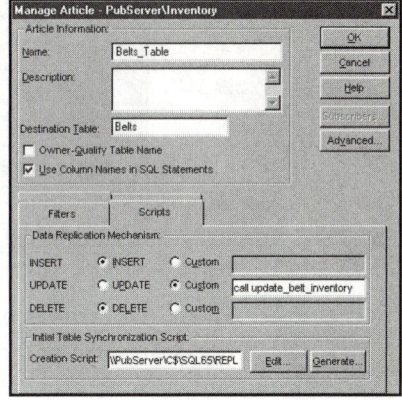

The last of the general options for articles is the creation script. SQL Server Enterprise Manager defaults this to the path specified in the setup for the distribution files with the table name and a .SCH extension. The administrator may override this value but must be careful that the file exists and that read permission is allowed on the login account that SQL Server is using.

The creation script is used when synchronizing the destination table for the first time or when the administrator manually initiates the synchronization process. As shown in figure 11.15, the creation script performs a T-SQL statement that creates the destination table. This table only has the columns that are replicated. This script is normally generated when the administrator clicks the Generate button on the Create Article dialog box.

Figure 11.15

Editing the creation script.

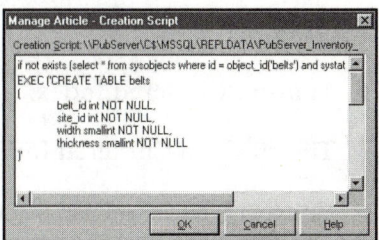

After the Generate button is clicked, the next dialog box contains settings that affect the manner of synchronization, as shown in figure 11.16.

Figure 11.16

The Auto-Generate Sync Scripts dialog box.

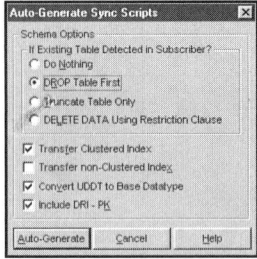

The first group of settings affects the actions of the destination database when the destination table already exists. If the administrator does not want any actions taken (rows deleted, table data truncated, or the table dropped) then the Do Nothing option should be selected. If the data must be exact, but there are triggers on the destination table that must be kept to ensure other operations, such as referential integrity, then the Truncate Table Only option may be selected.

When there are no triggers, or the work done by the triggers is duplicated elsewhere, then the DROP Table option is a good fit for a synchronization option. If the table participates in a "multiple publisher of one table" replication model, then the only reasonable option is the DELETE DATA Using Restriction Clause option. When this is set up correctly, it ensures that even when a synchronization event occurs, only that server's data is modified rather than all of the table data.

As shown in figure 11.16, there are a number of other options for the synchronization scripts:

▶ Transfer Clustered Index

▶ Transfer non-Clustered Index

▶ Convert UDDT to Base Datatype

▶ Include DRI-PK

If the clustered index on the source table is to be created on the destination table (very desirable if searches or reporting will take place), the Transfer Clustered Index option should be selected.

By default the index constraints are not included in the creation script file. However, selecting this option appends the syntax necessary to create the index on the destination table to the creation script file.

If the non-clustered indices are desired as well, then the Transfer non-Clustered Index option should be toggled on. In the case where user-defined data types (UDDT) have been defined for a table, but have not necessarily been created in the destination database, the Convert UDDT to Base Datatype check box should be selected. This ensures that errors will not occur in the initial table creation because the UDDT does not exist in the target database.

The final option, Include DRI-PK, allows the replication of primary keys, foreign keys, and other constraints on the source table to be created in the destination table as well. Because replication requires the primary key on the tables in order to function, this option should normally remain checked. If the indices either do not exist or are not wanted, then the transfer index options may not need to be chosen. Likewise if there are no UDDTs in the source table, or the administrator is certain that they exist in the destination table, this option may not need to be selected.

Advanced Options

There may be an instance when the filter clause may not be as simple as a field's value being compared to a constant. In this case a stored procedure that is created in the publication database may be used to determine whether a row will be replicated. The procedure must be of the following form:

```
IF sql_statement RETURN 1, ELSE RETURN 0
```

In the procedure, sql_statement is replaced by a Transact-SQL statement that performs filtering on a row-by-row level. For example:

```
If DATENAME(month, getdate()) = "July" RETURN 1 ELSE RETURN 0
```

This filter is executed for each record in the transaction log for the replicated table. To minimize the overhead cost of this operation, this filter should be as simple as possible.

Special Cases

There are a few special cases where it is difficult to perform replication.

The first case is one when the source table contains an identity column for referential integrity (RI) purposes. In this case it is necessary to use a stored procedure on insert to set the Identity_insert option for SQL Server to on, insert the data, and set identity_insert to off. An identity column also requires that the Use Column Names option be selected to ensure that the values go in the correct places. This allows replication to continue so the data will be the same.

The second case is when the source table contains a timestamp column for uniqueness or a key. Because replication is based upon a loose consistency model, the servers will not have the same exact time when the row is inserted. Therefore this must be dealt with in the same manner as the identity case or RI will be violated.

Recognizing the Role of the Distribution Server (Distributor)

Objective

The distributor contains the distribution database. It is responsible for storing the changes it receives to the published data in the distribution database. It then forwards the data to the servers that are subscribing to the publication.

Before anything can be replicated, the distribution database must be created. Figure 11.17 shows the dialog box from SQL Server Enterprise manager that pops up during this stage of replication installation.

Figure 11.17

The Install Repli-
cation Publishing
dialog box.

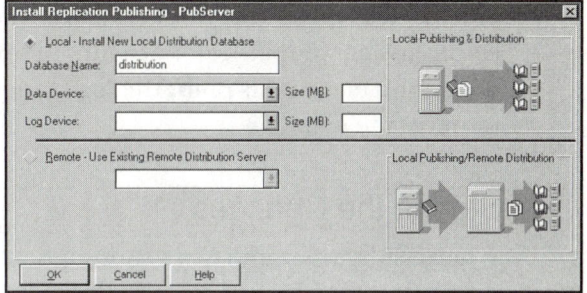

The default option for Enterprise Manager is to set up the distribution database on the local publication server. Although the database can be placed on any data device and log device, it is suggested that the database and log be placed on separate devices in case one gets corrupted. The size of the database and log should be at least the size of all the original data with additional space available to take into account the increased number of commands that replication creates in the log.

The distribution server is responsible for a variety of functions:

▶ Retrieving the data from the publishing server

▶ Storing the changes

▶ Applying the changes to the subscription server

▶ Keeping track of what changes have been processed

Retrieving the Data from the Publishing Server

The default for replication in SQL Server uses the same server for both the publishing server and the distribution server. This makes retrieving the data much simpler. On the same server, the log reader process can read the data out of the transaction log in the source database.

However in the case of the remote distributor model, additional steps are required. First the server must be able to connect to the server using Named Pipes, or the IP address. Once the distribution server knows the location of the publishing server, it must have been given at least SELECT permission. Because most installations use an administrator account of some sort, this is normally not a problem. At this point the log reader process takes over and retrieves the data.

Storing the Changes

When a subscriber initiates a subscription, an ID is created in the distribution database corresponding to the destination database. Once the command is picked up by the log_reader, it is stored in the distribution database. Next, a job is attached both to the command and then to the subscriber's ID.

Applying the Changes to the Subscription Server

Once the job has been separated and stored in the distribution database, the distribution server initiates a repl_subscriber process. This establishes a connection to the destination database on the destination server. This process actually retrieves the commands from the distribution database storage space and applies them to the destination database.

Keeping Track of What Changes Have Been Processed

Once the repl_subscriber applies the change to the destination database, it updates the status of the command and the entire job to a success or failure. If there is a failure, the task entry on the distribution server is updated to reflect the failure and the error that occurred.

Due to the manner in which the modifications are retrieved, manipulated, and forwarded to the subscription server, the distribution server incurs a large amount of overhead. For this reason, the distribution server is required to have a minimum of 32 MB of RAM, with a minimum of 16 MB allocated to SQL Server, or it will not run.

 **Tip**   If the distribution database will be used heavily, put the distributor on a separate server from that of the publishing database.

Recognizing the Role of the Subscription Server (Subscriber)

 **Objective**   This is the target database for the published data. It holds a copy and receives any changes from the publishing server that are forwarded by the distribution server.

In addition to the various partition methods and grouping of articles in publications, there also are mechanisms in place to change how the subscribing server gets the data.

Pull and Push Subscriptions

The first mechanism is the issue of how the subscriptions will be administrated and how servers can request that bands of data be replicated and synchronized.

When the subscriptions are set up on the publishing server's side, the subscription is known as a push subscription. This server gathers up all of its data and the appropriate modifications and pushes it down the link to all of the subscribing servers. This kind of subscription has the advantage of consolidated administration across multiple servers at the same time. One caveat on this type of subscription is that the administrator must have system administrator (SA) permissions on each of the subscribing servers. The other caveat is that the data cannot be selectively gathered by the subscribing servers; each time a synchronization event occurs, all of the data is replicated again.

The other type of subscription is a pull subscription. This type of subscription requires that the subscribing server take the administrative role once the publication has been created on the publishing server. With this method, the subscribing server can request that certain articles or entire publications be synchronized at any given time, without all of the data needing to be replicated. In addition to this, the administrator can determine what publications to subscribe to by selecting publications from a master list on the publisher.

Extended Replication

The second mechanism for the subscribing server is found in Microsoft SQL Server's extended replication abilities. With the extended replication commands, it is possible to publish data to non-SQL Server databases, including Microsoft Access, Oracle, and any other ODBC-compliant database. This ability allows SQL Server to interconnect and share data in environments where mixed databases are present. This also allows for easier distribution of data to areas where users require it, such as a small Microsoft Access database on a laptop used in the field.

Synchronization Options

Once the publication has been created and the subscription completed, the type of synchronization that occurs depends upon how the publishing administrator set it up.

If the administrator chose no synchronization, then the replication process continues without any other activity.

If the administrator chose manual synchronization then replication activity pauses until the administrator manually synchronizes the tables and then notifies SQL Server that the synchronization has been completed.

If the administrator chose automatic synchronization, then the table is modified according to the article settings and replication will continue.

Tracing the Replication Process

 Objective

The process of tracking changes from the publisher to the subscriber can be compartmentalized into where the steps occur: in the publisher, in the distributor, and in the subscriber. The replication process is actually composed of three processes: the log reader, the repl_publisher, and the repl_subscriber task.

Work Done by the Publisher

The publisher performs several tasks. The first task is handling the data modification. Depending upon the change, INSERT, UPDATE, or DELETE, triggers fire in the publishing database to perform the normal work. Once this work is done, the database must determine whether the transaction will be replicated by examining data in the *sysarticles, syspublications, sysobjects,* and *syssubscription* tables. The *sysobjects* table has a field in it that indicates if in fact the table is replicated. Next, the *sysarticles* table is checked using the ID from the *sysobjects* table. If indeed the data will be published, the command is then generated with ID numbers from the *syspublications* table for the appropriate publication and the ID of the subscriber from the *syssubscriptions* table. Once all of this data is gathered up, the row is written to the transaction log by the rep_publisher process.

Work Done by the Distributor

The log reader process picks up the modification from the transaction log and breaks it up into individual commands. The commands may be either in the short form or complete Transact SQL statements with column names, depending upon how the publication was set up. Once the commands are broken up, they are assigned job IDs in the MSjobs table. The actual detail is stored in the MSjob_commands table with the job ID being the joining field. The other tables involved in the storage of the modification are the MSjob_subscriptions table, which stores data linking the subscriber to the article, and the MSsubscriber_info table, which contains information used by SQL Executive to pass the job along. Once storage is completed, the information is sent to the repl_subscriber process. This process returns information to the distributor pertaining to the success or failure of the individual rows processed. This information is stored in the MSSubscriber_status table.

Work Done by the Subscriber

The repl_subscriber process performs several tasks in the subscription database. First it determines if the destination table exists as well as its synchronization status. If this is the initial synchronization for the table, it applies the synchronization method to the table. Next, it determines if the destination table requires that a stored procedure execute to manipulate the change, if so the procedure is executed. Otherwise, the change is made by simply executing the command as if it was initiated in the destination database natively. Once the command is executed, the repl_subscriber process returns the status to the distributor.

Summary

This chapter has covered a variety of subjects dealing with replication. You should now understand how to use the appropriate replication model for a situation. You have learned to recognize the different roles that a server may play in replication. You also learned how the replication process works and which tables the replication process uses. This should prepare you for the replication portion of the exam.

Exercises

Exercise 11.1: Choosing an Appropriate Replication Model

Your company has six sites that require common data distributed across them with the following specifications:

Sites A, B, C, and D all perform customer maintenance for additions, updates, and deletions, with the provision that each site may only update the customers that it adds.

Sites A, B, C, and D also perform real-time on-line transaction processing for the company and cannot afford to slow down processing of transactions to transmit data to the corporate server at Site E.

The company has provided Site F to act as a temporary storage repository for the transaction information from each site along its way to Site E.

The customer data must be distributed to sites A, B, C, and D such that each site can see each of the other site's customers.

Describe the replication models used to solve this situation.

Answer:

A, B, C, and D are publishers in a "multiple publishers of one table" model for customer data using F as a distributor.

1. A publishes its customers to F

2. B publishes its customers to F

3. C publishes its customers to F

4. D publishes its customers to F

5. A subscribes and receives B, C, and D's customers

6. B subscribes and receives A, C, and D's customers

continues

Exercise 11.1:   Continued

7. C subscribes and receives A, B, and D's customers

8. D subscribes and receives A, B, and C's customers

A, B, C, and D also are publishers in a "central subscriber" model with F as the distributor, and E as the subscriber.

1. A publishes its financials to F

2. B publishes its financials to F

3. C publishes its financials to F

4. D publishes its financials to F

5. E subscribes and receives financials from A, B, C, and D

See figure 11.18.

Figure 11.18

Hybrid replication models.

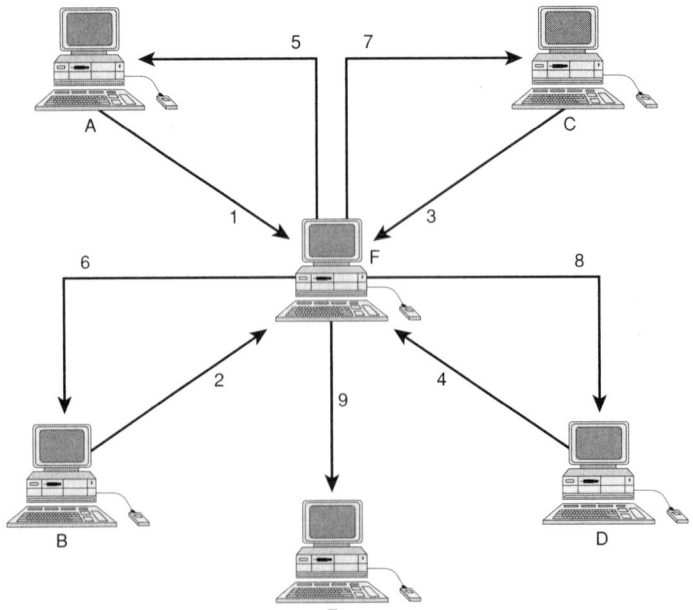

Exercise 11.2:   Publication Configuration

Your company has instituted a new program by which managers are paged if the inventory in the belts table on Server B is updated to a value below fifteen units. The managers only have access to Server A. Each morning at midnight, Servers A and B are synchronized. Once an hour between 8:00 AM and 5:00 PM, Servers A and B have data distributed between them for the inventory though Server B's inventory may change during the interval. Describe a method to set up replication between Servers A and B so that the managers will receive their pages appropriately.

Answer:

Servers A and B have replication set up normally with the following exceptions in the publishing setup. Instead of the interval being continuous, it is set to once an hour between 8:00 AM and 5:00 PM. In addition, the article that is defined for the belt inventory table has NONE assigned to the INSERT and DELETE scripts. Therefore the data only replicates on updates to the values in that table. The final component is to set up a task to synchronize the databases at midnight through the task manager.

Exercise 11.3:   Publication Security

Servers A, B, and C all contain sales, inventory, and financial data in respective tables. Due to the fact that the servers belong to different departments, security is an issue. The following security settings are desired:

Server A can only publish modifications to Server B and only for the sale data.

Server B can only publish modifications to Server C, and only for the financial data.

Server C can only publish modifications to Server A, and only for the inventory data. Due to a difference in the way that the group for Server B uses the data, Server B only receives the sale date and number of units sold from Server A.

For the same reason, Server A only receives data daily from Server C if inventory was received.

Describe a possible solution to this problem.

Answer:

Server A only enables publishing to Server B for the sale database.

Server B only enables publishing to Server C for the financial database.

Server C only enables publishing to Server A, for the inventory database.

The article on Server B is vertically partitioned for columns containing sale date and number of units sold.

Server C has an UPDATE clause of NONE, a DELETE clause of NONE, and the INSERT clause executes a filter to determine if new inventory has been received.

Review Questions

1. Choose two or more correct responses. The publishing server performs the following tasks:

   A. Creates subscriptions to articles

   B. Stores changes

   C. Applies changes to the destination database

   D. Creates articles and publications

2. The most complex replication model is

   A. Central subscriber

   B. Central publisher

   C. Multiple publishers of one table

   D. Remote Publisher with Central Distributor

3. Advantages of Native synchronization are (Choose two or more correct responses):

   A. Compatibility

   B. Speed

   C. Different target destination types

   D. Same target destination types

4. Vertically partitioned articles could possibly replicate:

   A. One of the columns

   B. All of the columns

   C. Selected columns

   D. Every even-numbered column

5. Choose two or more correct responses. Default options for creation scripts are:

   A. The server name, database name, article name concatenated with a .SCH extension

   B. The distribution directory

   C. Truncate Table

   D. Drop Table

6. Choose two or more correct responses.

   A. The minimum memory requirement for SQL Server is 8 MB of memory for a publisher.

   B. The minimum memory requirement for SQL Server is 32 MB of memory for a distributor with 16 allocated to SQL Server.

   C. The minimum memory requirement for SQL Server is 16 MB of memory for a publisher with 16 allocated to SQL Server.

   D. The minimum memory requirement for SQL Server is 16 MB of memory for a publisher/distributor with 8 allocated to SQL Server.

7. Choose two or more correct responses.

   A. Pull subscriptions are set up on the subscriber.

   B. Push subscriptions are set up by the publisher.

   C. Pull subscriptions retrieve modifications when the subscriber initiates a synchronization event.

   D. Push subscriptions send all of the data upon demand by the publisher.

8. Choose two or more correct responses. Tables used in replication are:

   A. Msjobs and syspublications

   B. *Sysarticles* and MSjob_status

   C. *Sysarticles* and MSjob_commands

   D. *Syspublications* and MSsubscriber_info

9. Choose two or more correct responses. Publications may be customized in terms of :

   A. Replication frequency

   B. Synchronization frequency

   C. Security

   D. Partitioning

10. Replication pauses until a particular operation is completed after a synchronization task. What task is this?

   A. Publishing is installed by the administrator.

   B. SQL Server is notified that a manual synchronization task has been completed.

   C. A pop subscription has been defined by the administrator.

   D. SQL Server creates a synchronization task for the subscriber and notifies the administrator.

Answers to Review Questions

1. A, D

2. C

3. B, D

4. A, C, D

5. A, B, D

6. B, D

7. All of the above

8. A, C, D

9. A, B, C

10. B

Answers to Test Yourself Questions at Beginning of Chapter

1. Two benefits that replication has, when properly implemented, are that it is log-based and fault tolerant. See "Introduction."

2. A server participating in a replication relationship may be a publisher, subscriber, or distributor. See "Recognizing Server Roles."

3. Valid replication models are central publisher, central publisher with remote distributor, central subscriber, publishing subscriber, multiple publisher of one table, and downloaded data. See "Apply the Appropriate Replication Model."

4. Depending upon how the data is required in the destination table, data may be published in rows, by columns, or in its entirety. See "Managing Articles."

5. The kinds of data that cannot be published without extra work are data with identity and timestamp columns. See "Special Cases."

6. Subscriptions fall into two categories, push and pull subscriptions. Push subscriptions are set up by the administrator of the publisher. Pull subscriptions are set up by the administrator of the subscriber. See "Pull and Push Subscriptions."

7. The three subprocesses that SQL Server uses in the distribution processes are the logreader, synchronization, and distribution processes. See "Managing Publications."

8. Three methods of synchronization for articles and publications are automatic, manual, and no synchronization. See "Synchronization Options."

Chapter 12

Application Development and Open Data Services (ODS)

This chapter helps you prepare for the exam by covering the following objectives:

Objectives

▶ Recognize and apply open architecture

▶ Recognize and apply Open Database Connectivity

▶ Identify the benefits of integrating OLE architecture with SQL Server

▶ Recognize how SQL Server takes advantage of the OLE architecture

Test Yourself! Before reading this chapter, test yourself to determine how much study time you will need to devote to this section.

1. SQL Server includes five mechanisms that allow it to interact with its external environment. What are they?

2. Name two ways that SQL Server implements open architecture.

3. Name two methods for fine-tuning ODBC data sources.

4. Name the two categories of OLE Automation applications and explain how they apply to SQL Server open architecture.

5. What is the underlying OLE architecture that SQL Enterprise Manager takes advantage of?

Answers are located at the end of the chapter...

Microsoft SQL Server is a powerful relational database tool. Within SQL Server, structures such as stored procedures, triggers, and replication allow data manipulation in many ways, including the distribution of data. SQL Server does the entire task on its own in each of these cases, without user intervention. This capability causes SQL Server to be classified as a back-end tool.

In today's client/server world, a front end of some sort is required to display the data to the end-user. These interfaces may be programmed in a variety of languages, such as Microsoft Visual Basic, Microsoft Visual C++, Delphi by Borland, and Powerbuilder by PowerSoft. Each of these languages handles database connectivity a bit differently, but they perform roughly the same function; they display the data to the end user.

As a means to an end, SQL Server includes several different mechanisms that make the interaction between the front end and SQL Server easier. Some of these methods include the following:

▶ Messaging Application Programming Interface (MAPI)

▶ SQL Distributed Management Objects (SQL-DMO)

▶ Open Database Connectivity (ODBC)

▶ DB-Library

▶ Open Data Services (ODS)

The Messaging Application Programming Interface (MAPI) component allows SQL Server to communicate with other MAPI enabled electronic messaging applications. MAPI enables SQL Server to use result sets and messages through electronic mail to achieve this communication.

Visual Basic, Microsoft Excel, Visual C++, and Microsoft Visual FoxPro are all capable of interfacing with SQL Server through SQL Distributed Management Objects (SQL-DMO). SQL-DMO is a set of 32-bit OLE Automation objects built for Microsoft Operating Systems. Each of the previously mentioned products can use SQL-DMO to manage and manipulate objects within SQL Server.

The Open Database Connectivity (ODBC) Interface is a universal set of APIs that provide an interface to SQL Server for the client. Each driver is specific to a particular product and is designed to provide database access to the client for development and manipulation.

A set of APIs that are designed to develop client-side (front-end) applications for SQL Server are grouped into the DB-Library component.

The Open Data Services (ODS) components define an API found on the server instead of the client. The component functions as a bridge between the client and the server, sending requests back and forth. These requests are made using the Open Data Services Library.

In order for you to understand application development and connectivity with SQL Server (and do well on that aspect of the exam), the rest of the chapter covers the following topics:

- ▶ Recognizing and applying open architecture

- ▶ Recognizing and applying Open Database Connectivity

- ▶ The benefits of integrating OLE architecture with SQL Server

- ▶ Recognizing how SQL Server takes advantage of the OLE architecture

Recognizing and Applying Open Architecture

 Objective

In order to understand how an open architecture applies to Microsoft SQL Server, it is first necessary to discuss the concept of open architecture. Once that is clear, then the next step is to discuss how it is implemented.

What Is Open Architecture?

When Microsoft created SQL Server, the product was built upon many different ideas with many technologies in mind. The designers realized that though they may have programmed a wide variety of features into SQL Server to make the product the best relational database tool they could, some functions would either not make the final cut or were not in the design. In order to get around this problem, Microsoft SQL Server is designed with an open architecture in mind.

An open architecture can be thought of as a design that provides for further expansion. The group that implements this expansion may be the company that makes the product or a third-party vendor.

How Does SQL Server Implement Open Architecture?

The open architecture in SQL Server allows it to interact with objects both internal and external to its process.

Internal Open Architecture

Internally, there are several ways that SQL Server may be extended out from its normal set of operations. The open architecture may take the form of user-defined data types (UDDT) that extend the base data types to allow the administrator to set up complex structures to hold information.

A common example of this type of extension is an updater_id column in a table. The updater_id data type is based upon a varchar data type (used to store character data) but has a length of 30. Once this UDDT has been created, any table that would have a varchar(30) column in it that was used to store user names can be recreated with an updater_id data type to make it easier to remember. Another benefit of UDDTs is that if the definition changes, the next time a table is created, the new definition will apply.

External Open Architecture

Another way that SQL Server implements open architecture is with extended stored procedures. The name extended stored procedure seems to be something of a misnomer when you consider the fact that the functions are not actually stored procedures. Instead, they are functions located in external dynamic link libraries (DLLs) that were created at various times. These functions emulate the actions of normal stored procedures and can be executed like normal procedures. In addition, they can return status values to the calling process as well.

System administrators (SAs) as well as developers can create the procedures, but only the SA has appropriate rights to add an extended stored procedure to the server. In addition, this procedure can only be added to the master database. Because the extended procedures are compiled externally to SQL Server, they add a great deal of flexibility to what SQL Server can accomplish.

Extended stored procedures are managed either through SQL Enterprise Manager or with the system stored procedures sp_addextendedproc, sp_dropextendedproc, and sp_helpextendedproc in the master database. The sp_addextendedproc uses the function name and library name parameters to register the function and library with SQL Server. Existing extended stored procedures may be deleted with sp_dropextendedproc.

An example of an application for an extended stored procedure is a financial dynamic link library for loan amortization. Within the DLL, functions to calculate the present and future values of loans and investments are created with an interface to return results to SQL Server. The code to perform the calculations may be easier to code in a language such as Visual C++ and therefore it is compiled this way. An extended stored procedure is called within SQL Server to the DLL, which does the calculations and returns the results to SQL Server. By using this type of open architecture, SQL Server may effectively perform complex financial calculations without actually needing to have the code created with Transact SQL.

Interacting with Mail

In today's enterprise a majority of communication between employees is done with electronic mail. SQL Server also may interact with the user environment by creating and sending messages through an existing e-mail system. The stored procedures used to facilitate this communication are:

- ▶ xp_startmail

- ▶ xp_stopmail

- ▶ xp_readmail

- ▶ xp_sendmail

- ▶ xp_deletemail

- ▶ xp_findnextmsg

- ▶ sp_processmail

The xp_startmail and xp_stopmail extended stored procedures are used to manage the mail session for SQL Server. The parameters for the xp_startmail command are composed of a user name and password that may be implicitly passed, or defaulted when SQL Server is set up, or in SQL Enterprise Manager by accessing the Server, SQL Mail, Configure menu. The xp_startmail procedure attempts to initiate a mail session only if an existing mail session is not executing. The mail session initiated by xp_startmail may be configured to start automatically when SQL Server starts by setting the Auto Start Mail Client server option.

Once a mail session has been established, SQL Server may perform operations on the MAPI-compliant mail system by using xp_readmail, xp_sendmail, xp_deletemail, or xp_findnextmsg. The xp_readmail procedure retrieves the message and any attachments from the mailbox. The xp_sendmail procedure sends messages with attached query results out to users on the e-mail system. Deletion of messages is accomplished using the xp_deletemail procedure, while the xp_findnextmsg retrieves the next message in the mailbox for reading, responding, or deleting.

In situations where incoming mail contains only a single query, sp_processmail may be used to interact with the mail system. The sp_processmail procedure uses the xp_findnextmsg, xp_readmail, and xp_deletemail extended stored procedures to return the results of the query in the message text to the message sender. Once the results have been successfully created and sent back, the message is then deleted.

Normally, the administrator sets up the extended stored procedures to execute and send mail to the administrator when an error of a sufficient severity occurs. A common practice is to link the e-mail system with a paging system to alert the administrator when an error takes place.

Interacting with the Operating System

Additionally, SQL Server can interact with the operating system on the server using another important extended stored procedure, xp_cmdshell. With this procedure, the administrator can execute a command string as if a command shell was opened and the command was executed within the shell.

The command is executed under the account that SQL Server uses as a login. Because of this, the administrator must be careful to grant permission to this powerful extended stored procedure only to responsible users because they will then have the ability to remove important files and possibly crash the system. This procedure is highly useful in situations where file maintenance must be set up and completed when the administrator is not actively monitoring the server.

Recognizing and Applying Open Database Connectivity

 Objective

Another component of open architecture in SQL Server may be found in Open Database Connectivity (ODBC).

What Is ODBC?

ODBC is a client interface that enables developers to perform operations on several different database systems for which an ODBC driver exists, including Microsoft SQL Server. ODBC generally serves two major functions:

- ▶ Session manager

- ▶ Transact SQL translator

Session Manager

In its role as a session manager, ODBC may either act as a connector or a database engine, depending upon the target database. If the target database is a Microsoft Excel spreadsheet or perhaps a text file, then the ODBC driver acts as a database engine and is known as a single-tier driver. If, on the other hand, the target is Microsoft SQL Server or Oracle, then the driver acts simply as a connector between the client and the server.

Transact-SQL Translator

The other role that ODBC plays is that of a Transact-SQL translator. The SQL Access Group created a standard and from this standard ODBC was created to provide nearly all of the functions that are available in Microsoft SQL Server. As a translator, the driver is primarily responsible for returning result sets from queries in a format that the client can understand.

However, ODBC is not limited to only returning result sets. By using ODBC, the client application can perform bulk copy operations, launch database maintenance tasks, and initiate many other tasks within the server.

ODBC Components

The architecture that composes ODBC can be broken into four components:

- ▶ Application

- ▶ Driver manager

- ▶ Driver

- ▶ Data source

The application is the front-end component that the user operates to interact with the database. The functions performed by this component are: connecting with the database, executing ODBC functions to submit SQL statements and retrieve the results, committing and rolling back transactions, and terminating the database connection when the user is finished interacting with it.

The driver manager and driver generally appear to be the same unit although they have different characteristics and functions. Loading the driver is the primary function that the driver manager provides. After loading the driver, the secondary functions of the driver manager are the following:

▶ Processing information functions such as SQLDrivers, SQLDataSources, and SQLGetFunctions if the driver does not support the SQLGetFunctions call

▶ Processing connection functions such as SQLAllocEnv, SQLAllocConnect, SQLSetConnectionOption, SQLFreeConnect, and SQLFreeEnv

▶ Forwarding function calls from the application to the driver, such as SQLConnect, which it forwards to the driver after performing initial processing

▶ Checking parameters for functions and state transitions

▶ Checking for error conditions before forwarding calls to the driver to reduce the amount of error handling that must be coded into the driver

▶ Logging each called function in a trace file after checking for errors when requested

The driver is loaded from a DLL by the Driver Manager when the SQLBrowseConnect, SQLConnect, or SQLDriverConnect functions are called from the applications. The driver interacts with the data source using ODBC function calls. Depending upon the function that is called, the driver may initiate or terminate a connection to the source, exchange requests and results between the application and the data source, translate data to or from another format, or map errors to standard error codes and return the standard code back to the application.

The data source is a general name for the data the user will manipulate, the database in which it resides, the operating system containing the database, and the network that exists between the client and the source (if the network exists.) Depending upon the type of data source, different information may be required in order to connect, although a name for the data source, a user ID, and a password form the base set of information. Processing SQL requests that the driver sent and returning results are two of the functions the data source provides in addition to the general database functions—such as transactions, concurrency, and consistency of data.

How Is ODBC Used?

ODBC is used in a variety of front-end tools, such as Microsoft Visual Basic, Microsoft Visual C++, and Powerbuilder. Each of these languages can use ODBC as a base for a set of objects that conform to their programming metaphor.

ODBC Installation

Before ODBC can be used with SQL Server from any programming language, it must first be installed on the client. When the client utilities for SQL Server are installed under Windows NT, Windows 95, or Windows 3.11, the ODBC SQL Server driver is automatically installed.

Setting up Data Sources

Once the driver is installed, the user must create a data source for each SQL Server that will be used from the client, as shown in Figure 12.1. A data source is a collection of information about a server or data file that is used to exchange information.

Figure 12.1

ODBC SQL Server Setup.

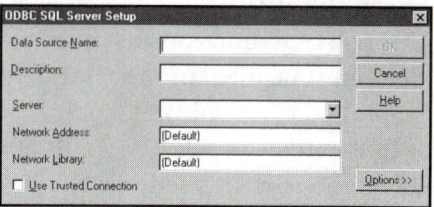

Data sources are divided into three categories:

- ▶ User data sources

- ▶ System data sources

- ▶ File data sources

All of the information about the data sources is stored in the Registry (other than file data sources information) but each type is slightly different from the others. User data sources are only visible under the account that created them and only on the machine on which they were created. System data sources including Windows NT services are visible to all users on the current machine. File data sources are visible to all users that have appropriate drivers installed.

The workstation maintains its list of ODBC data sources in a collection keyed by the data source name. Therefore, the data source must be given a unique name, usually the name of the server concatenated with the database or task name for later identification. In addition to the unique name, a longer description may be entered into the Description input box.

Next the server information must be entered, starting with the name of a SQL Server on the network. If the server has been entered from another source, such as SQL Client Configuration, then it will be selectable from the drop-down box. On a Windows NT machine, the server known as (local) is also selectable. The (local) server points to the SQL Server service that is running on the current workstation.

The address of the SQL Server must be entered so that the server may be located. This is very similar to registering the SQL Server through SQL Enterprise Manager. Likewise, the Network Library field must be filled in so that the driver knows which SQL Server Net-Library dynamic link library will be used to communicate with the network software. Both of these options may normally be left at the (default) setting. The default network library setting tells the server to use the library that was set up in the SQL Client Configuration utility.

In cases where a trust relationship exists between the Windows NT Domain of the workstation and the domain that the SQL Server resides in, it is possible to specify that the ODBC SQL Server driver will use a secure or trusted connection. Simply toggle the Use Trusted Connection checkbox. Under trusted connections, SQL Server ignores any login security on the server instead of using integrated security to make the connection to the data source. Along with this, the login ID or password that is supplied to initiate the connection is not used, as it would be under secure connections.

Clicking the Options button extends the setup dialog box as shown in figure 12.2, allowing for even more customization.

Figure 12.2

ODBC SQL Server Setup—Options.

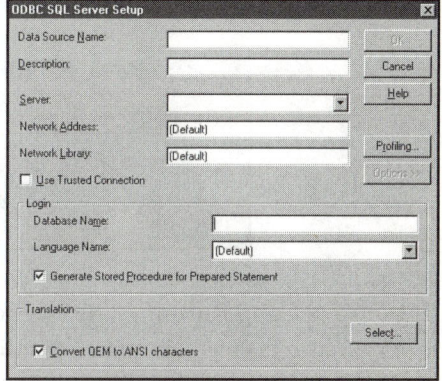

The Login information is used as the connection is made, allowing the connection to change its database to whatever database is named in the Database Name field. If for some reason the user does not have access to this database, ODBC changes to the first available database that the user is allowed in.

The Language drop-down box contains a selection of each of the international languages (character sets) installed on the SQL Server so that the user may pick which one will be used.

One of the benefits of using some ODBC drivers is the ability to prepare statements for later use. This technique allows the time spent compiling the command to be eliminated after the first time the command is run. This is known as "preparing a statement." When the Generate Stored Procedure for Prepared Statement check box is selected, it takes this one logical step further. Instead of just compiling the procedure and running it from a cache, it creates a temporary stored procedure in order to further speed up access.

The Convert OEM to ANSI characters option allows interaction between a server and client that are using the same non-ANSI character set. If the character sets are not the same, then a Translator must be chosen.

Configuring Data Source Profiles

Clicking the Profiling button from the extended dialog box with the full set of options for ODBC setup allows the data source to be fine-tuned in a couple of ways (see figure 12.3).

Figure 12.3

Configuring a data source profile.

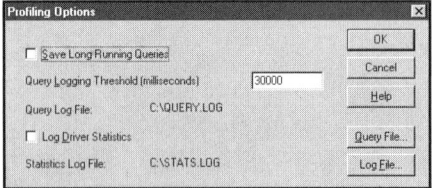

If the Save Long Running Query check box is checked, then any query that runs over the time specified in the Query Logging Threshold box in units of milliseconds is logged to the file specified by the Query File button.

Statistics on the driver also may be logged to a file specified by the Log File button if the Log Driver Statistics button is clicked.

Once the data source is set up, there is a general formula for accessing the data through ODBC that is independent of what programming language is used. The steps of the formula follow:

1. Allocate a connection handle

2. Open the data source

3. Access the data

4. Close the data source

5. Return the connection handle to the connection pool (which is managed by the driver manager)

Using ODBC from Visual Basic

Like the other programming languages, Visual Basic adds a layer between raw ODBC and the developer so that the developer does not have to memorize complicated parameter syntax combinations. In Visual Basic, the layer above ODBC goes in two distinct directions:

▶ Data Access Objects (DAO)

▶ Remote Data Objects (RDO)

DAO is primarily used with client-side databases such as Jet databases (.MDB files normally created with Microsoft Access), or ISAM databases such as Microsoft Visual FoxPro, Microsoft Excel, or text files where the work is done by the client. In addition, when an ODBC driver is used with DAO, DAO may be used to interact with Microsoft SQL Server or other remote databases where the work is done on the server. Using ODBC drivers with DAO enables the source database to be switched to another database type without modifying a substantial amount of code if the drivers are completely compatible.

RDO is used mainly for connectivity between the client application and a server-side database such as SQL Server or Oracle. When combined with a RemoteData control, the application written using Visual Basic offloads the work done to process queries and resultsets to the server instead of on the client. By offloading the work, the client processor is freed up to do more work while the server (which most likely is much larger in terms of computing power) processes the query and returns the results to the application. In addition to offloading the work to the remote server, using RDO also has the following benefits:

▶ Multiple result sets may be requested in a single batch.

▶ Result sets may have any cursor type that the ODBC driver supports (contingent upon options set when the request is made).

▶ Processing may be synchronous or asynchronous, which may or may not force the application to wait for query results to be returned before continuing execution, respectively.

▶ Execution of stored procedures may pass return values and output parameters back to the calling application.

Because of the RDO and DAO layers, a Visual Basic developer does not need to know all of the intricacies of ODBC. Instead, the developer accesses properties and methods of DAO or RDO object collections as if they were any other object in order to perform data manipulations on the target database.

Another benefit of using ODBC data sources with programming languages is database portability. Without having to change much code, the data source can be changed to any other kind of data source by redefining the data source in Control Panel. For applications that may be pointed to Microsoft SQL Server databases, Microsoft Access databases, or Excel spreadsheets, this is a definite plus. If the drivers are 100% compatible, the same code works on all three, reducing the time necessary to change the application for the new database structure. If the drivers aren't completely compatible, adjustments need to be made to work around the inconsistencies, but the time to implement the database change will most likely be much less than that to recode the entire application.

In the general formula for using ODBC automatically, Visual Basic takes care of steps 2 and 3 with methods attached to the objects, whether they are DAO or RDO. When a remote data control (a Remote Data Object) connects to its target server, behind the scenes it is allocating a connection handle from the connection pool. The OpenResultset method wraps the commands necessary to open the data source and selects data corresponding to the parameters passed to the method. The action of closing the data source and returning the connection handle to the connection pool takes place without the developer issuing any more commands when the control is unloaded.

ODBC and Replication

Another use for the ODBC drivers is replication, which may distribute data modifications to any destination database that conforms to the following requirements for the driver:

▶ ODBC Level 1 compliant

▶ Thread safe and 32-bit

▶ Has the capability to wrap commands in transaction blocks

▶ Executes the distribution process on one of the following platforms: Intel, Alpha, Power PC, or MIPS

▶ Is not read-only

▶ Supports the data definition language (DDL)

The stricture that the driver is ODBC Level 1 compliant ensures that there is a common functional base that can be used to perform data modifications.

If the driver is not thread safe then there is a possibility that the threads the driver uses may be affected or blocked by other threads, reducing concurrency, and possibly making data inconsistent.

Replication is implemented by sending the commands to the destination database in blocks of transactions. Therefore, the driver must be able to support multiple commands in a transaction block or replication will not work as designed.

The reason that the driver must execute on the selected distribution is that the distribution process only runs on those platforms.

If for some reason the driver is read-only, then it will not be able to make any of the data modifications that replication normally makes, thereby negating the point of replication.

One of the many components of replication is that the destination schema must be created upon synchronization through the use of a creation script. Because this script is created using the data definition language, the driver must support it in order to create the schema.

The Benefits of Integrating OLE Architecture with SQL Server

 Objective ▶ Another way that SQL Server may be extended out of its environment to interface with client applications is through the use of OLE architecture and Automation.

OLE Automation

OLE Automation servers provide interfaces to objects and their properties and methods to any application that is using them. The applications that use OLE Automation can be divided into two categories: Controllers and Objects.

Controller applications, as their name implies, provide a controlling or programmatic interface to the objects. In many situations, these applications function without any user intervention. They may be broken up even further into in-process and out-of-process servers.

In-process servers are compiled into dynamic link libraries (DLLs), and execute in the process of the client application. Because they execute in the process space of the controller application, they cannot be executed as stand-alone objects. Out-of-process servers execute in their own process space and are compiled into executable code (EXEs.) Because objects used in out-of-process servers require a switch in process space, calls to in-process objects execute faster.

An example of this type of application is a financial component implemented in a Dynamic Link Library (DLL). This particular library provides a financial object to the client. The client application passes the object data in-process server (an OLE Server since it "serves" the object interface to the client application and is contained in a DLL) then manipulates the data and returns the result to the client. In this case the code necessary to perform the financial function in question is encapsulated within the object and the client does not have to know anything about the actual function.

In effect, this is a sort of Black Box that information is passed to and values are returned from (see figure 12.4.). If the objects were exposed in a stand-alone executable file, the server would have been an out-of-process server instead.

The object applications contain the actual structures, properties, and methods. Any structure may have one or more methods and properties that are exposed through an interface.

Figure 12.4

Black Box technique.

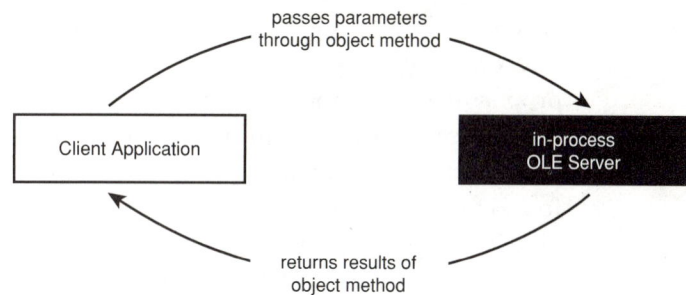

passes parameters
through object method

Client Application

in-process
OLE Server

returns results of
object method

OLE automation serves two main purposes: to expose the objects, and to manipulate the objects. The objects that are exposed may be used in any front-end application that supports OLE Automation, such as macros in Microsoft Excel. The application that exposes these objects is referred to as an OLE Automation Server. The controller application may also use OLE Automation objects from other applications. An example of one such controller application is Microsoft Visual Basic. It allows the developer to use objects from any of its internal libraries, as well as other objects that have a reference in the active project. Controller applications can create objects from other OLE Automation Servers as well as manipulate them by using properties and methods that the object supports.

SQL Distributed Management Objects (SQL-DMO)

One of the aforementioned components is SQL-DMO. This 32-bit library is actually an OLE server for a set of objects. The main function of this OLE server is to provide objects that allow a controller application to communicate with SQL Server and reference the SQL Server object library.

Unlike Remote Data Objects and Data Access Objects, SQL-DMO is not designed to support data access, but to encapsulate all of the administrative functions of SQL Server. SQL-DMO exposes each of the administrative functions as OLE objects, properties, and methods. In fact, there are over forty unique objects with over one thousand properties and methods combined.

If SQL Server was installed in its default location, the SQL-DMO type library is contained in the file named SQLOLE65.TLB in the

C:\MSSQL\BINN directory. Otherwise it is in the BINN directory wherever SQL Server was installed. Information on each object, property, and method exposed by SQL-DMO is contained in this file for use by any OLE Automation controller, such as Visual Basic. The file that contains the objects is SQLOLE65.DLL, which is found in the same directory as the type library file. Because the library is compiled into a dynamic link library (DLL), the objects are created in the client application's workspace, making it an in-process server.

The general formula for using SQL-DMO corresponds to the following:

1. Define the object

2. Connect to the server

3. Choose the database

4. Perform the operations

5. Disconnect from the database

6. Destroy the object to free memory

SQL-DMO Object Model

Before discussing the SQL-DMO Object model, the differentiation in the object model between a list and a collection must be clarified in terms of the SQL-DMO Object model.

Lists are groups of objects that have a many-to-many relationship. Typically, lists are names of objects contained in a collection instead of the objects themselves. In SQL-DMO, lists may be used in the same manner as collections except that items may not be added or deleted from the list because it is only a reference to the collection. Items in a list may be referenced by their zero-based index number. Databases and devices form good examples of list relationships—in other words, a database can be stored on one or more devices and a device may contain one or more databases. The return value of this method contains several string constants in a row.

Collections are groups of objects that have a one-to-many relationship. Each of the objects contained within a collection is of the same type and they share a common parent. Collections return the objects instead of the names of the objects. Objects that are members of the collections are added and removed with the .Add and .Remove methods of the collection object. A good example of a collection is a collection of databases for a server. This relationship works one way only, because a server may have many data bases but a database may only have one server.

Because the SQL-DMO library provides so many objects, properties, and methods, the objects must be organized in some fashion. The method that was chosen was that of a hierarchical tree. This model simplifies the normal administration and maintenance tasks of managing SQL Server by grouping the functions into a SQL Server Object Model, as shown in figure 12.5.

The top-level object under the application is the SQL Server object, which contains collections of objects. The objects directly under the SQL Server object are as follows:

▶ Databases

▶ Devices

▶ Logins

▶ Languages

▶ Remote servers

▶ Configurations

▶ SQL Server Executive

▶ Registry

▶ Integrated security

▶ Alerts

▶ Operator

Figure 12.5

The SQL Distributed Management Object Model.

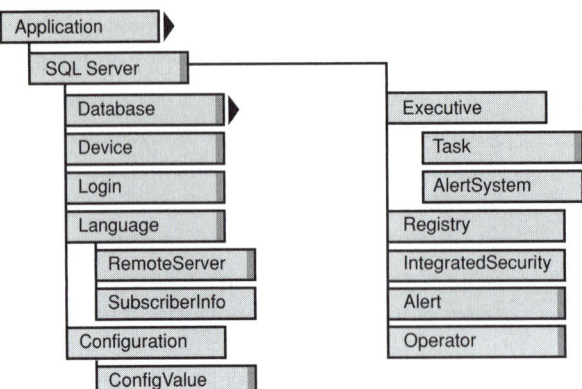

The majority of these objects are relatively easy to relate to objects that administrators work with every day. Conveniently, the names are the same in the SQL-OLE library.

Some objects that are accessible to the client through SQL-DMO are not normally accessible to the same degree through SQL Enterprise Manager. These include the SQL Server Executive, the Registry, Integrated Security, and Operators.

Through SQL-DMO, the Executive object under the SQL Server Object contains information regarding scheduled tasks and alerts. The Executive also includes properties to modify whether SQL Executive starts when Windows NT starts and how many rows the history contains before it overwrites old history rows. The Executive object also can be used to determine what interval SQL Executive will wait until it restarts SQL Server if it stops. It also includes a property to determine if in fact SQL Executive will restart SQL Server at all. One of the most useful functions of the Executive object is the ability to reassign multiple tasks to another login.

Because SQL Server stores many of its setting in the Registry, the Registry provides quick access to these settings. Many of the settings that normally require the SQL Server Setup program to be rerun are accessible through this object. Some of these settings include the following:

▶ Whether SQL Server has a case-sensitive sort order

▶ What character set SQL Server is using in terms of code pages

▶ Where the error log is stored

▶ Mail account name and password

▶ Information about the file locations for the SQL Server executable, and the master database

Not all of these settings may be changed, but the ability to retrieve them through a common object and modifying the entries in the Windows NT registry makes the job much easier.

The Integrated Security object holds a variety of information about logins, path expansion, and connection information. Some notable properties of the Integrated Security object include Map-DollarSign, MapPoundSign, and MapUnderscore. Each of these determines how the dollar sign, pound sign, and underscore within a username is resolved to interact with SQL Server. Other important properties are DefaultDomain and DefaultLogin. These properties set the domain and login, respectively, that SQL Server uses for trusted connections across domains.

The Operator object is used mainly to set up alerts and to determine who will receive them. The times that an operator may receive pages for specified alerts may be customized through the WeekdayPagerStartTime, WeekdayPagerEndTime, SaturdayPagerStartTime, SaturdayPagerEndTime, SundayPagerStartTime, and SundayPagerEndTime properties.

The extended model in figure 12.6 shows the other objects that are attached to a database object.

Advantages of SQL-DMO

By using SQL-DMO, the developer gains several advantages.

First, SQL-DMO enables the developer to use properties and methods instead of memorizing long lists of parameters for complex Transact SQL statements.

Second, SQL-DMO keeps track of many variables automatically, such as task IDs and object numbers. A use for this can be found in iterating through a publishing database's articles. Under normal circumstances, the developer would have to know the task ID for the synchronization tasks in order to change the frequency. By using SQL-DMO with Visual Basic, the developer can simply use the For Each construct to iterate through the article collection for each publication and gain access to all of the properties.

Figure 12.6

The SQL Distributed Management Object Model —Database.

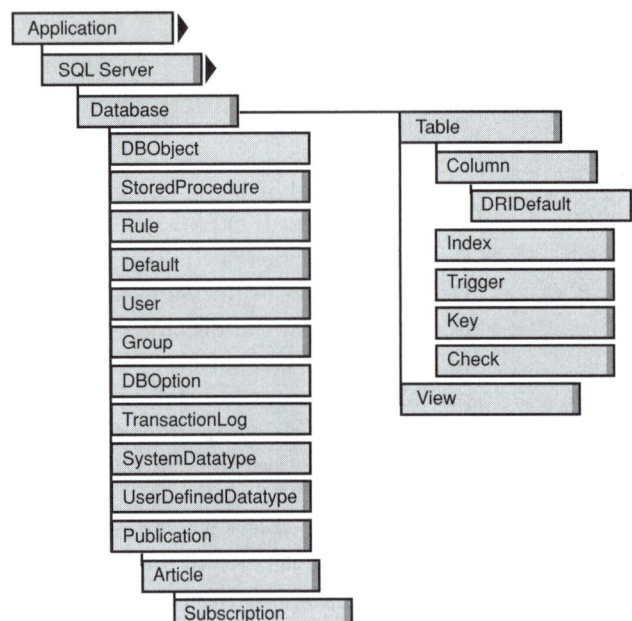

Third, SQL-DMO as an OLE Automation library may be used to extend any Automation-compliant programming tool. This set includes Microsoft Excel for reporting purposes, and any other language that supports Component Object Model (COM). This allows even more flexibility because the developer gains the benefits of the programming tool's normal functions in addition to the power of SQL-DMO.

Fourth, operations that were performed at the database level may now be performed at the object level for ease of use. An excellent example of this is the DBCC Checktable command. Without using SQL-DMO, this command must be run on each table, setting the parameter each time from the database level. With SQL-DMO, an iterative loop may be set up for all of the tables in a database because CheckTable is a method defined for the Table Object of SQL-DMO.

Fifth, the creation of new objects may in many cases be done with a .Add method instead of complex sets of Transact-SQL statements.

Disadvantages of SQL-DMO

On the other hand, SQL-DMO also has a few disadvantages.

Some developers find its interface to be not quite as malleable as they would like because it's designed to manage instead of provide result sets. With that in mind, if data retrieval and modification is the desired outcome, then another OLE Automation server that provides objects to perform these tasks is probably a better choice.

Another disadvantage of SQL-DMO is actually its power. By using the GUI front end of SQL Enterprise Manager, many of the more powerful features are safely hidden away from the administrator. Once the administrator begins to use SQL-DMO directly, the ability to set an improper setting, such as changing the replication working directory, is possible, along with its potential serious consequences.

Using SQL-DMO

The following Visual Basic code snippet is an example of a way to run a DBCC Checktable on each table in the database.

```
Dim objServer as SQLServer
Set objServer = CreateObject("SQLOLE.SQLServer")
objServer.Connect( servername, user_id, password)
Dim objDatabase as Database
Set objDatabase = objServer.Databases(dbname)
Dim objTable as Table
For Each objTable in objDatabase
objTable.CheckTable
Next
Set objDatabase = Nothing
objServer.Disconnect
Set objServer = Nothing
```

The first two lines of code declare the variable that will hold the SQLServer object. The next line opens the connection to the SQL Server using the server name, login ID, and password. Lines four and five set up another variable to serve as a reference to the database named dbname. A variable does not need to be declared to reference the database—line eight could read as follows:

```
For each objTable in objServer.Databases(dbname)
```

However, declaring a variable to serve as a reference to the database is more efficient. Line six sets up a variable to iterate through all of the tables in the database while line seven serves as an iterative loop through the database tables. Calling the .CheckTable method of the table reference in the loop executes a DBCC CHECKTABLE command on each of the tables in the database. Once the operations have been performed, setting the database reference to nothing frees up the memory allocated to that variable. Next, you disconnect from the server and set that variable to nothing, freeing up all of the memory that you have used for this operation.

If SQL-DMO was not used, then DBCC Checktable statements would have to be written for every table in the database.

Recognizing How SQL Server Takes Advantage of the OLE Architecture

 Objective
SQL Server takes advantage of OLE architecture through its use of Distributed Management Framework.

SQL Distributed Management Framework (SQL-DMF) is a set of objects, components, and services that are tightly integrated in order to manage SQL Server. The advantages of SQL DMF are as follows:

▶ Flexible

▶ Scalable

▶ Adaptable to specific needs

▶ Lessens need for user-attended maintenance tasks

▶ Provides services that interact directly with SQL Server

SQL-DMF is flexible enough to use in any OLE-compatible programming language and as such provides the ability to scale large enough to manage an entire enterprise from a central location.

Limited only by the developer that is using it as an OLE Library, SQL-DMF provides access to services that can be used for specific needs, such as unattended maintenance tasks that report results to an operator through e-mail.

Figure 12.7 shows the relationship between SQL-DMF components.

The third-tier layer (top down) is a layer of graphical administration tools. Whether a tool is made with Visual Basic, Visual C++, or any other Automation Compatible programming language, the language must support collections and lists in order to get the maximum level of usability from SQL-DMF. Enterprise Manager is a prime example of what kind of graphical interface may be created with SQL-DMF.

The second-tier layer is composed of SQL-DMO. SQL-DMO provides the object interface to SQL Server's database engine and services to the front-end application.

Figure 12.7

SQL-DMF relationships.

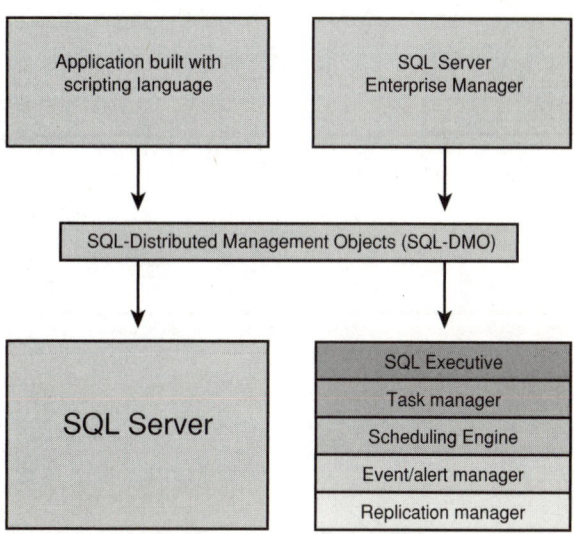

The bottom layer is composed of the base engine (SQL Server) and the SQL Executive. The base engine performs the majority of the work, but important tasks such as scheduling, event and alert management, and replication management are handled by the SQL Executive. This bottom layer provides command line access to SQL Server and the Executive using Transact SQL.

Summary

In this chapter you have been exposed to the various means by which front ends may be used to communicate with SQL Server. Both client side and server side approaches were covered. The uses of messaging were covered as well. SQL Server provides you with any number of approaches to linking users to the databases.

Exercises

Exercise 12.1:   Implement Replication with SQL-DMO

Your company wishes to perform replication across multiple sites. The table names, article names, and publication names are stored in a Microsoft Access Database.

Describe the process using Visual Basic in terms of the object model to perform the most efficient solution.

Answer:

Declare variables to store references to SQLServer objects. Connect to the server using the .Connect method with the server name, login name, and password. Declare a variable to hold a reference to the publishing database. Set the variable to the publishing database using the SQLServer.Databases collection. For each publication, create a new publication with the attributes found in the Microsoft Access database. For each article under the publication, use the .Add method for the Articles collection for each publication to add the article and set the properties appropriately. Destroy the temporary objects that have been created. Disconnect from the server. Destroy the SQLServer variable.

Exercise 12.2:   Interacting with the External Environment

You are the administrator for the SQL Server for your company and have been assigned the task of notifying users that their procedures have failed on weekends. The users have e-mail that is accessible through an alertuser function located in an external dynamic link library named WkdMail.Dll.

For some reason, the management team has mandated that you may not use OLE Automation because they feel it is inherently dangerous to the company's security. What is a possible solution to this problem without using SQL-DMO?

Answer:

Because you're the administrator, use your SA privileges to register the external dll with the sp_addextendedproc procedure in the master database using the syntax sp_addextendedproc alertuser, WkdMail.Dll. Set up an alert for the error conditions through the alert manager to execute the alertuser function. Be sure to set the appropriate options to only fire the alert on weekends.

Review Questions

1. Which of the following databases can extended stored procedures be added to?

    A. tempdb

    B. master

    C. Pubs

    D. model

2. Which of the following is not a valid extended stored procedure for interacting with the mail subsystem?

    A. xp_startmail

    B. xp_sendmail

    C. xp_getmail

    D. xp_stopmail

3. What does xp_cmdshell enable the user to do?

    A. Open a command shell.

    B. Define a command shell.

    C. Execute a command as if a command shell was open.

    D. All of the above.

4. Choose two or more correct responses from the following. Which of the following roles may ODBC drivers play?

    A. Transact sql command compiler

    B. Translator

    C. Session manager

    D. Transact sql command validation

5. What is the difference between the types of databases opened with ODBC for DAO and RDO

   A. DAO is usually used with databases on a client, and RDO is usually used with databases on a server.

   B. RDO is usually used with databases on a client, and DAO is usually used with databases on a server.

   C. DAO connects to multiple remote databases with a single connection, RDO connects to client databases with multiple connections per result set.

   D. RDO connects to multiple remote databases with a single connection, DAO connects to client databases with multiple connections per result set.

6. The major benefit of ODBC is _____.

   A. Accessibility

   B. Portability

   C. Speed

   D. Security

7. What is meant by ODBC Level 1 compliance?

   A. The highest level of functionality

   B. Basic functionality (core functions)

   C. The driver will work with ODBC

   D. The database will work with ODBC

8. What are the two categories of OLE Automation?

   A. Properties and methods

   B. Controllers and objects

   C. Objects and properties

   D. Objects and methods

9. An example of an OLE Server that may be used to interact with SQL Server is _____.

   A. Microsoft Excel

   B. Microsoft Transaction Manager

   C. SQL-DMO

   D. RDO

10. Choose two or more correct responses. Which of the following exposes more functionality through SQL-DMO than SQL Enterprise manager?

   A. Alerts

   B. Database

   C. Registry

   D. SQL Server Executive

Answers to Review Questions

1. B

2. C

3. C

4. B C

5. A

6. B

7. B

8. B

9. C

10. C D

Answers to Test Yourself Questions at Beginning of Chapter

1. Mechanisms that SQL Server uses to interact with its external environment are Messaging Application Programming Interface (MAPI), SQL Distributed Management Objects (SQL-DMO), Open Database Connectivity (ODBC), DB-Library, and Open Data Services (ODS). See the introductory paragraphs of this chapter.

2. SQL Server implements open architecture through user-defined data types (UDDT), which extend the base data types for ease of portability, and through extended stored procedures, which allow functionality that is easily coded in another language to be executed within SQL Server through a call to a DLL. See "How Does SQL Server Implement Open Architecture."

3. In the Profiling Option dialog box in the Options dialog box for setting up an ODBC data source there are two options for fine-tuning. Fine-tuning may be done in terms of when a long running query is logged to a query file, and that the statistics for the driver are saved to a log file. See "Configuring Data Source Profiles."

4. OLE Automation applications may either be controllers or general objects. The controller applications manipulate the objects using methods and properties within the client application, such as Visual Basic. The General objects may be business or work units that contain methods and properties used to manipulate SQL Server. See "OLE Automation."

5. SQL Enterprise Manager is built as a third-tier graphical management tool in the SQL Distributed Management Framework, with SQL-DMO as the OLE Server. See "Recognizing How SQL Server Takes Advantage of the OLE Architecture."

Appendix A

Overview of the Certification Process

To become a Microsoft Certified Professional, candidates must pass rigorous certification exams that provide a valid and reliable measure of their technical proficiency and expertise. These closed-book exams have on-the-job relevance because they are developed with the input of professionals in the computer industry and reflect how Microsoft products are actually used in the workplace. The exams are conducted by an independent organization—Sylvan Prometric—at more than 700 Sylvan Authorized Testing Centers around the world.

Currently Microsoft offers four types of certification, based on specific areas of expertise:

▶ **Microsoft Certified Product Specialist (MCPS).** Qualified to provide installation, configuration, and support for users of at least one Microsoft desktop operating system, such as Windows 95 or Windows NT Server. In addition, candidates may take additional elective exams to add areas of specialization. MCPS is the first level of expertise.

▶ **Microsoft Certified Systems Engineer (MCSE).** Qualified to effectively plan, implement, maintain, and support information systems with Microsoft Windows NT and other Microsoft advanced systems and workgroup products, such as Microsoft Office and Microsoft BackOffice. The SQL Server 6.5 Design and Implementation exam can be used as one of the two elective exams. MCSE is the second level of expertise.

▶ **Microsoft Certified Solution Developer (MCSD).** Qualified to design and develop custom business solutions using Microsoft development tools, technologies, and platforms, including Microsoft Office and Microsoft BackOffice. MCSD also is a second level of expertise, but in the area of software development.

▶ **Microsoft Certified Trainer (MCT).** Instructionally and technically qualified by Microsoft to deliver Microsoft Education Courses at Microsoft authorized sites. An MCT must be employed by a Microsoft Solution Provider Authorized Technical Education Center or a Microsoft Authorized Academic Training site.

 Note

For up-to-date information about each type of certification, visit the Microsoft Training and Certification World Wide Web site at `http://www.microsoft.com/train_cert`. You must have an Internet account and a WWW browser to access this information. You also can call the following sources:

▶ Microsoft Certified Professional Program: 800-636-7544

▶ Sylvan Prometric Testing Centers: 800-755-EXAM

▶ Microsoft Online Institute (MOLI): 800-449-9333

How to Become a Microsoft Certified Product Specialist (MCPS)

Becoming an MCPS requires you pass one operating system exam. Passing the "Implementing a Database Design on Microsoft SQL Server 6.5" exam (#70-27), which this book covers, does not satisfy the MCPS requirement.

The following list shows the names and exam numbers of all the operating systems from which you can choose to get your MCPS certification:

- ▶ Implementing and Supporting Microsoft Windows 95 #70-63

- ▶ Implementing and Supporting Microsoft Windows NT Workstation 4.02 #70-73

- ▶ Implementing and Supporting Microsoft Windows NT Workstation 3.51 #70-42

- ▶ Implementing and Supporting Microsoft Windows NT Server 4.0 #70-67

- ▶ Implementing and Supporting Microsoft Windows NT Server 3.51 #70-43

- ▶ Microsoft Windows for Workgroups 3.11-Desktop #70-48

- ▶ Microsoft Windows 3.1 #70-30

- ▶ Microsoft Windows Architecture I #70-160

- ▶ Microsoft Windows Architecture II #70-161

How to Become a Microsoft Certified Systems Engineer (MCSE)

MCSE candidates need to pass four operating system exams and two elective exams. The MCSE certification path is divided into two tracks: the Windows NT 3.51 track and the Windows NT 4.0 track. The "Implementing a Database Design on Microsoft SQL Server 6.5" exam covered in this book can be applied to either track of the MCSE certification path.

Table A.1 shows the core requirements (four operating system exams) and the elective courses (two exams) for the Windows NT 3.51 track.

Table A.1

Windows NT 3.51 MCSE Track		
Take These Three Required Exams (Core Requirements)	Plus, Pick One Exam from the Following Operating System Exams (Core Requirement)	Plus, Pick Two Exams from the Following (Elective Requirements)
Implementing and Supporting Microsoft Windows NT Server 3.51 #70-43 *AND* Implementing and Supporting Microsoft Windows NT Workstation 3.51 #70-42 *AND* Networking Essentials #70-58	Implementing and Supporting Microsoft Windows 95 #70-63 *OR* Microsoft Windows for Workgroups 3.11-Desktop #70-48 *OR* Microsoft Windows 3.1 #70-30	Implementing and Supporting Microsoft Exchange Server 4.0 #70-75 *OR* Implementing and Supporting Microsoft Exchange Server 5.0 #70-76 *OR* Implementing and Supporting Microsoft Systems Management Server 1.0 #70-14 *OR* Implementing and Supporting Microsoft Systems Management Server 1.2 #70-18 *OR* Microsoft SQL Server 4.2 Database Implementation #70-21 *OR* Microsoft SQL Server 4.2 Database Administration for Microsoft Windows NT #70-22 *OR* System Administration for Microsoft SQL Server 6.5 #70-26 *OR* Implementing a Database Design on Microsoft SQL Server 6.5 #70-27 *OR* Implementing and Supporting Microsoft SNA Server 3.0 #70-13

Take These Three Required Exams (Core Requirements)	Plus, Pick One Exam from the Following Operating System Exams (Core Requirement)	Plus, Pick Two Exams from the Following (Elective Requirements)
		OR Implementing and Supporting Microsoft SNA Server 4.0 #70-85
		OR Microsoft Mail for PC Networks 3.2-Enterprise #70-37
		OR Internetworking Microsoft TCP/IP on Microsoft Windows NT (3.5-3.51) #70-53
		OR Internetworking Microsoft TCP/IP on Microsoft Windows NT 4.0 #70-59
		OR Implementing and Supporting Microsoft Internet Information Server 3.0 and Microsoft Index Server 1.1 #70-77
		OR Implementing and Supporting Microsoft Proxy Server 1.0 #70-78
		OR Implementing and Supporting Microsoft Proxy Server 2.0 #70-88
		OR Implementing and Supporting the Microsoft Internet Explorer Administration Kit for Microsoft Internet Explorer 4.0 #70-79

Table A.2 shows the core requirements (four operating system exams) and elective courses (two exams) for the Windows NT 4.0 track. Tables A.1 and A.2 have many of the same exams listed, but there are distinct differences between the two. Make sure you read each track's requirements carefully.

Table A.2

Windows NT 4.0 MCSE Track

Take These Three Required Exams (Core Requirements)	Plus, Pick One Exam from the Following Operating System Exams (Core Requirement)	Plus, Pick Two Exams from the Following (Elective Requirements)
Implementing and Supporting Microsoft Windows NT Server 4.0 #70-67 *AND* Implementing and Supporting Microsoft Windows NT Workstation 4.0 in the Enterprise #70-68 *AND* Networking Essentials #70-58	Implementing and Supporting Microsoft Windows 95 #70-63 *OR* Microsoft Windows for Workgroups 3.11-Desktop #70-48 *OR* Microsoft Windows 3.1 #70-30 *OR* Implementing and Supporting Microsoft Windows NT Workstation 4.0 #70-73	Implementing and Supporting Microsoft Exchange Server 4.0 #70-75 *OR* Implementing and Supporting Microsoft Exchange Server 5.0 #70-76 *OR* Implementing and Supporting Microsoft Systems Management Server 1.0 #70-14 *OR* Implementing and Supporting Microsoft Systems Management Server 1.2 #70-18 *OR* Microsoft SQL Server 4.2 Database Implementation #70-21 *OR* Implementing and Supporting Microsoft SNA Server 3.0 #70-13 *OR* Implementing and Supporting Microsoft SNA Server 4.0 #70-85

Take These Three Required Exams (Core Requirements)	Plus, Pick One Exam from the Following Operating System Exams (Core Requirement)	Plus, Pick Two Exams from the Following (Elective Requirements)
		OR Microsoft SQL Server 4.2 Database Administration for Microsoft Windows NT #70-22
		OR System Administration for Microsoft SQL Server 6.5 #70-26
		OR Implementing a Database Design on Microsoft SQL Server 6.5 #70-27
		OR Microsoft Mail for PC Networks 3.2-Enterprise #70-37
		OR Internet-working Microsoft TCP/IP on Microsoft Windows NT (3.5-3.51) #70-53
		OR Internetworking Microsoft TCP/IP on Microsoft Windows NT 4.0 #70-59
		OR Implementing and Supporting Microsoft Exchange Server 4.0 #70-75
		OR Implementing and Supporting Microsoft Internet Information Server #70-77
		OR Implementing and Supporting Microsoft Proxy Server 1.0 #70-78

continued

Table A.2 Continued

Windows NT 4.0 MCSE Track		
Take These Three Required Exams (Core Requirements)	Plus, Pick One Exam from the Following Operating System Exams (Core Requirement)	Plus, Pick Two Exams from the Following (Elective Requirements)
		OR Implementing and Supporting Microsoft Proxy Server 2.0 #70-88
		OR Implementing and Supporting the Microsoft Internet Explorer Administration Kit for Microsoft Internet Explorer 4.0 #70-79

How to Become a Microsoft Certified Solution Developer (MCSD)

MCSD candidates need to pass two core technology exams and two elective exams. The "Implementing a Database Design on Microsoft SQL Server 6.5" (#70-27) exam does apply toward these requirements. Table A.3 shows the required technology exams, plus the elective exams that apply toward obtaining the MCSD.

Table A.3

MCSD Exams and Requirements	
Take These Two Core Technology Exams	Plus, Choose from Two of the Following Elective Exams
Microsoft Windows Architecture I #70-160	Microsoft SQL Server 4.2 Database Implementation #70-21
AND Microsoft Windows Architecture II #70-161	*OR* Implementing a Database Design on Microsoft SQL Server 6.5 #70-27

Take These Two Core Technology Exams	Plus, Choose from Two of the Following Elective Exams
	OR Developing Applications with C++ Using the Microsoft Foundation Class Library #70-24
	OR Microsoft Visual Basic 3.0 for Windows-Application Development #70-50
	OR Microsoft Access 2.0 for Windows-Application Development #70-51
	OR Developing Applications with Microsoft Excel 5.0 Using Visual Basic for Applications #70-52
	OR Programming in Microsoft Visual FoxPro 3.0 for Windows #70-54
	OR Developing Applications with Microsoft Visual Basic 5.0 #70-165
	OR Programming with Microsoft Visual Basic 4.0 #70-65
	OR Microsoft Access for Windows 95 and the Microsoft Access Developer's Toolkit #70-69
	OR Implementing OLE in Microsoft Foundation Class Applications #70-25

Becoming a Microsoft Certified Trainer (MCT)

To understand the requirements and process for becoming a Microsoft Certified Trainer (MCT), you need to obtain the Microsoft Certified Trainer Guide document (MCTGUIDE.DOC) from the following WWW site:

```
http://www.microsoft.com/train_cert/download.htm
```

On this page, click on the hyperlink MCT GUIDE (mctguide.doc) (117k). If your WWW browser can display DOC files (Word for Windows native file format), the MCT Guide displays in the browser window. Otherwise, you need to download it and open it in Word for Windows or Windows 95 WordPad. The MCT Guide explains the four-step process to becoming an MCT. The general steps for the MCT certification are as follows:

1. Complete and mail a Microsoft Certified Trainer application to Microsoft. You must include proof of your skills for presenting instructional material. The options for doing so are described in the MCT Guide.

2. Obtain and study the Microsoft Trainer Kit for the Microsoft Official Curricula (MOC) course(s) for which you want to be certified. Microsoft Trainer Kits can be ordered by calling 800-688-0496 in North America. Other regions should review the MCT Guide for information on how to order a Trainer Kit.

3. Pass the Microsoft certification exam for the product for which you want to be certified to teach.

4. Attend the Microsoft Official Curriculum (MOC) course for the course for which you want to be certified. This is done so you can understand how the course is structured, how labs are completed, and how the course flows.

 **Warning**

You should use the preceding steps as a general overview of the MCT certification process. The actual steps you need to take are described in detail in the MCTGUIDE.DOC file on the WWW site mentioned earlier. Do not misconstrue the preceding steps as the actual process you need to take.

If you are interested in becoming an MCT, you can receive more information by visiting the Microsoft Certified Training (MCT) WWW site at http://www.microsoft.com/train_cert/mctint.htm; or call 800-688-0496.

Appendix B

Study Tips

Self-study involves any method that you employ to learn a given topic, with the most popular being third-party books, such as the one you hold in your hand. Before you begin to study for a certification book, you should know exactly what Microsoft expects you to learn.

Pay close attention to the objectives posted for the exam. The most current objectives can always be found on the WWW site `http://www.microsoft.com/train_cert`. This book was written to the most current objectives, and the beginning of each chapter lists the relevant objectives for that chapter. As well, you should notice a handy tear-out card with an objective matrix that lists all objectives and the page you can turn to for information on that objective.

If you have taken any college courses in the past, you have probably learned what study habits work best for you. Nevertheless, consider the following:

- ▶ Study in bright light to reduce fatigue and depression.

- ▶ Establish a regular study schedule and stick as close to it as possible.

- ▶ Turn off all forms of distraction, including radios and televisions; or try studying in a quiet room.

- ▶ Study in the same place each time you study so your materials are always readily at hand.

- ▶ Take short breaks (approximately 15 minutes) every two to three 3 hours or so. Studies have proven that your brain assimilates information better when this is allowed.

Another thing to think about is this: there are three ways in which humans learn information: visually, audially, and through tactile confirmation. That's why, in a college class, the students who took notes on the lectures had better recall on exam day; they took in information both audially and through tactile confirmation—writing it down.

Hence, use study techniques that reinforce information in all three ways. For example, by reading the books, you are visually taking in information. By writing down the information when you test yourself, you are giving your brain tactile confirmation. And lastly, have someone test you out loud, so you can hear yourself giving the correct answer. Having someone test you should always be the last step in studying.

Pre-Testing Yourself

Before taking the actual exam, verify that you are ready to do so by testing yourself over and over again in a variety of ways. Within this book, there are questions at the beginning and end of each chapter. On the accompanying CD-ROM, there is an electronic test engine that emulates the actual Microsoft test and enables you to test your knowledge of the subject areas. Use this engine over and over and over again, until you are consistently scoring in the 90 percent range (or better).

 Note

This means, of course, that you can't start studying five days before the exam begins. You will need to give yourself plenty of time to read, practice, and then test yourself several times.

TestPrep, the electronic testing engine on the CD-ROM, we believe, is the best one on the market. Although the test engine is described in Appendix D, "All About TestPrep," here it's just important for you to know that TestPrep will prepare you for the exam in a way unparalleled by most other engines.

Hints and Tips for Doing Your Best on the Tests

In a confusing twist of terminology, when you take one of the Microsoft exams, you are said to be "writing" the exam. When you go to take the actual exam, be prepared. Arrive early and be ready to show your two forms of identification and sit before the monitor. Expect wordy questions. Although you have 90 minutes to take the exam, there are 56 questions you must answer. This gives you just over one minute to answer each question. This may sound like ample time for each question, but remember that most of the questions are lengthy word problems, which tend to ramble on for paragraphs. Your 90 minutes of exam time can be consumed very quickly.

It has been estimated that approximately 85 percent of the candidates taking their first Microsoft exam fail it. It is not so much that they are unprepared and unknowledgeable. It is more the case that they don't know what to expect and are immediately intimidated by the wordiness of the questions and the ambiguity implied in the answers.

For every exam that Microsoft offers, there is a different required passing score. The SQL Server 6.5 Implementation passing score is 760, or 76 percent. Because there are 56 questions on the exam (randomly taken from a pool of about 150), this means you must correctly answer 43 or more pass.

Things to Watch For

When you take the exam, look closely at the number of correct choices you need to make. Some questions require that you select one correct answer; other questions have more than one correct answer. When you see radio buttons next to the answer choices, you need to remember that the answers are mutually exclusive and there is but one right answer. On the other hand, check boxes indicate that the answers are not mutually exclusive and there are multiple right answers. Be sure to read the questions closely to see how many correct answers you need to choose.

Also, read the questions fully. With lengthy questions, the last sentence often dramatically changes the scenario. When taking the exam, you are given pencils and two sheets of paper. If you are uncertain of what the question is saying, map out the scenario on the paper until you have it clear in your mind. You're required to turn in the scrap paper at the end of the exam.

Marking Answers for Return

You can mark questions on the actual exam and refer back to them later. If you get a wordy question that will take a long time to read and decipher, mark it and return to it when you have completed the rest of the exam. This will save you from wasting time on it and running out of time on the exam—there are only 90 minutes allotted for the exam and it ends when those 90 minutes expire, whether or not you are finished with the exam.

Attaching Notes to Test Questions

At the conclusion of the exam, before the grading takes place, you are given the opportunity to attach a message to any question. If you feel that a question was too ambiguous, or tested on knowledge you did not need to know to work with the product, take this opportunity to state your case. Unheard of is the instance where Microsoft changes a test score as a result of an attached message. However, it never hurts to try—and it helps to vent your frustration before blowing the proverbial 50-amp fuse.

Good luck.

Appendix

What's on the CD-ROM

C

This appendix is a brief rundown of what you'll find on the CD-ROM that comes with this book. For a more detailed description of the newly-developed TestPrep test engine, exclusive to Macmillan Computer Publishing, please see Appendix D, "All About TestPrep."

TestPrep

A new test engine was developed exclusively for Macmillan Computer Publishing. It is, we believe, the best test engine available, because it closely emulates the actual Microsoft exam, and it enables you to check your score by objective, which helps you determine what you need to study further. Before running the TestPrep software, be sure to read CDROM.hlp (in the root directory of the CD-ROM) for late breaking news on TestPrep features. For a complete description of the benefits of TestPrep, please see Appendix D.

Copyright Information and Disclaimer

Macmillan Computer Publishing's TestPrep test engine: Copyright 1997 Macmillan Computer Publishing. All rights reserved. Made in U.S.A.

Appendix

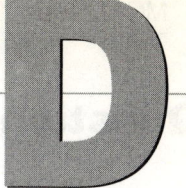

All About TestPrep

The electronic TestPrep utility included on the CD-ROM accompanying this book enables you to test your SQL Server knowledge in a manner similar to that employed by the actual Microsoft exam.

While it is possible to maximize the TestPrep application, the default is for it to run in smaller mode so you can refer to your SQL Server Desktop while answering questions. TestPrep uses a unique randomization sequence to ensure that each time you run the program you are presented with a different sequence of questions—this enhances your learning and prevents you from merely learning the expected answers over time without reading the question each and every time.

Question Presentation

TestPrep emulates the actual Microsoft "Implementing a Database Design on Microsoft SQL Server 6.5" exam (#70-27), in that radio (circle) buttons are used to signify only one correct choice, while check boxes (squares) are used to imply multiple correct answers.

You can exit the program at any time by choosing the Exit key, or you can continue to the next question by choosing the Next key.

Scoring

The TestPrep Score Report uses actual numbers from the "Implementing a Database Design on Microsoft SQL Server 6.5" exam. For SQL Server Design and Implementation, a score of 760 or higher is considered passing; the same parameters apply to TestPrep. Each objective category is broken down into categories with a percentage correct given for each of the 12 categories.

Choose Show Me What I Missed to go back through the questions you incorrectly answered and see what the correct answers are. Choose Exit to terminate the application.

I n d e x

P

Q

REGISTRATION CARD

MCSE Training Guide SQL Server 6.5 Design and Implementation

Name _____ Title _____

Company _____ Type of business _____

Address _____

City/State/ZIP _____

Have you used these types of books before? ☐ yes ☐ no

If yes, which ones? _____
_____

How many computer books do you purchase each year? ☐ 1–5 ☐ 6 or more

How did you learn about this book? _____

Where did you purchase this book? _____

Which applications do you currently use? _____
_____

Which computer magazines do you subscribe to? _____
_____

What trade shows do you attend? _____
_____

Comments: _____
_____
_____

Would you like to be placed on our preferred mailing list? ☐ yes ☐ no

☐ **I would like to see my name in print!** You may use my name and quote me in future New Riders products and promotions. My daytime phone number is: _____

New Riders Publishing   201 West 103rd Street ◆ Indianapolis, Indiana 46290 USA

Fax to 317-817-7448

Fold Here

||||

BUSINESS REPLY MAIL
FIRST-CLASS MAIL PERMIT NO. 9918 INDIANAPOLIS IN

POSTAGE WILL BE PAID BY THE ADDRESSEE

**NEW RIDERS PUBLISHING
201 W 103RD ST
INDIANAPOLIS IN 46290-9058**

MACMILLAN COMPUTER PUBLISHING USA

A VIACOM COMPANY

Technical ---- Support:

If you cannot get the CD/Disk to install properly, or you need assistance with a particular situation in the book, please feel free to check out the Knowledge Base on our Web site at **http://www.superlibrary.com/general/support**. We have answers to our most Frequently Asked Questions listed there. If you do not find your specific question answered, please contact Macmillan Technical Support at **(317) 581-3833**. We can also be reached by email at **support@mcp.com**.

MCSE Training Guide: Windows 95

ISBN: 1-56205-746-4 $59.99 USA/$84.95 CDN   784 pp.   1 CD-RC

This resource contains all the insider tips, notes, tricks, strategies, and helpf advice users need to achieve Microsoft certification on Windows 95. The eas to-read, concise format provides users with the most valuable information— quickly and efficiently. CD-ROM contains New Riders' exclusive TestPrep te: engine, which simulates the actual Microsoft exam better than anything els on the market.

Covers: Implementing and Supporting Microsoft Windows 95—Exam 70-63

MCSE Training Guide: Windows NT Server 4

ISBN: 1-56205-768-5 $49.99 USA/$70.95 USA   560 pp.   1 CD-ROM

This must-have guide to the Implementing and Supporting Microsoft Windows NT Server 4.0 exam will save users countless hours and thousands of dollars in MCSE courses. Filled with insider tips and notes from MCSEs and MCTs, the training guide also includes a CD-ROM with hundreds of questions to help users practice taking the exam.

Covers: Implementing and Supporting Microsoft Windows NT Server 4.0—Exam 70-67

MCSE Training Guide: Networking Essentials

ISBN: 1-56205-749-9 $49.99 USA/$70.95 CDN   512 pp.   1 CD-ROM

This updated edition has all the information users need to pass the Networking Essentials exam. Organized in a concise easy-to-read manner, this must-have resource saves users countless hours and thousands of dollars in training courses. T series is the fastest, most effective, and least expensive study tool for achieving Microsoft certification. CD-ROM contair New Riders' exclusive testing engine, TestPrep, with hundreds of questions to prepare users for the actual exam.

Covers: Networking Essentials—Exam 70-58

Inside Windows NT Server 4, Certified Administrator's Resource Editi

ISBN: 1-56205-789-8 $59.99 USA/$98.95 CDN   1,344 pp.   2 CD-ROI

This book ensures you will have the skills you need to be a success. This proven bestseller is the best book available for the vast majority of Windows NT Server administrators. It contains numerous tutorials that quickly bring new administrat up to speed, but is organized as a reference that serves the needs of even the most technically savvy and experienced Windows NT administrator. Certified by Microsoft as an Approved Study Material, this book is ideal for those preparing fo the MCSE Exam 70-67. Two CD-ROMs contain New Riders' official TestPrep testin software; an electronic version of the text; utilities, and administration tools.

Covers: Windows NT Server 4.0 and MCSE Exam 70-67

Inside Windows NT Workstation 4, Certified Administrator's Resource Edition

ISBN: 1-56205-790-1 $59.99 USA/$98.95 CDN   1,145 pp.   2 CD-ROMs

This book offers Microsoft-certified training material, enhanced with hands-on, performance-based exercises and incluc advanced peer-to-peer discussions, in-depth Registry analysis, and troubleshooting scenarios. Two CD-ROMs contain N Riders' exclusive TestPrep testing software; an electronic version of the text; utilities, and administration tools.

Covers: Windows NT Workstation 4.0 and MCSE Exam 70-73

Networking with Microsoft TCP/IP, Certified Administrator's Resource Edition

ISBN: 1-56205-791-X $55.00 USA/$77.95 CDN   672 pp.   1 CD-ROMs

This bestselling title is enhanced with end of chapter review and self-test sections that greatly increase the reader's chance of passing the Microsoft TCP/IP certification exam. Key information markers provide the necessary testing information at the reader's fingertips. CD-ROM contains New Riders official TestPrep testing software; an electronic version of the text; utilities, and administration tools.

Covers: Microsoft TCP/IP for Windows NT Server 4.0 and MCSE Exam 70-59